A SENSE OF THE SACRED

A
Sense
of the Sacred

Theological Foundations of
Christian Architecture and Art

R. KEVIN SEASOLTZ

continuum
NEW YORK • LONDON

2005
The Continuum International Publishing Group Inc
15 East 26 Street, New York, NY 10010

The Continuum International Publishing Group Ltd
The Tower Building, 11 York Road, SE1 7NX

Library of Congress Cataloging-in-Publication Data

Seasoltz, R. Kevin.
    A sense of the sacred : theological foundations of sacred architecture
and art / Kevin Seasoltz.
        p. cm.
    Includes bibliographical references and index.
    ISBN 0-8264-1701-9 (pbk. : alk. paper) — ISBN 0-8264-1697-7 (hardcover :
alk. paper)
    1. Liturgy and architecture. 2. Church architecture. 3. Christian art
and symbolism. I. Title.
NA4605.S43 2005
726.5'09—dc22
                                                    2005006991

Continuum Publishing is committed to preserving ancient forests and natural resources. We have elected to print this title on 60% postconsumer waste recycled paper. As a result, this book has saved:
15 trees
688 lbs of solid waste
6,239 gallons of water
2,509 kw hours of electricity
1,351 lbs of air pollution
Continuum is a member of Green Press Initiative, a nonprofit program dedicated to supporting publishers in their efforts to reduce their use of fiber obtained from endangered forests. For more information, go to
www.greenpressinitiative.org.

Contents

Acknowledgments

THE RESEARCH FOR THIS BOOK WAS SUPPORTED BY A GENEROUS Sabbatical Grant from the Louisville Institute. I am also grateful to Father Hugh Witzman, O.S.B., and Father Richard Vosko for their kind help with photographs, and to Frank Oveis, Senior Editor at Continuum, who has graciously seen this book through publication.

1

Culture: The Context for Theology, Liturgy, and Sacred Architecture and Art

SINCE THE MIDDLE OF THE TWENTIETH CENTURY, SIGNIFICANT advances have been made in reconciling a rather wide range of competent architects, artists, and craftspersons with the ministry of Protestant, Catholic, and Anglican churches. Not only have some of the world's most prestigious architects been commissioned to design churches, but also some of the most outstanding artists have been asked to create works that find a prominent place in our churches and liturgical celebrations. Various denominations have issued constructive directives on the art and environment of the liturgy and also on sacred music; likewise liturgical scholars have written extensive commentaries on these issues.[1] Although the relationship between theology, liturgy, architecture, and art is being clarified and cooperation among practitioners of the various disciplines is increasing, since the Age of the Enlightenment in the eighteenth century, the relationship of artists and architects to the churches has often been strained. In particular the relationship of artists with the Western world and technology has been ambiguous.[2] It must be acknowledged, however, that when Christ or his mother is mentioned, many people admit that it is not the words of the Bible that come to their minds but rather concrete images or pictures. Although most people would not recognize the name Warner Sallman, his head-and-shoulders portrait of Christ, painted in 1940 and entitled *Head of Christ*, finds immediate recognition among millions of people, for this most popular portrait has been reproduced more than 500 million times and distributed around the world.[3]

In order to have a deeper understanding of the importance of the role of the various arts and their relationship to theology and especially to liturgical celebration, we should have some general understanding of the history

1

of the arts in Western society at large and particularly within our churches; we should also have some grasp of the major shifts that took place in that history following the Renaissance. Above all we should be aware of the sharp conflicts that have existed between religion and the arts since the Enlightenment, especially in the last century.[4] That understanding, however, should be contextualized in terms of the broad cultural developments that have taken place in the Western world, since the diverse cultures of the world have reacted and responded quite differently to technological developments.[5]

CATEGORIES OF CULTURAL DEVELOPMENT

Culture has been defined in various ways, but it is basically a set of meanings and values informing a common way of life.[6] It is a coherent system of meanings embodied in images and other symbols that enable people to relate cognitively, emotionally, and behaviorally to the world and to communicate that appreciation and understanding to others. It is a prism through which communities and individuals view the whole of their experience—domestic, political, social, and economic.[7] It is preserved and transmitted by institutions. A specific culture is often analyzed in terms of space and time, for they are the fundamental perceptions in which people tend to cast reality. In terms of space, culture provides people with a structure in which to live and function; in terms of time, it manifests an internal dynamic, a historical movement, and various stages of development. If culture is the meaning system for people, it provides, above all, meaning for the organization, production, and reproduction of life.

Religion is certainly the preeminent cultural institution if by religion we mean that institution which seeks to disclose the deepest meaning of human experience or what is ultimate in life. Religion itself is communicated, shared, and transmitted above all through symbols, rituals, myths, stories, and metaphors rather than through doctrinal statements and creeds. Theologians speak of symbols, myths, metaphors, and rituals as constituting *theologia prima*. Doctrinal creeds and theological statements are usually the result of conscious reflection on and interpretation of the former. Hence, they constitute what theologians describe as *theologia secunda*.[8] In that sense religion is not divorced from the social, political, and economic aspects of human life; it rather seeks to expose the deepest meaning of all those aspects of human existence.[9] In theological terms, it is through creation, through human bodiliness, language, texts, and other institutions that divine revelation takes place. All meaning is personal, but meaning that has cultural implications is above all social. Interpreted at its deepest level, meaning is religious.

Culture is mediated through institutions that have the task of sustaining and cultivating meaning and naming it so people can own it. More specifically, culture is mediated through both verbal and nonverbal symbols, including myths, rituals, stories, and metaphors. Unless the symbols are cultivated and sustained, social structures are apt to collapse; they enable the social system to produce and reproduce. Without them chaos results because meaning becomes exclusively personal and privatized.[10]

One of the complex aspects of human life today in the Western world is that we have not one dominant culture but rather many diverse cultures that are regularly impinging on one another. As Christopher Dawson noted in his various studies of Western culture, the major reason that Western culture was so creative in the past was that it regularly interacted with other cultures. Because it had a sure sense of its own identity, it was able to assimilate certain aspects of other cultures to itself, which resulted in an eventual enrichment rather than impoverishment of Western culture.[11] At the present time what might be described as Western culture is itself so pluriform that diffusion rather than enrichment is often the case.

When cultural institutions interact with one another and try to relate and respond to historical changes in society, three things can happen: new symbols can be created; old symbols can be preserved and protected from contamination; or extant symbols can be transformed through inculturation. One of the major questions facing the Christian religion in the West today is whether it is the proper time to create new symbols, simply preserve the old, or transform those that already exist. What has become increasingly clear is that religious symbols cannot easily be isolated from the rest of human life. When political, social, and economic institutions change, culture changes too. Since religion involves the interpretation of those institutions on the deepest level, religion and its symbolic expressions will be modified too. In the midst of such developments, what is imperative is to discern which changes are creative and which are destructive of human life, and ultimately to discern which changes foster idolatry and which promote true worship of the divine.[12]

For purposes of analysis, human culture in the West might be analyzed in terms of four broad categories that are useful for understanding various cultural experiences and interpretations of life today. These categories are: (1) primal culture; (2) classical culture; (3) modern culture; and (4) postmodern culture. It is important to realize that all four categories of culture are to be found in the West today, sometimes existing side by side within our churches.

PRIMAL CULTURE

The primal cultural form began perhaps one and a half million years ago when *homo sapiens* emerged. It continued as the dominant form until perhaps 2000 B.C.E., but it is still found among the Amerindian tribes in the United States and the Aborigines in Australia and Canada as well as among the peoples of Africa and South and Central America. Various aspects of primal culture are being brought to many countries in the Western world today through widespread immigration.

In primal culture, the social form is tribal and the religious form is shamanistic. Primal culture tends to view space in terms of a circular web; everything in life is thought to be part of a single circular communion. The web is vital rather than restrictive; it is permeated with religious mystery. It provides the context in which the divine is revealed; in fact, the divine is known primarily in and through creation. In primal culture the spiritual energy is animistic, so that the divine is revealed immanently, that is, in and through the sacramental mystery of the regenerative cycles of nature. The divine is transparent in nature.[13]

This natural spirituality of immanence continues to exist in the Western world as a powerful substratum carried by the folk traditions of peasant people, including the Celtic tradition. In Africa it is reflected in many of the dance steps that tend to thrust the feet into the ground rather than upward, as is common in dance steps in the West. The African steps symbolize the desire to be rooted in the earth, in creation, for the divine is believed to be not only transcendent in the heavens but immanent in all of creation.[14] Primal culture is being rejuvenated today by the advocates of the New Age movement and so-called creation spirituality.[15]

Primal culture tends to view time in terms of a moving arrow, driving forward but in the form of a circle or spiral. Time is rhythmic; it is circular and cyclical. Hence great emphasis is placed on the natural seasons, months, weeks, and days of the year.

Primal culture has tended to be polytheistic because spiritual energy surfaces in many places, resulting in a belief in many gods. In particular, however, it has stressed the sky father, symbolic of divine transcendence, but above all the earth mother, symbolic of divine immanence. She has been linked especially to rivers, wells, caves, and fruit-bearing plants.

Early European evangelizers, following the Christian principle that grace builds on nature, carefully grounded the Christian faith in that primal spirituality. In the case of the British evangelizers, they were encouraged by the pope to retain the Druid shrines and to transform them into Christian centers.[16] Thus, ancient earth-mother shrines still survive today in the area of British churches built on the sites of holy wells. Similarly in Ireland, the shrine of the goddess Brigit of Kildare was supposedly converted into a Christian monastery, though there is no direct contemporary evidence for this.[17]

Closer to our own day, the manifestation of Mary in Mexico known as Our Lady of Guadalupe took place at the site of a former shrine dedicated to an Indian earth goddess named Tonantsin, which means "Beloved Earth Mother." In the apparition, Mary wore the robes of Tonantsin. Thus, while not herself divine, Mary was the symbol of the feminine face of God. Until that mystical communication of the earth-mother symbol, many of the native Mexicans were not able to accept the gospel from their cruel Spanish oppressors. With the apparition of Mary as Tonantsin, the earth mother who consoled her defeated children, Mexico was dramatically evangelized.[18]

The same phenomenon happened in Europe much earlier. Time and time again, the image of Mary and Jesus as mother and child was transposed from the pagan worship of the earth mother and her young child. The famous black madonnas of Europe suggest an African origin for this primal mother-goddess image.

In primal culture, the dominant forms of communication are nonverbal gestures and rituals as well as speech. The development of speech, possibly invented by women in the context of the mother–child relationship, represented a major stage in the development of primal culture, for it certainly facilitated communication and the sharing of nuanced meanings.

Aboriginal art is especially expressive of the religious character of primal culture.[19] Aboriginal religion yields a rich reservoir of symbols that are deeply rooted in the consciousness of the people; the symbols are closely associated with myths that tell the story of people who have never lost contact with their ancestor spirits in the land and who see divine power living in and energizing every plant, animal, and human being. Their religion is vitalistic in that it is centered in the life force that circulates through everything. In the same way that their religious rites both express certain realities and actually bring them about or make them real for the practitioners, so their works of art are not merely objects to be looked at; they have an active religious role in the lives of the people.[20]

The basic characteristics of primal culture can be illustrated by a brief analysis of several forms that are still found in our world and churches today.

NATIVE AMERICAN CULTURE

Native Americans are very religious people; in a sense the earth is their church and the sky is its roof. A great variety of Native American tribes existed in the Northern Hemisphere before the arrival of the white people, for whom religion has often occupied a niche reserved for what is remote in their lives and has been a reference point reached only after death. By contrast, many Native American tribes have looked upon religious experience as something that surrounds them all the time. Each tribe maintains distinctive myths, symbols, and rituals for explaining the universe, for making sense of what cannot be easily understood, for assuaging grief and misfortune, for obtaining good fortune and health, for ensuring an abundance of food, plants, and animals, and for predicting the future.[21]

Most significant is the Native American's deep sense of oneness with all of creation. For the Native Americans, religion involves an ongoing conversation with their Creator and the forces of creation. They listen to the universe and have a deep sense of reverence for solitude and silence. All objects, living or inanimate, belong to one great system of an all-conscious and interrelated life system. Hence anthropomorphism and animism are essential attributes of the Native American religion: plants, trees, and stones have human characteristics and all of nature has conscious life. There is energy and power in every living being and object in the environment, which is mysterious and wonderful. Native Americans have always believed in this mysterious power, which is manifested in a special way in the sun.[22]

The various manifestations of life are not objects of worship in themselves but are more like media of communication with the permeating occult force within. They are like stopping places for God. As a result Native Americans stand abreast of nature; they do not face it and cannot master or coerce it or view it scientifically. They have deep reverence for their everyday environment, which they regard as integrally interwoven with their lives. They are mysteriously devoted to nature, especially the soil—they sit on it and walk on it with their bare feet.

The presence of the Spirit is especially evident in growing things, in the four-legged and two-legged beings of the earth and in the winged beings soaring through the sky, especially in the flight of the eagle. They feel that human beings have only to place themselves in relation to the six special points of reference—up, down, east, west, north, and south—to feel themselves contained, protected, and immersed in that mysterious reality from which all healing and invigorating power come to them. Awareness of this numinous power throughout the entire cosmic order establishes among the Native Americans a most integral form of spirituality—the cosmic, the human, and the divine being are all present to one another in a unique way. This mode of experience is sometimes described as "an earth mysticism."[23]

The drum is the only instrument regularly used in sacred rites because of its round form, which represents the whole universe, with its steady strong beat portraying the pulse, the heart throbbing at the center of the universe; it is the voice of the Great Spirit stirring the people up and helping them understand the mystery and power within all things.[24]

Native Americans measure time by how many suns and moons have elapsed. For them it is important to stay attuned to the rhythms of the universe and of the gods. Time is experienced as cyclic and rhythmic, not linear, with a dependence on sacred time so that the eternal is happening even now.[25]

The Native Americans relate to animals in a distinctive way; they see themselves as part of an evolutionary process that has taken place over the years. What they see of the world with their physical eyes is only one dimension of reality, for they also see with the eyes of their mind. Sacred centers in their tepees and houses establish the perimeters of their space. The center created by either a fire or by a tree planted in the center defines for them the actual center of their world; it is their bridge between heaven and earth. Many of the Native Americans ritualize their rootedness in the universe by sharing the smoking of the pipe; they believe that through the agency of their breathing, the apparent multiplicity and separateness of the grains of tobacco are absorbed within an ultimate unity. After the communal smoking of the pipe, they explain, "We are all related."[26]

Native American children are taught to listen respectfully to the elderly, who can teach them the wisdom of life and good conduct. The aged are considered so close to the next world as to possess a unique quality of holiness. This reverence for elders and the significance given to oral traditions are closely associated with Native American respect for their ancestors.[27]

As the devotion to ancestors is basic to the culture of many Native American tribes, so the ghost dance is prominent among their rituals. The underlying meaning of the dance is that a time will come when an entire Native American race, the living and the dead, will be reunited on a regenerated earth to live a life of happiness without death, disease, or misery. The time of its fulfillment can be hastened by a good life and by attendance at the ghost dance, in which the dancers join hands, move in a circle facing inward, with a tree or pole planted in the center. Singing and moving according to the course of the sun from right to left, without drum, rattle, or any musical instrument, the dancers perform all night until they collapse in a trance, which is often stimulated by the hypnotizing efforts of the medicine men whirling eagle feathers and colored scarfs before the participants and looking intently into their eyes.[28]

As already noted, the circle is frequently employed ritually and is intuitively sensed rather than logically understood. Often a cross is inscribed within the circle, thus reinforcing the symbol of the universe by including reference to the four directions. The circle with a cross inscribed within it is often painted on ritual objects and on the bodies and heads of those who participate in tribal ceremonies.

Dances are essentially ritualistic in Native American culture. The Indians speak of dancing as the breath-of-life made visible. This breath-of-life is discovered everywhere in their world. Their dance steps are regularly downward in thrust because the dancers want to be grounded in the earth and so grounded in the Great Spirit who permeates the earth. So many of their symbols and symbolic actions—the peace pipe, their practice of inhaling the first light of day, and their belief that in exhaling they confer a blessing—are all associated with the wind and with the breathing of the universe. It is the wind that gave them life, and it continues to do so when they exhale. When the wind within them ceases, they die.[29]

These basic characteristics of Native American culture are regularly expressed in their architecture and their artifacts, in their totems and their sacred art. Their ceremonial clothing reflects their spirituality: for example, the eagle feather represents the Great Spirit, and the rosette of eagle feathers or of porcupine quills represents the sun. To wear an eagle-feather headdress implies that one is identified with the sun. Likewise, fringes on clothing suggest the rain. Native American masks include complex sacred geometric diagrams or forms. The masks are worn primarily in sacred dances, often organized around the winter and summer solstices. Their purpose is to increase and renew the spiritual forces that animate the physical world and its natural cycles.[30]

At heart, Native American culture represents the embodiment of primordial, archetypal spiritual truths. Their myths, their symbols, and their way of life affirm what they believe it means to be human and alive on this earth.[31]

AFRICAN AMERICAN CULTURE

In the second half of the last century, African American communities made considerable efforts to retrieve their roots and to rediscover the rituals and art forms characteristic of their rich traditions.[32] In terms of cosmology, they discovered that they held some tenets in common with Native Americans. African peoples tend to perceive reality as one related whole rather than as separate compartments. There is no clear distinction between the sacred and the secular. The rhythm of life is bound up in the cosmos—a harmonious world, created and ordered by God. While postmodern schools of thought are now returning to the interrelatedness of disciplines in theology, black peoples have continuously reflected this method of theologizing. The African heritage is not a monolithic heritage, but some branches of that heritage were involved in the origins of Christian worship and played a major role in the development of worship patterns and their theological underpinnings. Certainly a number of the most important church fathers came from or ministered in Africa, including Clement of Alexandria, Origen, Tertullian, Cyprian, Dionysius, Athanasius, Augustine, and Cyril.

Hence African primal worldviews that shaped foundational belief systems also undergird African American theologies of church life and worship. Worldviews determine and affect cultural symbols through which beliefs are expressed and transmitted.[33]

While there are some differences in the various worldviews in the understanding of the presence and activity of God in the world, creation is undoubtedly looked upon as the work of God. The cosmos is understood as a whole unit or body that is alive and sacred; it is the foundation of religious values. Modalities of the sacred and of being are revealed through the natural world and cosmic rhythms. The harmonious structure of the cosmos is a means by which God's transcendence is remembered. Divine connectedness is activated through symbols. Water, for example, symbolizes the origin and sustenance of life as well as death and rebirth. Contact with water signifies a reincorporation into creation or pre-creation.

African peoples respond to God's presence in a variety of ways. Worship is generally expressed vocally and physically rather than through meditation or contemplation. Beliefs as well as ritual actions are related to the lived experience of the community. Worship is more experiential than rationalistic. Its focus is on the communal sharing of reality rather than simply on the transmission of information. Since the emphasis is primarily experiential, common symbols, shaped by the community, are the major means of communication. Through nonverbal symbols the community expresses what might be difficult to verbalize. Symbols help free the mind of clutter so that clarity can be given to phenomena that might otherwise be incomprehensible. Music, movement, physical gestures, colors, shapes, and the gifts of nature common to the community are very important symbols.

A composite of fundamental beliefs based on primal worldviews has emerged as African Americans make deliberate efforts to theologize from within the African American experience. Unlike the Western-oriented Christians, whose theology is most often rooted in Greco-Roman concepts and culture, African and African American people tend to seek to know God personally rather than to know about God through doctrines and creeds. Everybody, including children, knows that God is, as if by instinct. Christian faith, for traditional Africans, does not mean that one has to assent to or recite certain written doctrines or creeds to prove that one knows about God. What matters is that one seeks to know God through God's revelational activity in one's own life and in the life of the community.

African peoples in America have expressed in a number of ways the importance of experiencing and knowing God in Jesus Christ. In gospel songs, African Americans continue to document the importance of knowing God. The language of these songs reflects a reaching out through space and time as singers identify with the lived experience of others, so that characters, scenes, and events in the Bible become present and provide evidence of hope.[34]

One of the strongest forces in traditional African life that continues among African Americans is a deep sense of kinship or relatedness. From the perspective of primal worldviews, God is the continuing source and sustenance of all that is good. Since God called forth the cosmos as an orderly, complete, and perfect entity, all creation and the inhabited universe are sacred to God. Humanity is part of the created order; thus, human beings are to exist in unity with one another and with all of creation. To be human is to be defined by a sense of belonging, for it is not enough to be a human being; one must participate in and demonstrate a sense of belonging to the community. Religion, understood as one with life, is not an isolated part of the community's life, but permeates every facet of the community's existence. The sense of kinship is not limited to human relations. It involves all of nature, including animal and plant life. Kinship is the basis for an understanding of the community, including the living, the living-dead (the deceased who are alive in the memories of the family), and those yet unborn who are still in the loins of the living. The anticipated arrival of future generations yet unborn provides hope in the continuation of God's ongoing family. The deeply ingrained urge for expression is represented in art and art forms that evolved as functional adjuncts to African religious rites. The blending of music and rhythmical movements is a universal expression of the interrelatedness of lived experience.[35]

In the past and even at present most African churches have been built as rectangles, following the Western manner. This type of architecture was imported by the missionaries and the colonizers. However, it is not the square or the rectangle but the circle that plays an important role in African life. For example, the daily meal is taken in a circle, signifying unity and equality. Once in the circle, age, social status, and gender are unimportant. Everyone shares in what is available in the circle.

The circle is used for other purposes as well: for example, the people dance in the form of a circle, expressing their common joys and concerns. Family, clan, or public meetings are also held in the form of a circle. The participants stand or sit in a circle to listen to stories. The chief gathers his advisers in a circle to listen to their advice. The ground-plan of many traditional houses is also a circle. The round hut provides a maximum of space and uses up a minimum amount of material.

In some parts of Africa, a hexagon, a derivative of the circle, is being used as the basic design for the Christian church. Worshipers sit in the form of a circle to listen to the scriptures proclaimed and shared; the people are united in a circle around the table of the Lord, where they share in his meal. The altar itself often takes the form of a circle. The circle thus becomes a symbol of the unity of the community in Christ.[36] These churches are regularly adorned with art objects that are native to Africa.

African Americans have generally inherited church buildings. Hence, they simply adjust to what they have been given. Protestant and Evangelical churches tend to emphasize the pulpit; Roman Catholic churches tend to stress the importance of the altar. However, an effort has been made to adorn these churches with African artifacts, often of distinguished quality. Especially prominent are images of the African Christ. The people have a special interest in the principal events in the life of Jesus, such as his birth, death, and resurrection, and have hope for the resurrection of those who have been incorporated into the body of Christ. Hence, Jesus is often viewed as the "victor," the one who triumphs over the powers of evil, disease, fear, and even death itself. Africans and African American Christians are often quite aware of the various powers of evil in their lives and their environment. Jesus, as the perfect human being, suffers and dies in order to complete his identification with human beings. The cross then is not a sign of shame and humiliation. What happened before Easter happens to all people; what happens after Easter happens only to the God-man and constitutes the uniqueness of the Christian gospel.[37]

One of the most impressive churches built since Vatican II in the African American style is Saint Benedict the African Church in the Englewood area of Chicago. It was designed by the distinguished architectural firm Belli and Belli. Regina Kuehn was the liturgical consultant for the church. The exterior of the building is a circle with scalloped walls. One enters the building through a spatial narthex, where the community gathers. Then one approaches what is the most striking feature of the church: a circular baptismal pool, surrounded by a wall of boulders and holding several hundred gallons of water. The importance of baptism cannot be lost on the many parishioners, especially those baptized as adults. Walking around the pool, one encounters circular and curved shapes in order to enter the circular nave, which resembles an African hut. The altar, ambo, and presider's chair are carved in walnut, African style. Around the walls of the nave are trees and plants, reminding the community that they are born out of nature as well as grace. About three hundred chairs are arranged antiphonally with the altar, ambo, and presider's chair completing the circle. The tabernacle is placed in a walnut tower off to one side, a place of honor but not a focal point during the liturgy. There is a clear sense of openness and hospitality—no platforms, rails, no sense of separation but an authentic sense of God's creation in the natural light, the plants and trees, the water, and above all in the gathered community.[38]

HISPANIC AMERICAN CULTURE

Those living in the United States whose native language is Spanish do not constitute a completely homogeneous population; however, they do tend to share many cultural elements, including a common language, similar values, and some form of the Christian religion. Although the majority of these people were probably baptized as Catholics, many Protestant groups, especially storefront, evangelical, and Pentecostal sects, have in recent years made deep inroads into Hispanic American Catholicism. One of the most cherished values among all of these people is family life. Flowing out of that value are an appreciation for and love of children, special devotion to the mother of the family, and deep reverence and compassion for the elderly. Children are shaped by the values of their elders, who are looked to as the transmitters of wisdom. Parents and God-parents play an important role in the life of children; in fact, God-parents are often viewed as co-parents. Hospitality is also a distinctive characteristic of Hispanic people, manifested in a genuine concern not only for visitors but even for strangers. They look upon death as an awakening to real life; hence, they consider themselves as pilgrim people.

A basic and constant aspect of these Christians is a sense of the presence of God, who is found above all in the arms of the Virgin Mary. Strong emphasis is placed on the humanity of Jesus, particularly as a weak infant, as a suffering servant dying on the cross, or as an understanding person whose symbol is the image of the Sacred Heart. The favorite images of Jesus are the Sacred Heart, the crucifix, and the infant. Mary is at the heart of Hispanic spirituality, though each Hispanic community tends to have its own particular devotion to Mary. Spirituality is expressed above all in popular devotions and in the use of symbols, gestures, and rituals.[39] It is also expressed in behavior and human attitudes. Prayer and hospitality, endurance and hope, commitment and forgiveness tend to be prominent character traits. Christian faith is kept alive at home through religious practices in daily life, particularly during the principal seasons of the liturgical year, such as advent and lent. All celebrations are looked upon as communal events; most of them include prayer and sharing of food, as well as singing, dancing, and reciting poetry or telling stories. The people rarely pray for themselves but regularly for others.[40]

Hispanic peoples in the United States inherit their spirituality from indigenous people. Hence, they often cultivate the seeds of their religion as found in pre-Hispanic customs and ideas that sometimes seem to be less than Christian. Many of their practices, especially those belonging to Mexican Americans, were brought to North America by sixteenth-century missionaries from Spain.

In southern California, Texas, and New Mexico, Hispanic people have generally inherited church structures built in the baroque tradition.[41] These churches are usually cruciform, in conscious imitation of the Latin cross. Altar screens are placed not only above the main altar but also at the side altars throughout the nave. Frequently sculptures rather than paintings dominate these altar screens, with the iconography of Mary and the saints set out so as to elicit a very direct, emotional response. Mary and the saints are not looked upon as transcendental beings but rather as intimate friends. The statues are often carefully dressed for special occasions. In the tradition of medieval passion plays and the Holy Week processions of Spain, large images of Christ are frequently carried in procession to reenact the events of the passion, beginning with Jesus' arrival in Jerusalem on Palm Sunday and continuing throughout the week. During lent, statues of the various saints associated with the passion of Christ, especially the Mother of Sorrows, Mary Magdalen, Veronica, and the apostles, are given special places of honor in the churches. Likewise elaborate nativity scenes are given prominence during the Christmas season. On the occasion of other festivals, the churches are decorated with candles, flowers, and streamers, and the images of particular saints are clothed in special attire and taken in procession outside the church. Such processions were common ritual occurrences in medieval Europe and have been maintained by immigrant peoples in the New World.[42]

In other parts of the United States, especially in major urban areas where there are large concentrations of Spanish-speaking people, the churches that originally were associated with German and Irish immigrants have in recent years been populated by Spanish-speaking immigrants, not only from Mexico but also from Cuba, Central America, and Puerto Rico. When these churches have been redecorated, the patterns described above have been incorporated and the popular devotions and rituals have been carried out.

ASIAN AMERICAN CULTURE

Asian culture has traditionally been very sophisticated; it would undoubtedly not have many of the characteristics associated with primal culture, but neither does it have characteristics associated with classical culture in the West. Like those in primal cultures, Asians tend to think of the world as a circle, whereas Westerners think of it as a line. Asians believe in constant change, but believe things always move back to some earlier state. They attend to a wide range of events and search for relationships between things; they likewise think they cannot understand the part without the whole, in contrast to Westerners, who tend to live in a simpler, more deterministic world and who focus on salient objects or people instead of the larger picture.[43]

Because it is such an important component of present life in this country, Asian culture deserves special attention. Like Native Americans, African Americans, and Hispanic Americans, the diverse cultures of Asiatic peoples are radically different in many ways from the cultures that predominate in North America. There is little doubt that Asians and Westerners think very differently and consequently express themselves in distinctive ways in their art and architectures. Since the Second World War, but above all during the latter part of the twentieth century, the number of Asians and Pacific Islanders in this country—defined by the U.S. Census Bureau as any of the original peoples of the Far East, Southeast

Asia, the Indian Subcontinent, or the Pacific Islands—has increased dramatically. Many of these Asian and Pacific newcomers are Christian, both Protestant (mainly Presbyterian and Baptist) and Catholic (Roman as well as Eastern). These new immigrants and refugees, all with distinctive cultural and religious traditions, pose enormous challenges to the churches in North America.[44]

Asian spirituality is generally rooted in an experience of the sacred based on the Vedic scriptures (1800–500 B.C.E.) and encompasses several religious traditions—Hinduism, Buddhism, Confucianism, and Taoism. Many Christians today have incorporated into their own spirituality elements of Asian Spirituality, for example, the practice of yoga.[45]

There is a widespread perception that European and American theologies are not meaningful to Asian Americans; consequently, a significant number of Asian and Asian American theologians have tried to build an alternative theology based on Asian resources.[46] These resources include, first of all, the daily stories of suffering and joy, despair and hope, hatred and love, oppression and freedom experienced by Asian people. These accounts are not found in official books but are simply kept alive in the dangerous memories of Asian people.[47] In a special way their Christian faith is kept alive by their deep faith in God in spite of their countless struggles against oppression, especially in recent decades by Communist regimes.

The second source, actually a subset of the first, is the account of their lives by women. Asian societies are predominantly patriarchal, and women often experience oppression and poverty. Women's stories occupy a dominant place in Asian theology; they provide a hermeneutical tool for interpreting the stories in the Bible.[48]

The third major source is found in the sacred texts and ethical and spiritual practices of Asian religions that have shaped the spirituality of Asian people thousands of years before the advent of Christianity to their lands. These sources continue to nourish the spirituality and practice of Asian people.[49]

The fourth source is Asian philosophy, understood as a whole way of life and of being in the world. For example, the metaphysics of yin and yang has been pressed into service in an effort to explain the Christian understanding of christology and trinitarian theology.[50]

The fifth resource is found in Asian monastic traditions, with their distinctive rituals, ascetic practices, and ethical commitments. It is significant that Asian monks have regularly been involved in social and political struggles through their voluntary commitment to simplicity of life.[51]

The final source, and an extremely important one, is found in Asian cultures in general in their immense storehouse of symbols, rituals, stories, myths, songs, and dances.[52] It is the Asian cultures that provide the images that are regularly expressed in sacred art and architecture. In Asiatic countries there are numerous Shinto and Buddhist temples. Shinto shrines are often found in places of natural beauty or places with an atmosphere of mystery or grandeur about them. Natural materials are used for the building of shrines. Modern shrines are built in a variety of styles, but most are located within a garden or in the midst of trees. A clear boundary separates the shrine from the secular world. The shrine itself usually consists of one or more halls, and an inner room reserved for the priest and containing an image of the deity or *kami*.[53] Shinto shrines are found primarily in Japan. In North America, Japanese devotees of the Shinto religion are apt to incorporate images of their traditional gods into their homes but they have not established Shinto shrines.

Buddhist temples are found in India and throughout Asia. They often manifest a great diversity of art and architecture. The temple is the primary Buddhist sanctuary, in which the laity attend services and make offerings to the Buddha. It is often attached to a monastery where monks meditate and pursue self-enlightenment. Many temples are built on the plan of a mandala and contain numerous images for both worship and instruction.[54] In North America there are Buddhist temples that are often attached to monasteries. They attract many North Americans who have been converted to Buddhism.

Asian Christians have generally been assimilated to established parishes and congregations in North America; as a result, they do not have churches built in the style of Shinto or Buddhist temples. Where there are large numbers of Christians, they have often tried to incorporate Christian art executed in an Asian style. The Asian Christian Art Association was established in 1978 and has already published books, sponsored art exhibitions and the education of young artists, and promoted Christian art in the Asian tradition. For example, the Indian artist Alphonso Doss has painted a striking picture entitled *Christ Preaching*. It portrays Jesus as a man of severe grace and great dignity. The right hand is extended in a preaching posture, with the first two fingers pointing upward and the third finger held against the palm by the thumb. In his left hand, Christ holds an egg, symbolizing the source of life.[55] Hatigammana Uttaranda, a Sri Lankan artist, painted a portrait of Jesus that reflects Buddhist iconography. It shows Jesus with lowered eyes and eyelids half closed in an attitude of renunciation and compassion.[56]

The Christian Conference of Asia has promoted the construction of churches that are faithful to gospel values but firmly planted in the culture and community of native peoples.[57] The indigenous styles, however, have yet to influence the construction of new churches built for Asian immigrants and refugees in North America.

CLASSICAL CULTURE

From about 3000 B.C.E. and the development of the ancient Greco-Roman world, the classical form of human culture emerged and developed.[58] It was dominant until about 1500 C.E. Called "civilization," this classical form began to gather people into the large structures of empires.[59] This imperial form began probably first in Africa, then in Asia, later in Europe, and still later in the Americas. Monotheism began to displace polytheism. In stressing that God is one, classical culture should have stressed at the same time the unity of life. However, it tended to emphasize the transcendence of the divine, symbolized by the primal sky father, but it neglected the immanence of God, symbolized by the primal earth mother. In fact the latter image was frequently suppressed in classical culture. It likewise emphasized the primal image of the divine as light but suppressed the image of the divine as nurturing darkness. Darkness, like woman, became a symbol of evil. The end result was often the exaltation of the divine but the denigration of the human.

In classical culture the innovative means of communication was writing, invented by people after the metalurgical revolution, which created tools and weapons necessary for imperial civilization based on tribal conquest and large-scale production. The use of writing instruments enabled treaties to be enacted across wider tribal confederations, censuses to be taken of large populations, and records to be kept of sacred tradition. With these records, organizational structures became possible on an imperial scale.

Enormous religious organizational structures also became possible, generating what we know today as world religions of a holy book. With handwritten texts, religious traditions and teachings could be standardized over vast geographical areas, even gathering large numbers of tribes into monotheistic belief systems. Leadership in religion belonged no longer to nature-rooted shamans but rather to temple-based priests, and later to cloister-based monks who carefully copied and interpreted the written word and adorned the pages with beautiful illuminations. These priests and monks were often the only educated people who had the skills of writing and reading.

To some extent Judaism and to a great extent Christianity, both religions of the Bible, a holy book, were historically rooted in classical culture. Both, however, have deeper origins in oral traditions of speech, and both emerged in many ways as prophetic, marginal, countercultural forces to the imperial civilization.

Classical culture maintained that there is but one normative culture whose values and meanings are universal in claim and scope. It affirmed an abstract ideal that is unchanging; it was preoccupied with universals rather than particulars. As it developed in the West, it was rooted in a dualistic philosophy structured especially according to Aristotelian logic. Likewise it issued laws that were thought to be universally applicable and truths that were considered eternal. The circumstances of time and space, so important in primal culture, were merely accidental in a classical framework. Human nature itself was thought to be a universal concept denoting an unchanging reality.

Although classical culture destroyed the circle and the web, it did introduce a sense of creative responsibility into the human race. In the biblical tradition, men and women were to cultivate the earth and make it productive. In primal culture, human beings were simply expected to commune with and stand in awe of the divine mystery in creation. Classical culture allowed human beings to become involved in the ongoing process of creation or in its transformation. The overall goal, however, was to rise above the cycle of nature and the web of human life, to break out of the horizontal circle of time and to rise above the normal structures of society. Historically the result was the replacement of the web with a hierarchically structured pyramid. Those at the top of the pyramid were thought to be freed from temporal and spatial concerns so they could transcend the material world. Classical spirituality was one that stressed transcendence, but the experience was generally reserved to an elite group of people who contemplated and communed with the divine mystery beyond the material world. Historically the result was the development of two classes in society, the aristocracy, or higher class, and the peasantry, or lower class.[60]

In spite of the classical emphasis on transcendence, the art and architecture of the early Greeks and Romans appear to have concentrated on this world. In Athenian society it was the free-born citizens who were the patrons of the arts. Their motto was to live beautifully and happily here and now because they did not look upon death with faith in the future nor did they dwell upon it with a sense of morbid regard. Life after death had little interest for them, so they did not confront the mystery of suffering and death. The Greek temperament sought to master the world by knowing it and reducing it to simple mathematical formulas. Their gods were basically human beings endowed with greater physical beauty and more wisdom than most human beings. Because Greek philosophy was concerned with the mind, it is natural that Greek art reflected mathematical precision and proportion. In their limited world, however, the Greeks found the idea of space quite difficult to comprehend; it was intangible and did not have convincing reality.[61]

The early Romans were concerned mainly with increasing their power and controlling large areas of space. They were practical, proud, and mercenary people who loved sensual pleasure, lavish living, and grand parades. Their religion was akin to that of the Greeks, but they placed more faith in military arms than in their gods. They had a vague notion of life after death but put little credence in any idea of immortality. Their religion was centered in the home, so they had household gods for each family activity.[62]

Christianity developed against this background of early Roman and Greek classical culture, but it developed its own distinctive interpretation of reality. Early Christian theologians simply discoursed on the given character of reality, and once Aristotelian philosophy was available in Latin translation theologians articulated their reflections as clearly as possible. Eventually liturgy came to be looked upon as the uniform worship of God; it reflected the unchanging character of both God and creatures. As a complex of symbols and rituals, the liturgy was in a special way a cultural expression of the life of the church; it also manifested an understanding of the church as a hierarchically structured society. Increasingly it reflected an institutional model of the church and a descending model of christology whereby the divine Logos came down from on high to take on a human nature; he redeemed humanity from its sinfulness by his death on the cross and then rose from the dead to take his place with the Father at the right hand of God on high. The permanence and uniformity of the liturgy were eventually expressed by Latin as a common language;[63] its unchanging character was ensured by well-defined, universally applicable rubrics that became increasingly uniform as cultural controls, such as a strong, authoritarian papacy and the accessibility of printed books, became available.

The dualistic structure of classical culture was expressed in the church by clear distinctions between clerics and religious, who constituted the higher class, and layfolk, who constituted the lower class. As Christianity assimilated itself to the classical model of Roman imperial culture, monasticism in its eremitic and cenobitic forms emerged as prophetic counterpoints. As the Roman imperial structure collapsed, patriarchal monasticism developed and preserved the classical tradition. Indeed in the postimperial period, monasteries became the central institutions for producing written documents. Monasticism thus carried the classical tradition after the imperial structure collapsed. Later, religious life took on a mendicant form, especially among the Dominicans and Franciscans. The friars constituted a transitional stage between the classical handwritten forms and the modern print-based apostolic forms of religious life and spirituality.

Class consciousness was given a strong theological foundation in the late Middle Ages with the development of the so-called state of perfection, which consisted of a formal commitment to a life of chaste celibacy, poverty, and obedience. Through celibacy, professed religious and clerics were thought to be freed from the biological aspects of the life cycle; through a commitment to simplicity of life and poverty they were thought to be freed from material concerns; and through obedience they were thought to be freed from self-will and immersion in secular affairs. By removing themselves from the secular cares of life, those in the state of perfection were thought to be free to contemplate the divine. What was considered ideal in regard to these commitments was certainly not always achieved in practice.

The lower class was forced to live according to the biological cycles of the secular world. They had to marry and beget children, attend to material cares, and fulfill their personal needs and desires. Layfolk were immersed in the lower cycles of life here below from which they could be liberated only by death. Sanctity was identified with the transcendent experience of the higher class; the lives of the lower class were spent in a valley of tears to be endured until death brought them the reward of eternal life.

Classical culture did not succeed in entirely repressing primal culture in the church. It continued to find some expression in the sacramental rites, especially the rites of passage, in the liturgical year, and in the liturgy of the hours, all of which relied on symbols rooted in creation and in the human life cycle. Furthermore, monasticism, particularly in its Benedictine and Cistercian forms, continued to stay close to the earth and to maintain a sense of stewardship over creation. Although the classical tradition more or less suppressed the image of darkness as a bearer of the divine by unambiguously asserting that God is light, mystics surfaced within the classical tradition who retrieved the image of darkness as a path to the divine which cannot be captured or confined in any way. The *via negativa* developed along with the *via positiva* as an approach to the divine. In general, however, classical spirituality emphasized the transcendent. It sought escape from nature, from biology, from the life cycles, and from woman.

A critical turning point in the history of Western culture occurred in the thirteenth century, sometimes referred to as "the greatest of centuries." There is no doubt that extraordinary achievements were accomplished in that era, especially in the areas of architecture, sculpture, and stained glass, but as with most major shifts in culture, there were losses as well as gains.

The university might be cited as a condensed symbol of major changes that took place in that century. As a cultural institution, the university had no counterpart in the ancient world or in the earlier Middle Ages. The central intellectual problems of the period were debated within the faculty of theology, where Greek philosophy, especially in its Aristotelian form, confronted the Bible. In other words, the confrontation was between reason and divine revelation, or the achievements of human culture and transcendence. Another cultural development that affected the theological faculty was the ongoing movement in the Western world from an oral to a literate culture. The thirteenth century probably witnessed the most significant advance in that direction.

In the thirteenth century, theology moved out of the monasteries and cathedrals into the classrooms. Up until the development of the universities, it had existed primarily in a liturgical context. In the university it became professedly academic and scientific. The Bible shifted from being a book of prayer and holy reading to a data base, a source of concrete information about the sacred with which one could confront the natural theology of the Greek philosophers, especially Aristotle. One has only to read the sermons of Augustine in the fifth century or those of Bernard, the twelfth-century Cistercian, to grasp the difference in style and content from thirteenth-century treatises. Certainly both Augustine and Bernard were theologians, but they practiced their discipline quite differently from the Scholastics of the thirteenth and following centuries. Although the sermons of both Augustine and Bernard eventually took written form, they carry many of the traits of an oral culture. Both were influenced by the power of the spoken word. They usually began their sermons by quoting a text from scripture, but as they developed their reflections on the biblical texts, their discourse is distinguished by the use of mnemonic devices and other traits characteristic of oral cultures. Their sentences are marked by a conscious use of rhythm; hence, their style is closely related to music and consequently appeals to human emotion. Their sermons speak not only to the mind but also to the heart.[64]

Nothing was more characteristic of the Scholastics, the university professors of the thirteenth century, than their penchant for definition, argumentation, and precise conclusions. They usually opted for a literal interpretation of the Bible rather than an allegorical or poetic interpretation. Likewise, under their direction, doctrine underwent a significant redefinition, and it came to mean abstract propositions to which one was obliged to give intellectual assent. As a result, the affective dimension of theology, so characteristic of the church fathers, was undercut.

The Scholastics were responsible for what might be called the doctrinalization of Christianity. Faith, instead of involving the Christian in a whole way of life, became more or less equated with intellectual assent to propositions. Grace, instead of being the presence and power of God in human hearts and communities, became an abstract power that enlightened one's intellect and fortified one's will so that a person believed the right doctrines, worshiped the right way, and lived a moral life in accord with prescribed laws. This resulted in a subtle shift in Christian priorities as proofs marginalized affections, as analysis displaced poetry, as mind took precedence over heart, and as religious language changed from communication charged with affective and aesthetic overtones to one dominated by critical analysis and rigorous argumentation. These significant developments led the institutional church in many areas to assign secondary importance to the emotional life of Christians and consequently to the role of art and architecture in developing the faith life of individuals and communities. In a sense, the artistic and affective dimensions of Christianity were left to those humble layfolk who could not get seriously engaged in the pursuits of intellectual Christianity. Nevertheless, classical culture was expressed by extraordinary achievements in architecture, sculpture, and painting, all analyzed, appreciated, and promoted down to the present time in what came to be known as Romanesque and Gothic. Scattered throughout Europe, these works manifested the power and majesty of God revealed above all as a transcendent reality.[65]

MODERN CULTURE

The dualistic understanding of the universe—spirit and matter—began to collapse in the fourteenth century under the impetus of several cultural revolutions.[66] The first was the development of nominalism, a theory of knowledge that denied the reality of universal concepts and affirmed the existence only of particulars. Associated above all with William of Ockham (ca. 1298–1347), the theory challenged the contempt for matter that seemed to be implied in Platonic and Aristotelian philosophy and emphasized a return to rootedness in the earth.[67]

The second revolution was the Protestant Reformation with Martin Luther (1483–1546) as the focus. Above all Luther undermined the hierarchical structure of both church and state. He emphasized the basic dignity and equality of all Christians through baptism and the freedom of human conscience.[68]

The third and most powerful revolution was the scientific revolution, symbolized by the demonstration made by Galileo Galilei (1564–1642) that the earth moved around the sun. His experimentally rigorous and verifiable method of investigation lay at the heart of the seventeenth-century conflict between religion and science; it was science that put one in touch with what was real.[69] The development of empirical investigation dislodged the place of religion in the lives of many people. The Roman Catholic Inquisition's condemnation of Galileo and the church's efforts to curtail the scientific revolution only served to isolate the Roman Catholic Church from the dominant intellectual currents of the time.

What was in the seventeenth century primarily a movement among scientists developed in the eighteenth century into a broad cultural outlook that eventually affected either directly or indirectly much of Western society. The scientific revolution begun by Galileo induced the industrial revolution in the middle of the eighteenth century and also spawned the economic revolution of laissez-faire capitalism inaugurated by Adam Smith in 1776.

In a sense, modern culture really eliminated the natural cycles as well as transcendence. The direction of human life was simply linear; the goals were production and progress. Compulsive work and competition tend to take over so that there is no time for human beings to renew themselves socially. The result is individualism, fragmentation, specialization, differentiation, and a loss of the sense of the whole of reality. Modern science has so stressed the parts of reality that people have lost a comprehensive sense of the whole. Religion is naturally dislodged because its focus is on the meaning of the whole of life at its deepest level.[70]

The expression of modern culture was due in many ways to the development of printing, which revolutionized Europe. It enabled power to be taken from the landed aristocracy, who used handwriting as their means of communication. Power was assumed then by the expanding urban bourgeoisie, who enthusiastically embraced print as truly congenial to their fragmented and individualistic cultural consciousness.

Print supports individualism, both in religion and in society at large, because printed books are normally read alone. Handwritten documents usually required collective assemblies in which the texts were read aloud.

When handwritten documents were the rule, people went to church or to monasteries to hear the Bible read aloud, but with the beginning of printing, individuals acquired their own Bibles and devotional books. The Protestant Reformation was successful partly because of the print revolution, since Luther's Bible, which was printed in the vernacular, followed quickly on the heels of Gutenberg (b. ca. 1394–1399; d. 1468).[71] It was Gutenberg who invented movable type, thus facilitating the mass printing of books in a quick and efficient manner. As a result, scholarship became more and more an individual enterprise, for individual scholars were able to collect their own books and establish their own libraries. Individual scholarship also meant lay bourgeois scholarship, which eventually broke the aristocratic, clerical, and religious control of scientific information.[72]

By marginalizing religion, by eliminating tradition and community, and by extolling the value of science, the proponents of modern culture thought they were freeing humanity from both temporal and spatial restraints. Modern culture certainly inflamed the spark of creativity within large sectors of humanity, a power that both primal and classical culture would have associated with divine endowment. By the individualist in modern culture, creativity was proclaimed to be a human prerogative, dependent not on God but simply on human genius, science, and technology. The result was the erection of science and technology as idols, false gods of society. In spite of their divinization, however, they failed to answer deep questions about the meaning of human life.

In 1736, Alexander G. Baumgarten wrote a tract in which he introduced the term *aesthetics* to apply to those philosophical reflections that dealt with all human experiences that were not clear and easily analyzed and that were based on sensory cognition or feeling.[73] As a result, a distinction came to be made between science and the arts. Before the Age of the Enlightenment in the eighteenth century, artists were primarily craftspersons who made things according to the rules of their trade. They were skilled workers who knew how to design and construct buildings, how to bind books and tool leather, how to weave tapestries and make clothes, how to work in stone as well as in gold and silver. Good work was the goal rather than originality, yet within the inherited framework of skills and high standards, there was room for freedom and originality. Quality was of prime importance; nevertheless, craftspersons were expected to be true to their own talents. Beauty, however, was not a distinct quality for which one worked; it was simply the result of working skillfully with appropriate materials. What we currently call art was but the natural beauty and truthfulness that resulted from humanly made things that were well executed.

There was no sharp distinction between crafts and what today is known as the arts, though even today the distinction is becoming increasingly blurred.[74]

The understanding of art and the role of artists began to change radically during the Age of the Enlightenment. In the eighteenth century much was written about the notion of the beautiful, the sublime, and the principles of art, resulting in the removal of art from normal everyday life in the world. Art became what we would today call fine art as distinct from crafts, which were concerned with making things that were necessary for daily life.

With the writings of Immanuel Kant (1714–1804), Georg Wilhelm Friedrich Hegel (1770–1831), Friedrich Schelling (1775–1845), and Arthur Schopenhauer (1788–1860), art was radically separated from ordinary enjoyment; it was posed as the means whereby humanity could move beyond the mechanistic universe and find refuge from the tensions and travail of daily life. As a result, the artist became the person with special genius capable of mediating an experience of transcendence into the lives of people. In a sense, art replaced religion.

Until the Age of the Enlightenment there were no works of art as we would use that expression today. Sculpture, painting, and portraits were designed to fulfill a specific function, either to adorn a place or to set out significant values to be appropriated, especially as those values were realized in important personages. Following the Enlightenment, works of art came to be considered apart from their content. Subject matter declined in importance so that the way was prepared for the nonfigurative art of the twentieth century. Subjective dispositions were thought to be unimportant. Life was a closed system in which a rationalistic human race struggled to relate to an objective nature that was ruled by firmly fixed laws. God or any other non-natural or nonhuman force had no place in such a complex.

Hence, the Enlightenment produced a world that was, if not overtly antireligious, at least a-religious. Religion was tolerable as long as it was a private affair that did not interfere with science, philosophy, the fine arts, or scholarship in general. A principle of neutrality developed which maintained that in scholarship one should leave behind what is subjective, including religious convictions, which are ultimately irrelevant. Scholars should concern themselves with what is objective and true regardless of religious faith.

This understanding of objective reality not only influenced the vision of artists but also the interpretation of art given by historians, who did not concern themselves with the driving forces in the lives of artists or what they believed or what principles they held. Such subjective concerns were set aside, leaving the impression that artistic masterpieces of the past were simply created by artists out of their own special genius. Although the subject matter of the masterpieces was often religious, a religious interpretation was thought to be irrelevant.

It is important to realize that the scope of reality was increasingly circumscribed. The only things that were thought to be real were those that were natural; science alone could expose and analyze that reality. As a result, what previous generations had considered sacred and mysterious was reduced to fundamental instincts for power, pleasure, and survival. Human life, instead of being appreciated in terms of the varied and profound meanings that it has in the Bible, became mere biological life expressed by the beating of the heart and the urge for sexual pleasure, food, and drink.

Science certainly provided the tools for acquiring amazing insights into the structure of reality and for improving the living conditions for many people, but it was elevated by the rationalists into the tool for knowing all the truth worth knowing. The world was no longer open to the transcendent God. It was an enclosed web in which humanity was confined. The application of the scientific method to the natural sciences progressed rapidly in the nineteenth century; before long the same method was applied to other fields of human endeavor, including anthropology, sociology, economics, and psychology. For many, scientism became the new religion. Human persons became objects determined by natural laws to be studied by scientists using scientific method. They were not essentially different from animals and plants, simply more complex. It was in that context that Charles Darwin (1809–1882) could set out his evolutionary vision of what human beings really are and could become through the mechanics of natural selection. It was logical then, in Herbert Marcuse's terms, to speak of "one-dimensional man."[75]

Much of the contemporary Western world still operates on the principles of the Enlightenment. The overriding interest is still in the scientific method, which is looked upon by many people as the only way in which to make a better world. In the nineteenth century, Søren Kierkegaard posed significant questions about the human condition; so did the German romanticists. In the last century it was the existentialists who pondered the absurdity of life in a world turned in on itself. Worldwide catastrophes above all have convinced many people that the idols of science and technology have clay feet.

There is a basic crisis of meaning in the contemporary world because the dream of liberation at the heart of the Enlightenment has turned into the threat of the destruction of humanity as well as the whole world. In religious language, the Enlightenment vision of the modern world implicitly rejected the divine in human life, but at times it ended up extolling the demonic. From an artistic point of view, it is significant that the punk rock and rap culture has celebrated the satanic in modern life. Punk rock and rap groups maintain that they are simply mirroring back to humanity in their art what Western civilization has become.

There is no doubt that cultural developments in the West have been clearly mirrored in the various arts, especially since the beginning of the nineteenth century. Architecture was profoundly affected by the industrial revolution beginning in the eighteenth century. Both the increase in population and the shift from rural to town areas posed architectural problems that were eventually confronted by the use of newly discovered and refined materials such as steel, concrete, and glass, and by developments in engineering. Functionalism and efficiency were often the overriding concerns. However, in spite of technical advances, the satisfaction of deep human needs on the part of the poor and the middle classes of society was frequently neglected. The overall result has been the development of the complex phenomenon known as modern architecture.

Painting has reflected cultural shifts in a preeminent way. Naturalism, impressionism, expressionism, abstraction, cubism, surrealism, and pop and op art have all reflected the modern world. Music, too, has captured the modern mood in the development of jazz, blues, rock, and rap. Similar developments have taken place in the verbal arts, especially the novel, drama, and poetry. Perhaps above all it has been the new art forms of dance and theater and the film arts of photography, motion picture, and television that have symbolized most realistically what has been happening in the modern world.[76]

Out of all this has come a crisis for art and its role in society. It has often been asked to provide what religion has traditionally mediated, namely, an experience of transcendence, a mystical answer to the deep-seated questions that have been asked, and a satisfaction of the hunger for ultimate meaning that has been felt by many people in the Western world. But artists themselves have frequently been alienated and hungry for meaning. Artists have often been removed or perhaps more often have removed themselves from the mainstream of everyday life. Their art has frequently been taken out of the realm of ordinary commerce and placed in museums, galleries, and concert halls, which have become in a sense religious temples where the avant-garde can worship with appropriate catalogues and programs providing a liturgical guide to the experience.[77]

Art following the Enlightenment degenerated in many instances into art for art's sake, and interest in art functioned as a kind of irreligious religion for people living in a world where religion itself was a nebulous phenomenon exercising no clearly defined role. Because art often became so esoteric, people had to be initiated into its mysteries through lectures, catalogues, and courses in art appreciation.

What has appeared on the surface to be a crisis in the world of art was in fact a cultural crisis in Western society, a spiritual crisis affecting all aspects of human society, including morality, economics, and technology. Alienation, loneliness, despair, and isolation have characterized many segments of the Western world in recent decades. Since the Enlightenment, Western culture has focused above all on the relationship of humankind to the natural world in order to master that world and to take advantage of the benefits it can offer. However, the constantly increasing ability of many people to control their environment and shape the conditions in which they live has been an important cause of change in both the outlook and the lifestyles of many in the Western world.

The extraordinary success of modern technology and the scientific method in the Western world has induced people to concentrate on the satisfaction of their material needs and wants. This preoccupation with the material world, combined with the ruthlessness and impersonalism of modern industrial societies, has resulted in a vacuum of meaning in the lives of many individuals. They are not able to find satisfaction for their deepest longings in the worldviews that are set out by the communications media, nor are they often able to find the meanings they are searching for in traditional, organized religions. This is reflected in the large number of middle-class people in the United States who attend the so-called seeker service churches.[78] Some people attempt to fill the vacuum in their lives through sexual activity or the use of chemical substances, through Eastern religions or fundamentalist churches, through techniques of prayer or through revolutionary efforts to overthrow the various establishments thought to be responsible for the existing alienation. But on the part of many individuals there is simply an apathetic refusal to confront any of the social problems of the contemporary world and a consequent withdrawal into a privatized world. In the midst of the uncertainty and insecurity, it is not surprising that there has been a strong reactionary conservatism seeking to counteract what is perceived to be rampant permissiveness in a world that has lost its bearings.

Initially, modern culture was expressed by Renaissance architecture and art; it then progressed to the development of numerous art and architectural forms, culminating in various twentieth-century styles that have more or less given way to what is known as the "postmodern."

POSTMODERN CULTURE

Any discussion of postmodern culture must attempt to grapple with the obscure terminology and various distinctions that appear in the literature.[79] The work of French philosophers has dominated postmodern thinking, especially that by Georges Bataille and Jacques Lacan, followed by Emmanuel Levinas, Jacques Derrida, and Julia Kristeva, and eventually by a group of neo-Nietzscheans including Gilles Deleuze, Michel Foucault, and Jean-François Lyotard. It was in Lyotard's work above all that the term "postmodernism" referred not to a cultural expression or a period concept but to a form of philosophical skepticism.[80]

There are various contemporary theologies that purport to be postmodern in the sense that they agree that the ground of much modern theology has proved to be baseless and that a theological alternative must be radically different and deeper. There are three basic categories of postmodern theology with different commitments to premodern theology and philosophy. First is the deconstructionist type exhibited by the later work of Jacques Derrida and John Caputo. Then there is radical orthodoxy, represented by John Milbank, Catherine Pickstock, Graham Ward, Stanley Hauerwas, George Lindbeck, and Peter Ochs. Their aim is to give a more profound account of the transcendent in terms of Christian faith.[81] The third type is represented by the work of Jean-Luc Marion, who brings together classical negative theology with post-Heideggerian phenomenology. Three themes dominate his work: idolatry, the gift, and love. He explores ways of thinking about God as beyond being. Especially important is his distinction between idol and icon. An idol is something that simply reflects our own gaze, whereas an icon points our sight beyond ourselves to something we cannot master. The ultimate icon is Christ, who intervenes in person in the celebration of the eucharist.[82]

The term "postmodernity" refers to a specific culture, frequently understood as one fashioned out of late capitalism. It is dominated by the media and is characterized by eclecticism and the exaltation of the popular and the occasional. It is characteristic of the work of certain writers, such as John Barth and Thomas Pynchon, and certain architects, such as Robert Venturi and Frank Gehry. The turning point for this development was the publication in 1966 of Venturi's *Complexity and Contradiction in Architecture,* which acknowledged the ambiguous character of good architecture and the various levels of meaning in each structure.[83] Various terms were used to describe the new scene, including personalism, new rationalism, high-tech, and romantic pragmatism. During the 1980s, however, these terms gradually coalesced to form several main trends in architectural design: late modern, high-tech, postmodern classical, and neo-vernacular. Parallel to the postmodern developments was the conservation movement, which was concerned with finding new uses for old buildings.[84]

Above all, postmodernity in art and architecture posits itself against the abstract, purist characteristics of what has traditionally been called modern.[85] It is very consciously a countermovement.[86] The technical changes, however, have not been so much in the basic materials used in modern architecture, such as steel, glass, and concrete, as in the greater use of plastics for components as well as structures, resulting in sophisticated geometric forms and warped surfaces.

If, however, one speaks simply of postmodern culture, one invariably includes under that name a great variety of reactions and responses to the crisis of the modern Western world. This culture, developing above all among young people, is in some ways a return to primal culture, to nature, to the images of good and evil, and to symbols, myths, and rituals that are thought to enable people not only to deal responsibly with the mystery of iniquity in human life but to triumph over that evil.

Modern culture emphasized individual subjectivity, interiority, and personal autonomy. Postmodernism, however, is more fully aware that the human person is a relational being existing with an orientation toward others and within a complex of traditions. In general, postmodernism describes a current philosophical, political, and artistic climate that contrasts with both classical and modern culture.

Many interpreters of the postmodern world are nihilistic in nature as they call for a complete deconstruction of the philosophical and religious systems that have supported classical and modern culture. Others are more optimistic. Those who are rooted in the Christian tradition assert that human hope is grounded not ultimately in human achievements but rather in the power of the God who in Jesus Christ has conquered evil and has promised to save the world in Christ and through the power of the Holy

Spirit. This renewed trust in divine providence accompanies an effort to deconstruct the modern conviction that the human person is a self-determined, autonomous being who has no need for religion or tradition; it posits that the human person is really a network of relationships dependent ultimately on God but immediately dependent on community and traditions. This strain in postmodern culture is characterized by humility, which acknowledges that the human grasp of truth is always partial. Both human persons and communities are fragile and finite; hence, their discourse about themselves and about God must be tentative. This does not mean that truth is relative; it means that the human grasp of any revelation about God is open to the possibility of further revelation, understanding, and clarification. In a postmodern perspective, the world is understood not as a coherent whole but rather in terms of a multiplicity of constructs that sometimes fit together and sometimes do not. Claims to universality are suspect.

Postmodern sensibility maintains that views of reality do not constitute a given but are rather constructed. The disjunctive character of history and the magnitude of evil in the world call into question all claims to a complete grasp of truth. While recognizing the fragmentary character of the human grasp on reality, postmodern culture is suspicious of modernity's affirmation of the need for and usefulness of specialization and compartmentalization. Hence, it has sought to develop as much as possible a sense of continuity in what is known and achieved. Special effort is made to understand the human person not as a composite of various faculties but as a thrust toward unity achieved through relationships and rootedness in tradition. Wholeness is not thought to be irreconcilable with particularity; in fact, the two are dialectically inseparable.

Postmodern culture acknowledges that there is interruption, disorientation, and discontinuity in much of the world; this has encouraged Christians to reclaim the God of the Jewish and Christian scriptures not as one providing simple order and providence but rather as one who is above all active in history and present to creation, even in its experience of suffering and death.[87]

Communication in postmodern culture is above all by means of electronic devices. As with earlier technological revolutions in communications media, this new electronic form is transforming the organizational structures of society and its institutions and making possible for the first time a truly global society and truly global institutions.

The transition from late modern to early postmodern culture is a threatening one, for the later modern forms of technology and their supporting

privatized spiritualities continue to threaten and destroy the life systems of
the planet earth. In addition, they have been leading to a profoundly individualistic disintegration of our social relationships, beginning with the
family, and of our public value systems and spiritualities. A direct result of
this disintegration has been the serious erosion of institutionalized forms
of Christianity in the West. However, a strategic contribution of the electronic age is that, with its incredible connecting of information and its
holistic synthesizing of symbols, the destructive crisis of the Western
world is being powerfully revealed to all who have eyes to see.[88]

In postmodern culture science has gone beyond the Cartesian-
Newtonian-Darwinian paradigm. Physics is the dominant scientific discipline in postmodern culture, but unlike Aristotelian physics, which
dominated classical culture, postmodern physics, at least in some of its
expressions, maintains that the universe is a creative unity; it is a mystical
communion that continues to unfold creatively. The changes in the universe are thought to be not the result of shifting forces but the result of a
divine mind immanent in the universe. Human beings are thought to get
in touch with that divine mind not primarily by going beyond or outside
the universe but by going deeper and deeper within it.

In postmodern culture the thrust is toward convergence. The great challenge facing both science and religion is not only to tap the creative energies inherent in the world but also to address the need for redemption and
deliverance from evil. Life must be seen as both a creative and a redemptive
process.

Obviously many difficult questions face Christianity as its seeks to
relate to postmodern culture. Many Christians still live in an amalgam of
classical and modern culture. Following the Protestant Reformation, the
Roman Catholic Church constituted in many ways a classical ghetto in the
modern world. Its response to cultural pluralism has been mixed. Roman
Catholic Church leaders have often been uneasy when cultural diversity
exists; pluralism has sometimes been looked upon as intrinsically hetero-
dox. In recent times there has been a nostalgia for the unity and security
that classical culture brought to the Roman Catholic Church. The modern
rupture between religion and secular life has been curiously reflected in the
fact that some Roman Catholics openly acknowledge the legitimacy of
both modern and postmodern cultures in all areas of their lives except religion, where they want and expect everything to remain unchanged and to
continue to function in a classical framework. They can accommodate
their lives to contemporary technology, sociology, economics, and psychology, but they want classical religion, especially as it was expressed in

late medieval and Tridentine theology and liturgy. In other words their church should always be the same, *semper idem.*

There are some Christians who tend to have a very superficial understanding of culture and identify it simply with artistic forms and styles. Disgruntled by what they think is little more than a trendy pursuit of cultural fads in the areas of music, art, and architecture, and nostalgic for the aesthetic experiences they either had or imagined they had before the late-twentieth-century ecclesial and liturgical reforms, they oppose any ecclesial or liturgical inculturation and insist that culture must adapt itself to what they think should be an unchanging church and unchanging liturgy. There are others who wholly reject the contemporary approach to culture and stand firm in their conviction that classical culture, based as it is on a *philosophia perennis*, is the only legitimate culture and that it should be preserved and defended at all costs.

In spite of divergent views on culture among Christians, the contemporary world has generally left classical culture behind. Since the 1960s most mainline Christian churches have made an effort to relate to the technological developments in the contemporary world. Ironically, this change in attitude has taken place at a time when modern culture is in so many ways collapsing and giving way to postmodern culture. One cannot help but wonder whether Christianity is not often one cultural revolution behind the times.

As the Western world moves more and more into postmodern culture, religious experience is being interpreted in new ways. Religion has traditionally manifested itself in terms of doctrinal statements to be believed, rituals or liturgies to be executed, codes of behavior to be observed, and structural forms to be appropriated because they unite in communities or congregations those people who share the same religious experiences and convictions. Together these manifestations constitute the institutional character of religion. Obviously new experiences and interpretations of religion will call for new institutional forms.

In postmodern culture, the Christian religion must find institutionalized forms that affirm both the basic goodness of creation and the ongoing need for redemption in Jesus Christ and through the power of the Holy Spirit. Likewise, Christians must find forms that express and support the conviction that God is not only immanent in creation but transcendent as well. While recognizing the legitimacy of distinct roles in the church, Christians must affirm not only basic racial equality but also equality between men and women, ordained persons and laypeople, single and married, young and old, those who are physically and emotionally disabled and those who are strong and well. The structures must challenge people to involve themselves in both the ongoing creation of the universe and the critical transformation of the world. But if such structures are truly Christian, they will both support and challenge people in their conviction that it is not humanity that ultimately saves the world and brings it to fulfillment; it is God—God alone in Jesus Christ and through the power of the Holy Spirit. Art and architectural forms should play an important role in that process of supporting and challenging human values in light of the Christian tradition.

2

The Response of the Churches
to Cultural Shifts

THE WORLD BEGAN TO CHANGE RADICALLY WITH THE RENAISSANCE
in the fifteenth century. With their direction set on a humanistic track,
men and women looked upon themselves as the dominant figures in the
universe, where power and pleasure, achieved primarily through money,
became principal values. Although there were numerous Christians in the
Western world, they had relatively little effect on the direction that culture
was taking. The mainstreams of Christianity became so introverted that
they had minimal influence on the wider secular world. Broad areas of life,
such as science, philosophy, politics, economics, and the arts, were generally left in the hands of the secularists, while Christians concentrated on life
hereafter. Christianity became increasingly spiritualized as it lost interest
in the created world. In various ways it has often lived what has been
described as a ghostlike spirituality without a body; it seemed to espouse a
nonhistorical form of orthodoxy. Although Christians preached the
gospel, celebrated the sacraments, and engaged in charitable works, they
concentrated on saving souls and seemed to forget the incarnational principle that God is the God of the living and the God who has become incarnate in Jesus so that people might learn to live responsibly in the world and
deal with that world which is God's own creation.

There is no doubt that the church was in dire need of reform at the end
of the Middle Ages. Criticism of the church from within its own ranks
should have stimulated revitalization of the institution, but the criticism
resulted only in polarization and eventually in the divisive reform of the
early sixteenth century. Prophetic and apocalyptic visionaries separated
themselves from the authority of the Roman Catholic Church, thus leaving traditional Roman Catholicism with the complex task of reconstruct-

ing itself as a Christian church standing up and over against Lutheran, Zwinglian, Calvinist, and Anglican churches.[1]

Martin Luther (1483–1546) set out the foundation for all Protestant worship in his 1520 treatise *The Babylonian Captivity of the Church*,[2] which energetically attacked the whole late medieval system of worship. He did not attempt to find in scripture detailed prescriptions for worship, since he did not consider liturgical forms essential to the gospel. However, his interpretation of scripture led him to reject any sacrificial language in the eucharist, as well as invocation of the saints and veneration of relics. He emphasized the sermon as a primary feature of every liturgical celebration and likewise stressed congregational song. In general, Luther and his followers retained more visual and kinesthetic components in worship than did other Protestants, a situation that prevailed until the Anglican revival in the nineteenth century. Luther's *Formula Missae et Communionis* (1523) was a very conservative creation, retaining Latin and much traditional text and ritual; however, his *German Mass* of 1526 replaced Latin with German, paraphrased the ordinary of the Mass, and simplified the rituals. This was the liturgy that continued to be used until recently by European Lutherans and also by some German-speaking congregations in North America.[3]

The reforms in text and ceremony inaugurated by Ulrich Zwingli (1484–1531) in Zurich and John Calvin (1509–1564) in Geneva were much more radical; they emphasized strong biblical and didactic characteristics. Zwingli's liturgy, *Epicheiresis* (1553), was an almost completely new ritual. Preaching was not linked to any lectionary, and all music was forbidden. Calvin's *Form of Church Prayers* (1542) survives in worship ordos used in Reformed and Presbyterian churches; there are directions but no texts. The eucharist was to be carried out only quarterly, although Calvin advised weekly celebration. Calvin's tradition, which influenced Presbyterian worship in Scotland, England, and North America, is remembered above all for the method of singing psalms, but hymns and organs were forbidden. In more recent times, hymns have largely replaced psalms, and instrumental music is allowed.[4]

Anglican worship has traditionally been distinguished from other Protestant worship because of its conformity to prescribed texts, a factor that has given Anglicanism a sense of cohesion. It centers on the Book of Common Prayer, first issued in 1549 and revised three years later, largely by Thomas Cranmer (1489–1556). The prayer book provided complete texts for daily, Sunday, and occasional services, and its use was mandatory in Anglican churches. Historically the Book of Common Prayer is quite

Lutheran in its conservative approach to liturgy, but Calvinistic in its theology. All editions have provided daily and eucharistic lectionaries.[5]

The term "Free Churches" includes those groups that broke off from the original Protestant Reformers in the sixteenth and following centuries. They have placed emphasis on preaching, the pastor's prayer, and congregational singing. They emphasize lay leadership, including that by women, and seek to recover the practices of apostolic times. Baptism is the only sacrament that tends to be emphasized.[6]

The task of responding to the Protestant Reformation was entrusted by the Roman Catholic Church to the Council of Trent, which extended over eighteen years from 1545 to 1563. The council clarified a wide range of disciplinary and doctrinal questions and set in motion extensive reform measures, most of which were directed at the church's clerical leadership. The result was the development of a uniform Catholic culture expressed in clearly defined doctrinal teachings to be believed, precise disciplinary measures to be implemented, moral laws to be observed, ecclesiastical structures to be maintained, and sacramental rites to be performed.[7]

It was above all the Council of Trent that sought to respond to developments in the various Protestant communities. Although the commission that prepared the agenda for the council outlined an extensive project for the reform of the liturgy by Roman Catholics, the defensive mentality of the majority of the council fathers precluded their interest in executing such proposals, because they were looked upon as either concessions to the Protestants or distractions from major doctrinal and moral issues. By the end of the late Middle Ages, the church's liturgy had become very distant from the ordinary people; it was the worship of a clericalized elite celebrated in a language that the common people could not comprehend. A retrieval of the scriptures and the liturgy for the people was certainly one of the most positive objectives of the Protestant Reformation, for although ordinary laypeople often had deep religious piety, their spirituality was often divorced from the Bible and distant from the liturgical prayer of the church. The liturgical books that were issued after the Council of Trent did in fact eliminate certain medieval abuses, but they did not succeed in establishing a liturgical or biblical spirituality for the Roman Catholic Church at large. What they did was stabilize the Roman rite at a period of its development when it was an almost exclusively clerical preserve. That status was further ensured by the establishment of the Sacred Congregation of Rites on January 22, 1588, which asserted that the rubrics set out in the liturgical books and interpreted by juristic methods provide the clear and indisputable norms for regulating the liturgy.[8]

The dominant philosophical system affecting the majority of the fathers at Trent was nominalism. Rather than construct an integral doctrine of the Christian mysteries, they were inclined simply to maintain that Christian teachings were the result of divine decrees; hence, in the area of sacramental theology and practice they opened the way for an extrinsicism that plagued Roman Catholicism down to the time of the Second Vatican Council. In such a theology, sacramental validity is the overriding concern. Sacraments are administered rather than celebrated; they simply require one ordained or entitled by the church to perform the action, an intention to do what the church wants done, the correct matter and form established by the church, and the intention of the recipient to receive the sacramental grace. Like the rite itself, the sacramental grace is reduced to a very impersonal level. Rather than a share in God's own life, it is looked upon as an abstract power that enlightens one's intellect and strengthens one's will so that one believes the correct doctrines, observes the right laws, and carries out the proper rituals. So much emphasis is placed on the proper execution of the sacramental rites that little attention is given to the faith and devotion of either the minister or the recipient, and none to the wider community of the church and the effective proclamation of God's Word in conjunction with the sacramental rites. The aesthetic aspects of sacramental celebrations are of little or no concern.[9]

The Counter-Reformation, more properly spoken of as the Roman Catholic Reform, took place in an age when bourgeois humanism and court life were highly esteemed in the secular world. Both had an effect on the style of Roman Catholic life and worship. It was thought that in the same way as an earthly king was honored by an elaborate etiquette of court ceremonial, so also Christ the King, enthroned in the tabernacle or in the monstrance on the altar, awaited the homage of his subjects in an exuberant and sumptuous church resembling a salon. External pomp and grandeur became the most desirable aspects of Roman Catholic worship. The absence of intelligibility on the part of ordinary layfolk was thought to enhance the mysterious atmosphere and to promote a sense of awe. Those who were not ordained were generally kept at a distance from the sanctuary and were reduced to mere spectators and auditors admiring a scene of majesty and splendor.[10]

Through their art and decoration, the baroque churches emphasized the continuity of earth and heaven. The edifices and the rites carried out within them were meant to draw the believers' attention from the seen to the unseen, and from earth to heaven. As a result of their inability to participate actively in the rites, laypeople devised various ways of praying or otherwise occupying their time while in church. Their methods of assisting at Mass were usually unrelated to the meaning of the specific rites. Since most people could not understand Latin, the liturgy of the word did not constitute for them an effective proclamation of God's Word. Following Pope Alexander VII's condemnation of missal translations in 1661, the possibility of participating intelligently in the Mass became even more remote. Consequently, practices continued and were further developed that were not only at variance with the rites being celebrated but also at odds with sound theology. These included the recitation of the rosary and exposition of the Blessed Sacrament during Mass, and prolonged sermons unrelated to the scriptures or other liturgical texts delivered all during the Mass. These practices were generally attractive to the laity because they were comprehensible and sometimes even entertaining.[11]

Since much emphasis was placed on the eucharist reserved in the tabernacle or exposed in the monstrance for adoration, the Mass as the central focus of the liturgy tended to be displaced both in theory and practice. Both eucharistic devotion and Holy Communion, rarely received by the laity, were supported by an incomplete and sometimes distorted sacramental theology, often detached from the theology of the eucharistic action of the Mass. The latter focused on the Mass as a sacrifice to the neglect of the Mass as a meal. The only mode of Christ's real presence generally appreciated by Roman Catholics was the real presence under the eucharistic species of bread and wine. Although theologians spoke of the ordained priest acting in the liturgy *in persona Christi,* that assertion was understood more in terms of juridical efficacy than in terms of a dynamic encounter with Christ present and operative in the person of the minister. In general, the sense of presence appreciated at the time was not an active presence transforming the community through the mediatorial role of Christ in the Mass; it was a static presence of the Lord reserved under the species of bread alone so he could receive the adoration of his faithful subjects. This static understanding of presence was consistent with the dominant christology of the period, which was a descending christology articulated in terms derived from classical Aristotelian philosophy and emphasizing the two natures of Christ, one human and the other divine, both subsisting in one divine person. It was also consistent with the dominant ecclesiology of the period, which was based almost exclusively on a static institutional model of the church.

In general, the sacraments were looked upon as signs bringing individuals into contact with a transcendent God through grace, understood as a reified power that enlightened one's intellect to believe Christian truths and fortified one's will to perform Christian actions. This concept of grace was quite removed from the New Testament understanding of grace as the intimate presence of the risen Lord in the hearts of individual persons and in the midst of communities through the power of the Holy Spirit. New Testament imagery was not widely appreciated in either the Renaissance or the baroque periods. It was fashionable to employ Greco-Roman mythology as an artistic and literary medium; consequently, those who were brought up in such a tradition often found the biblical imagery employed in the church's liturgy quite remote and not readily intelligible. Furthermore, both the Renaissance and baroque periods were characterized by an intense interest in natural life on both the physical and intellectual levels. The flamboyant attitudes of these periods were at odds with the discipline and sobriety that characterized the Roman rite and were requisite for full, active, intelligent participation in that rite. Hence the official liturgy, apart from devotions, was often looked upon as austere and cold.[12]

Another factor that influenced the Catholic Reformation was that unflinching loyalty was expected of Roman Catholics toward the institutional church. That loyalty, however, often lacked a critical theological and biblical foundation. The theologians of the Catholic Reformation period were confident that the concise doctrinal statements contained in their theological manuals preserved the church's magisterial teaching, but the link between the *lex orandi* and the *lex credendi* was often tenuous. So long as the liturgy did not contradict Catholic doctrine, it was presumed to be legitimate to embellish the rites and the church buildings with artistic elements appropriated from secular culture but without any critical appreciation of the essentials of the Roman rite and its historical evolution.

In the history of art and architecture, the baroque period falls roughly between the years 1600 and 1725. It was followed by the Age of the Enlightenment, but in art history the years between 1725 and 1800 witnessed the development of two distinct styles of sculpture, painting, and decoration. The first was rococo. It flourished among the wealthy, especially in France but also to some extent in Germany and Italy. Its primary characteristics were its luxurious display of elegance and its sentimentality. The second movement, neoclassicism, developed toward the end of the eighteenth century. It stood at least partially in opposition to the superficial elegance of the rococo and partly in continuity with the baroque. It was based on a conscientious return to the classical ideals of the ancient world expressed in the use of models derived from ancient Greece and Rome and also from the Italian Renaissance.[13]

Obviously, all of the complex factors discussed above and taken together had decided effects on the interior designs of churches, the place-ment of the furnishings, and the decor of the buildings in the period fol-lowing the Protestant Reformation. The Roman Catholic churches not only expressed the self-understanding of the worshiping community but also clearly shaped the identity of those Roman Catholics in accord with a firm institutional model of the church, which emphasized the rights and powers of the officiating clergy. In those churches, the assembled laity were primarily passive beneficiaries of the clergy's rights to teach, rule, and sanctify.

In reaction to the artistic forms of the seventeenth and eighteenth cen-turies with their predilection for neoclassicism and their use and abuse of mythology, the romantic period, extending throughout the nineteenth century, extolled the culture of the Middle Ages, especially the external achievement of that period, because it was viewed as the most human, most religious, most Christian era of the church. Consequently, neoclassicism gave way to the neo-Gothic forms in architecture, vestments, liturgical ves-sels, music, and poetry.[14] Since the Gothic style naturally commanded a sense of awe, it was looked upon as admirably suited for places of worship. Augustus Welby Pugin (1812–1852), an English convert to Roman Catholi-cism and one of the most distinguished church architects of the period, maintained that Christian architecture should illustrate Christian beliefs. He saw the doctrine of redemption demonstrated in the cross plan of medieval churches, the doctrine of the Trinity in the triple arches and win-dows of the buildings, and the resurrection in the vertical thrust of the structures. Although Pugin felt that the Roman Catholic Church was the only one in which the grand Gothic style could really be restored, his ideas were primarily implemented in England by architects who belonged to the Anglican Church. Pugin's interests were shared too by some of the leaders of the Oxford Movement who were encouraging Anglicans to discover the history of the church before the Protestant Reformation.[15]

Shortly after the beginning of the Oxford Movement in 1833, a society called the Cambridge Camden Society was founded by J. M. Neale and Benjamin Webb for the study of ecclesiastical art. In 1841 it began to issue a monthly periodical, *The Ecclesiologist,* which survived until 1868. It greatly stimulated interest in traditional Catholic worship and church architecture and thus promoted the liturgical and ceremonial revival in the Anglican Church in the later nineteenth century.[16]

On the Continent it was above all in the monastic movement launched by Dom Prosper Guéranger at Solesmes in 1833 that the Gothic forms were brought to bear on the celebration of the liturgy and its environment.

Gregorian chant was restored, and the rubrics prescribed in the liturgical books were carefully implemented, resulting in a liturgy that was austere, impressive, and cleansed of much of its baroque theatricality.[17]

Although the romantic period generally retained the baroque understanding of the eucharist, with its emphasis on adoration of the reserved sacrament rather than on the sacrificial action of Christ, there were significant theological developments that helped to lay the foundation on which the modern liturgical movement was built. Historians such as Johann von Döllinger (1799–1890), emphasized the recovery of early manuscripts so that Christian tradition could be separated from legend. Following their restoration in 1814, the Jesuits did much to recover the past, including the writings of Thomas Aquinas. Pope Leo XIII (1810–1903) not only supported sound academic efforts in the Roman Catholic Church but also issued significant documents himself in an effort to relate the Roman Catholic Church to the modern world and its problems.

Especially important was the theological work done at the University of Tübingen, first by Johann Sebastian von Drey (1777–1853), who tried to think through the relationship between the particulars of Christian scripture and tradition and the Christian faith, and then by his colleague Johann Adam Möhler (1796–1818), who rethought the nature of the church. In 1832, Möhler published his major work, *Symbolik*, in which he tried to integrate the understanding of the church's visible structure with a more complete and vital understanding of the mystery of the church as set out in both the New Testament and the writings of the church fathers. Möhler's ecclesiology was characterized by insistence on both the visible structure of the community and the interior reality nourished by God's Spirit through the life of grace.[18] This approach was furthered by Jesuits in Rome, including Carlo Passaglia (1812–1887), Klemens Schrader (1829–1875), and J. B. Franzelin (1816–1886); and also by Matthias Scheeben (1835–1888) in Germany and John Henry Newman (1801–1890) in England.[19]

In preparation for the First Vatican Council (1869–1870), a schema on the church, prepared largely by Klemens Schrader, defined the church primarily in terms of the Mystical Body of Christ. Opposed by many of the council fathers, the image was relegated to secondary importance with the result that the council defined the church above all as a visible society. However, a more biblical understanding of the church was further developed in the twentieth century, specifically between World War I and World War II, through the writings of Karl Adam (1876–1966) and Emile Mersch (1890–1940). In 1943 Pope Pius XII issued his encyclical *Mystici Corporis,* which incorporated the patristic and medieval insistence on the interior reality of God's Spirit within the church together with the theology of the church as a visible, hierarchically structured society. Following the Second World War, Roman Catholic ecclesiology was greatly influenced and enriched by the ecumenical movement as well as by further developments in the scriptural, patristic, and liturgical movements.

This scholarship had a dominant influence on the understanding of the church set out in the documents of the Second Vatican Council, especially the Constitution on the Sacred Liturgy (*Sacrosanctum Concilium*), the Dogmatic Constitution on the Church (*Lumen Gentium*), and the Pastoral Constitution on the Church in the Modern World (*Gaudium et Spes*). In *Lumen Gentium*, the church is described in terms of a rich complex of images that complement the traditional image of the church as a hierarchically structured society. It is the people of God, a holy communion, the body of Christ, and the sacrament of salvation. What is important for architectural purposes is that the emphasis has shifted from a pyramidal image of the church dominated by a clerical elite to an image of the church as an assembly of the faithful, who by Christian initiation are basically equal but who exercise various ministries on behalf of the community, some because of Christian initiation, others because of presbyteral and episcopal ordination.

Since the Second Vatican Council the church has been analyzed in terms of various models, including those of institution, herald, communion, servant, sacrament, and community of disciples.[20] Since no one model is in itself adequate for understanding the nature of the church, the various models must be used to complement one another. As an image or expression of what the church itself is, the church building must both express these various images and also form Christians so they internalize the identity that is set out in the images themselves.

Other theological developments have also had a significant influence on the Roman Catholic understanding of liturgy, its artistic forms, and the environment in which it is celebrated. Because of its central role within Christian theology, christology very largely determines both the content and the style of sacramental theology and ministry. Until recent times, christology was one of the most stable tracts in dogmatic theology. Cast in classical metaphysical terms, it firmly asserted that Jesus Christ is one divine person with two natures, one human and one divine. Such a christology yielded a sacramental theology that was preoccupied with the Christian's ontological union with Christ through the sacraments functioning as instrumental causes of grace. Great care was taken to maintain the priority of Christ's action over the liturgical action of the minister.

Since this model of christology relies so heavily on categories drawn from the philosophy of nature, when it is used to underpin a theology of the liturgy, it leads to an impersonal, if not mechanical, understanding of the sacraments, one that does not encourage an active participation on the part of the recipients or, more properly, those who celebrate the sacraments.[21]

Reflection on the Council of Chalcedon occasioned by the fifteenth centenary of that council in 1951 prompted Roman Catholic theologians to raise and tackle new christological problems. Karl Rahner's commemorative essay, originally titled "Chalcedon: End or Beginning?" had special impact.[22] Protestant christology in modern times has been deeply rooted in the Bible; that is especially evident in the work done by outstanding theologians, including Karl Barth, Rudolf Bultmann, Ernst Käsemann, Jürgen Moltmann, and Wolfhart Pannenberg. Roman Catholic christology has been much more shaped by the dogma of Chalcedon. As a result of biblical renewal, however, Roman Catholic theologians have tried to grapple with the issue of Jesus' self-knowledge as well as the historical Jesus. In more recent times, theologians have tried to relate christology to the pressing issues of social justice, peace, and ecology, as well as those raised by feminism and liberation theologies. Hence various christological models have developed in recent years, among which the psychological and revelational models have proved especially attractive.[23]

The psychological model has been influenced by modern phenomenology. The category of the "self" is important in this model; it seeks to set out the feelings, purposes, motivations, and in fact the mind of Jesus Christ. It is not so much the ontological union of God and humanity in Jesus Christ that is stressed as the I–Thou relationship between Jesus and the Father, which is highlighted in the New Testament, above all in John's Gospel. Likewise, it is not so much our union with Christ understood in metaphysical terms that is emphasized as it is our union with him through faith and love in mind and heart. This model emphasizes the reality of the church as the body of Christ constituted as such by the communication of Christ's own Spirit through Christian initiation and the other sacramental rites. Hence it stresses the sacramentality of human persons and communities as the bearers of the Spirit of God.

The model takes the incarnational principle seriously; it seeks to draw out the implications of Christ's consubstantiality with human beings in terms of intersubjectivity and the personal encounter between human beings and Christ. Christ's presence and action in the sacraments must be expressed, then, in some form of personal communication between Christ and human beings. The sacraments are for human persons, not in the sense that they are impersonal instruments for human salvation, but rather in the sense that they are expressions of human life on the level of deep needs and longings, and of God's response in Christ to the human situation. In other words, the sacraments are celebrations whereby human persons grow more and more into the image of God in Christ through the power of the Holy Spirit.

On a sacramental level, the psychological model of christology emphasizes how important it is that the sacramental rites actually communicate the meaning intended. The model implicitly asserts that the Christian life of human persons and communities must be authentic and their faith vital if the encounter with Christ in the sacraments is to be transformative of persons and communities.[24]

The revelational model seeks to interpret Christ as the Word of God and the unique revelation of the Father. It situates Christ within the purview of salvation history and looks upon all creation as a manifestation of the divine Logos. The model is obviously very biblically oriented; hence it seeks to mine the revelatory content of the biblical notions of word and image. It is especially useful for Roman Catholics in their efforts to retrieve the place of the scriptures and sacramental word in the liturgy. Just as the historical humanity of Jesus Christ was a sacramental expression of the divine Logos, so the scriptures proclaimed in the liturgy are sacraments of the divine Logos. The model affirms that it is not only ritual action that is sacramental but the word accompanying the action is sacramental as well. Because it views all of creation as a sacramental revelation of the divine Logos, this model is useful at a time when there is the threat of ecological disaster; it can incorporate the view that not only human beings but all earthly creatures and the whole universe are destined for final redemption and blessing in Christ through the power of the Holy Spirit.[25]

Certainly these theological developments have had important effects on both the verbal and the nonverbal symbols in liturgy, as well as preaching, teaching, prayer, and pastoral ministry. The major emphasis in the revelational mode is on God's creative and redemptive initiative in Christ speaking to human persons; however, human persons must hear and respond actively to God's initiative with faith and love if their lives are to be transformed.

Above all, in the last forty years or so, serious efforts have been made by many theologians, Protestant, Roman Catholic, and Anglican, to relate their discipline to contemporary developments in the physical and social sciences. To some extent this effort has been made in response to the challenges of secularization rooted in the Enlightenment. Until the Second Vatican Council, many Roman Catholics took modernity seriously only if it did not threaten traditional Catholic beliefs and practices. In recent years, however, conscious efforts have been made to develop theological methods whereby scripture and the other confessional expressions of Christian faith found in doctrinal formulas, theological discourse, liturgy, and pastoral practice may be correlated with one another and with human experience. In other words, an effort has been made to develop interdisciplinary methods enabling theology to relate to a wide variety of arts and sciences, to take account of their findings, and to evaluate their assertions. This is not a case of theology simply adapting itself to the modern or postmodern world or of translating theology into terms that are set out by the world. The church itself and its sacramental expressions have an identity and an intrinsic value of their own. It is not only a question of the church being confronted by contemporary cultural developments; it is also a question of contemporary culture with its physical, social, and artistic developments being confronted by the church.

As a result of this enterprise, one of the most important areas in theology today is Christian anthropology, which is the study of human beings insofar as they are related to God. The discipline seeks to understand human persons in the light of revelation, particularly the revelation of God in the humanity of Jesus Christ. Hence, Christian anthropology is especially dependent on the revelation model in christology. It inquires how people can relate to God's Word and work in the world; consequently it also seeks to understand the nature of the world itself. Certainly this area of theological investigation is important for the light it can shed on human persons and communities as the subjects of worship, how they are to relate to the world in which they live, and how they are to be accommodated and addressed in the worship environment.[26]

The contemporary approach stands in marked contrast to that generally taken since the seventeenth century, when theology became quite dependent on philosophical idealism and so discoursed in an abstract way on what was essential to human nature. Instead of asserting clear divisions between nature and grace and the natural and supernatural orders, many theologians now take the direction set out by Maurice Blondel at the end of the nineteenth century and follow an existential method. Beginning with the concrete unity of human persons as they exist in history, they concentrate on the one, actual, supernatural order established by the incarnation and redemption of Jesus Christ and the outpouring of the Holy Spirit on all of creation. In pursuing this approach, theologians must be in dialogue with philosophical existentialism.[27]

Henri de Lubac, Karl Rahner, Edward Schillebeeckx, and Johann Baptist Metz have made significant contributions to the new approach to the Christian understanding of human persons and their world. A number of theses have been prominent in their writings that have bearing on the sacramental life and ministry of the church and consequently on the art and environment of that ministry. The most important point stressed in contemporary Christian anthropology is that human beings are beings-in-the-world; they are finite historical beings without a firm grasp on existence. Their awareness of reality cannot be achieved in isolation from the cultural forces that shape their lives. Although language itself is always culturally conditioned, it plays an essential role in the human effort toward self-understanding and self-fulfillment. It not only provides means of communication for human beings but also a medium in which revelation about the meaning of life takes place. Because of the divine creation, incarnation, redemption, and outpouring of the Holy Spirit, God does not stand over against people but is really the metaphysical ground of all human being. Although human persons are beings of finite, limited resources, they are oriented toward the infinite; they are not satisfied with what is confined and limited. Religion and revelation are intrinsic to the human spirit. The fulfillment of the human aspiration is manifested in the incarnation of God's Word, the perfect union of God and humanity. The divine incarnation in Jesus Christ therefore sets out the paradigm for all human persons in their effort to relate to God.[28]

If human beings are oriented in and through their finiteness toward God as the end and goal of all human activity, then God will be revealed and available to human persons not only in their interior religious experience but also in and through the various social and historical processes of human life. Any dichotomy between matter and spirit or between body and soul is rejected as a contradiction of the fundamental unity of both creation and redemption. However, theologians emphasize that although human persons are ordered toward union with the divine, they are free to reject God. The concrete existential order in which human persons are drawn toward God through God's own initiative does not preclude either the possibility of unbelief or the rejection of God's self-gift. But only insofar as human persons freely respond to the offer of God's self-gift do they become fully human.[29]

If God is not conceived of as absolute Being standing over against all people but rather as the absolute metaphysical ground of all being, then all being can be revelatory of God's presence. The Eastern Christian traditions have regularly appreciated the created world as a medium for the presence of God; creation has not been an enemy of either God or God's people. An important theme in Eastern Christian theology has been that of *theōsis*, or deification, which implies the transformation of humanity into the image of God. The created world has been esteemed and venerated because the creator of the world became incarnate as an integral part of the world in the flesh of Jesus. Through that sacred humanity God achieved the redemption and transformation of the world. In Jesus, God restored the divine image in human beings, who had distorted that image through sin. Consequently the doctrines of creation, incarnation, and redemption have been at the heart of Eastern Christian life. But those doctrines have taken on life and meaning for Eastern Christians in and through the celebration of the liturgy. In the context of the whole world as sacrament, the liturgy has regularly held primacy of place in the lives of Eastern Christians.[30]

The Western tradition has been much more fragmented. Contemporary efforts by theologians working in the area of Christian anthropology have resulted in a more integrated systematic theology related to both ethical behavior and worship. Their emphasis on the intimate relationship between God and human persons and God's presence in their lives as well as in all of creation has resulted in a shift in the understanding of the sacramental theology and ministry of the church. The liturgy is not looked upon as a complex of signs pointing to a reality wholly other than the signs themselves but rather as a sensible expression of God present and operative within the signs themselves. The liturgy truly makes the transcendent God immanent and available to human beings; it enables people to share in God's being, revealed and offered to humanity in and through creation itself.

Both Christian anthropology and ecclesiology affirm that the church does not exist in isolation from the world; it is now and always has been bound up with the whole process of human history, in spite of its efforts at certain periods to isolate itself from the rest of the world. As a living organism, the church is bound to change and develop and is subject to influence from the cultural phenomena of the wider world. This influence is operative not only on a superficial or external level as though the church were wholly distinct from secular history but willing to make an occasional concession to secular culture by adopting some of its expressions and modes of operation.

Certainly the church possesses an intrinsic identity of its own, but it is dependent on cultural phenomena as it seeks to give an expression of its own identity in terms that can be appropriated by contemporary people. As history shows, all aspects of the church's life, including its governmental structures, its religious language, its art and architecture, and its ministry, give clear evidence of this interdependence. In its most vital periods, the liturgy, as the primary cultural expression of the church, has clearly reflected this interdependence. It must continue to do so if it is to be constitutive of the identity of the church for people living in the contemporary world.

Efforts to relate contemporary Christian theology and ministry to the diverse cultural systems of the world are fraught with many difficulties. As noted above, very basic questions about life and death are being urgently asked by men and women struggling to find meaning in their existence during this transitional phase from a modern to a postmodern culture. The very questions have often brought Christian theologians and behavioral and social scientists into dialogue with one another as they try to suggest answers to the existential questions that are being asked by men and women struggling to find meaning in their existence in this period during which we find a curious mix of primal, classical, modern, and postmodern cultures. In their efforts to collaborate, they have often found common ground in their common concern for symbols, rituals, and myths, which have traditionally played important roles in shaping and sustaining the lives of individual persons and communities.

Many cultural anthropologists are also keenly interested in rituals. Like myths, rituals are constitutive elements in religion. Since they can be observed, they are often more easily described and understood than myths, at least on a superficial level. Rituals are generally described as patterned, repetitive, formal behavior; when they are used in religion, their goal is to relate human persons to the transcendent. By taking part in religious rituals, individual persons acquire a sense of identity with particular religious groups; they likewise internalize the religious values espoused by those groups.

The anthropological insights concerning ritual that have been set forth by such social scientists as Clifford Geertz, Mary Douglas, Margaret Mead, Victor Turner, Ray Rappaport, Catherine Bell, and Ronald Grimes have been both provocative and useful to sacramental theologians and liturgical scholars, but it must be noted that though Christian liturgy has much in common with ritual behavior, the two may not be equated. Christian liturgy is a celebration of a mystery that is both transcendent and immanent. It is not only a remembrance of what has occurred in the past but also a celebration of what is made present here and now in the liturgy. It likewise proclaims an expectation of what is yet to come. The formal, repetitive aspect of liturgy must make allowance for the creative life of God to break into the lives of persons and communities. In that sense liturgical behavior is both programmed and spontaneous. The God whom Christians relate to in the liturgy is both creator and redeemer. By sharing in God's life, they share in the divine ability to create and transform what has already been created; they also open their lives to the redeeming power of God, which overcomes the mystery of iniquity in the universe. God offers humanity that redemption in Jesus Christ through the power of the Holy Spirit.

Just as social and behavioral scientists attempt to analyze human life and invite human persons and communities to reflect on their experience, so also contemporary Christian theologians invite persons and communities to reflect on their experiences here and now; but they also and above all challenge people to find God present and active in their lives. Responsible Christian living involves experience coupled with exploration of the meaning of the experience situated in the context of faith. In other words, it involves efforts to understand the divine revelation that life holds for us. The world we live in confronts us with countless problems, many of which can be solved. The technological revolution has helped us solve many of those problems, or it has convinced us that they are solvable even if we ourselves cannot find the solutions. But in spite of our extraordinary scientific advances, the world we live in also confronts us with mysteries that can only be lived with and contemplated. Solutions would be useless. There are the everyday mysteries of birth and death, the mystery of energy within the atom, and the endless expanse of space; there are the mysteries of freedom and beauty as well as the mysteries of good and evil in the world. It is the contemplation of these mysteries that has given rise to both religion and art.

The mysteries of life have given rise to religion because in a world that does not readily make sense, men and women have searched for some meaning that does make ultimate sense. They have tried to establish a relationship with that sense of ultimacy through cults, creeds, and codes of behavior. Likewise, through common structures they have joined together with others who share in the same interpretation of ultimacy. The mysteries of life have also given rise to art because men and women have discovered that the ultimate meaning they find can be expressed only through works of the creative imagination: through poetry and painting, through architecture and sculpture, through music and drama.

Imagination is not the same as mere fantasy, which is sometimes contrasted with objective fact. Imagination is the human mind's capacity to see meaning beyond what is immediately evident, to make connections among various individual components, and to envision new possibilities. In a holistic view of the human person, reason and imagination are not rivals, not pitted against one another in a tug-of-war that neither side wins. Rather they are mutually enhancing powers, mutually enriching dimensions of the one act of human knowing. Imagination is the faculty that enables artists to create works of art and enables others to participate in what they have created. In a sense, the act of creation does not finish with the work of the original artist.[31] As Ernst Barlach, the German sculptor who died in 1938, remarked, "Two are needed for every art—one who makes it and one who needs it."[32] Naum Gabo, the Russian artist who died in California in 1977, expressed the same idea: "A work of art, restricted to what the artist has put into it, is only a part of itself. It only attains full stature with what people and time make of it."[33]

Artists and architects, poets and composers invite us to participate creatively in what they have begun. We must not hesitate then to bring our experience, our own lives, into dialogue with the life experience expressed by the artists. That is precisely what art is meant to do: to stimulate our own imaginations, to set us free to explore our experiences. A good work of art prompts and challenges us to reflect on our encounters with life at its deepest levels. It encourages us to dare to explore the mystery that lives at the heart of religion. Perhaps it is not so much a question of what we see in a work of art as what the work of art sees in us. For example, it has been suggested that in Mark Rothko's dark panels of black and red hanging in the meditation chapel in Houston and in the Tate Gallery in London we do not see a reflection of the terror, madness, and despair of our times, but rather we see what God is seeing and feeling as God looks out on our suffering world as it seems to collapse into its own death. Likewise, in Barnett Newman's *Stations of the Cross,* abstract paintings like those of Mark Rothko, but vertical rather than horizontal, bright rather than dark, we are not called to see the walk of the suffering Jesus along the Via Dolorosa but rather we are called to hear his words to us, "Why? Why did you forsake me? To what purpose?" This means that religious forms and symbols need to be reinterpreted in the light of each new generation's experience. Only in this way can the truth they point to be rediscovered and so once more be communicated and shared.[34]

Men and women expressed their sense of mystery, their relationship with the numinous and the ultimate in life through painting and poetry, through sculpture and dance, music and myth, story and parable long before they came to formulate it in any creeds or doctrinal statements. This does not mean that creeds and codes of behavior are not important components of institutionalized religion. Religion and religious experience are sustained and communicated primarily by symbols and rituals, myths and metaphors, not primarily by doctrinal propositions or theological reflections. Theological reflections, however, distilled in creeds and propositions, are important for all of us but especially for ministers in the church, because they provide us with the criteria by which we understand and evaluate our own religious experience and the experience of others. In light of those criteria we are called to make judgments about the rightness or wrongness, the truthfulness or falsity of our experience, and in the light of those judgments make responsible commitments and help others to do the same. It is the application of sound theological criteria that keeps our faith from degenerating into fundamentalism, quietism, individualistic piety, or enthusiastic sentimentality. It is on the doctrinal level that we are able to identify the paschal mystery of Jesus Christ, open our lives to the light of the Spirit, and then make commitments so we become one with the experience of Jesus Christ through the power of the Holy Spirit.

Traditionally religious communities have found their identity above all in commonly accepted doctrinal statements or creeds. That emphasis on creedal statements, however, has had its serious limitations, especially in an age of doctrinal pluralism within religious institutions. As a result, religious communities today are often in search of a clear sense of identity. As Archbishop Rembert Weakland has pointed out, a formed and informed Catholic identity is not easily found in the United States at the present time, even though the quest for such an identity seems to permeate many of the institutions of the Roman Catholic Church in this country—from universities to elementary schools, from hospitals to social services. He suggested that a useful way to remedy the lack would be to retrieve, restore, and support the role of the arts in the transmission of Catholic culture.[35] He wrote, "We have not given form to our belief. . . . We have often focused on the transmission of precise verbal formulas that encapsulate the essentials of our teaching."[36] Although formulaic assertions of beliefs memorized by Catholic adherents are important, they are intellectual formulas that need to be incarnated in a common Catholic culture, a meaning-system that pulls together and makes sense of the great variety of human experiences. A Catholic culture is a way of looking at the whole of life—at life and death, at good and evil, at past, present, and future, at human relationships and relationships with God.[37] In an earlier age, the *Baltimore Catechism*, the Latin Mass, weekly novenas, abstinence on Friday, Catholic education at the elementary and high school levels, pictures and statues of the Sacred Heart and the Blessed Mother all went a long way in giving an identity to Catholics in this country, even Catholics from diverse ethnic backgrounds.[38]

A lack of denominational identity is reflected among Anglicans and Episcopalians. Many Anglican bishops from the Southern Hemisphere seem to be willing to depart from the traditional emphasis on a spirituality based on the Book of Common Prayer and to emphasize instead the primary importance of personal conversion and a fundamentalist approach to scripture. A confusion about identity is reflected also in those Lutheran congregations which have taken a "seeker-service" approach to worship and try to respond to individual needs and promote personal fulfillment rather than celebrate Sunday worship according to the prescribed Lutheran rituals.[39]

In the United States, the aesthetic aspects of culture, above all the artistic, musical, literate, and architectural components, have not found a profound or distinctive Roman Catholic expression. Since the Second Vatican Council, Roman Catholics in this country "have produced very little in these fields that has been or could be claimed by the overall Catholic population as truly expressing who or what they believe and are."[40] There are at present many cultural expressions among Catholic people, but those expressions are generally undistinguishable from the culture of many others in the country. What is true of Catholics is probably true of the majority of the mainline Christian churches in this country.

In his monograph entitled *Seeing Theological Forms,* Thomas O'Meara has challenged professors of theology, religious educators, liturgists, and other church ministers. He wrote:

> Little has changed in much of education since the time of Aristotle. A teacher still lectures to a silent class, and the students listen and memorize. But education and thinking are more than that passive enterprise. Recently teaching, recognizing that Americans are intellectually formed by the electronic media, has begun to incorporate into the classroom the new technology. Clearly, in colleges or universities where lectures are complemented by transparencies, films, and interviews, the purely aural era of education is yielding to new pedagogies. . . . Contemporary theology still remains too often synonymous with a text: faith is pursued not in human life but in books, a cerebral construct, or a method.[41]

O'Meara's hope is that theological students will see both visually and intellectually, since in human life the two seeings are joined.

Other contemporary scholars, including Margaret R. Miles and Caroline Walker Bynum, have rightly complained that historians have read the development of Christianity almost exclusively through doctrinal statements and have neglected to show how art and architecture shaped the understanding of Christians and, in fact, served as significant media through which their religious experiences were basically sustained and communicated.[42] Although historians have fashioned a reasonably coherent account of Christian leaders and their doctrines, controversies, and struggles with secular powers, they have often neglected the religious experiences of ordinary Christians who left no literary account of their faith, worship, and community life.[43]

Both the Old and New Testaments speak to us in word pictures. There are pictures of a burning bush, a pillar of cloud, a humiliated son returning home to his father's embrace, a traveler beaten and left half dead by the roadside, a shepherd searching for a wandering sheep, a woman sweeping her house as she looks for her lost coin. We see Jesus himself embracing little children, touching a blind beggar's eyes, bending compassionately over a woman taken in adultery. We see him hanging on a cross and then appearing three days later to a grieving woman in a garden. When Jesus wanted to teach us about God, he painted pictures with words and parables. Through pictures we glimpse the basic truths of Christianity.[44]

Artists create pictures to stimulate our creative imaginations and to help us grasp a broader scope of reality. They paint particular men and women to help us get new insights into the lives of men and women in general. Great artists paint more than their eyes can see; they paint the possibilities of what we may see. But artists are neither mere photographers nor historians. They are not literalists. Art is a means of communicating the truth. It is not an invitation to live in a self-indulgent world of fantasy. Rather it is an invitation to bring our creative imaginations to bear on all of life and to see that the world and our life in it need not always be the way they are now.

Bad art does not simply fail to tell the truth; it tells a lie. For example, when Christ is portrayed as a rather spineless figure of sentimental benevolence surrounded by lambs in a romantic landscape, such a representation is deceptive; it has unfortunate effects on theology, prayer, and worship. As Edward Robinson has observed, "Kitsch degrades by satisfying the heart or mind with an inadequate or false image of reality. It is this, and not its failure to appeal to the finer feelings of a cultivated mind, that makes it an enemy of true spirituality."[45] Kitsch is sentimental art; its fault is that it does not hint at the whole truth but sets out only the part of the truth that people are apt to want to see. If the ultimate object of Christian worship is to get beyond the here and now to experience a transcendent relationship with God, then any form of mere naturalism should be ruled out as at best inadequate and at worst distorting.

The sacred images that surround people and the architecture in which they worship certainly communicate meanings. Although most people probably act their way into thinking and so liturgize first and then theologize, it has been asserted that it is increasingly common today that people come to liturgy after they have espoused a certain set of doctrines or theology rather than come to espouse doctrine because of the way they have worshiped. The mind sometimes defines before the emotions exult. Likewise, Christians who have a well-defined sense of the Christian mystery and its personal and social implications often withdraw from liturgical assemblies that espouse either no awareness of social responsibilities or one that is contrary to the doctrines the worshipers think are compatible with their understanding of Christianity. They take advantage of the mobility that is available to them and the liturgical possibilities from which they are able to choose and so worship where they sense a consonance between liturgy and Christian life in the world. Those options unfortunately are usually not open to the poor and the elderly.

There is also what has been called the phenomenon of reversionism, which involves a search for transcendence in the midst of what is thought to be an obsession with the human.[46] But the transcendence of God must not be recovered at the expense of the human. As Richard Gaillardetz has noted, the experience of transcendence without community is not Christian, nor is the experience of community without transcendence.[47]

Christian life is really a way of living out the call from Jesus Christ to grow into the image of God through the power of the Holy Spirit; it is a way of living out the paschal mystery. Jesus Christ is for Christians the primary symbol of the passage from death to everlasting life. He not only shows us the way to make that passage; he also empowers us through the Holy Spirit to follow his way. His death and resurrection were continuous with his lifelong willingness to embrace the creative gift of new life offered moment by moment in the context of a community, and in that context to embrace the God who comes to people with the gift of new life. His great desire is to share the Holy Spirit with us so we might come to live on deeper and deeper levels and overcome the alienation and isolation that characterize so much of human existence. Jesus died to the human tendency toward isolation, self-centeredness, and self-preoccupation. He inserted himself into the human community and entered deeply into the healing and corrective dimensions of human life. Through the outpouring of the Holy Spirit, he empowers us to do the same.

Depth of experience for Christians is always grounded in Christ. His life and person are always normative. His life sheds light on their lives. Christianity is basically a mutual sharing in life that comes from Jesus Christ, whose Spirit is communicated through everything and every person alive. It is mediated in a special way through the symbols that Christians have traditionally called the sacraments.[48]

The ability to appreciate artistic forms, to open one's life to the meaning they seek to communicate, and to hear the questions they try to ask is really the outgrowth of a particular kind of life. Above all, it is dependent on a sense of awe and wonder at everyday life. But our technological culture, at least in its modern forms, tends simply to convert the mystery of life into a long series of problems to be solved; postmodern technological culture is in some ways perhaps more inclined to respect the mystery of life. Modern culture also tends to dissipate any sense of gratitude for the gift of life and its continuance and to replace it with a sense of greed, as we are reminded by the media of all the material things we do not yet possess. Consequently we are often obsessed with the quantity of things we have rather than with the quality of our experience.

One of the primary requisites for effective celebration of the liturgy and for an appreciation of its artistic forms and environment is the ability to experience the liturgy as a complex of symbols rather than simple signs. Before the Second Vatican Council, Roman Catholic catechisms and theology manuals used to define the sacraments as "outward signs instituted by Christ to give grace." Contemporary sacramental theologians are apt to explore the meaning of the sacraments as symbols mediating participation in the paschal mystery of Jesus Christ. One of the problems that Christians face in dealing with symbols is semantic. For many people in the past, if something was only a symbol, it was not the real thing. Roman Catholics, for example, sometimes tried to distinguish their notion of the eucharist from what they thought Protestants held by asserting, "For us Christ's presence is real but for them it is only symbolic." In recent years, however, scholars working in various fields have tried to clarify the meaning of symbols by carefully distinguishing between signs and symbols.[49]

The principal role of a sign is to set out information or to expose data. It stands for a particular object, person, event, or circumstance—"Washington 75 Miles," "Harrods," "Danger," "Scenic View." Hence a sign is pragmatic and functional. Since signs are meant to denote something, they should be clearly recognized; however, sign language must be learned, since signs are meaningful only by convention. They are sensitive to the culture that creates them and change as the culture changes. In order to function effectively, signs should be unambiguous. Because they are so obvious, they require little intellectual investment and elicit little or no emotional response; they allow people to remain uninvolved. They rely on a brief but total message that provides all the necessary information without demanding any direct action or response.

Signs operate on the level of what might be called object thinking. They have but one meaning and stand in a one-to-one relationship to that which is signified. They are invented and established by convention. Hence, signs constitute a social phenomenon insofar as their meaning is accepted socially. They may become universal when the conventions underlying them become universally accepted. For example, across the world, rest rooms are usually indicated by stick figures of a man and a woman. A change of signs simply means a change in convention. Since they simply and overtly provide information, they do not demand any commitment on the part of individuals or communities.

Unlike a sign that points away from itself, a symbol is the sensible expression of a present reality. In a sense it stands for another reality, but it reveals that reality in its own structure. Of its nature a symbol is limited, but it reveals a reality that goes beyond the limits of the symbol itself. Symbols operate on the level of subject thinking. They push the participant beyond the experience of empirical objectivity toward a subjective experience and appreciation of the transcendent, something that transcends the limits of the symbol itself. The task of a symbol is to make the transcendent or some aspect of the transcendent available and to mediate participation in that which is revealed. A symbol, then, cannot simply be equated with what it symbolizes. For example, the human body is the primary symbol of the human person, but the human person is more then the human body; likewise, speech is a symbol of inner human experience, but inner human experience is more than speech.

Symbols invite people to come to terms with their meaning; the interpretation will, of course, depend on the experience and understanding that people bring to the task. Because they supply a limited amount of explicit information, symbols require that we fill in the blanks. Consequently, exposure to symbols is apt to result in diverse interpretations and experiences on the part of various participants. In that sense, symbols have polyvalence, a multiplicity of possible meanings. They are in a one-to-many relationship with what is symbolized. They always possess a surplus of meaning that signs do not have.

Symbols not only open up dimensions and aspects of reality that otherwise would remain closed to us; they also unlock dimensions and aspects of our own inner lives that correspond to the dimensions and aspects of reality. For example, a great novel gives us not only a fresh vision of the human scene; it also opens up deeper levels of reality in our own being. There are certainly aspects of our own lives that we do not become aware of unless they are revealed to us through symbols, such as lines and colors in a painting or melodies and rhythms in a symphony.[50]

Furthermore, symbols cannot be invented or produced intentionally. They are born out of life. They grow out of the individual or collective unconscious and cannot function unless they are accepted by the unconscious level of our being. Symbols are a social phenomenon insofar as they are grounded in a common experience of a social group and a common way of interpreting that experience. They become universal when that common experience and common way of interpreting them are universally shared.

Like human beings, symbols develop and sometimes die. They flourish when they find appropriate acceptance and interpretation; they die when they lose their power to transcend and no longer elicit the response in the individual or group where they originally found expression. When they take on a one-to-one relationship with what is symbolized, they degenerate and become mere signs rather than symbols.

Symbols may be verbal, as in poetry and novels; nonverbal, as in architecture, sculpture, and dance; or they may be a combination of both verbal and nonverbal, as in drama, opera, and liturgy. Like the liturgy as a whole, the language of liturgical celebration is essentially symbolic. It is meant to reveal the transcendent which is immanent in the symbols but goes beyond the symbols themselves. As such, liturgical language is meant to be the medium in which God's revelation takes place and participation in that revelation is realized. Liturgical language invites believing persons and communities to open their lives to its meaning and to inhabit its world. Because of the divine incarnation and the outpouring of the Holy Spirit on all of creation, the presence and power of God permeate not only the assembly gathered for liturgy but also the language used to express and realize those relationships with God, with other human persons, and with oneself which are the goal of liturgical worship. In both verbal and nonverbal symbols, liturgy is addressed to God, who is present in the midst of people through Christ and in the power of the Holy Spirit. God, however, also extends infinitely beyond creation. God is other in the sense that the divine fullness always extends beyond our human boundaries. Through the divine indwelling, human persons and communities are the bearers of God's life, but they are not God.

Liturgical celebrations should be occasions for affirming and deepening our awareness of human worth springing from the divine indwelling.

Good liturgy relates to both persons and things in such a way as to highlight the fact that there is more to both than meets the senses. Persons, as the primary symbols in the liturgy, reveal a transcendent, a beyond, a mystery with what is present. They point to the invisible with what is visible, the inaudible with what is audible, and the untouchable with what can be touched.

In a sense, liturgy itself is an art form that serves to communicate meaning, ultimate meaning, beyond the complex of symbols that comprise the various celebrations. Its goal is to communicate that, even when the world is experienced as chaotic and one's life is fragile or even broken, life has ultimate meaning, which sustains us even in time of suffering and disappointment. The primary purpose of liturgy is not to communicate Christian truths or ethical values but to share a vision of what life is really all about. In other words, because of what happens in liturgy, Christians should be able to look at life differently, just as they look at sunflowers differently because of the way Van Gogh painted them, or at a Campbell soup can because of Andy Warhol's art.

Liturgy is meant to satisfy the human need for form, order, coherence, and integrity. This is especially evident in the liturgical calendar, the liturgy of the hours, and the various sacramental rites of passage that express both order and transition in the lives of people that are often inchoate and fractured. Liturgical celebrations provide us with the means by which we appropriate the really real, by which we affirm that life is shaped not by arbitrariness but by a provident God who has a plan for the whole world and its people.

It follows, then, that liturgical ministers must be artists capable not only of reciting the right words, singing the proper melodies, and moving in the correct way, but also of setting out a vision of the universe that is so compelling that it inspires hope and banishes doubt. Apart from the celebrations of liturgy, the world may be experienced as fractured, but the actual celebrations of the liturgy should so strongly communicate a vision of healing, wholeness, and integrity that after the celebrations, Christian persons and communities view the fractured world with a new vision of wholeness superimposed upon it. Hence, there is an essential link between the celebration of the liturgy and social justice and ethical behavior.

Worshipers, however, often bring what has been called a flat-minded literalism to the celebrations. Living in a technological environment, people do not easily develop a contemplative disposition that enables them to interpret experience on deep levels and to look beneath the surface of events. Moving rapidly from experience to experience, they find it difficult to interpret life on the level of what Philip Wheelwright called "tensive" symbols, which do not simply convey information and agreed-upon meanings but rather break through conventional understandings. Tensive symbols point beyond themselves to open up new insights into the meaning of life. Unlike Wheelwright's "steno" symbols, tensive symbols involve people emotionally; they appeal to the whole person, including the intellect. This is the category into which liturgy should fall, including its language.[51]

Much of ordinary language is one-dimensional, directed simply at the understanding of the listener. By contrast, liturgical language is designed not primarily to communicate information but to give vocal expression to the convictions of faith and to articulate and constitute relationships between Christian persons, communities, and God. The purpose of liturgical language is to awaken in human hearts dispositions of devotion and reverence and to elicit commitment to God, and in God's name, commitment to the human community. Its effectiveness, however, is often frustrated by the flat-minded literalism that characterizes so much of the contemporary world. For many people the scientific mode of acquiring knowledge is often considered the only way to grasp reality. Likewise, the communication process is often understood simply as a process of conveying information. This cultural mood induces the flat-minded literalism that prevents religious symbols from being experienced symbolically and converts them into signs whose meaning can be captured in static statements about an ontological deity. But the primary role of liturgical language is not to convey supernatural facts; it is rather to engage us in relationships with God and with each other.[52]

In the celebration of liturgy, language is regularly joined with symbolic gestures. A gesture is a physical movement, but some physical movements are technical gestures and others are symbolic. Symbolic gestures differ from technical gestures above all because their primary purpose is not to achieve some practical end but to communicate meaning. Giving a glass of water to a thirsty person is a performative or practical gesture, but giving a friend champagne in Waterford crystal is meaningful. Symbolic gestures are rooted in performative actions but the human meaning underlying the action is more important than the practical aspect. Because symbolic gestures are invested with human meaning, they mediate relationships.

Symbolic gestures are also invested with excess or redundancy. Both water and champagne will quench a person's thirst, but the champagne carries with it a certain elaborateness that goes beyond what is necessary to satisfy thirst. The excess or redundancy indicates that the gesture is a medium for communicating meaning, a way of relating to another in a distinctive way. Furthermore, symbolic gestures are formal or conventional; they are ritualistic rather than spontaneous. They are meant not primarily to express feelings but to convey attitudes. Feelings are often not able to be controlled, but attitudes in fact determine a person's character and often shape feelings in accord with those attitudes.

Liturgical language and gestures are not executed to accomplish a task; they are rather meant to reveal meanings and express dispositions. The experience of Christian liturgy is meant to be an in-depth experience in which symbols unfold and invite our interpretation and participation. Unfortunately many Christians interpret the liturgy primarily in terms of an educational enterprise. Homilists, for example, often look upon the Sunday eucharist as the principal occasion when they can communicate a system of doctrine and morals to an assembled congregation. Although the communication of doctrinal and moral systems to the faithful is important, it is not the primary goal of liturgical celebration. The principal goal of the liturgy is an encounter with the mystery of God, an encounter that generates both insight and commitment. Liturgical celebration presupposes that the participants have some creative imagination and that they are willing and able to bridge the distance between themselves and the liturgical forms so that the symbols will enable them to experience reality in a new way. They must be willing to enter into the symbols and to expect transformation to take place. It is for this reason that liturgical celebrations must be accompanied by a reflective or contemplative disposition and a life of personal prayer on the part of those who participate. The dawning of understanding and the disclosure of fresh meaning usually come gradually and often unpredictably to those who do involve themselves in the symbols and who spend time with them imaginatively.

The God of Jews and Christians is a God revealed in the midst of human life; that God is the all-living God and the God of the living. God is to be found in human hearts, in other living persons, and in living encounters. It is for that reason that the assembly is the primary celebrant of the liturgy. However, the belief that God is really present in human lives requires deep faith and perception. Many Christians do not have great difficulty believing in the real presence of Christ under the species of bread and wine, but they often seem to have great difficulty in practice believing that the reason why Christ is present in the eucharistic species is so that he might be present in human hearts. This has traditionally been affirmed by the scholastic axiom, *Sacramenta sunt propter homines*, "The sacraments are for human persons." Christians often have great difficulty believing realistically in the Pauline doctrine that the community constitutes the body of

Christ. An appreciation of the community as the body of Christ would facilitate a belief in the other modes of Christ's real presence that have been emphasized in the Constitution on the Sacred Liturgy from Vatican II: his presence in the gathered assembly of the church, in his ministers, in his Word, and in the prayers and songs of the liturgy. As Salvatore Marsili noted, "Between the eucharistic real presence and the other real presences, there is no difference with regard to the presence of Christ and the reality of his presence. The difference lies in the manner in which these various presences are made real."[53]

An awareness of the primacy of persons over things and of the dignity of human persons springing from the divine indwelling was characteristic of the ancient Christian East; likewise it has been constant in the Christian mystical tradition. For good reason it is being asserted by many contemporary theologians. In light of the various threats to the dignity and worth of human life in contemporary society, such assertions are both important and countercultural.

Liturgical celebrations should be occasions for affirming and deepening our awareness of human persons and human values. Good liturgy relates to both persons and things in such a way as to highlight the fact that there is more to both than meets the senses. Persons, as the primary symbols in the liturgy, and then things, related to persons, reveal with what is present a transcendent, a mystery, a beyond; they point to the invisible with what is visible. Liturgy is concerned with that transcendent in order that we may rise above a utilitarian way of relating to both persons and things. However, it requires that we really contemplate and experience persons, places, and things deeply so that we are able to perceive them for what they really are.

Because of the contemporary emphasis on the symbolic foundations for religious experience, in recent years a strong interest has developed in the relationship between theology and aesthetics or in the development of what might rightly be called theological aesthetics. Classic among the works in this area are the seven volumes of Hans Urs von Balthasar's *The Glory of the Lord: A Theological Aesthetics.*[54] Certainly throughout the history of Christianity beauty in creation and in various artifacts has been appreciated as a revelation of God's own beauty. Sacred architecture and art have not only provided ways of leading human beings to God but also have been ways through which God comes to human beings.[55] Von Balthasar's work, important as it is, remains on the theoretical level; it does not deal at length with concrete expressions of the beautiful. What is needed are serious theological works that attend to and are integrated with aesthetic concerns and manifestations of the beautiful in the church and the world. In a church where so much emphasis is placed on doctrinal statements and belief systems, we need to come to a deeper appreciation of sacred architecture and art as revelatory texts themselves.

There are some forms of art, especially manuscript illustrations and vocal church music, that are intimately linked with literary texts of a creedal or theological nature, but there are also architectural and artistic forms that rightly serve as theological and revelatory texts in themselves. In other words, works of art and architecture can well be a locus of the Christian faith tradition. Sometimes they illustrate the history of theology. For example, Gothic and Romanesque churches, in their separation of clergy and lay people, express the hierarchical nature of the church as understood in the Middle Ages. At other times, sacred art forms embody Christian ideas and values and so constitute a form of theology. For example, paintings of Christ in the fourteenth century often portrayed him and gave expression to his identity as the suffering servant. Hence artistic forms can sometimes constitute an integral part of systematic theology and spirituality.

Sacred art and architectural forms also reveal diverse aspects of the human situation to which God's revelatory word is addressed. For example, Dinah Roe Kendall's contemporary painting *Woman Taken in Adultery* clearly portrays the human tendency to be harshly judgmental, which contrasts with Jesus' own sense of compassion and forgiveness. In this regard theology must reflect on sacred architectural and artistic forms as a source for understanding God's action in the world. Finally architectural and artistic forms often present a message in such a way that one is persuaded to moral action and conversion. For example, churches where the assembly is arranged antiphonally around the altar invite the community of believers to see Christ not only on the altar table but also in the diverse members of the community. Likewise, Fritz Eichenberg's woodcuts, for example, *Christ of the Breadline,* invite viewers to see Christ and to respond to his presence in the poor.[56]

Sacred architecture and art also provide an important source of information about the development of the Christian religion, revealing not only the content of Christian beliefs but also the attitudes and emotional responses of Christians to those doctrines. For example, the Swiss churches in the Zwinglian tradition, stripped of all images, reveal the fear of some Protestant reformers toward sacred paintings and sculptures. Visual texts, however, do not stand in isolation from Christian doctrine but can in significant ways illuminate the meaning of doctrine for various periods in the history of the church. In this regard sacred art and architecture provide an access to understanding the development of Christian spirituality and piety. Hence, there are significant parallels between the history of sacred art and architecture and the history of theology. It is imperative, then, that historians of theology should survey not only the development of theological texts but also the history of sacred art and architecture.

As symbols, sacred art and architecture both communicate to people of Christian faith information about the sacred tradition and are also part of the tradition itself in the sense that they hand on both the content and the attitude of faith. It is well known that sacred art and architecture served as effective mediators between abstract theology and the religious experience of uneducated people. In fact, much sacred art, especially in the Middle Ages, had an explicitly didactic function. However, the history of sacred art as expressive of popular piety always needs to be subjected to critique by sound theological principles lest it fall victim to sheer sentimentality and nostalgia. Throughout much of its history, Christian theology was produced by a small minority of scholars who were almost exclusively male and predominantly clerical. By contrast, folk art of a religious nature has tended to be much less elitist and has allowed for the emergence of what might be called a minority point of view.[57] Much so-called fine art, however, was commissioned by clerics or aristocrats and hence was intended for the edification of educated patrons. Consequently, the social context in which sacred art, both popular and fine, was produced must be taken into account.[58]

Sacred art and architecture are in a real sense sacramental; however, the West, unlike the Eastern tradition, has neither readily adopted such a view nor easily appreciated the revelatory power of art and architecture to mediate divine presence. The Eastern view has been well expressed by Leonid Ouspensky in his *Theology of the Icon:*

> The visible image is equivalent to the verbal image. Just as the word of Scripture is an image, so is the painted image a word. . . . In other words, the icon contains and proclaims the same truth as the Gospel. Like the Gospel and the Cross, it is one of the aspects of divine revelation and of our communion with God, a form in which the union of divine and human activity, synergy, is accomplished. . . . The icon is not art illustrating Holy Scripture; it is a language that corresponds to it and is equivalent to it, corresponding not to the letter of Scripture or to the book itself as an object, but to the evangelical kerygma, that is, to the content of the Scripture itself, to its meaning, as is also true for liturgical texts. This is why the icon plays the same role as Scrip-

ture does in the Church; it has the same liturgical, dogmatic, and educational meaning.[59]

Undoubtedly Ouspensky's claim that the icon is the equivalent of scripture would be disputed by many theologians, especially those in the Protestant tradition.

Certainly the meaning of sacred images in art or architecture may not be reduced to an illustrative role, for they always involve an interpretation of what is set out; they likewise elicit an affective response, provide a comment on what is portrayed, and invite a relationship with a transcendent reality. In other words, the message that is merely set out in a literary text is concretized, interpreted, and given emotional content when it is expressed in an artistic form. Hence, the goal of sacred art and architecture is not simply to communicate catechetical information but to stimulate a transcendent experience, hopefully an experience of the divine.[60]

As symbols, sacred art and architecture make present the transcendent; they point beyond themselves to what is other than themselves. In theological terms, they manifest the Spirit of God who is everywhere and always. Their goal is to facilitate the union of human beings with the divine.

In his *Analogical Imagination,* David Tracy observed that the classic works of Catholic theologians and artists tend to emphasize the immanence of God in the world, while the classic works of Protestants tend to concentrate on the absence of God from the world.[61] The lines of that difference, however, are certainly not so clearly drawn today. In the chapters that follow I will take a look at the history of sacred architecture and art, beginning with the Bible; I will emphasize the Western tradition in an effort to discern how best Christianity in the West might respond today through architecture and art to the great human need for an experience of both transcendence and immanence, transcendence and community.

3

Sacred Architecture and Art in the Bible and the Early Church

THERE IS CERTAINLY A RENEWED INTEREST IN THE WAY WE THINK
of sacred space, because it is seen today as having profound human, social,
political, and religious importance. When mosques are destroyed or
defaced, when Orthodox churches are reclaimed by Roman Catholics,
when Aboriginal and Native American peoples take up arms to protect
their ancestral sacred spaces, and when synagogues are bombed—these incidents raise profound challenges to our work for justice, peace, religious tolerance, and holiness of life.[1] In addition, there are various internal factors
that make the development of a profound theology of sacred space especially timely. First of all there is the interest in creation-based spirituality
and theology. A renewed understanding of the whole earth as somehow
sacramental and imbued with divine presence from its very beginning
forces us to attempt to rethink what we mean by the "fall of nature." Second, there has been a renewed interest in the biblical understanding of
place and how we understand the creation narratives as well as the place of
the land, temple, exile, and pilgrimage in the Old Testament. Then there
are the efforts by Protestant, Anglican, and Roman Catholic liturgical theologians to rethink the role of sacred places in the celebration of the
liturgy. Finally there have been the interdenominational dialogues among
Christians as well as dialogues with the major world and tribal religions in
an effort to understand how the world's diverse peoples relate to the physical world and in particular to those spaces that are designated as especially
sacred.[2]

There are, however, serious theological difficulties or at least questions that must be confronted if our understanding of sacred space is to be deeply rooted. Unfortunately, there has been little rigorous treatment of the topic by systematic theologians. As a result much of the discussion has been passed on to liturgists, specialists in ritual behavior, art and architectural historians, and historians of religion. The latter tend to base their reflections on how sacred space functions in Eastern or tribal religions; at times their work is intertwined with the findings of depth psychology and semiotics. Liturgical scholars have been concerned with how sacred places should function in the celebration of rites. The result has been that the theology of sacred space has often not been very theological, nor has it been profoundly Christian. Art and architectural historians who have an interest in Christian theology have tended to focus on how the theology of a given time and place has been translated into worship spaces; they have shown how shifts in ecclesiology, christology, and sacramental theology have affected architectural plans and the representation of Christ, his mother, and the saints. Although we have had superb histories of church architecture and to some extent histories of sacred art, we have not witnessed a careful correlation between those histories and the history of theology. Finally, the discussions of sacred space have been complicated by the challenges that have come from the serious issues raised by the defenders of social justice, mission, evangelization, and ethics. The renovation of extant churches and the building of new ones in recent years have regularly been challenged by those who object to the expenditure of large sums on religious buildings when so many in the world go hungry.[3]

With those serious concerns in mind, I turn now to a survey of the Old and New Testaments in search of the biblical foundations for a contemporary theology of sacred space and sacred place. In the seventh chapter of the Acts of the Apostles there is an account of Stephen's discourse before the Sanhedrin following his arrest. Peter and the other apostles taught that Christ was the Messiah, but like Christ they faithfully observed the Jewish law. Stephen, however, openly proclaimed the limitations of the law which was fulfilled by the new covenant. He spoke of the destruction of the Jerusalem temple, which was superseded by the temple of Christ's own body and concluded that "the Most High does not dwell in buildings made by human hands" (Acts 7:48).[4] Somewhat later, Paul proclaimed the same idea in Athens before the council of the Areopagus when he said, "The God who made the world and all that is in it, the Lord of heaven and earth, does not dwell in sanctuaries made by human hands" (Acts 17:24). In Athens,

Paul "grew exasperated at the sight of idols everywhere in the city" (Acts 17:16); hence, before the council he asserted the emptiness and the frivolity of their pagan temples.

The situation in Jerusalem was totally different from what Paul encountered in Athens, for the temple built in honor of the true God was not the abode of idols. It was natural that the Jews should be offended by Stephen, who, within a short distance of the temple, affirmed that God did not dwell in a house that human hands had made.

The two accounts of Stephen and Paul in the Acts of the Apostles touch on one of the basic truths of Christianity. The religion taught by Jesus is not tied down to a building erected by human hands; it is rather built up by God on the foundation of Christ through the power of the Holy Spirit. In proclaiming the uniqueness of Christianity in contrast to both paganism and Judaism, Stephen and Paul affirmed the universal character of the religion taught by Christ.[5]

In spite of the New Testament proclamation made by Stephen and Paul, there are Christian edifices called churches; however, they do not negate the teaching contained in the Acts of the Apostles. They rather reflect a marked shift in the understanding of worship edifices under the Jewish law and under the new covenant established by Christ. Even the history of Christian churches since the time of Christ reflects a changing understanding of sacred space and sacred place within the Christian economy.

As noted earlier in this book, time and space are the two most basic categories used to analyze culture, for they tend to be the fundamental perceptions in which people cast and interpret reality. Because of the creative work of Mircea Eliade in the comparative study of world religions, sacred time and sacred space have become common categories used to interpret diverse religious traditions.[6] Calendars organize time in categories of days, months, and years according to lunar and solar cycles. History counts time in relation to significant events. These secular categories, reflected in language, speak of a past, a present, and a future. Among biblical scholars, much attention has been given to sacred time because the God of both Jews and Christians has been recognized as a God who acts in history, conceived of as a purposeful series of divine–human encounters in which God intervenes to bring salvation to the world and its people. Sacred time introduces the temporary as it is ordinarily understood and makes past and future coterminus with the present. Sacred time is organized according to rituals and seasons that celebrate eternal mysteries. The liturgical calendars of the Christian churches measure time in terms of seasonal cycles, feast days, days of penitence, and other special occasions that commemorate the principal events in salvation history and the life of Jesus. The liturgy makes the effects of these saving events present to all who believe in Jesus Christ through the power of the Holy Spirit.

In one sense sacred space is something that is given; however, to appreciate the natural world as sacred one must always read it in the light of divine revelation. Alexander Schmemann, the distinguished Orthodox theologian, titled one of his books *The World as Sacrament*. He described the human person as a priest:

> He stands in the center of the world and unifies it in his act of blessing God, of both receiving the world from God and offering it to God. . . . The world was created as the "matter," the material of one all-embracing Eucharist, and man was created as the priest of this cosmic sacrament.[7]

For Schmemann the world itself only had meaning and value when viewed as the sacrament of God's living presence.[8] Living in the world demands that we cooperate with God in drawing out the potential of creation. We are called to respond to what God has given us; hence, sacramental action is essentially a matter not so much of co-creation as cooperation.[9]

Given the sacramentality of all of creation, traditionally authors have maintained that some places are especially sacred and become so because of the use to which they are put or because of the religious memories, reverence, and awe commonly associated with those particular places. Therefore, a place may be sacred and nonsacred at the same time, depending on the interpretation given to it. Since it is not a space of wholly human choice or construction, a sacred space is different from other spaces. Its significance is grounded in the fact that the divine has intervened or continues to intervene in a particular way at such a place. Hence, a sacred space is a symbol of divine mystery and presence.

A space is sacred because it fulfills a religious role, not because it has special aesthetic or physical qualities. It is customary to identify three functions of sacred space. First of all, it is a place of communion with the divine. Jewish, Christian, and Islamic traditions abound with stories of theophanies, visions, and auditory experiences wherein the divine presence has made itself felt. Hence, a sacred space is often marked by a special symbol, such as an altar, a statue, a mandala, or a pillar, which represents the presence of the divine in an intense way. Second, it is a special place where divine power manifests itself. The effect that the power of divine presence has on human life varies from one religion to another. In some traditions, the transformation is described as salvation; in others, as healing or illumination. Sacred places have often been the location of miraculous cures.

Third, a sacred place is often regarded as a mirror of what the human world should look like as it relates to the divine. It provides an orientation for human life and focuses attention on what is thought to be significant for human transformation. In some religious traditions, sacred places face in a certain direction.[10]

The Israelites experienced God in space, but unlike most of the ancient gods, their God traveled from place to place as a nomad with the people. The Lord guided Abraham in the promised land, liberated the Hebrews from Egypt, wandered with them in the wilderness, dwelt with them in Jerusalem, and accompanied them as exiles into Babylon. Even the wilderness played a special role in Israel's encounter with God. It was a wide-open space, unsurveyed and undomesticated. It stood in marked contrast to Egypt, which was distinguished by its order and neatness. The contrast is important, because the wilderness came to symbolize in Israel's history the very mystery of God. Egypt represented human control and order—and slavery for the Israelites—whereas the wilderness represented divine presence, the freedom of God, lack of control for the Israelites, and consequently true freedom for them as God's children.[11]

The land of Israel was the Lord's land; it belonged to the Israelites not by right but by promise. Its role in the divine plan, its climate, its topography, and its agriculture were all causes for awe and wonder. Salvation was to be found in the Lord's land; exile from that land was always catastrophic.

It should be noted, however, that in the Old Testament there is a theological dialogue between landedness and landlessness, between a people settled in a place and a people in exile. Biblical theology is rooted in both experiences. The God of the promised land is also the God of the wilderness and the exile; God could be encountered in Babylon as well as in Jerusalem. These paradoxes were woven together in a spirituality rooted in covenant, pilgrimage, belief and faith, promise and prayer—a spirituality in which place was always important. This commitment to place, however, was always threatened by the possibility of idolatry; the Israelites' worship of graven images was paralleled by their tendency to tie the omnipresent God down to a certain place.[12]

With the incarnation of God in Jesus Christ, the Lord became more intimately related to people in both time and space. In the physical body of Jesus, God's people were able to come face to face with their savior; in him they were able to find the fullness of God's revelation, for God was present in Jesus in a unique way. But Jesus' own assertions about place were both ambiguous and paradoxical. Jesus was the one who had nowhere to lay his head; the one who proclaimed that he would destroy the temple, the most sacred place for the Israelites, and would build it up again in three days; the one who told the Samaritan woman that the days were coming when God would not be worshiped on Mount Gerizim or in Jerusalem but rather in spirit and in truth; Jesus was the one who affirmed that wherever two or three are gathered together in his name, he would be in their midst. The central theme of Jesus' preaching was the establishment of the kingdom of God, which was certainly not identified with a place but involved an encounter with the living God that would result in reconciliation, peace, and love among God's people.

In spite of Jesus' detached attitude toward special places, the gospels manifest a deep concern for special places. They tell us where Jesus preached, where he performed miracles, where he prayed, where he died, and where he was seen after his resurrection. However, all of these places are important not because of their own special identity but rather because Jesus was in those places and made them holy by his presence. He transformed the meaning of places by his holy actions. Hence, the special places that are designated in the New Testament as holy are such not because of their geographical location but rather because of their association with the incarnate Word of God. Place, then, has a distinctive meaning in the New Testament economy. One might even say that in the Old Testament the revelation of God is related to certain places, whereas in the New Testament it is related to a person and his actions. The promises that were tied to the land and certain places in the Old Testament were fulfilled in Jesus.[13]

The early Christians' conviction that the risen Lord Jesus poured out the Holy Spirit on all of creation enabled them to find God sacramentally present in their own space and time, although the divine presence was mediated in a particularly intense way in certain places and at certain times. Certainly all created space is a potential place for divine revelation by reason of its divine origin and also because of the divine indwelling through the presence and power of the Holy Spirit. It was out of the sacramentality of all of creation that there grew an appreciation of the importance of special sacraments as symbols of God's saving presence to people through Christ and in the power of the Holy Spirit.

The importance of Jesus' actions in particular places as he made God's life and love visible and tangible for the transformation of the world naturally give a certain importance to the places where the church, as the sacrament of Christ's presence in the world today, ministers in the name of the Lord Jesus. All ecclesial ministry by believers is meant to extend the work of Christ. Just as his ministry of healing, teaching, preaching, and forgiving was identified with certain places, and just as those places derived their special meaning because of what Jesus did there, so certain places in the history of the church derive their special meaning because of what the church does there. Nevertheless, the sacred significance of those places always derives from and is dependent on the essential relationship that such ministry has with Christ. Consequently, the christological and ecclesiological foundations for the sacredness of church buildings have been regularly emphasized in the rites for the consecration of churches, which date back to the early sixth century.[14]

The anthropological work of Victor Turner provides categories for analyzing sacred space in both Jewish and Christian traditions. In a number of important studies, Turner investigated the symbols and behavior manifested in various social and religious phenomena of transition, such as rites of passage, pilgrimage, and millenarian movements. All of these events took place in space that both expressed and constituted at least to some extent the meaning of the experience. Following the work of Arnold van Gennep, Turner identified three phases in these rites: (1) separation of the ritual subjects from their role in the traditional social structures; (2) a marginal, liminal, or transitional stage; and (3) reincorporation of the subject into the traditional social structures but with new roles. In the second phase, Turner found symbols and behavior patterns that provided him with a key to understanding the ritual process and its role in the lives of the participants.[15]

In the liminal state, the ritual subjects are "betwixt and between" the places assigned them by custom, law, or ceremonial. They have undergone a symbolic death to their old status in life and are in the process of being reborn to a new status. Turner describes the social relationships among the liminal subjects in terms of *communitas,* which is a kind of bonding that does not depend on social status, wealth, class, or rank; it is different from the normal modes of human relationships in society. As Turner notes, the bonds of communitas are undifferentiated, egalitarian, direct, extant, nonrational, and existential. The relationships among liminal subjects are spontaneous, immediate, concrete, boundless, and potentially universal; they are not shaped by the customary norms of social behavior. By submitting to the authority of the ritual elders, the liminal subjects experience the equality of sharing in a common state. Hence, their modes of acting, thinking, and relating are different from those of people in customary social positions.

Liminality and the communitas it engenders have social and religious significance beyond the rites of passage. For example, millenarian movements may be described as liminal because they usually occur when societies are undergoing major structural shifts. Such enthusiastic movements set themselves against the traditional structures of society; they are open, free, and unrestricted to particular social groups. Likewise, in historical religions, pilgrimages function analogously to the initiation rites in preindustrial societies.[16] The pilgrims leave their familiar lives behind and join for a time an egalitarian community on a liminal journey toward a sacred space or place. Following their journey, which may be penitential, transformative, or devotional in character, the pilgrims reenter society as new persons who have been changed by the experience of communitas.

Not only the rituals but also the space or place in which the rituals occur can produce the experience of liminality and engender communitas among people. A sacred space puts people in a place that is "betwixt and between"; it is distinct from the secular places that people occupy most of their lives, but it is not the final resting place where people hope to find their lasting home. While in the sacred space they leave behind the structures that often pit them against one another. Although there are different roles executed in the places, the members of the communitas are basically equal. In their liminal spaces, Christians are gathered for penitential purposes, to acknowledge their need for the saving presence of God, and to be transformed so that they might be able to live in the secular structures of society in a way that is consonant with their calling to be faithful disciples of God and brothers and sisters to one another in Christ and through the power of the Holy Spirit.

Turner's theory is indeed helpful for understanding not only social process in general but also liturgical process in particular. Since he focuses his attention not only on fixed social states but on change and on the processual view of society, his insights can illuminate the conversion process that is inherent in both Judaism and Christianity, a process that should both be reflected in the structures of the sacred places in which the liturgy is celebrated and be deepened and facilitated by those places. For example, the placement of the baptismal font at the entrance of a Christian church is both a call to conversion in Christ through the Holy Spirit and a regular reminder to the faithful of the ongoing need for conversion so they might be true to their vocation to discipleship.

DIVINE PRESENCE IN THE OLD TESTAMENT

One of the important contributions of scholars working in the comparative study of religion has been the decoding of symbols common to many traditions and the revelation that similar preoccupations are common to religious people and are expressed in symbols common to diverse religious traditions. In his study of sacred space in the history of religions, Mircea Eliade has analyzed various images that he clusters under the heading "symbols of the center."[17] The ladder, pillar, mountain, vine, and tree each symbolize a link between heaven, earth, and the underworld; they constitute the places where the divine presence has manifested itself in a special way. In keeping with their liminal character, such places or objects constitute a break with ordinary space; they also constitute a focal point from which ordinary space is viewed. The task of the history of religions is to elucidate the patterns in which particular sacred places have been retained, developed, or forgotten by religious groups and to ascertain the reasons for such patterns. As the religious experiences of groups change, so also do the symbolic representations of those experiences.

The sacred places and objects in the history of both Judaism and Christianity manifest patterns of development that enable analysts to discern the religious experiences of those people, the character of their relationships with God, themselves, and others, and their understanding of the effects that religious experience should have on their lives in the world. Long before they found God especially in the Jerusalem temple, the Israelites encountered God in less pretentious places. In a special way the wilderness was a liminal place for the Israelites. They were separated from Egypt by the exodus and the crossing of the Red Sea; they wandered for forty years in transition; and they were reincorporated by the crossing of the Jordan and the conquest and resettlement of a new land. They then journeyed to Mount Sinai, where a theophany bonded them in a fresh way. Mountains in general were special places of divine encounters.[18] Like most ancient peoples, the Israelites lived close to the land. Their natural environment affected the way they looked at the world; it shaped their perceptions. Above all, mountains captured their religious imagination as places where God intervened in the human sphere. Mount Sinai and Mount Zion were the two most important pivots in their sacred history.

Mountains had religious significance because they offered security, they were high, and they symbolized fertility. The mountains were a witness to the order and stability of the created world; they symbolized the power and permanence of God. Their height not only witnessed to the splendor of God's creation but pointed to God in the heights. They linked God with the world, for they extended from the heavens, where God was thought to dwell, down to the foundations of the earth. Because of the sense of authority they evoked, they were often the settings from which God's words of blessing and curse were delivered. The mountains symbolized fertility because they were a prominent feature of the promised land, which was fertile. Their fertility, however, depended on Israel's obedience to God, who was the ultimate source of all blessings, including fertility. The point of all this is that, for Israel, God's presence was sacramentalized in the world not only in a general way but in very specific places.

Although the Israelites encountered God in what we would call sacred places, there was no temple during the period of the patriarchs. Abraham was a nomad; wherever he happened to be, he adored the Lord. In making the covenant with Abraham, God said, "Walk in my presence and be blameless" (Gen. 17:1). The command was simply a matter of living in the presence of God, who existed everywhere and at all times but beyond all times and places. Nevertheless, Genesis notes that in several places Abraham built an altar to the Lord and there invoked his name (Gen. 12:7; 13:4; 13:18). Although Abraham walked in the Lord's presence, he felt a need to express his worship of the Lord not only in his heart but also visibly and audibly. Hence, he set aside a time and place for special encounters with God (Gen. 12:6–7; 12:8; 13:8). Wherever he dwelt, Abraham built a place of sacrifice. Since the Lord encountered Abraham at these places, they became important sites in the history of salvation and for that reason were remembered as holy places.[19]

On his way to Harran, Jacob had a dream in which he saw angels going up and down a ladder, and he heard the voice of the Lord. When he woke from sleep, he proclaimed, "Surely the Lord is in this place and I did not know it. . . . This is none other than the house of God; it is the gateway to heaven" (Gen. 28:16–17).

The religion that Moses proclaimed was linked with the religion of the patriarchs; both religious experiences were rooted in the Lord's special intervention in the lives of the people. Whereas Genesis portrays the Lord as speaking immediately with the patriarchs, in Exodus Moses is delegated by the Lord to speak to Israel in his name. Although the Lord sometimes manifested his presence to all the people, only rarely did he communicate his commands directly to them, as he did when he gave them the Decalogue (Exod. 20).[20]

The Lord made his covenant with Israel as a whole, not with the individual tribes, but that election did not mean that the Lord rejected other nations. In keeping with his presence everywhere and always, the Lord was not a national God; he was a guide and a protector to other tribes and nations as well (Exod. 28; 29; Lev. 8–10). Israel's special responsibility was to mediate the presence of the Lord to other people. In that sense the

Israelites were holy people, priestly people, transformed from uncouth slaves into free men and women.

During the time of Moses, there was the development of a special priesthood (Exod. 25:23–30; Lev. 2–8; 10:1; Num. 16:6; 17:11), and the structures and appointment of the ark of the covenant (Exod. 25–29). The ark was not stationary; it accompanied the Israelites wherever they went, and it organized their wanderings. The ark was rather the living symbol of God's presence in the midst of his people (Exod. 29:45–46). The Lord, then, was present everywhere—in Egypt, on Mount Sinai, in the wilderness, and in Canaan.

As the Israelites moved about, the ark too was moved, with the result that God was, so to speak, made a nomad among nomads. This mobility lasted from the time of Moses up to the time of David, who led the ark triumphantly into Jerusalem (2 Sam. 6). He sensed the impropriety of housing the ark in a tent and so laid plans for the erection of a temple. When Nathan informed him that this task was reserved for his successors (2 Sam. 7:4–16), David was content to make preparations by collecting funds and materials, by purchasing the site, and by erecting an altar in Jerusalem (2 Sam. 24:18–25; 1 Chr. 22; 28).[21]

The author of the First Book of Kings recounts the building of the temple with such solemnity that the special importance of the event is clearly emphasized (1 Kgs. 6:1). The account is an architectural description, but it indicates the love with which the author speaks of the temple. It climaxes with the actual dedication (1 Kgs. 8:10–13). Solomon built the temple from the goods of the earth and according to humanly devised plans, but God ratified the work of the builders and chose the temple as a very special dwelling place by a manifestation analogous to that which accompanied the exodus.

After he affirmed God's special presence in the temple, however, Solomon suddenly exclaimed in the course of his dedicatory speech, "Can it indeed be that God dwells among men and women on earth? If the heavens and the highest heavens cannot contain you, how much less this temple which I have built" (1 Kgs. 8:27). From the text of this prayer, it is clear that God did not literally dwell in the temple, since God could not be confined within the enclosure of a sanctuary. The temple was only a privileged place for prayer, a special meeting place between God and the people.

The temple modified the relationship between God and the people. The solemn transfer of the ark marked the end of an era, for God no longer appeared as a nomad in the midst of nomads but rather as a sovereign in a palace, a king whom no one sees except his special servants, a king dwelling in the privacy of his own chamber.[22]

Four centuries after the dedication of the temple, the Jews returned from exile and reconstructed the demolished edifice, but just as Nathan had cautioned David against building the original temple, so also a prophetic voice was raised against the restoration project (Isa. 66:1–2). On both occasions the plans were realized, apparently with God's blessing, for God both accepted the construction of the temple and made it a place of divine favor. Although pilgrimages continued to be made to Israel's other places of sacrifice, the temple in Jerusalem gradually became Israel's primary place of worship. The temple was the great place for prayer; it was there that the people went periodically on pilgrimage, and it was there that they assembled in a special way as God's chosen people, just as of old they assembled about the ark of the covenant. For ten centuries the temple played a significant role in the history of Israel.

But God regularly tried to arouse the consciences of the Israelites to a mission nobler than that of mere ritual cult. The invectives of the prophets against those who placed a blind trust in the temple were less a criticism of the temple than an invitation to return to the basic call to love the Lord and seek his face. The temple required of those who approached it a ritual purity, but according to the prophets, God sought a holiness that sprang up from within the human heart. Although the temple seemed to be the property of the Israelites since it was located in Jerusalem, the prophets proclaimed that all the nations would come to adore the God of all the earth.[23]

In salvation history, the capture of Jerusalem by Nebuchadnezzar, the destruction of the temple, and the exile of the chosen people played essential roles. Many times the prophets had announced that God would abandon the temple. Finally in 586 B.C.E. what seemed to be an extravagant oratorical ploy became a reality, for Jerusalem was captured, the temple was razed, and the Israelites went into exile in a foreign land, where they lived for half a century. After the first exiles returned to Judea, they had to wait twenty years for the reconstruction of the temple, a project that was finally completed in 515 B.C.E. For seventy years, then, the Israelites lived without the temple.

Even before the destruction of Jerusalem, Ezekiel had prophesied the departure of the Lord (Ezek. 10:4–5; 10:18–19; 11:22–23). In fulfillment of his words, the glory of the Lord left the temple, not because the enemies of Israel had entered the city, but because idols had invaded the courts of the temple. In a sense, then, God freely left the temple just as God had freely come there of old. But God did not abandon the people. Rather, God went with them into exile. Far from Jerusalem and its temple, God remained with those who suffered and hoped in the Lord. Although Jeremiah had prophesied the destruction of Jerusalem and the exile of the Israelites, he had also foretold a new alliance of God with the people (Jer. 31:33–34). It was God's intent that the new Jerusalem should be founded on the principles of justice and righteousness.

Ezekiel prophesied the building of a new temple where God's glory would dwell, but not until he had first announced a new covenant (Ezek. 36:25–26). During the exile, then, God prepared a holy people, purified by suffering, a people who loved God and were filled with God's spirit of love, which they shared with one another.

THE SYNAGOGUE

Although synagogues are not mentioned in the Old Testament, they were actually one of the most important religious institutions in the centuries immediately preceding the coming of Christ. Whether they developed as a substitute for the temple during the exile or as a supplement to the temple for the benefit of those who could not get to Jerusalem frequently, the synagogues fulfilled both roles. Their services have always been nonsacrificial and have been based on readings and prayers. The activity that every synagogue had to sponsor was meetings: gatherings of the faithful assembly, the elders, and the notables.[24]

In the exilic literature of the Old Testament there are indications that the dispersed Israelites gathered in assembly. One rightly presumes that some of these meetings were for religious purposes, above all to hear the scriptures proclaimed on the sabbath, and perhaps on other days as well. After the return of the exiles to their own land, the scribe Esdras called the people together and had the word of the Lord proclaimed to them. When the solemn reading was finished, however, there was no offering of sacrifice. Instead, the people took a vow to carry out the sacrifice when the city had been rebuilt and the temple reconstructed. The people would have come together regularly because they knew that God dwelt with them in a special way as a united people and that they found God's presence especially in the Torah.[25] Whereas the Jews originally had assembled in the temple because it was a sacred edifice, the dispersed Jews would have constructed synagogues because they sought to be united as God's chosen people.

The worship of the synagogues gained in importance after the reconstruction of the temple, for then the people realized that the temple, as it was rebuilt, failed to fulfill the hopes expressed by Ezekiel; they also sensed that it was not even the equal of the older temple. However, the ritual in the synagogue was in no way opposed to the cult in the temple, nor did it interfere with the great annual pilgrimages to Jerusalem. The synagogue worship fostered the eschatological expectation stressed by Ezekiel of a true and lasting worship, an eternal sacrifice. When the people recalled God's great deeds in the work of their salvation, they did not praise them as a final accomplishment, but rather recalled them as a pledge and a foreshadowing of those far greater works that God would accomplish in the future. This partly accounts for the increasing decline in the importance of the temple ritual, even after it had been restored.

In addition to the temple and the synagogue, the home was also a special place of worship. The sabbath celebration really began there, just as it was in the home that the family gathered each year to celebrate the paschal meal. The Jews also gathered outdoors in order to pray together. In addition they continued to honor their fathers, the patriarchs, as well as the kings and prophets, who played significant roles in the history of the people. From Hebron through the Kidron Valley to Shechem, the monuments erected in their memory were objects of special veneration because the people realized that God had intervened in their lives through their leaders. We see, then, that there were really five special places of worship in the life of the Old Testament Jews: (1) the temple, (2) the synagogue, (3) the out-of-doors, (4) homes, and (5) sites of monuments.

DIVINE PRESENCE IN THE NEW TESTAMENT

From the time of Moses to the coming of Christ or from the time of the ark to that of the new covenant, the chosen people were a people set apart. Moses had led them into the desert, where they were separated from other nations. The believers were separated from nonbelievers, especially by the observance of food ordinances, the sabbath rest, and circumcision.

Both Jesus and his disciples worshiped in the tradition of the chosen people. After gathering his first disciples on the bank of the Jordan River, Jesus proclaimed the arrival of a new age in the synagogue in Nazareth (Luke 4:14–20). He taught in the synagogues of Galilee and made the required pilgrimages to the temple in Jerusalem for the feasts of Passover, Pentecost, and Tabernacles. There he taught in Solomon's portico (John 10:23). But the family dwelling also played a significant role in the religious life of

Jesus. It was there that he would have taken part in the sabbath meal throughout his life; it was in Peter's house at Capernaum that he taught and cured the sick (Mark 1:32–34); it was in the upper room of a house that he shared his last special meal with his disciples before his own passion and death (Matt. 26:18; Mark 14:14; Luke 22:10–12); and it was at a household table that he broke bread with his two companions in Emmaus (Luke 24:29–30).[26]

The coming of Christ, and more precisely the mission of the Holy Spirit, inaugurated a regime of dispersion. There was geographical dispersion: the new Christians lived not only in the towns where up till then there had been only Jews, but also in every place where the gospel was proclaimed. There was ethnic dispersion: in the church of Christ there was neither Jew nor Greek nor barbarian nor free person. John could truly write that the church was made up of men and women of every race, language, and nation (Rev. 5:9–10). The first Pentecost, that of Mount Sinai, had created a people separated from other peoples, but the new Pentecost tossed the seed of the gospel to every wind and carried the word of God to all parts of the world. Although the converts to the new church belonged to various nations (Acts 2:5–11), they nevertheless formed a single people, the people of God. They were not united by social origin, geographic location, or common language, but they were united by the Spirit of God. Ezekiel had prophesied that God would assemble the people of every nation through the gift of the Spirit (Ezek. 36:22–38). The unity attained by the Holy Spirit was and still is a true organism in spite of widespread dispersion. The people of God form one body (1 Cor. 12:12).

Although Paul developed the image of the church as a body, he was accustomed also to employing another figure—that of the temple (1 Cor. 3:16–17; 6:19–20).[27] The theme of building is further developed in the Epistle to the Ephesians (Eph. 2:20–22). House of God, building, holy temple—these terms call to mind the temple of Jerusalem. But the temple of which these letters speak is not built of inert stone, nor is it built only of people of good will, but rather of all those who are members of Christ through baptism. In the First Letter of Peter the community of the faithful is also spoken of as a temple (1 Pet. 2:4–10).

Some of these texts were most likely drawn up while the Jerusalem temple was still in existence and when no one suspected that it would shortly be destroyed. The New Testament writers were loyal to the temple. In comparing the Christian community to the temple of the Lord, the writers were not referring to the transitory character of the Jerusalem temple, but rather, in a long line of prophets, they announced simply that God would dwell in the hearts of the people. At the same time, they described the church which had been born from the side of Christ on Calvary. The church springs wholly from Christ, is animated by the Holy Spirit, and through his life develops into a splendid structure that is the dwelling place of God.[28]

The church is wholly of Christ; this is what was written to the Colossians (Col. 2:9) in anticipation of what John would later say in his gospel: "The Word became flesh and made his dwelling among us" (John 1:14). The expression that John used to describe the dwelling of the Word in humanity recalls the sojourn in the desert and the dwelling of the Lord with his people: the Word was made flesh and pitched his tent and camped among us. The Godhead, however, is wholly in Christ, for he is at one and the same time divine and human. When one looked upon his body, one saw both God and the dwelling place of God (1 John 1:1–3). Never before had God dwelt in this way among the people—neither in the ark nor in the temple. In Christ, in his body, united to his body, men and women saw their God. God's temple, then, is not a material edifice. It is rather the body of Christ, a body which the apostles had seen and touched. Since the outpouring of the Spirit, God's true temple is the community of the baptized in whom the Spirit of Christ truly abides.

What surfaces with great clarity in these reflections on the New Testament is the primacy of the community over the material edifice. First of all, the temple of God is the body of Jesus Christ, then through the outpouring of the Holy Spirit, the temple of God is the community of the faithful disciples of Jesus Christ. If material edifices have any intrinsic Christian meaning, it is because of the community who assemblies there and what they do when they are gathered—namely, hear the Word of God proclaimed, break that Word for one another, and celebrate the life, death, and resurrection of Jesus Christ in the various sacramental rites.

APOSTOLIC PERIOD

After Pentecost the disciples of Jesus continued to frequent their customary places of worship. They would most likely have felt at home in the Jerusalem temple until it was destroyed. The apostles also taught in the synagogues, as is evident from the account of Paul's mission. Likewise, the early Christians gathered in private homes to teach and break bread together. Households constituted the basic organizational structure in the early church. In the beginning of the Acts of the Apostles, Luke depicts the apostles, Mary, and others gathered for prayer in an upper room, which must have been spacious enough to hold a large group (Acts 1:13–14). Later when Peter was released from prison, he went to the house of Mary, Mark's mother, where many Christians were gathered together in prayer (Acts 12:12–14).

Early Christians would also have celebrated baptism. There are several explicit references in the Acts of the Apostles, including the baptism of the three thousand believers (2:41), the baptism of the Ethiopian eunuch (8:36–38), and the baptism of the centurion Cornelius along with his whole household (10:34–42). Presumably these were all baptisms by immersion in a river or other natural body of water.

Although the Christian communities that sprang from Judaism would have naturally retained close ties with the temple and synagogues, those that originated in non-Jewish environments would most likely have frequented only the houses of other members of the community as places for assembly. These would probably have been spacious rooms such as can be pictured from the ruins at Ostia and Pompeii. It was in such a room that Paul addressed the Sunday gathering at Troas, for there were many lamps in the upper room where the community had assembled (Acts 20:7–8).[29]

The destruction of the temple in 70 C.E. did not modify anything that the apostles had taught concerning the dwelling place of God, for the veil of the temple had been rent after the death of Christ on the cross. For some time before the destruction of the temple, the Christians had understood that the true temple of God is the body of Christ. Nevertheless, the actual destruction of the Jerusalem temple, an event foretold by Christ, was a providential sign that marked the end of an epoch. The temple at Jerusalem disappeared just as the new temple of the church, the body of Christ, was beginning to spread throughout the world.

After Christ's resurrection, the disciples gathered regularly to listen to the word of God and to share in the breaking of the bread. Since Christ had promised his followers that he would be in the midst of those who gathered in his name (Matt. 18:20), the actual place of assembly was not of primary importance. It was more a matter of convenience and availability, for they knew that God is not confined within the walls of a building but rather dwells within the assembly of the faithful. Nevertheless it was practical to have places that could be used for worship as well as ordinary secular functions. Motivated by a need for a place of assembly, then, the early Christians used private dwellings, especially those of the wealthier members of the community. These domestic churches provided a context for community life, a platform for preaching, a lodging for itinerant preachers, and economic stability for the group. Membership in the church included people from all social ranks, indicating Christianity's ability to transcend the class distinctions that were so respected in the Greco-Roman world. Women are listed as prominent members of these churches; they were probably heads of households and so also were leaders in the church community that met in their homes.[30]

It can be said that Christianity was nurtured in its early days in what would be described as nonsacred places; it developed in the ordinary transactions of daily life; and it was localized in small communities, probably made up of not more then thirty or forty people.

The early domestic churches expressed the fundamental values of community life, but those Christian communities had to guard against exclusiveness and the kind of intergroup rivalry that developed in Corinth. Each local house church would have been a symbolic expression of God as the head of humanity with the Christians as children adopted in Jesus Christ through the power of the Holy Spirit. But each local house church would have had to relate to other house churches, all as brothers and sisters in Christ. Hence, the early church was both local and universal.

SECOND, THIRD, AND EARLY FOURTH CENTURIES

As the size of the Christian community increased, the family dwellings naturally became too small for large assemblies. In the second century, however, it does not seem that the Christians yet had any places set aside exclusively for worship.[31] Extant literary evidence suggests that meetings continued to be held in households and other private dwellings throughout the second century. The *Martyrdom of Justin* indicates the situation in Rome at least until 165.[32] When Justin Martyr was asked by the prefect Q. Junius Rusticus where the Christians customarily met, he gave a vague answer, hinting that there was no single meeting place, but admitting that he gathered in an assembly that met in the same place where he lived and taught.[33] It is the same Justin, however, who provides us with the earliest description, written about 150 C.E., of the Sunday assembly of the Christians: "On the day which is called Sunday, we have a common assembly of all who live in the cities or in outlying districts."[34]

Until the beginning of the third century, assembly and worship by Christians would have taken place in the homes of wealthier members. The meal setting would have taken place in the dining room (triclinium) or possibly in other larger rooms as they were available. However, no architectural specialization would have occurred to accommodate religious functions.[35]

In the third century, Christians began to hold church property in common. This practice was facilitated by the peaceful existence of the church, the increased number of Christians, and by legal developments that allowed property to be held in common. We know, for example, that in Rome the Christians competed with a tavern keeper for the purchase of a house that belonged to the state. The emperor Alexander Severus (222–255 C.E.) gave preference to the Christians since he felt that a place of worship was better than one for drinking.[36] Writing from Carthage, St. Cyprian (d. 258) specifically mentions the ambo as the place from which the word was proclaimed. This reference indicates that the room where the ambo stood must have been reasonably large and the assembly sizable.[37]

The best textual evidence regarding special places for Christian worship in the second and third centuries is of Syrian provenance. The *Didascalia Apostolorum,* or *The Teaching of the Twelve Apostles*, probably written in northern Syria during the first half of the third century (ca. 230), provides a graphic description of the liturgical assembly.[38] It notes that the bishop's seat should be placed at the east, surrounded by places for the presbyters. The laypeople also have places, the men in front, the women after them, with the young girls on one side and the widows on the other. Mothers with small children are to sit apart. The deacons are to stand at the doors so as to be able to identify those who enter the assembly.[39]

Before the period of Constantine, concrete evidence of church buildings is rare. In the nineteenth century it was believed that the first Christians met in the catacombs, but it is certain that any places for worship in the catacombs are late and derive from the development of pilgrimages to the martyrs who were buried there. Archaeological searches were later made beneath the urban churches of Rome, called *tituli* and distinguished by a personal name in the genitive, for example, *Titulus Equitii*; some scholars thought they could identify churches set up in the houses of such persons, who had presumably donated their property to the church. As a matter of fact, the earlier buildings beneath the Roman churches are varied and have no definitive layout. Hence, that theory has been more or less abandoned. Archeology, however, has given us valuable evidence of a Syrian house that was modified for Christian worship and used between 240 and 256 C.E. The site is at Dura Europos, a small town in the Syrian desert on the Euphrates, originally established about 300 B.C.E. as part of the Greek expansion into Asia Minor; it served as a fortress for the Greeks. Throughout the second century B.C.E. it was under regular siege, first by Parthians, then by

Romans, and finally by Persian Sassanians, who destroyed the town in the middle of the third century C.E.

Christianity was introduced into Dura Europos by the Romans during their occupation about 163 C.E. Various buildings have been excavated, including a synagogue and a small Christian church. Information about the life of the Christian community has been gained from the excavation of the church built about 249 C.E. When the town was destroyed in 256 C.E., the church community was dissolved.[40]

The house church at Dura Europos originally was a private house that was remodeled by Christians in the middle of the third century. It originally had eight rooms, including a courtyard, portico, vestibule, gathering hall, baptistery, and three additional rooms. The baptistery is clearly identified by the presence of a raised pool standing under an arch adorned with stars. On the surrounding walls are biblical paintings, including representations of the Good Shepherd and his sheep, the fall of Adam and Eve, the women bringing spices to anoint the body of Jesus in the tomb, the healing of the paralytic, Jesus walking on the water, the woman at the well, David and Goliath, and Peter saved from drowning on the lake of Tiberius. There are also paintings of grapes, wheat, and pomegranates over the font, perhaps referring to the celebration of the Eucharist following baptism. Both sacraments symbolized the new life after death, promised by Christ and celebrated in the rites of baptism and eucharist.[41]

A wall was removed from one of the rooms opening off the central courtyard in order to create a large room for the assembly. More than two hundred square feet in area, it contained a slightly raised platform for the presider, but there was no fixed altar. We do not know whether the walls of the assembly room were decorated like those of the baptistery or were simply left unadorned.[42] Upper rooms of the house may possibly have been used by the original owners or by visiting Christians, though L. Michael White maintains that it was no longer used as a residence after renovations, since it had become a church building in a more formal sense.[43] In outward appearance the church building at Dura remained essentially a house, indistinguishable from the other houses excavated in the town.

A short distance from the house church is a similar house synagogue with distinguished wall paintings.[44] Not far away is a building dedicated to the worship of Mithras, a cult often popular in Roman garrison towns.[45]

Another example of a house church is the so-called house of Peter in Capernaum. Ancient homes in the vicinity consisted of various rooms opening off a courtyard that in turn opened onto the street. One such house, near the lake of Capernaum, is thought by some to be Peter's house.

It dates from the first Christian century but was remodeled in the middle of that century for use by the local Jewish-Christian community, as seems to be clear from various inscriptions and wall paintings. The building was apparently renovated at the end of the third or the beginning of the fourth century. In the middle of the fifth century the whole area was cleared and an octagonal church was constructed. Mosaics cover the floor, and a portico and baptistery were added. What is of interest is the sequence in which this site developed. First there was a private home used for worship; then it was converted into a house church, and finally into a formal church of a completely different style.

In his *Ecclesiastical History*, Eusebius (ca. 260–340) notes that the church flourished so much in the period prior to the persecution under Diocletian (303 C.E.) that it was impossible to describe "those mass meetings, the enormous gatherings in every city, and the remarkable congregations in places of worship. No longer satisfied with the old buildings, they raised from the foundations in all the cities churches spacious in plan."[46]

It is important to note the significant shift in terminology used to describe Christian worship spaces by the end of the third century. The extant texts speak primarily of houses of prayer and churches. By discarding the word "temple," Christians indicated their separation from both paganism, which surrounded them, and also their inherited Jewish tradition. Words less inclined to carry sacral overtones came to be used for places of worship. Included here were the expressions "house of prayer," "house of God," "house of the Lord," and "church." In northern countries the word *kyriakon* (house of the Lord) prevailed, whereas in Greek and Latin regions the word *ekklēsia* was regularly used. The term designated, first of all, the assembly of those baptized and those preparing for baptism. The transferral of the word to the place where the assembly gathered was contemporaneous with the construction of the first edifices explicitly designed for worship. The association of the community and the building would have been suggested by the New Testament, which speaks of building the church (Matt. 16:18) and of constructing it on the foundation of the apostles and prophets with Christ Jesus himself being the cornerstone (Eph. 2:19–22).[47]

In the fourth century, Christians also used secular terminology, especially *titulus* and *basilica*, to designate worship spaces. The term *titulus*, followed by the name of the owner of the dwelling, indicated a house where the early Christians assembled. From Rome there is evidence to support this assertion. The name of the owner was usually inscribed on a slab above the entrance to the building.[48]

By the beginning of the fourth century, there were at least twenty-five churches in Rome known as *tituli*. Only ruins of these houses remain, usually under church buildings constructed at a later date. Just before the peace of Constantine (313 C.E.), the first buildings constructed specifically for Christian worship were erected in Rome. But in the decade following his victory at the Milvian bridge, new shapes and types of ecclesiastical buildings appeared. Externally these buildings were unexceptional; they generally looked like ordinary Roman assembly halls.

The house churches were places for Christian celebration. They were not sacred monuments built to give glory to God, nor were they simply gathering places for the proclamation and study of the scriptures or for socializing by members of the community. They were places where the assembled community experienced the paschal mystery. It is reference to that central mystery of Christian faith above all in its baptismal and eucharistic expressions, all related to and transforming the ordinary life of the gathered community, that distinguished the Christian churches from all other secular or religious buildings.

In the house churches the primary emphasis was on the assembly. The interior arrangements of the house churches had no specific design. Objects had no predetermined place, nor did they have any sacral meaning apart from the community and its celebrations. The important thing for Christians was to gather in the name of the Lord to celebrate his saving presence in their midst through the power of the Holy Spirit and to share the power of that presence so as to transform the world. Communion and mission were the goals of the early Christian assemblies. The achievement of these goals allowed for the multiplication of house churches because it was the Holy Spirit who brought Christians into unity, not one particular temple or one special church building.[49]

Hence, the early house churches stood in marked contrast to the Jewish temple, which was a sacred monument, unique and static. It was a symbol of God's stability and order. In design as well as in its furnishings, it was meant to reflect the immutability of God; thus, the ceremonial carried out in the temple was both carefully regulated and minutely detailed.

In contrast to that rigid system, the liturgy of the house churches was designed to highlight the centrality of Christ and the dignity of the Christian community gathered in Christ's name through the power of the Holy Spirit. The symbolism of the temple was transposed so that it was applied first of all to the risen Christ and then to the community of his disciples, who became the temples of the Holy Spirit. Unlike the temple of the first dispensation, which was firmly established in Jerusalem, Christians were scattered throughout the Roman empire but were one in Christ.

During the age of the house churches, the celebration of the liturgy was essentially a communal action, carried out by a small assembly interacting with its leader, who presided over the group in the name of Christ. Unlike the priests of the Jewish tradition, the Christian presiders did not function as solitary delegates of the Lord. The presider was a symbol of unity in the community, one whose ministry was service, exercised through prayer, proclamation, and ritual action—all designed to build up the community as the body of Christ. A distinction between the presider and the rest of the community was in place, but it was not accentuated so as to divide the community. The entire ethos of the liturgical celebrations was that of profound unity in Christ through the power of the Holy Spirit.[50] Christian sacrality was expressed primarily by actions: eating, drinking, proclaiming, bathing, and anointing. Unfortunately, in the years that followed the period of the house churches, the emphasis tended to shift from persons to places and things as attitudes were increasingly borrowed from the sacrality of the Jewish people or from secular society; in the process, liturgy increasingly was thought of as a noun rather than a verb.

IMAGES IN THE PLACES OF WORSHIP

The beginnings of Christian art cannot be dated earlier than the end of the second or beginning of the third century, when carved or painted expressions of Christian beliefs appeared. This relatively late date raises the question of whether earlier Christians were more observant of the biblical injunction against idolatry or were reserved about images because they believed in a transcendent God who required them to abstain from luxuries and to be more spiritual.[51] The late appearance of Christian art is somewhat curious, since Christian literature in various forms, including apology, exhortation, and poetry, as well as distinctive forms of liturgical worship were quite well established by the middle of the second century. As a matter of fact, the appearance of Christian art in the late second and early third century actually parallels certain developments in Christian theology. There is no incontrovertible evidence that there was any direct conflict between theological text and Christian images.[52]

In general the subjects of Christian art fall into four broad categories: (1) subjects derived from the pagan religious world but adapted to serve Christian doctrines; (2) neutral subjects found in traditional decorations but given a specific Christian symbolic meaning; (3) images derived from biblical accounts; and (4) portraits of Christ, Mary, and the saints. The Christian art of the second and third centuries was based primarily on the first three categories. Fragments of fresco paintings in house churches and burial places reveal consistencies both in subject matter and in the treatment of the subject.[53] Some themes that one would naturally look for in churches were apparently never treated directly. According to Margaret Miles,

> [There are] no surviving depictions of the resurrection or ascension of Christ, and the Eucharist cannot be positively identified in pre-Constantinian art. There are no portraits of Christ and no depictions of the crucifixion. Scenes of the Last Judgment are also conspicuously absent. Human figures are depicted praying in the customary position, standing with raised arms, and there is at least one depiction of a woman holding an infant, most likely a portrait of the deceased. Numerous symbols appear again and again, such as a fish, loaves of bread and the chi-rho monogram.[54]

Particular subjects, however, appear with great regularity and in usually consistent style, for example, the Good Shepherd, Jonah, Abraham and Isaac, Noah, Daniel, and the baptism of Jesus. The mood of the art is consistently serene, even when martyrdom is depicted. As the art historian Emile Mâle noted, "In those tragic years when the blood of the martyrs was flowing, Christian art expressed nothing but peace."[55] The early Christian art is simple and humble in style. Although it has sometimes been described as expressionistic, its expression is one of inner experience. The bodies are especially expressive. For example, the eyes of the *orantes* are large, expressing the inner disposition of the whole person.[56] Although some patristic texts preceding the peace of Constantine give the impression that the early Church was opposed to artistic representation because of its eagerness to distinguish Christian from pagan practice, the texts do not in any way support an interpretation of unambiguous iconoclasm. However, the message that is communicated by these early images is complex and their message is symbolic rather than precise.[57]

Most of the extant examples of early Christian art originated in the environs of Rome and from the catacombs and sarcophagi. In fact the first important examples of Christian art are frescoes on the walls of the Christian catacombs along the Via Appia Antica in Rome. The oldest of these subterranean burial grounds, the Catacomb of Callistus, was named for one of the early bishops of Rome (ca. 217–222) who, while still a deacon, was made responsible for these tunnel-like burial grounds. The adornment of these burial places with Christian images did not reflect an effort on the part of Christians to hide their Christian identity from Roman officials. Certainly the excavation and decoration of the catacombs was quite public and would have been undertaken with the full knowledge of the secular authorities.

It seems that the creation of a distinctively Christian iconographic language should not be looked upon as the work of individuals; it was rather the result of a gradually emerging public Christian face of a religion that was developing its own identity. The existence of such burial places indicates that the Christian community had achieved both the funds and the right to own property and to bury their dead in places that were purchased specifically for that purpose. Certainly the development of early Christian art reflects changes in the economic and social condition of Christians and the development of Christianity itself as a religion over time. Although there was a strong transcendent thrust to Christianity and a clear focus on divine laws and other-worldly expectations, nevertheless Christians themselves lived in the midst of political, economic, and other cultural factors of the time. Hence, the visual arts reflected not only civil circumstances but also developments in Christian doctrine and church life. External as well as internal developments would have affected the face of Christianity. Theological debates, interpretations of scriptural data, and liturgical practices would have been part of the overall environment in which images were developed. It was at the end of the second century and the early years of the third that Clement of Alexandria, Origen of Alexandria, Hippolytus of Rome, Irenaeus of Lyons, and Tertullian of Carthage were in their prime. Gnosticism, Montanism, and monarchianism were the subjects of theological debate. The Roman empire itself was especially unstable during the third century. All these events and circumstances must be taken into account in any effort to understand both the theological texts and the artistic images that were produced in this early period in the life of the Christian church. Although historians differ in their interpretation of the images, it seems certain that they were not simply accidentally or arbitrarily chosen. In fact the interpretation of early Christian art may be profitably advanced by considering the contemporary written documents. Literary texts and visual images did not in fact represent divergent belief systems but emerged from the same or similar religious communities and hence manifest a common purpose and outlook.[58]

Robin Jensen has summarized the place and role of Christian images in the early period with clarity; she also demonstrates the necessary correlation that should exist between visual and literary texts:

Those writers who expounded their understanding of the Christian faith in

words frequently illustrated their prose with metaphors, and scriptural illustrations whose parallels appear in visual form in the paintings, mosaics,
sculpture, and other crafts of the early church. Many of these metaphors
remain constant through centuries. . . . Central religious images, both visual
and literary, balance and reinforce each other. Historians cannot give pride
of place to texts, assuming they speak more clearly or accurately for a particular community than do material objects. In isolation, textual data only
give a partial view of things. Images are articulate and complex modes of
expression that make no sense in isolation and have no meaning apart from
ideas that emerge in a local community and engage that community's values.[59]

Many of the popular early Christian images had parallels in contemporary pagan images; hence, we may conclude that there was not a strict separation between Christian and pagan imagery in the third and early fourth
centuries. In fact the optimism found in pagan funerary imagery was easily
carried over into early Christian art as an expression of belief in the resurrection of the dead to eternal life. Such a transition from pagan imagery to
Christian symbolism found a parallel in the texts of some of the second-
and third-century theologians, including Justin Martyr and Clement of
Alexandria, who emphasized the continuity between late Hellenistic philosophy and Christian truths, especially concerning human virtues and the
nature of the divine being.[60]

Early images were often rooted in biblical themes, a fact that underscores the distinctive place that biblical narratives played in the faith and
life of early Christians, especially during an age when formal theologians
were preoccupied with the philosophical foundations of Christianity, the
refutation of heresies, and the proper formulation of doctrinal statements.
Old Testament stories and subjects were especially prominent in the Christian art of the second through the fourth centuries. The story of Jonah was
quite popular, as was the account of Noah, Moses striking the rock in the
wilderness, Abraham sacrificing Isaac, Adam and Eve, and Daniel in the
lions' den. Of the New Testament narratives, only representations of the
baptism of Jesus and the raising of Lazarus found much popularity.[61]

The style and subject matter of Greco-Roman art seem to have influenced the way Christian images were presented. For example, Daniel was
represented as a heroic nude; the prophets were shown in philosophical
garb; and the altars in the scenes of Abraham sacrificing Isaac were typical
Roman altars. We may conclude, then, that the most obvious source for
much of the early Christian iconography as far as style is concerned was the
surrounding Greco-Roman environment.

Various theories have been proposed to account for the popularity of Old Testament themes but the simplest explanation is probably that particular Old Testament narratives were chosen because they represented God's deliverance from danger, especially during times of persecution.

In fact, the artistic themes that were drawn from biblical narratives served the important exegetical function of commenting on the biblical texts themselves. They gave a symbolic or metaphorical interpretation to the biblical texts. This style of exegesis certainly had roots in Hellenistic Judaism, particularly in the writings of Philo of Alexandria. The artistic images would have been polyvalent, and so would have been interpreted on various levels by viewers. The paintings in the catacombs would quite certainly have communicated various meanings depending on the experience and background of the viewers, who would have found messages hidden behind the literal or illustrative level.[62]

Many of the images in the catacombs or on sarcophagi seem to refer to the sacraments of baptism and the eucharist. For example in the catacomb of Callistus there are representations of the baptism of Jesus, Jonah, Moses striking the rock, a fisherman, the resurrection of Lazarus, the Good Shepherd, seven young men eating a meal, the Samaritan woman at the well, and Abraham offering Isaac. Some of these images had more than one meaning; for example, the fisher and especially the fish carried both baptismal and eucharistic connotations. Likewise, Jonah's fall into the sea and his resurgence would have symbolized both the sacrament of baptism and the death and resurrection of the Lord Jesus.[63]

The meaning of these artistic images would have found resonances in the biblical and patristic writings. For example, Paul identifies the Israelites passing through the Red Sea as a figure of baptism; likewise, the author of 1 Peter 3 presents Noah, who was saved through water, as anticipating the sacrament of baptism. Tertullian provides a number of scriptural types for the sacrament of baptism, including the crossing of the Red Sea, Jesus' own baptism, the miracle at Cana, Jesus walking on the water, and water springing from the side of Christ on the cross. Cyprian also refers to Moses striking the rock and the Samaritan woman at the well as anticipating the sacrament of baptism.[64]

Decorating a tomb or a burial place with symbols of baptism and the eucharist should not be surprising, since belief in those sacraments was considered essential for eternal life. Other images are, of course, not so easily interpreted. Some figures, such as Daniel in the lions' den, Susannah, and the three young men in the fiery furnace seem to refer above all to deliverance from danger; hence they are not clearly sacramental in their reference.[65]

Robin Jensen draws a sound conclusion to her book that helps us understand theologically the complex issues involved in the production of early Christian art:

> Art crystallizes, or perhaps materializes certain points of doctrine which, while based on scripture, are sometimes more often encountered in theological arguments than in ordinary daily experience. Images can make the bridge between the material and the intellectual via an interesting kind of hypostatic union—logos and icon. Complex and sophisticated symbols that communicate on many levels and refer to different stories, ideas, and matters of faith, visual images also speak directly and clearly, even to the simplest believer. Thus "religious pictures" are not merely for the theologically untrained, or for the illiterate, or for the practitioner of popular religion at all, even while they serve the needs of persons in those categories. By the same token, neither is the deepest value of art restricted to the elite, the intelligentsia, or to those trained in the lore or techniques of its interpretation.[66]

Certainly the interpretation of sacred images cannot be accurately done without clear reference to the community in which they originate and to the many values and meanings which that community chooses to articulate in its literary texts, its rituals, and its artifacts.[67]

4

Post-Constantinian Period

BY THE FOURTH CENTURY, A MORE OR LESS STANDARD LITURGY
had developed throughout the Roman empire, at least in its very basic elements.[1] The liturgy required a nave, an apse, an altar, an ambo, a baptistery,
and rooms in which the catechumens could be instructed. The liturgy itself
was peripatetic, with various processions from one part of the church to
another. Certainly the form of the liturgy would have been conditioned by
the shape of the church buildings themselves. The eucharistic celebration
would undoubtedly have been experienced differently if the altar were
placed in the middle of the nave than if it were in the front or rear of the
apse. The liturgical texts would have been interpreted and reinforced in
light of the mosaics and frescoes on the walls and the floor of the buildings.
In addition to the actions and words of the liturgy, the overall experience
of the participants would have been greatly affected by the inner atmosphere of the buildings.

During the fourth century, the term "basilica" was regularly applied to
church buildings, above all in the Mediterranean world. Although it means
"royal," it has no specific connection with court language. In Rome, the
first basilica at the Forum dates back to the time of the Republic (ca. 500–31
B.C.E.). It was essentially a large hall used for public gatherings and the
transaction of official business. Unlike the family house, which protected
domestic life from outside intrusions, the basilica facilitated social communication. Architecturally it was generally a clerestoried nave with two wide
aisles, one on each side created by a double colonnade, all covered by a
prominent roof, though the roofs of the side aisles were usually lower than
that of the main nave. The lower roofs made space for clerestory lighting.
The nave terminated in an apse, sometimes having transverse wings flank-
ing a chancel area. Structurally it was a simple building that could be
adorned with mosaics, frescoes, and marble and could accommodate large

groups of people because of its open space. If used for judicial purposes, the bench for the judges was placed in the apse at one end and was set off by a railing. The entrance from the street was located along the longitudinal axis.[2]

In religious basilicas, however, the entrance was located on the shortest side, facing the apse. An open quadrangle, serving as a place of transition from the outside world, was often found inside the main entrance. Occasionally there was a double apse, one at each end of the building. The basilica would have been but one building, a meeting place, among a number of buildings that would have served the needs of the religious communities in an urban setting.[3]

With Constantine's victory over Maxentius in 312 and the consequent freedom from persecution that was extended to Christians, the number of Christians rapidly increased, thus necessitating larger buildings for worship assemblies. They naturally took over the basilica, which became the reception hall of the Lord, the *basilica dominicana*. It was the place where the Lord convoked his people so he could share his word with them in the sacred scriptures and nourish them at the eucharistic table.[4]

The Christian basilicas were distinguished not by any architectural innovations but by their interior arrangements. They contained an apse and usually an atrium with a fountain for ablutions located before the entrance to the basilica proper. Within the basilica itself there were three focal points called for by the liturgy: the bishop's chair surrounded by benches for the presbyterium, the ambo for the readings, and the altar for the celebration of the sacrificial meal (though there is some evidence that the altar was portable and was brought into the assembly just in time for the liturgy of the table). The location of these foci varied from region to region.[5]

The assembly room and the ambo would have been common elements in the synagogue; so would the presider's chair. The table for the eucharist, however, would have distinguished the Christian church from both the synagogue and pagan temples. Just before 312, the first buildings constructed specifically for Christian worship were built in Rome.[6] The edifices constructed after the peace of Constantine were mainly erected outside the city walls of Rome rather than within the already densely populated city.[7]

Ordained ministers, bishops, and presbyters, who were often outlawed or held in suspicion before the peace of Constantine, were gradually assimilated into the ranks of civil officials. This phenomenon paralleled a development in the theology of ordained priesthood as clearly distinct from that of the nonordained. In earlier periods, the emphasis was on the unity of the assembly with the presider functioning as a servant of the community and as a symbol of unity in the group. After the peace of Constantine, the bishop, and eventually the presbyter, was looked upon as the personal representative of Christ, both theologically and juridically. Increasingly the liturgy appeared not primarily as the worship of a local community of faithful disciples of Christ but rather as a public act expressing the universality of the church. The bishop presided over the community as teacher, governor, and sanctifier, exercising those roles as a vicegerent incorporating in his own person the power of Christ.[8]

As worship was experienced more and more as a public celebration, the architecture became more and more an expression of the public character of the church. The Christian basilica became a monumental place for public gatherings, not so much in terms of its exterior appearance as in terms of the richness of its interior decoration. The bishop's chair, located in a special place of honor in the center of the semicircular apse, facing outward and overlooking the nave, clearly symbolized his headship in a hierarchically structured church. His position would have paralleled the position of the emperor in a secular gathering place. By the second half of the fourth century the bishop was accustomed to entering the basilica in a grand procession following a ritual that accompanied the entry of the highest court magistrates. The cultic objects that were carried in procession—the cross, gospel book, portable lamps, and incense—accompanied the presider as symbols of special reverence toward him; they were only indirectly related to Christ. It has been suggested that the marvelous mosaics that eventually adorned the apsidal walls of most of the basilicas were related above all to the bishop himself as a living symbol of Christ.[9]

Clearly, as the Christian basilica developed, it became an impressive, hierarchically arranged hall with one area carefully set off for the clergy and another for the lay folk. However, we should not exaggerate the sumptuous character of the basilica. Apart from its interior decorations and occasional vastness, it was exteriorly a simple building, quite unassuming, utilitarian, and integrated with the other buildings in an urban setting. The basilica itself would have been but one of a complex of buildings which would have accommodated the Christian community, including the baptistery. Exteriorly these buildings would have looked no different from any other complex of secular buildings.[10]

The interior of the basilica was designed to delight the eyes of the worshipers. It is likely that fourth-century Christians prayed, as the *orantes* of the catacombs are pictured, with eyes open. In addition to the action and movement of the liturgy, the worshipers would have sensed that bright light was a marked feature of fourth-century churches. Constantine himself had a commitment to the cult of the sun, which he apparently never renounced. Furthermore, the emphasis on the divinity as light was a distinctive characteristic of classical culture. It is not surprising that a bright, open atmosphere was normal in the fourth-century basilicas. It was light along with color that brought the basilica to life. Mosaics and wall paintings, covering a wide range of subjects, both instructed and pleased the worshipers.[11] Certainly the visual images of fourth-century Christian art provided an important source of orientation and catechesis for the worshipers in the churches of that time.[12]

There is no clear disjunction in the use of images before and after the peace of Constantine. The fragments of fresco painting in catacombs and house churches show consistencies in subjects depicted and their treatment. The mood of Christian art from this early period is consistently peaceful. The lines and colors are serene, but the postures indicate inner tension. The visual evidence indicates a generally accepted use of images in the places of early Christian worship.[13]

Eusebius (ca. 260–340), the bishop of Caesarea in Palestine from about 315, is a primary source for the history of the church from the apostolic age to his own day. In a panegyric on the building of churches addressed to Paulinus, bishop of Tyre, he wrote:

> For when he had thus completed the temple, he also adorned it with lofty thrones in honor of those who preside and also with seats decently arranged in order throughout the whole, and at last placed the holy altar in the middle. And that this might be accessible to the multitude, he enclosed it with frame lattice work, accurately wrought with ingenious sculpture, presenting an admirable sight to the beholder.[14]

Although the artistic works that lavishly adorned the interior of these churches were executed in various styles, materials, subjects, and themes, the overall impression communicated was that Christianity was the universal way of salvation. The images were regularly arranged so that they focused on the bishop's chair and on the altar; they not only reminded the viewers of the biblical episodes presented but communicated that the viewers themselves were being caught up in the same saving experiences through the celebration of the liturgy. The fourth-century pagans who were in the process of becoming Christian or those who were recently bap-

tized would have been initiated into the Christian faith by the visible splendor of the churches; their transition from paganism to Christianity would
have been facilitated by the ease with which many of their old symbols
were taken over by Christianity but given a fresh interpretation compatible with the Christian faith, a clear indication that inculturation was taken
seriously in the early church. This visual experience assured new converts
that their cultural heritage was not to be exterminated but converted.

Examination of the visual evidence of the fourth-century churches
shows that Christianity accepted and placed within its own context a wide
variety of pagan, Jewish, and imperial images and themes in an effort to
build all human beings into the church of Christ who was the way to truth
and the life of salvation for all God's people.

END OF THE EARLY CHRISTIAN PERIOD

During the fourth and fifth centuries, numerous Christian churches were
built by bishops and their people, assisted by civil authorities. These were
constructed both to accommodate the large numbers receiving baptism and
also to honor the places where God had intervened in the lives of people,
especially through God's Son, Jesus Christ. In Palestine the new churches
perpetuated the memory of Jesus Christ and the principal New Testament
events; in Rome and throughout the empire, they often commemorated
the martyrs, who lived out the paschal mystery of Christ in the church.[15]

Where the Christian faith was well established, the community often
constructed three distinct buildings, grouped together to serve the needs of
the faithful: the church, the baptistery, and the martyrium.[16] The baptistery was usually separate from the basilica. It was ordinarily the central
room of a whole complex used for the formation of the catechumens,
including dressing rooms for the men and women to be used at the time of
baptism, and a place for the postbaptismal consignation conferred by the
bishop. Either hexagonal, octagonal, or circular in shape, the design of the
baptistery was taken over from the burial mausoleums, especially the Anas-
tasis, the rotunda over the tomb of Christ in Jerusalem.[17]

The martyrium was a structure built over the tombs of early martyrs.
Since their cult flourished from the fourth century onward, their tombs
became popular places for pilgrimage. The most important tombs were
those reputed to be the burial places of Christ in Jerusalem, and Peter and
Paul in Rome.[18]

MEANING OF EARLY CHRISTIAN ARCHITECTURE

From an architectural point of view, the early Christian basilica manifested a profoundly symbolic interpretation of Christian life in the world. The concepts of center and path were especially important. An emphasis on interiority was common to all early Christian churches. In a sense they were conceived as interior worlds representing the eternal city of God. A simple treatment of the exterior served to emphasize the inward thrust.

The center of the Christian world was something more than a concrete place. Christ was the center, for he was the mediator between God and the people; he was Savior and Lord. His presence, however, was symbolized above all by the Christian community, the assembly of individual persons who were all initiated into the paschal mystery of Christ through baptism and who, as a result, formed the church as the body of Christ and the people of God. They realized that the celebration of the Eucharist not only expressed their identity as the body of Christ but also their union with one another. For the early Christians, following Christ did not mean that the goal of life is achieved all at once; they realized that Christianity is a way of life. In architectural terms their conviction was expressed as a longitudinal axis, as a road leading to the altar which symbolized Christ and union with him through the power of the Holy Spirit. When Christians returned from the altar to their normal life in the world, they hoped that they had been somewhat transformed so as to be able to contribute to the transformation of the world into the true *civitas Dei*, the city of God.

As a manifestation of the *civitas Dei*, the church building represented the heavenly Jerusalem; hence, it naturally took over forms from the Roman city, such as the colonnaded street and the apse, which contained the seat of the *paterfamilias*, the head of the family, or the throne of the emperor. The bishop's seat was ordinarily placed in the apse and became a focus and symbol of unity among the people in the same way as the altar and the ambo were unifying symbols of Christ who nourishes his body the church by means of the word of wisdom, the bread of life, and the cup of salvation.[19]

The cross was also integrated into the place of the early church. Though it did not appear in pre-Constantinian art, it surfaced as an important Christian image after Constantine's victory in 312 and the freedom given to the Christian church. The integration of the cross in the spatial layout of the church would have been natural, since Christ conquered the cosmic order of sin and death by his own death on the cross and his resurrection from the dead.[20]

The extensive building activity all over the Mediterranean world during the fourth century largely came to a halt in the West in the fifth century by the successive invasions of the Visigoths and the Vandals. Although the Eastern empire was able to offer some effective resistance to the barbarians, it too suffered the loss of many of its important early Christian monuments during the Arab invasions of the seventh century. When church buildings were erected in the West during this period and well into the Middle Ages, they were patterned after the early Christian models. Once Palestine fell into the hands of the Arabs, Rome gained even greater importance for Christian pilgrims, but Palestinian monuments were often duplicated in Rome. Hence the architect's aim as the church moved into the Middle Ages was to build *more Romano*, after the manner of the early churches at Rome.

In the Christian East, a distinctive style of architecture known as Byzantine developed above all during Justinian's reign in the sixth century. It flourished again from the ninth to the eleventh century, following the spread of Byzantine liturgy. As an architectural form, it evolved around the religious use of the dome. The first masterpiece of Byzantine architecture appeared in the church of San Vitale in Ravenna, the principal center of Justinian's rule in Italy.[21] In technique the greatest Byzantine achievement, however, was the building of Hagia Sophia (532–537), where the dome reached a volume not attained again until the Renaissance. As the principal church in Constantinople, it set the decisive pattern for church architecture in all the provinces of the Eastern empire.

SACRED IMAGES

During the fourth century, when Christianity emerged from being an oppressed minority religion with a carefully controlled system of visual images to a public religion patronized by the Roman emperor, new images and new contexts for those images developed. The large, newly built churches in Rome, Constantinople, and the Holy Land gave artists an opportunity to exercise their skills in presenting images of Jesus Christ, his mother, and the saints. At the end of the fourth century, Paulinus of Nola commissioned artists to adorn a new church built to house the relics of St. Felix with images of Christ and the saints as well as scenes from certain biblical narratives . He defended the commission as a way of counteracting the continuing popularity of pagan idols. He felt that the colorful paintings attracted people inside the church and "nurtured their believing minds with representations by no means empty."[22] Although he probably hoped that the images would edify the faithful, he seems to have felt that the images would be able to mediate holiness to the people in the same way as the relics of the saints who were buried in close proximity to the church.[23]

The development of a new kind of image took time and contrasted rather markedly with the images painted and carved in pre-Constantinian times. During the third and early fourth centuries, the images of Jesus were symbolic references to his character and teaching; he was either the Good Shepherd or a philosopher, or he was represented as Orpheus or Sol. He was also represented as a character in a biblical narrative. Usually pictured as a beardless young man wearing a long tunic, he was set out as the central figure in a scene that included other people. With the exception of his baptism by John, where he was often shown as a naked young man, Jesus was portrayed in the act of healing, teaching, or working miracles. The other figures in such scenes were usually the same size as Jesus and wore similar attire. For the most part they did not manifest awe or reverence in the presence of Jesus. These images were not portraits in any sense but were illuminations of biblical events that in no sense sought to set Jesus apart as the Son of God.[24] It was the human nature of Jesus that was primarily presented.

The new type of image that developed in the middle of the fourth and the early fifth centuries included paintings of Christ enthroned in glory, presenting the new law to the apostles, triumphantly entering Jerusalem, washing the feet of the disciples, as well as incidents from his passion, including his arrest, his trial, and his carrying the cross. These new images, which were not related to specific scriptural texts, gradually replaced the older iconography. By the late fourth century, burial in the catacombs seems to have ceased and with that the type of funerary decoration that was familiar in such burial sites. However, the end of catacomb painting did not mean that narrative images ceased altogether. Christian images continued to portray biblical narratives. In the fifth century and throughout the sixth, liturgical objects made of ivory or precious metals were decorated with such scenes as Abraham offering Isaac, Daniel among the lions, the raising of Lazarus, Moses striking the rock, the healing of the paralytic, and the man born blind.[25]

From the late fourth century on, illuminated manuscripts developed which juxtaposed artistic images with biblical texts, making those images quite clearly illustrative but no less capable of communicating allegorical meanings. The juxtaposition of text and image did not necessarily imply that the image was a mere illustration, for illuminations in themselves often played an important exegetical function.[26]

In the British Museum there are four ivory reliefs dating from the early fifth century; they formed the sides of a small casket, possibly used to hold a relic or a consecrated host.[27] The emphasis is on Christ's divinity expressed through his physical strength and endurance rather than on his humanity and suffering. There is Christ taking up his cross, then the crucifixion, which appears to be the earliest surviving representation of that event in a narrative form; then there is the empty tomb, and finally Christ giving his commission to the apostles. The notion of a triumphant Christ was surely the one promoted up until the Middle Ages.[28]

The gradual shift in the style and content of the images that began in the late fourth century reveals that a new message was emerging concerning the character of the Christian faith in the post-Constantinian period. This iconography was intended to stress the glory, majesty, and power of Christianity as a triumphing religion, closely related to the power and triumph of the Roman emperor and indirectly indicating the demise of traditional Roman paganism and the imperial cult itself.[29] Thus, there was the development of images of the so-called imperial Christ in contrast to the human Jesus.

In the early 1990s, Thomas F. Mathews, a professor of the history of art at New York University, produced a very important book, *The Clash of the Gods: A Reinterpretation of Early Christian Art*.[30] It is a critical study of the period of art history between the third and the sixth century and focuses on the images of Christ. Mathews surveys the various artistic images and religious interpretations of Christ produced during that period and asserts that the Christian images were above all dependent on the rival images of the ancient gods, so Christ is presented as a magician, a philosopher, and an androgynous figure. He is convinced that the images of Christ during the early history of the church affected not only the history of art but also the history of Christianity itself, for the images of Christ had significant effects on the way people thought of him not only in the early centuries but ever after. In other words, the history of the images of Christ provided Christians with what might be called a nonverbal christology.[31] Mathews challenged a tradition in art history established by distinguished scholars and their disciples who maintained that images of Christ produced from the third to the sixth century were derived primarily from images of the Roman emperors, an approach that Mathews described as the "emperor mystique."[32]

He calls it a "mystique" insofar as it involved "a reverence bordering on cult for everything belonging to the emperor."[33] The formulation of the theory can be traced to the work of three brilliant European scholars working between the First and Second World Wars: Ernst Kantorowicz, Andreas Alföldi, and André Grabar.[34] Grabar was the most eloquent spokesperson for the theory. He believed that with their own divine emperor, Christians adapted, for their own distinctive purposes, the images used to promote the emperor into motifs which expressed the identity of Jesus Christ.[35]

Scholars of the classical tradition, in both art and literature, have generally been unwilling to grant that the Christians of the pre-Constantinian and immediately post-Constantinian periods created anything of their own. They regularly assumed that the culture and art of the Christians were almost nonexistent and that they needed support from imperial and worthy patrons to develop at all. Although more recent work on the third century has challenged that supposition,[36] Mathews has sought to exclude totally the emperor and the art and ceremonial associated with his person from the artistic and imaginative world of post-Constantinian Christianity. His work speaks to legitimate and long-felt reservations on the part of some scholars working in the classical tradition.

Constantine's conversion did not make Christianity the established religion, nor did it undermine the entrenched power of the pagan aristocracy of the empire. It did, however, give the church a new prominence and an opportunity for bishops to be involved in state affairs. Constantine himself was actively involved in the building projects of the church; his role as a patron of Christian art and architecture was considerable.[37]

There is no doubt that, like music played in the wrong key, images of Christ in early Christian art have been misleadingly interpreted. The great art historians of the 1930s and their disciples proposed to interpret the imagery of Christ as an adaptation of the images of the emperor. They interpreted the identity of Christ in that light in order to give Christ the dignity and majesty that the early Christians thought were his due. As a matter of fact, Christ was not in competition with the emperors, for his kingdom was not of this world. Hence, he did not assume the guise of the earthly Roman emperors in early Christian art. It was not until the Romanesque period, and then only occasionally, that Christ assumed imperial attributes, with a crown on his head and a globe in his hand. In the East, Byzantine art never knew an image of Christ the King. Christ coexisted with the emperors for centuries. The Christ who emerges from early Christian art is vigorous in his own right. In one sense his place is among the gods of the ancient world, not among the emperors, for it is with the pagan gods "that he engaged in deadly combat, and it is from them that he wrested his most potent attributes."[38]

Christ, in fact, assumed a multiplicity of roles in ancient Christian art; his imagery drew upon a variety of sources—principally pagan gods, philosophers, and magicians. The New Testament left no account of the physical appearance of Christ. Certainly gospel claims went beyond the possibility of any clear visual symbols. How could an artist interpret Christ's claim, "Before Abraham was, I am," or "He who has seen me has seen the Father"? Early Christian painters, sculptors, and mosaic workers rose to the challenge. In a sense they rewrote the gospels by representing as many facets of Christ's identity as possible; they tried to express somehow what was in fact an unimaginable mystery. Their distinguished achievements certainly gave birth to a distinctively new Christian art, above all in the post-Constantinian period.[39]

In the course of the fourth century, Christianity made a significant transition from being more like an oppressed minority cult to a public and influential religion supported by the Roman emperor himself. This change provided not only an impetus for artists to produce new images but also a fresh context in which the images could be displayed. The newly constructed churches in Rome, Constantinople, and the Holy Land lent themselves to a grand exposition of images and especially new ways of portraying Christ, his mother, and the saints.[45]

At the end of the third century and in the early decades of the fourth, new healing and miracle scenes were added to the Christian repertoire, including the changing of water into wine at Cana, the raising of Jairus's daughter or the son of the widow of Nain, and the healing of the man born blind. In all these representations, the humanity of Jesus was quite clearly set out. He was portrayed as a man of ordinary stature and physical appearance and simply equal in appearance to the other figures portrayed. His divine nature may have been implicit but was in fact not emphasized. [41]

By the mid-fourth and early fifth centuries, new themes developed, including Christ enthroned in glory, Christ presenting the new law to the apostles, Jesus as an infant receiving homage from the magi, Jesus triumphantly entering Jerusalem, Jesus washing the apostles' feet, and Jesus being arrested and carrying his cross. These new themes, often not directly associated with a particular biblical text, gradually replaced the older images, particularly those on sarcophagi. Catacomb frescoes continued to portray biblical scenes, but new themes were included. By the late fourth century, however, it seems that burial in the catacombs was discontinued and along with the practice went the funereal type of decoration and many of the subjects portrayed there.[42]

The end of catacomb decoration, however, did not end narrative iconography, for Christian art continued in new contexts and new media. In the fifth century and through the sixth and seventh centuries liturgical objects made of ivory and precious metals continued to show biblical scenes, including Abraham offering Isaac, Daniel in the midst of the lions, Moses striking the rock, the healing of the man born blind and the paralytic, and the raising of Lazarus.[43]

From the late fourth century, there was a significant shift in the style and content of Christian iconography with the result that a new message was communicated concerning the identity of the Christian faith. The new art emphasized the glory of Christ and the consequent power and majesty of Christianity, perhaps subtly relating both to the power of the emperor who supported the Christian faith and contrasting that importance with the dying aspects of the traditional Roman paganism and the old gods.[44]

In the fourth century a new category, the portrait, appeared in Christian iconography. Certainly the portrait tradition had been strong in both Greece and Rome. Perhaps Christians shied away from the portrait form because devotional images in pagan religions regularly took that form. In fact, portraits of the emperor were frequently used to test the faith of Christians. Nevertheless, portraits of Christ began to appear in the fourth century. Jesus' divinity was the subject of much debate in the fourth and fifth centuries, the conclusion being that Jesus was both human and divine and that the two natures were united in one person. However, there was no document that discussed the challenge of portraying Christ in terms that were being discussed by theologians.[45] The development of portraits certainly changed the nature of images of Christ from illustrations to icons. In fact, the earliest extant portraits fall along a line that begins with images that interpreted biblical passages and end with images that are icons worthy of veneration in themselves. The older story-based images were generally quite simple and often staccato, whereas the new representations focused on Jesus as the transcendent savior professed in the Christian creeds.[46]

The sense of transcendence was often communicated by halos. The halo was frequently used in Greek art as a symbol of divinity and was sometimes used to adorn the portrait of the emperor. It was initially applied to Jesus and the *Agnus Dei*, but was eventually used in portraits of Mary, the angels, and the saints. It was sometimes gold but also blue, green, or white. From the fifth century on, Christ's halo was ornamented by a Greek cross, a *chi-rho* monogram, or the Greek letters *Alpha* and *Omega*.[47] The so-called mandorla, a round or egg-shaped disk, probably imported from Buddhist iconography and originating in central India and differing from the halo, was sometimes used to surround the whole body of a divine being. These iconographic devices were used to communicate teachings concerning the nature of Christ and his role in the Christian economy. Such awe-inspiring images of Jesus from the fourth through the sixth century sought to represent Christ's divine essence as well as his human nature and as such elicited not only an intellectual response on the part of viewers but also a sense of veneration.[48]

Although the images of Jesus from the fourth through the sixth centuries sought to portray him as both divine and human, there were significant variations on that theme. Some of the images portrayed him with a beard and dark skin; others showed him as youthful, beardless, and light-haired. Certainly a full-bearded face suggested majesty, authority, and power, as seen in the portraits of the male deities in the Roman pantheon; whereas the clean-shaven face recalled the eternal youthfulness of God and the various divine attributes associated with the pagan savior gods. Christian iconography borrowed freely from the classical portrayals of the gods in order to stress the divine attributes of Jesus. He was most frequently shown as a youth in scenes portraying his miracles and acts of healing; in this way he was associated with suffering humanity. By contrast, the bearded Christ emphasized Jesus' majesty and power over the universe.[49]

In some of the paintings and mosaics created both before and after Constantine, Jesus carries a wand (*virga*), especially when raising Lazarus from the dead, multiplying the loaves and fishes, and changing water into wine at Cana. Such a prop, not given to Jesus in the New Testament, was, however, closely associated with Moses in scenes where he parts the Red Sea or strikes the rock in order to bring forth water for the thirsty Israelites. In the fourth century, it was Peter who took the place of Moses and was shown striking a rock with a wand and baptizing his Roman jailers.[50] The link between Moses and Peter is meant to show both as significant leaders of their people. We have no biblical account of Jesus holding a wand when he healed people; rather he achieved such miracles by touching the person to be cured, or by speaking a healing word, or pointing to the one to be cured. Such portrayals are in accord with the gospel text.[51]

One of the curious characteristics of the images of a beardless Christ is that he is often shown with feminine traits and characteristics, including long curly hair and small protruding breasts. In this regard he contrasts markedly with representations of the apostles, who are usually given clear male characteristics, such as clipped beards, short hair, and broad shoulders. These feminine characteristics were probably intended to indicate that Jesus possessed not only the qualities associated with the pagan male deities but also those associated with the female gods. In other words he possessed all the divine qualities in his one person.[52] It seems that throughout history artists sought to portray the kindness and compassion of Jesus with characteristics that appear to be feminine.[53]

IMAGES OF THE SUFFERING, DEAD, AND RISEN LORD JESUS

Although the fourth century witnessed a gradual shift in Christian iconography away from biblical narratives depicting Jesus as healer and wonderworker and to images emphasizing his divinity and transcendence, curiously missing from the new images are representations of Jesus' suffering and death on the cross.[54] Apart from a few extant examples, Christ is generally represented as victorious over death but not undergoing death. The cross dominated both Byzantine and medieval iconography, but early Christian art apparently deliberately avoided any graphic portrayals of Christ's suffering and death. The absence of early images of Christ on the cross continues to amaze theologians and church historians, since the death of Christ on the cross is such a central event in the mystery of Christian salvation. Apart from two extant carved gems dating from the fourth century and a disputed second-century wall inscription in Rome, the earliest images of Jesus crucified date from the early fifth century and are very rare until the seventh century.

The earliest certain examples of an image of Christ crucified are not at all monumental in size. The first is a wood relief sculpture on the door of the Basilica of Sta. Sabina in Rome and is dated about 430; there Jesus is shown hanging on a cross between the two thieves who were crucified with him.[55] The second is a panel of four ivory reliefs dating from the early fifth century, perhaps a decade earlier than the Sta. Sabina image. As noted earlier, they formed the sides of a small casket, possibly used to hold a relic or consecrated host and are now housed in the British Museum.

Gnostic and docetic Christians in the early church tended to deemphasize Christ's suffering and death, not because they wanted a purely human savior but because they were repulsed by the idea that a divine savior might undergo an ignominious death on a cross. However, such a denial of physical suffering on the part of Jesus implied a denial of his incarnation, a dogma that the early Christian writers firmly believed and asserted. The suffering and death of Jesus were set out as a unique offering which reconciled humanity with God and made the need for any other sacrificial offering superfluous.[56]

Various theories have been proposed to account for the absence of crucifixion images in the early history of Christianity. Some have held that the Christians, still close to the actual event of Jesus' crucifixion, might have been opposed to representing their savior as one who suffered such a gruesome death. That portraying Jesus on a cross would have offended early Christians may have been linked with the threat of idolatry. The problem was not simply whether the incarnate God could be represented visually but also how the sacred mystery of an incarnate deity could be expressed truthfully without profaning a transcendent mystery in finite material.[57]

Others have proposed that artists may have been reluctant to depict Jesus on a cross because the mystery of his death and resurrection was too profound to be expressed in any way in front of those who were not initiated into the church. Still others have suggested that crucifixion was such a barbaric mode of execution, reserved for slaves, foreigners, and traitors, that it was simply too much to ask that Christians openly represent the cross as the means by which Jesus was put to death, especially in times of persecution and ridicule.[58]

What is perplexing is the fact that though the cross of Jesus is very prominent in early dogmatic and liturgical texts, the subject is absent from art. Jensen proposes a caution in drawing conclusions:

> Scholars will need to reconsider whether there is, in fact, a complete absence of crucifixion image in early Christianity. Possible indirect references to the passion include such signs and symbols as simple crosses, "crypto-crosses" (Anchors, ships' masts, trees, plows, axes) and *tau*-crosses. More complex figures that may refer symbolically or typologically to the Crucifixion include the image of the Lamb (agnus Dei) or a type taken from the Hebrew scriptures—Abraham offering his son Isaac as a sacrifice.[59]

It must be admitted, however, that plain crosses, *tau*-crosses, and so-called crypto-crosses are not easy to interpret. The christological meaning is quite clear, however, in the image of a cross surmounted by a *chi-rho* that dates from the late fourth century and is now in the Vatican Museo Pio Cristiano.[60]

With the edict of Constantine the display of the cross as a symbol of the crucifixion of Jesus was no longer subject to the derision of Christians living in a pagan world. Two events especially marked the turning point. First, Constantine himself claimed to have seen the cross in the heavens and then adopted the labarum of chrism traced on the shields of his soldiers and on their banners. He subsequently abolished crucifixion as a death penalty in his empire. Second, the discovery of the true cross in Jerusalem by Helena, Constantine's mother, inspired subsequent pilgrimages to the Holy Land and devotion to the true cross. These events led to the development of images of the crucifixion that initially showed Jesus on the cross with open eyes and a physically robust stance. In the British Museum is an ivory plaque that shows Judas hanging to the left of Jesus on the cross, but there is a marked contrast between the hanging Judas and the alive Jesus. In an illumination from the Syrian Rabbula Gospels, Jesus is attired in a gold and purple robe rather than a loincloth and is shown with a halo. These examples and others place an emphasis on the dignity and transcendence of Jesus rather than on his human suffering and death.[61]

Another important symbolic image of Christ and his passion is the lamb, which derives from the frequent biblical references to Jesus as the sacrificial lamb, the *Agnus Dei.* Before the middle of the fourth century, images of the lamb usually appeared in conjunction with the images of the Good Shepherd and never in isolation. Even these early representations of sheep may have had sacrificial overtones in light of Jesus' statement that as the Good Shepherd he lays down his life for his sheep (John 10:15); however, it is the self-offering of the shepherd rather than the sheep that is affirmed in the text. New Testament texts certainly highlight the lamb as a symbol of Christ's passion.[62] By the fifth and sixth centuries, the Lamb replaced Jesus standing on the rock from which flowed the four living streams. This image appeared in the vault of the baptistery of St. John Lateran, on ivory gospel book covers, and in the presbytery vault of S. Vitale in Ravenna.[63] Although there were not explicit references to the crucifixion, such Lamb images, especially those placed in close proximity to altars, signified Christ as both victim and victorious, winning salvation for his faithful people.

In the fifth and sixth centuries, the victory won by the cross was signified by jewels embedded in the cross. In 619, however, the Council of Toledo forbade images representing Christ as the Lamb because it was felt that such depictions undermined the reality of Christ's human nature and his sacrificial redemption.[64]

Christ's suffering and death were also represented by the image of Abraham offering his son Isaac, a very common representation in early Christian painting and sculpture. Several pre-Constantinian catacomb paintings and several sarcophagus reliefs portraying the scene have been identified. It also appears in the fourth and fifth centuries in many more catacomb frescoes and sarcophagus reliefs as well as images on ivories, lamps, and bowls.

The scene is also found in the Dura Europos synagogue. There are various interpretations of these images, some affirming passion symbolism, others opting to view the images as a simple indication of deliverance and rescue in time of persecution.[65]

In the basilicas of S. Apollinare in Classe and S. Vitale in Ravenna, there are sixth-century mosaics that show the offerings of Melchizedek, Abraham, and Abel as types of the eucharistic sacrifice, which would be renewed at the altar standing beneath the mosaics. Without showing the crucifixion explicitly, the link among the Old Testament offerings, Jesus' sacrificial passion and death, and the church's celebration of the eucharistic sacrifice would have been quite clearly indicated through the medium of the rich visual images that would have surrounded both the altar and the presider at the eucharist.[66]

As we have seen, the Christian iconography of the mid- to late fourth century was considerably enlarged by the development of images related to the gospel accounts of Christ's arrest and trial. Appearing above all on sarcophagus reliefs, these biblical narratives included images of Jesus' arrest, his crowning with a wreath, usually of laurel rather than thorns, Simon carrying the cross, and Pilate washing his hands. None of these scenes, however, included the actual crucifixion. Sometimes the composition included a figure of Jesus triumphantly enthroned and handing the law to the apostles or an image of Christ's victory in the form of an empty cross mounted by the chi-rho monogram, which clearly expressed the idea that Christ's passion and death were the port of entry to victory and new life. In the fourth century, images of the simple cross were created in which the cross was carried by Simon of Cyrene or held by Jesus as a sign of triumph. In some instances Jesus is shown flanked by his apostles, who carry crowns or are shown greeting Jesus with gestures of affirmation and acclamation.

In the fourth and fifth centuries the simple cross appeared frequently: in gold mosaics such crosses were shown against a starry night sky; crosses were mounted on empty thrones; crosses were held by the Good Shepherd, the Lamb, Peter, and other saints; crosses were studded with jewels and planted on mountaintops from which four rivers flowed. In all these representations the cross would have referred not simply to Jesus' suffering and death but above all to his resurrection, his victory over death. The cross as a symbol of both Christ's death and his resurrection was undoubtedly encouraged by the finding of the true cross in Jerusalem and the spread of relics of the true cross throughout Europe.[67]

The earliest examples of the crucifixion image show Jesus as a robust figure, eyes open, not dying but quite alive. He is indeed a man of great dignity whose transcendence shines forth through his suffering humanity.[68] Between fourth-century images that manifested a reluctance to show the crucifixion realistically and the sixth- and seventh-century images of Jesus' actual crucifixion a theological debate had surfaced concerning the meaning of Jesus' suffering and death. The controversy flourished throughout the Middle Ages, played a role in the iconoclastic dispute in the East, and continues today in the question, Does God suffer?[69]

In conclusion one may say that the empty cross and the crucifix gradually assumed a central role in the iconographic history of the church. At different times and in different contexts, emphasis was placed either on the suffering of Jesus or on his victory. The challenge has been to portray both aspects of the paschal mystery—the Lord Jesus both dead and risen. As the tree of life, the cross has replaced the tree of Eden and opened the way for all to enter eternal life with God. As a sign of victory, the cross portrays God's benevolent attitude toward his people and his willingness to give his Son so that we might share in God's own eternal life through the death and resurrection of Jesus. What is perhaps most curious is that the role of the Holy Spirit is scarcely ever portrayed in the images of the passion and death of Jesus, a lacuna that still stands in need of correction today, especially in the West. In time the cross and even pilgrimages to the Holy Land became symbols of the inward journey that Christians must make in order to die to their own self-centeredness and self-preoccupation so that they might rise with God in Jesus through the power of the Holy Spirit.

IMAGES OF THE RESURRECTION OF JESUS
AND THE HUMAN BODY

Belief in life after death developed only gradually in the Old Testament period, but belief in the resurrection was an essential part of Christian faith in the early Christian period and was expressed in the paintings in the catacombs and sarcophagus reliefs. Christians believed that their time on earth was simply a prelude to life eternal, a belief that was symbolically enacted in the rites of Christian initiation. Such faith was clearly articulated in the early creeds and baptismal professions of faith. Belief in a fleshly resurrection characterized Western creeds in general, whereas the Eastern creeds offered variants, but the more dominant Eastern tradition spoke of the resurrection of the dead, a wording that is supported by New Testament texts, including Matthew 22:3–32 and 1 Corinthians 15. In any case, Christians believed in a general resurrection, modeled after Christ's own resurrection from the dead on Easter morning. Whether the creeds spoke of "flesh," "body," or "dead," they emphasized a physical resurrection as contrasted with a different belief in the immortality of the soul.[70]

By the second century the urgency about Christ's second coming had been dissipated, so that the teachings concerning the time and meaning of the resurrection became increasingly vague. The major question was whether the resurrection included the earthly flesh or whether it simply involved a transformation into something merely spiritual. At stake was an affirmation of the essential goodness of matter over against the Hellenistic, Gnostic, and Marcionite rejection of matter, including the human body. This has been a subject of considerable speculation down to the present time. Gnostic writers tended to deny or at least deemphasize the bodily nature of Christ's resurrection and to assert that it involved something other than the physical body he had while he was on earth. Over against these tendencies to devalue or deprecate matter, and especially the human body, orthodox Christian writers affirmed the essential goodness in general and the human body in particular. The doctrine of the resurrection continued to develop through the end of the fourth century and climaxed with the teaching of Augustine on the subject. He argued that human bodies would be transformed but would still be *substantia*. For him, Paul's "spiritual body" was a fully enfleshed body but one that was fully united with and subject to the spirit. This affirmation was supported by contemporary iconography and linked with belief in the resurrection of the body to life after death.[71]

Many of the artistic images referring to the resurrection included symbols that addressed specifically the transformation or incorruptibility of the flesh, including the dolphin, the phoenix, and the peacock. These three images do not appear in any specific biblical texts but were found frequently in non-Christian contexts. The dolphin, an image borrowed from Greco-Roman iconography, was commonly found in funereal art, as well as in simple decorative maritime scenes in both pagan and Christian art. As it was used on tombs, its meaning was probably derived from various myths that portrayed dolphins carrying persons to safety or immortality. The phoenix and the peacock, non-narrative images, both clearly referred to resurrection, the phoenix because it was reputed to have risen from its own flames and ashes, and the peacock perhaps because of the belief that its body was incorruptible. Like dolphins, peacocks were especially popular as images for decoration and appeared regularly in the catacombs, on the sarcophagus reliefs of Christians, and later in the decoration of Christian churches.[72]

Many of the patristic writers illustrated their teaching concerning the resurrection of the physical body by citing biblical typologies, including the story of Jonah, Jesus' raising of Lazarus, the resurrection of the dry bones, the three young men in the fiery furnace, the translation of Elijah and Enoch, the transfiguration of Jesus, and the creation of Adam and Eve. When such representations appeared in art, they seemed to serve as allegories or illustrations, since the art and the texts paralleled one another. Representations of both paradise and the last judgment were rare in early Christian art.[73]

In his First Letter to the Corinthians (15:20), Paul speaks of Christ's resurrection as the "firstfruits" of the rest of those who had fallen asleep. Hence, the resurrection of Christ is a promise of future resurrection. However, just as images of the crucifixion were rare, so explicit images of Christ's resurrection, ascension, and even the empty tomb are not known before the fourth century. The only exception may be a painting in the baptistery at Dura Europos that perhaps shows the three women on their way to Jesus' tomb on Easter morning. Beginning in the fifth century, however, images of the empty tomb, watched over by an angel and visited by two or three women, began to appear regularly. For example, there is an ivory diptych from Rome that shows the tomb as a strong building topped by a cupola and two women kneeling or bowing before a seated, young haloed man holding a scroll and gesturing a blessing or a greeting. Above the figures are the traditional symbols for Matthew (a winged man) and Luke (an ox). Small scenes of Jesus raising Lazarus and conversing with Zachaeus are pictured on the doors of the tomb. Since the young man has a halo, some interpreters maintain that the figure is actually Christ appearing to the two women after his resurrection. Another image, on ivory and probably from the same period, may be either a representation of Christ's resurrection or ascension or a conflation of both. It shows Christ climbing a hill to heaven and reaching up to grasp God's right hand. Two apostles are shown crouching below at the foot of the hill. On the left there is an empty tomb similar in design to one on the Roman ivory.[74]

A somewhat later ivory casket from Rome (ca. 420–430) has four plaques, representing scenes from Christ's passion and resurrection. There is Pilate washing his hands, Christ carrying his cross, Judas hanging from a tree, Christ crucified, the women at the empty tomb, and Thomas touching the side of Christ. Reference has already been made to the wooden doors of the basilica of Sta. Sabina in Rome, where a different kind of resurrection sequence was carved. Two women approach an angel who guards an arched structure and greets the women; there are no further details. The doors also include an image of Christ's ascension in which Christ is shown being lifted up to heaven by three angels, while four apostles stand in awe. There is also an image of the second coming of Christ, in which he is presented in a mandorla, while standing on earth below is a personification of the church in the orant position being crowned by Peter and Paul.[75]

The late-sixth-century Rabbula Gospel book, which, as we have seen, contained one of the earliest representations of the crucifixion, also portrays an empty tomb directly under the crucifixion panel. There is an angel seated to the left of a small tomb, who greets two women. From the tomb's door rays of light strike down three Roman soldiers. On the right, Jesus is shown greeting the same two women who kneel in adoration before him. Christ, the angel, and one of the women have halos.[76] In the same Gospel book, there is an image of Christ's ascension. Jesus is shown from the front, enclosed in a mandorla and being carried aloft by four winged creatures. Underneath the mandorla is a wheeled and winged seraph comprising the four beasts from the vision of Ezekiel (1:4–15). This seraph carrying Christ up into heaven surrounded by a mandorla came to represent the ascension in the East from the sixth century onwards. On the ground is a group of apostles with Mary, in an orant position, at the center.[77]

In the early artistic tradition, Christ's resurrection is imaged as the prototype of the final resurrection of all the faithful from the dead. Images of the last judgment were not popular; instead the early church emphasized the resurrection. The expectation of corporal or fleshly resurrection was artistically represented through various types, including the dry bones described in Ezekiel 37, Jesus' raising of the daughter of Jairus and the widow's son, and the raising of Lazarus.

The raising of Lazarus is an especially popular subject, found in sarcophagus reliefs, catacomb paintings, in ivory on diptychs, pyxes, and reliquaries, and in mosaics. Usually Jesus is shown holding a wand; he points at a small mausoleum at the door of which stands the small mummified figure of Lazarus. The location of many of these images in burial places suggests that the message to be conveyed is one of life beyond death through the resurrection of the dead. Although Lazarus died again, his first raising is proof that God has power over life and death and can bring the dead back to life again. The representations of Christ raising Lazarus are often found in close proximity to presentations of other healing and miracle stories and are often part of an integrated program referring to Christian initiation, healing, death, and life after death.[78]

In some of the Lazarus scenes, a small nude figure stands at Christ's side, probably representing Lazarus as raised from the dead. But why is the figure naked? And why is he diminutive? It has been suggested that both the nudity and the childlike size refer to the status of the newly baptized Christian.[79] Artistic representations of Jonah can shed light on that subject.

The figure of Jonah was one of the most frequently reproduced images in early Christian art. He is frequently shown being tossed into the sea, being swallowed up by the fish, emerging on dry land, sitting under a withered gourd vine, and as one who has come to life. Sitting under the gourd vine, Jonah is shown as a nude figure. Underlying the images is surely the theme of resurrection, and it is directly linked with the text in Matthew 12:39–40 in which Jesus says that just as Jonah was three days and nights in the belly of the fish, so will the Son of Man be three days and nights in the earth. Christian baptism is itself a ritual expression of Jesus' death and resurrection, and so the baptismal connection between Jonah and Jesus would be logical. Jonah and the initiate are both immersed in water. Jonah's nudity is reflected in the nudity of the initiates as they were immersed in the baptismal pool and were reborn to new life in the womblike waters of the font.[80]

Daniel also appeared as a nude figure in early Christian iconography, perhaps explained by the fact that in the Greco-Roman iconographic tradition the hero was often shown as a nude figure. Most representations portray him as beardless, facing out, with his arms lifted in prayer like an orant. Lions sit at his sides. Daniel's significance in early Christian art was either that of a martyr willing to die for his faith or of a prophet who predicted the coming of Jesus as the Messiah. His nudity perhaps points to his prefiguration of Christ's resurrection, making both Jonah and Daniel symbols of new life or rebirth.[81] Thus, there is a positive link with Christian initiation. Baptism is the sacrament through which new life, healing, strengthening, and rescue from eternal death are communicated to those being initiated who were immersed after they had disrobed. Nudity at baptism had three symbolic meanings. First of all, it symbolized the stripping off of the old self; second, it symbolized the original state of innocence of Adam and Eve in paradise; and, third, it symbolized the way that children are born from their mothers' womb.[82]

In the early church, the newly baptized received a mixture of milk and honey, not simply because they were like little children but also because they were like the Israelites who journeyed across the Red Sea and the Jordan before they entered the promised land. They journeyed from death to new life. The promised land, however, was not like the land of Israel; it was rather like the newly restored Eden symbolized by the baptismal font.

Hence, each new initiate was a second Adam or Eve restored to the original Garden of Eden. Certain aspects of the baptismal ritual symbolically enacted the Adam and Eve typology. The ritual often included a renunciation of Satan while facing the West, after which the initiates faced the East, the direction of Eden, to proclaim their faith. It seems, then, that the many representations of Adam and Eve in early Christian art were not references to their disobedience and fall from grace, but rather referred to their restoration and resurrection. This interpretation would explain their inclusion over the font at Dura Europos. In conjunction with symbols of baptism and resurrection, this iconography would have been most appropriate in a funerary context.[83] The association of Adam with baptism and resurrection and with creation and the new creation would have resonated with Paul's theology of "being in Christ" as a new creation in which the old creation has passed away and everything has become new (1 Cor. 15:2; 2 Cor. 5:1–17).

Both textual evidence and early iconography make it crystal clear that Christians had a firm belief in eternal life after death and that such a life would include the whole human person, body as well as soul. Such a belief was rooted in belief in the incarnation of the divine Logos and the bodily resurrection of Jesus Christ, whose own resurrection was a promise of resurrection for his faithful disciples. These beliefs, affirmed in early Christian creeds and ritually enacted in the sacraments of Christian initiation, were represented in the art of the early church, above all the art that was meant to both decorate and illuminate Christian burial places. The artistic images concretize beliefs rooted in scripture and articulated in doctrinal statements. The images, however, were not simply illustrations of doctrine but often communicated in subtle ways levels of meaning that could not be clearly expressed doctrinally. The theological writings of the fathers of the church and the doctrinal statements contained in early creeds often illuminate the meaning of the images, but the images often illuminate the meaning of the theological statements and creeds. The artistic images often served as a concrete bridge between the intellectual and the material worlds of the early Christian community.[84]

Certainly Jesus Christ, as both human and divine, as well as the complex nature of Christianity itself could never be portrayed adequately in any form of art; hence, the great variety of images should be seen as complementary rather than contradictory. Speaking of Jesus to fourth-century catechumens, Cyril of Jerusalem captured the artistic challenge effectively:

> The Savior comes in various forms to each person according to need. To those who lack joy, he becomes a vine; to those who wish to enter in, he is a

door; for those who must offer prayers, he is a mediating high priest. To those in sin, he becomes a sheep, to be sacrificed on their behalf. He comes to be "all things to all people" remaining in his own nature what he is. For so remaining, and possessing the true and unchanging dignity of Sonship, of physicians and caring teachers, he adapts himself to our infirmities.[85]

5

Romanesque and Gothic Architecture and Art

THERE IS LITTLE DOUBT THAT MONASTICISM, ESPECIALLY IN ITS Benedictine form, played a major role in the civilization and Christianization of Europe during the Romanesque period. St. Benedict of Nursia, in his sixth-century rule, legislated for a cenobitic monastery, which should constitute a community under its abbot, elected for life by the monks.[1] The vow of stability bound the monk to the monastery of his profession; that of *conversatio morum* obliged him to follow a monastic way of life according to the Rule of Benedict; and obedience bound him to follow the directives of the rule under his abbot. The daily life consisted of the public celebration of the liturgy of the hours, serious reading (*lectio divina*), and manual labor. Everything, including ascetical practices, was subject to the abbot's discretion. The spiritual program, grounded on obedience, silence, and humility, and flexible enough to take account of diverse strengths and weaknesses among the brethren, was intended to promote a faithful following of the gospel. Through his *Dialogues*, Pope Gregory the Great promoted Benedict's reputation in the West and the adoption of his rule. The wisdom and moderation of the rule itself, as well as the missionary zeal of the monks and the papal patronage, were the chief factors contributing to the preeminence so quickly acquired by the Rule of Benedict in Latin Christendom. By 800 it had supplanted most other monastic observances. By the same date most monks were priests, and many of them had become bishops. Intellectual work came more and more into favor, while manual labor was left to the uneducated. The numerous monasteries were centers for civilizing the neighborhoods as well as houses of worship; they were rich sources of the Western Christian civilization that was coming to birth.

For most of Christian monastic history, monks have been either artists or patrons of the arts. It is in monastic ritual, chant, architecture, sculpture, and painting that historians of theater, music, and the visual arts locate the origins of Romanesque culture.[2] In keeping with the incarnational character of Christianity, Benedictine monasticism rendered visible and tangible the iconic dimension of Christianity in imitation of Christ himself, who was, as noted in the epistle to the Colossians, the icon or image of the unseen God (Col. 1:15). Benedict's rule explicitly invokes that analogy when it compares the monastery to an artist's workshop. The whole monastic enterprise is looked upon as a creative process. In Benedict's mind, the monks were meant to channel their human energies into exercising the spiritual craft; their tools were the moral instruments of the Christian life, *instrumenta artis spiritalis* (RB 4:75).[3] Benedict's figurative use of these images eventually became literally true, as the monasteries became important centers of the creative arts, thus preserving and developing what eventually became known as Romanesque architecture, sculpture, and painting.

THE ROMANESQUE PERIOD

With the death of Justinian in 565, the Roman empire withered. Church architecture also declined until stability was restored in the middle of the ninth century and a second phase of church building emerged in which the structures were both more modest in dimension and more monastic than imperial in character. Although basilicas continued to be built until about the year 800, most newly constructed churches consisted of a barrel-vaulted cross imposed on a rectangle, with a dome over the center generally elevated on a drum. Apses were multiplied in the eastern end of the buildings, and minor domes were constructed in the angles between the arms of the cross. The overall effect was one of fresh elegance with greater emphasis on the vertical line and decorative detail. The earlier plain brick exteriors gave way to alternating bands of brick and stone or tile; the flat wall surfaces were ruptured with tall narrow niches. The colonnade separating the sanctuary from the nave was hung with icons, thus preparing the way for the iconostasis. Throughout the interior, the iconography portrayed the divine hierarchy in descending order from the image of Christ Pantocrator in the dome down through choirs of angels and bands of patriarchs and apostles, ending with the local saints appearing in the church calendars. The church thus became a rich symbol of the supernatural cosmos in which the God of heaven gloriously lives and reigns with all the angels and saints.[4]

The Romanesque style of art and architecture developed above all in Italy and western Europe between the decline of early Christian art and architecture and the development of the Gothic. Countless Romanesque churches, monasteries, and castles still mark the European landscape. They are records of an age that was distinguished by a strong cultural unity in spite of much political unrest and division. By the end of the eighth century, the western world was ready for a retrieval of many of the things that antiquity had cherished. Although civil strife was rampant during the period, energetic personalities like Pepin (714–768) and his son Charlemagne (768–814) were centers around whom the forces of order rallied. Through his strong ecclesiastical and political ties with Rome, Charlemagne synthesized Germanic and Roman culture, but it was a synthesis that also integrated various Byzantine and oriental influences which found their way to the West through the trade centers of Venice, Ravenna, and Marseilles.[5]

The most obvious characteristic of Romanesque buildings was their combination of massive enclosure and strong verticality. For the first time in architectural history, the tower became a formal element of primary importance. In early Roman architecture, square, round, and octagonal towers were used to reinforce city walls; city gates were often flanked by towers. The towered facades of Romanesque churches should be related to the earlier Roman use of towers, thus combining existential significance with that of transcendental aspiration.[6]

After the fall of the Roman empire and especially after the expansion of Islam during the seventh century, urban civilization degenerated. Hence, the churches that were built during the Carolingian period were intended to serve relatively small groups of people, since the towns were few and the countryside was sparsely populated. The impulse for a new form of architecture came above all from the monasteries, some of which served the needs of a thousand or more people. Monasticism itself was given a strong Roman imprint during the Carolingian period by the imposition of the Rule of Benedict on all monasteries of the empire. Down to the eleventh century, the monasteries were cultural and economic centers; like the feudal castles, they gave rise to new settlements. As they developed into imposing territorial, financial, and educational institutions, new architectural problems developed. The solutions that the monks offered in building their churches laid the foundations for the church architecture of the whole period.

Geographically the monasteries were quite isolated from one another, but since they were committed to the same basic values and general way of life, they formed a network of institutions that established a unity of European culture, in spite of individual differences, political divisions, and ineffective systems of communication. With the growing importance of local saints and interest in relics, certain ecclesiastical centers, such as Santiago de Campostela, grew in importance and attracted large numbers of pilgrims. These pilgrimage centers gave a visible expression to the history of Christianity and provided Christians themselves with a sense of psychological security and identity in a world that was in many ways both dangerous and frightening. Together with the monasteries, these sacred places exercised both spiritual and temporal functions for the common folk.

Whereas early Christian architecture represented the human tendency to turn inward to find God, the Romanesque style was the creation of people who wanted to bring God to the world. In the basic plan, the Romanesque church was T-shaped. To enlarge the capacity of the edifice, the chancel was lengthened and transepts, usually of the same width as the nave, were added. The barbarian invasions, which had razed many towns and churches, induced architects to construct fireproof buildings. Consequently the timber roofs that had been used in the basilicas were replaced by vaulted stone ceilings supported by thick walls often reinforced by internal flying buttresses. The chancel was usually elevated above the level of the nave and rested on piers above a vaulted crypt. This marked division between the chancel and the nave had been prompted by the fourth canon of the Second Council of Tours in 567, which forbade laypeople to stand among the clergy during the celebration of the liturgy and which reserved the chancel for the clergy.

In some of the later Romanesque churches, an aisle connecting the aisles of the nave wound completely around the sanctuary to form an ambulatory. With this arrangement, the people could visit the various votive shrines that were often constructed behind the chancel. Since the church was both the largest and most substantial building in the neighborhood, the people often gathered there for protection in time of invasion. The towers housed the church bells, and when pierced with windows, they admitted light into the otherwise dark church interiors.

Several characteristics of the Romanesque churches were affected by the development of the liturgy that took place from the eighth to the thirteenth centuries. About the middle of the eighth century Pepin decreed the general acceptance of the Roman liturgy throughout the empire. When the Roman liturgy was introduced into Franco-Germanic territory, it found a home where only a small fraction of the population made up of clerics and monks understood the Latin language of the liturgy. Consequently, in the Carolingian empire intelligent participation in the liturgy was reserved almost exclusively to the clergy and the monks. In practice a *disciplina arcani,* or discipline of the secret, developed in which holy things were concealed, not from the uninitiated, as in the early church, but from the initiated Christians themselves.

Furthermore, the church was no longer thought of as a communion of the redeemed people of God united to the risen Christ, the head of his body the church, all gathered together by the power of the Holy Spirit. Instead, great emphasis was placed on the hierarchical structures of the church, symbolized by a pyramid, with the clergy at the top representing Christ as head, ruler, sanctifier, and teacher of the layfolk. Since the clergy in fact constituted the governing class in society because of their social position, education, and prestige, they were often estranged from and lifted above the laypeople.

In France and Spain the fight against Arianism so accentuated the divinity of Christ that his humanity in general and his role as mediator in particular were overshadowed, resulting in a changed understanding of the eucharist. The apostolic church had appreciated the eucharist as the great ritual prayer of thanksgiving which the whole Christian community celebrated in union with Christ. Strongly influenced by the teaching of St. Isidore of Seville (ca. 560–636), the Romanesque church emphasized the significance of the eucharist as the great gift of divinity which God grants men and women and which descends on the altar at the consecration of the Mass. The eucharistic anaphora became veiled in special mystery since the priest recited it in a quiet voice. He alone was deemed worthy to enter into the mystery, while the rest of the people were left to pray silently at a distance from the sanctuary. In the patristic period there was an appreciation of the distinctive roles of the ordained ministers and the baptized laity, but during the Romanesque period that distinction developed into a line of demarcation and a wall of division.

As a result of these liturgical and theological developments, the altar was moved to the rear of the apse, seemingly as far from the laypeople as possible. In the cathedral churches, this necessitated moving the bishop's throne from a central place near the rear wall to a place at the side of the altar. The benches for the clergy, which formed a half-circle around the altar in many of the early Christian basilicas, were set in rows facing one another on either side and in front of the altar. This arrangement prepared the way for the development of the rood gallery or choir, which in the late

Romanesque period became the rood screen. In most cathedrals and collegiate and monastic churches, the rood screen consisted of a massive wall constructed between the chancel and the nave and surmounted by a cross, a rood, and the figures from the crucifixion scene on Calvary. The precise origin of these screens is not known; what is certain is that they hindered the laypeople from participating actively in the liturgy, by obstructing a clear view of the celebration. The layfolk were free to participate in the many so-called private Masses that were celebrated quietly and with little ceremony at the many side altars in the churches, but they were generally excluded from taking part in the solemn celebration of the liturgy in the major churches where they could no longer see but only hear what was going on in the sanctuary.

Since the people could not see what was going on at the altar, their attention was drawn to the music, which became increasingly elaborate. In the cathedrals of France, polyphonic song accompanied by various musical instruments was introduced into the church's liturgy for the first time. This prepared the way for the eventual development of a splendid art form from within the church itself. Naturally celebrations in small churches with very limited resources would have been much more simple.

Another modification in the Romanesque churches was the introduction of the communion rail, which was effected by the gradual change from the use of leavened to unleavened bread and the decline in communion under both kinds. The increased sense of unworthiness among the faithful, together with a growing sense of reverence for the Blessed Sacrament, brought about the use of small, thin, round wafers, which could be distributed without crumbs. They could easily be placed directly on the tongue, rather than in the hand of the communicant. Later in the Romanesque period, the faithful began to receive communion while kneeling rather than standing. Thus, a low communion railing, distinct from the barrier that was commonly placed between the nave and the chancel, was introduced.

In their efforts to bring God into the world, Christians during the Romanesque period tried to instill in civil society the divine principles of living in accord with Augustine's understanding of the church and its mission. They were convinced that the church must permeate the state with Christian principles. Hence, God became a God leading people into the Godhead, a journey manifested above all in the vertical dimension that permeated Romanesque churches.

The priests no longer faced the people in the liturgy, either in the liturgy of the word or in the celebration of the eucharist. They took their places at the head of the congregation, forming a static unit directed toward the altar. Dialogue between the laity and their leaders was rendered impossible, and eventually the priests even took to themselves the parts of the liturgy that belonged either to the assembly as a whole or to special ministers in the celebration. In practice this resulted in the creation of two rooms in the church—the sanctuary reserved for the clergy and the nave set aside for the laity. The church was no longer a place where the community gathered as a unity. In fact, the church building acquired a monumental identity of its own. It came to be called the "house of God," even the "temple of God," rather than the house for the assembly of God's people.

God manifested the divine presence in the world through the lives of local saints, but above all through the establishment of a world order grounded in Christian values, which were promulgated especially through the numerous Benedictine monasteries that spread across Europe in the Romanesque period. The monasteries were not so much places of refuge from the world as vital components of the world itself, often deeply involved in the world's commerce. The monasteries and their churches made the *civitas Dei* visible in the world. Stability was reflected in the massive solidity of Romanesque architecture, which provided the spiritual dimensions of Christianity with a secure home on earth. In spite of God's proximity to the world, God was still an object of both aspiration and admiration during this period. For Romanesque Christians, God was above all the triumphant Christ, the *Rex tremendae majestatis*.

One of the most significant monasteries of the Middle Ages was the foundation made at Cluny by William the Pius, Duke of Aquitaine, in 909/910. Its objectives included a return to a strict interpretation of the Rule of Benedict, especially as it was expounded by Benedict of Aniane (ca. 750–821), the Carolingian reformer. It stressed the cultivation of a deep personal spiritual life on the part of the monks and the solemn celebration of choir office, which tended to grow to excessive length, with the result that manual labor was considerably reduced.[7]

As often happens, monastic complexes become so large that they tend to collapse under their own weight. That seems to be what happened at Cluny and its numerous foundations. As a result there were various reform movements in the late eleventh and the twelfth centuries, chief among them being the Cistercians. The order is named after the first foundation at Citeaux in Burgundy, France. It was founded by St. Robert of Molesmes (d. 1111), a former abbot of the Benedictine abbey at Molesmes. In 1098 he founded the monastery at Citeaux to institute a life of poverty, simplicity, and eremitical solitude under the Rule of Benedict. The order flourished, especially under the leadership of St. Bernard, who in 1113, with about thirty companions, applied for admission to Citeaux, became the founder and first abbot of Clairvaux, and died in 1153.[8]

The Cistercian order played an important role in the history of sacred architecture and art. Their buildings, especially the churches, were originally distinguished by their simplicity and absence of ornamentation. This style of architecture formed an integral part of Cistercian spirituality. The relationship between their spirituality and architecture was linked to the way in which they understood their relationship with God and consequently their relationship with the environment they created for themselves. They felt that the life of God was manifested in the material world. Their practice of *lectio divina* resulted in a careful pondering of their structures and their decoration. The mysterious quality of spaces that were open and closed, with clean lines and shadows and shafts of light, all invited the eye to behold the beauty of God, just as the play of sounds in their churches invited the ear to hear the word of God. They were convinced that the human mind and heart should be drawn beyond what it sees and hears. Hence they wanted space in their buildings for the eye to see in a way that inclined its vision to go beyond the sight and the ear to go beyond the word proclaimed. Their spirituality was one that emphasized the importance of place, light, and word, but they wanted all to sustain and foster the contemplative dimensions of their lives.[9]

The Cistercians wanted to be poor with Christ who was poor. As a result they sought to reject anything that might appear to be luxurious, whether in their worship, their clothing, or their food. In architecture, they rejected the construction of bell towers, paintings, and sculptures. These commitments were vigorously set out by St. Bernard in his famous *Apologia* addressed to his friend William, the Benedictine abbot of Saint-Thierry. He protested against the splendor of Cluniac churches and their grand size, as well as the decoration and ornamentation of the capitals in both the churches and cloisters. Bernard acknowledged that representations of biblical scenes could be instructive and could edify the faithful, but he wondered what use they could be for spiritual men vowed to a life of poverty.[10]

There is, however, really no such thing as an authentic original Cistercian architectural style. Just as the order evolved, so also the buildings were the result of complex cultural, organizational, and religious phenomena intermingling with and influencing one another. A great variety of building styles existed, reflecting the context in which they came into being. Furthermore, a description of a distinctive Cistercian architectural style is not to be found in the documents of the general chapters of the order. Although the order was in some sense quite centralized, a certain autonomy was always characteristic of each of the abbeys. St. Bernard has often been taken as speaking with the authority of the whole order; his prestige was great, but his views did not always reflect those of the other abbots. The general chapters sought to keep unity within the order, but unity was not the same as uniformity, since each monastery functioned within a complex web of ecclesiastical and secular politics.[11]

Drawing on the architecture itself, we can conclude that Cistercian art and architecture manifest many different forms of expression. Not surprisingly, the architectural style at the time of the great expansion of the order was Romanesque on its way to becoming Gothic. Hence, this style was adapted by many of the early Cistercian buildings in Burgundy and their daughter houses, but the style of these buildings is not much different from other abbeys in Burgundy. As the order expanded, local styles often fused with the styles that prevailed in the mother abbeys. Furthermore, the development of technology made it possible for the monks to improve their architectural designs as time went on.

The key element lying behind the architectural choices made by abbots and their communities was the silence prescribed by the Rule of Benedict. Life in community was meant to provide a context in which the monks could develop a deep interior life of solitude. The environment in which the monks lived and worked was just as important an instrument for formation as were the books, sermons, and instructions in the community. Although silence is normally a description of an auditory condition, it relates also to the visual realm. There is regularly a near-absence of narrative and color in Cistercian buildings. The decor is achieved by using bands and moldings of various widths, thickness, profile, or material to emphasize the architectural lines. In the twelfth and thirteenth centuries, figurative sculpture was quite uncommon in Cistercian churches. It was the crucifix in the refectory that had the greatest impact on the monks and nuns. Their imaginations were nourished above all by the images to be found in scripture and other sources of sacred reading. Perhaps what distinguishes Cistercian buildings most of all is the presence of much light. Sunlight animates the buildings by day, outlining the nooks and crannies, highlighting all the architectural details. It is the silence of the abbeys that draws attention to the visual subtleties, for there are few distractions.

After a long period of more or less faithful building in the Romanesque style, the Cistercians adopted the Gothic style and contributed to its expansion all over Europe. Ultimately they succumbed to the trends of their time and built enormous churches decorated with both sculpture and painting.

In addition to their important contribution to architecture, the Cistercians also produced distinguished illuminated manuscripts; the oldest coming from the scriptorium at Citeaux contained ornamented letters and illuminations of a high quality. But about 1150, under Bernard's influence, there was a decree of the order's general chapter, which ruled that only one color should be used for the initial letters of a text. As a result the copyists devoted their care to the quality of parchment, the outline of the letters, and the arrangement of the text on the page. But soon the chapter's prohibition was forgotten and illuminations reappeared.[12]

IRISH MONASTICISM: ITS ARCHITECTURE AND ART

In his writings, St. Patrick (ca. 390–ca. 460) speaks of the many sons and daughters of Irish chieftains who became monks and virgins of Christ. But how numerous these monks and virgins were or what style of life they lived one cannot say. Certainly they cannot have been as organized or as influential in the life of the Irish church as their successors were in the second half of the sixth century and for succeeding centuries.[13]

Toward the middle of the sixth century, about one hundred years after the coming of Patrick to Ireland, what is best described as a monastic movement began to stir the country. Its beginnings are associated with St. Finnian of Clonard, St. Cieran of Clonmacois, St. Colmcille of Iona, and St. Brendan of Clonfert.[14]

The monastic movement contributed in an important way to the growth of a distinctively Irish form of Christianity and an Irish way of praying and living the gospel. In the monasteries a cultural meeting took place between the native Celtic tradition of literature and art and the Christian tradition of western Europe. This encounter proved to be both positive and creative, one in which the Irish received important traditions from abroad and in turn contributed their own traditions to develop new forms of Christian life, literature, and art.

The Irish monasteries were very different in shape and style of life from the typical Benedictine monasteries of the period. The shape of the monastery, a cluster of small stone or wooden buildings surrounded by a protective wall, was modeled after the typical Irish habitation, the ringfort. The surrounding wall was not thought of as a monastic enclosure separating the community from the Christian community at large. Contact between the monastic community and the rest of the local community was assured by means of the monastic school and by the ever-increasing interest and involvement of the monastery in the material and spiritual welfare of the people.

The larger monasteries had flourishing schools and scriptoria. Teaching was given not only to prospective monks and candidates for orders but also to young men and women who would later inherit the family lands. They were taught Latin grammar and syntax; the psalms, hymns, and canticles used in the liturgy; scriptural interpretation; history; and traditional lore. The traditional lore was transmitted in the Irish language, often in the medium of verse and poetry. The Irish and Latin traditions, then, flourished side by side and influenced one another in various ways.

Celtic spirituality is grounded in creation, but its central focus is the cross of Jesus Christ, the one image that really sums up the Celtic way. The early Irish monks placed special emphasis on human effort and on the performance of good works of prayer and penance as their way of participating in the passion, death, and resurrection of Jesus Christ. Many of the early prayers and hymns show that in the foreground of the conscious faith of the monks was the conviction that it is Christ alone, through the Spirit, who makes them capable of living and persevering in the Christian life.

Many of the monastic sites were superbly situated along the bend of a river, on green southward-facing slopes, or looking out over bays and headlands, so that brightness seemed to fall on them. The monastic sites that have endured survived because they fulfilled certain requirements. Some were sited because the place was conducive to ascetic and contemplative life, others because the monastery played an important part in everyday society. The isolated houses are the ones that have survived best. The sites show the variety and individuality of the monastic life in a Christian context. The houses that played the most important part in social life were nearly all located in accessible places or on or near major land routes, in bays and harbors, or on lakes which acted as waterways.

Buildings for various functions were constructed on the monastic property. At Glendalough, for example, the beautiful valley is full of extant buildings—early churches, round tower, enclosure, and cells. At many midland and eastern sites, where wood must long have been the most important building material, there is little early work to be seen, but in the west, in a landscape where stone is readily available, many sites are rich in standing remains.

The first thing to be seen is the monastic enclosure, which provided a protective barrier. The enclosure delineated the legal area belonging to the monastery; this was regarded as holy and was to be free from aggression. A roughly circular outline was common. Within the enclosure the focal point of the monastery was the church. Irish churches are very difficult to date. Those that remain are very simple, lacking datable features; inscriptions are rare and written sources give little help in dating particular structures. The traditional Irish method of building was in wood, even as late as the twelfth century.

Always great travelers, Irish churchmen had plenty of opportunity to see stone churches, for example, in seventh-century Northumbria. If they adhered largely to timber until the eleventh and twelfth centuries, it was not through ignorance but by choice and tradition. It is possible, therefore, that many of the simple stone churches that survive on early Irish ecclesiastical sites are not earlier than the eleventh and twelfth centuries.

Most of the surviving early Irish churches are small, though a few larger ones exist, like the cathedral at Glendalough. The surviving small churches (sometimes as small as seven by eight feet) are simple and boxlike, a rectangle without porches, aisles, sacristies, towers, or other elaborations of plan or elevation. The door is customarily at the west, so that the people faced the east when at prayer, and when it is not, there may well be traces of a blocked west door or evidence that a north or south door had been inserted. Windows were usually few and small, with a rounded triangular or flat head. Some of these early churches were built without mortar. Thatch and shingles must have been used for roofing, but a few stone churches had all stone roofs. The stone-roofed churches, though rare compared with those with wooden and thatch roofs, were an Irish specialty, involving a great deal of labor and imposing a very heavy burden on the walls.

How were these early churches used? Large churches must have been designed for congregational worship. An early-eighth-century text indicates that two churches at Armagh were used by different groups—bishops, priests, and anchorites in one; and virgins, penitents, and lay monks in the other. The smallest church would not have held more than a half dozen people. Some small churches were near burial sites, and pilgrims would have gone there for Mass celebrated by a priest. For the most part, extant remains of early altars do not exist.

A distinctive feature of early Irish monasteries is the multiplication of small churches. The legendary number seven is not uncommon. It seems to have been the practice to build another small church rather than rebuild or enlarge an existing one. Sometimes a special church seems to have been built for the nuns in the area. Because in was not permitted for a woman to pass her property on to anyone outside her immediate family, monasteries of nuns apparently did not exist over a long period of time.[15]

Another important building within the monastic enclosure on many sites was a round tower, usually standing close to the church. The extant ones are tall and slender, ranging from about seventy to one hundred and twenty feet in height, tapering gradually and gracefully upward and finishing in a conical cap. In those instances when the internal arrangements can be traced, it is clear that there were wooden floors—some had four or five, but others six, seven, or even eight floors. The floors were supported by joints resting either in holes or on ledges contrived in the wall. Access must have been by ladders from floor to floor. The towers are peculiar to church sites. There were often four windows under the cap of the tower. The towers served as belfries, but they had other uses as well, especially the safekeeping of people and treasures. The idea was presumably to shepherd people into the tower in the hope of sitting out an attack by enemies.

There is no hint of the regular layout of buildings around the cloister, unlike the design that had certainly appeared in England in the twelfth century and perhaps earlier. Irish monasteries represent a different world. Benedictine monasteries emphasized the discipline of communal life in the shared dormitory, dining room, warming house (calefactory), and working rooms. Early Irish monasteries certainly had communal rooms; but there was much more emphasis on individual practice and observance, and so there was a contrast between individually and communally used buildings.

Apart from the church, the most important communal building was the refectory, for it seems that the monks usually ate together. The guesthouse is also prominent in written sources; it usually stood somewhat apart from the other buildings. Close to the church was the cemetery. It was believed that the relics of the founder or a revered saint brought great spiritual and material rewards to a monastery. Graves of special people, if not buried in the church, were marked in the graveyard by a special monument or stone cross or other structure.

These are the important ingredients that make up the plan of early monasteries: enclosure, church and cemetery, round tower, cells, and other necessary buildings. Of special significance, however, are the carved stones of the early Christian period. They often stand close to other remains, but sometimes a splendid cross survives where no other early features can be seen. The stone carving is often beautiful in itself, but it can also provide a commentary on the craftsmanship and foreign contacts of the church, on changing fashions, and even on the appearance of people and buildings.

Carved stones served different purposes, as the written sources indicate. They might mark burial places, and the most usual formulas in inscriptions ask for prayers or blessing for a deceased person. Burials were also made at stones already in place. Legislation ordered that the holy place, that is, the area in which sanctuary could be claimed, should be clearly marked by crosses. Crosses may have been used as a focus for outdoor services, and they were also sometimes set up to mark notable events, to commemorate grant of land, or to mark an important place. It seems they were also set up along travel routes. Hence the cross-carved stones and freestanding crosses were important markers in the topography of early Irish monasteries, and they should be viewed against this wide range of possible functions.

Stones that have crosses carved on their face in two dimensions are probably earlier than freestanding, three-dimensional crosses. The range of crosses varies enormously, from very simple, linear, unembellished forms to quite complicated ringed and expanded crosses and others made of segments of circles. The cross might be enclosed in a rectangular or circular frame. Sometimes there may be no decoration at all, or the cross may be elaborated with triangular or spiral terminals, small crosses, interlace, and occasionally birds or human figures between the arms and the shaft. The most easily available local material was usually employed, but fine stone was sometimes transported, especially when this could be done by water.

We know very little about the stone carvers and whether they also worked in wood or metal. Occasionally a cross asks for prayer for the craftsman. Upright cross-carved pillar stones are common at sites in the islands and coastal counties of western Ireland, but their distribution farther east is less dense. Features of some stones, especially in the southwest, suggest links with the Continent, especially France. The *chi-rho*, common in continental inscriptions from the fifth century onward, made up of the first two letters of Christ's name in Greek, were derived from continental models. Recumbent stones became the most popular form of grave marker from the seventh century onward and persisted until the end of the twelfth century.

Best known of the carved stone monuments are freestanding, three-dimensional crosses, often known as high crosses.[16] The Celtic cross combines the great circle of the world, of creation, with the cross of Jesus Christ. The poised holding together of the themes of creation and redemption is a great contribution that Celtic spirituality can make to a world split by divisions and polarized by conflicting values. The usual form is a tall, ringed cross set in a shapely base, but within this framework there is much scope for variation. The size ranges from tall examples, eighteen to twenty feet or more in height, to short, stubby crosses, six to eight feet high. The head is usually ringed, the ring sometimes solid but usually open. The inner circumference of the ring can be decorated with projecting semicircular disks. The most usual shape for the base is a truncated pyramid. Decoration includes figure carving, animals, and a wide range of geometrical motifs, including interlace, spirals, bosses, and key patterns.

In highly carved standing crosses, there is often a clear Old Testament/New Testament distinction between the two main faces, with the crucifixion occupying the head of the New Testament side, and Christ in glory or a judgment scene at the head of the other side, which served to remind the beholder to lead a good life. The central theme of almost all the crosses bearing figure sculpture is the crucifixion, which is placed at the center of the west face of the head of the cross. Christ usually stands at the center of a ring that symbolically may represent the cosmos. Old Testament scenes often illustrate incidents that occurred when God helped those in trouble—Noah and the flood, the sacrifice of Isaac, Daniel and the lions, and the children in the fiery furnace. Some of the New Testament scenes illustrate the feast of Christmas and epiphany, such as the annunciation to the shepherds and the adoration of the magi, but representations of the wedding feast at Cana and the triumphal entry into Jerusalem are also found. Like the early frescoes found in continental churches, the carvings encouraged meditation on the paschal mystery of Jesus Christ.

There are other kinds of carved stones that may be encountered at early Irish monastic sites. Certain stones with five crosses may be derived from an altar, for legislation shows that, although altars were meant to be made of stone, they were in fact often made of wood, and in these cases a stone was to be let into the top, big enough to hold the vessels for the celebration of the eucharist. The consecrated stone altar top was marked with five crosses, one in the center and one at each corner.

The monastic routine revolved around the regular services in the church. Hence, there are sundials that survive as carefully shaped, freestanding monuments. The most common form is a shaft, sometimes with a semicircular top expanded with three rays extending from the hole at the top of the semicircle, presumably indicating terce, sext, and none, the day hours of the monastic liturgy. However, time could scarcely depend totally on the sundial, since the sun certainly does not shine all the time in Ireland.

There is a final category of worked stones that were a common feature of early Irish monastic sites, often called bullauns. Sometimes there is only one, but at some sites there are several, and at Glendalough there are over

thirty scattered along the valley. The most common is a boulder, un-
worked except for the hollow, either loose and movable or very large. The
diameter is often between seven and fifteen inches and the depth between
three and nine inches. It is usually roughly circular. The stones are now
often filled with water, and the water is sometimes used to cure warts. They
are at times interpreted piously: a single hollowed one is explained as a
saint's pillow and double ones as knee marks from long hours at prayer.
But it is in the homely realm of subsistence that they should probably be
viewed. They would have been ideal for use as mortars, for grinding all
kinds of things with a pestle. But these stones have also been used for cura-
tive and superstitious purposes.

The carved stones of Ireland show us a church developing from rather
humble and dependent beginnings into a rich, powerful institution with an
elaborate decorative art, drawing inspiration from continental models,
from Anglo-Saxon England, from Carolingian Gaul, from Viking motifs,
and from Romanesque patterns, yet all the time transmuting what it
learned into the daily life of monasteries, clerics, and laymen and women
as well.

ROMANESQUE ART

Romanesque art emerged all over Europe in a variety of styles, but it was
generally subordinated to architecture, for painting, sculpture, and church
furnishings were designed to enhance the architectural conception. In the
early years of the period Romanesque art flourished under imperial spon-
sorship, whereas beginning with the late eleventh century it was associated
with the strong personalities advocating reform, including St. Bernard,
Odilo of Cluny, William of Volpiano, and Lanfranc, later the archbishop
of Canterbury (ca. 1010–1089). The attractive, didactic quality of tympanums, such as those of Moissac (the vision of the Apocalypse), of Vezelay
(Pentecost), and of Autun (last judgment), are superb achievements involving a highly organized iconography.

Figurative Romanesque sculpture often sought inspiration from the
Apocalypse and developed images from it: Christ enthroned in glory, symbols of the evangelists, and terrifying representations of the last judgment.
The Virgin Mary was often represented as a queen. Episodes from the Bible
were frequently set forth on the frieze of capitals in the cloisters. Much of
the art was moralistic, warning people of the perils that faced poor fallen

humanity. For example, greed was sometimes presented as a man with a purse hanging from his neck; lust, as a nude woman attacked by serpents or toads; and pride, by a horseman being hurled over a precipice by a rearing horse. The goal in designing the tympanum was to fuse a vision of the known world with the unknown so as to portray an ordered theological synthesis and a credible cosmology. A great variety of motifs was found in the decoration of the buildings which abound in geometric elements. Although artistic motifs from flora were rarely used, representations of real fauna were found everywhere. Often the animals had symbolic values—for example, the centaur symbolized bestial lust; the siren-bird or sea nymph, seduction; and the lamb symbolized innocence. Narrative scenes from the Bible were often placed on the capitals of the cloisters in such a way that Old Testament personages and events from the New Testament were juxtaposed, thus shedding light on one another. There were also everyday scenes, such as making hay, harvesting, pruning vines, and bands gathering grapes.

Fresco painting on the walls and ceilings of Romanesque churches appeared in the twelfth century. The solemn themes of Christ and the Virgin in majesty and of the Ascension and Pentecost were shown on the vaulting of the apse; the apostles were depicted in the sanctuary; and the last judgment was often painted on the back of the church facade. Mosaics were frequently used to adorn Italian churches because of the abundance of colored marble that was available. The technique of painting on glass made significant advances and prepared the way for the splendid achievements of thirteenth-century stained glass. In the Cistercian churches, colorless glass was used but the sections were bound together by a lead network that formed interesting geometric patterns.

DRAMA AND LITURGY IN THE MIDDLE AGES

The terms "mystery play" or "miracle play" have been loosely applied to the vernacular religious drama of the Middle Ages. The origins of this drama are unclear; however, the shaping influence of the liturgy, especially the offices of Holy Week and Easter, is clear. The more immediate sources used by the dramatists were early vernacular paraphrases of the Bible, especially the New Testament.[17]

Historically the dialectic between public theater and Christian liturgy has been complicated. Early Christian worship was focused on the extended family, but eventually formality took over as solemn processions, role distinctions, and hierarchical stratifications became standard in post-Constantinian worship. In the large basilicas the liturgy replaced the drama, dance, and mime that had formerly been carried out in the temples and public theaters. Christianity rejected the frivolous acting and public displays of violent and sexually explicit themes in plays and mimes, all of which were regarded as demonic. Dramas and stadium events as well as the public or private use of secular music were all condemned.[18]

In the early medieval church, theologians such as Sophronius (560–638) in the East and Amalarius of Metz (780–850) in the West took the rubrics of the liturgy and turned them into dramas, in the East as mimes of the heavenly liturgy and in the West as historicizations of the life and death of Jesus. Christ was the real actor in the eucharist, but the priest acting *in persona Christi* took the place of Christ with the result that the priest became the primary agent in the eucharistic celebration, which was no longer concerned with what the eucharistic assembly is but with who Christ was for Christians in the past. Christ extended his actions of the past into the present through the actions of the priest. If and when the illiterate Christians were able to see what was taking place in the chancel of the Romanesque churches, they could watch while the clergy enacted the ritual drama of the Mass.

As theologians were linking the rubrics of the Mass and the history of salvation, monastic communities were creating plays about the virtues and saints, presenting them in the cloister, and writing passion plays for use during the liturgy itself. Liturgical tropes, especially those in the Easter season, were turned into dramas, as were those of the Christmas season. The boundary line between dramatic liturgy and liturgical drama became very blurred.[19]

Although there were occasional objections to the use of drama in worship, the reluctance generally did not hinder the development of religious plays. But opposition grew as the monastic culture that had originally nurtured liturgical drama began to reject it, since the penitential and ascetic discipline of the Benedictines and Cistercians forbade blatant displays of piety and the cultivation of bodily pleasures. In the fourteenth century, dissenters in England, especially the followers of John Wycliffe, opposed emphasis on seeing as the primary mode of participation in the liturgy and stressed the importance of personal faith and interior dispositions as well as the primacy of scripture.[20] In spite of the opposition, the mystery plays held an important place in late medieval Christian culture, even a sacramental role, for they attempted to join the sacred and the secular, Christ and the community.

GOTHIC ARCHITECTURE AND ART

There are various interpretations of the Gothic period in architecture and art,[21] a period whose spirit extended generally from the twelfth to the end of the fifteenth century. It originated in France whence it spread over most parts of Europe, assuming variations in each place. It clearly reflected classical culture, which was deeply embedded in the West, perhaps especially in the church. There seemed to be a human desire to strike out in new directions. The style is most closely associated with cathedrals and other church buildings, but it is generally agreed that the church building cannot be discussed reasonably apart from the medieval town in which it was built, for it was an integral part of the local environment. From the eleventh century on, a general process of what we would describe today as urbanization took place in western and central Europe because of the rapid growth in population. The process began in Italy, especially in Tuscany and Lombardy, then spread to Provence and to northern France and Flanders, where there developed a relatively dense concentration of people. It moved across England and the rest of the continent, spread to the Viking empire of Scandinavia, and even appeared in the Byzantine province of central Europe. By 1400 the Gothic was the principal style of building in the western world. Gothic architects designed royal palaces, town halls, courthouses, and hospitals, but above all they designed structures for the church, which was the most prolific builder in the Middle Ages. The Gothic flourished and found its best expressions in churches because its verticality did not lend itself readily to domestic buildings and its openness was not appropriate for military structures. Since the church was in fact the center of each town, it was fitting that the most splendid building on the landscape should be the church.

Although the towns were linked by a network of roads, communication among them was difficult during much of the year; hence, each medieval town was somewhat isolated and relatively self-sufficient. Regardless of their size, the towns shared some basic properties: enclosure, intimacy, density, and the allocation of certain streets and districts for use by special groups such as guilds. The town was of primary significance as a place where genuine community could be experienced. As a result, the cenobitic character of the monastery was extended to a more comprehensive unit of society. Surrounded by a wall, which provided necessary protection and enabled the town to function as a container and a magnet, the town was an area where human persons could be relatively free because law, order, and security were presumed to be in effect there. The walled town created a sense of being inside, of being somewhere. Although it was a physical enclosure, it was characterized by an interiority that took the spiritualized understanding of space common to the early Christian church and extended it to the town as a whole. The medieval town was a living organism in which the wall functioned as the hard shell and the church was the soft core. Thus, the whole town became an extension of the character that was previously symbolized by the early Christian church interior.

Whereas the exterior of the early Christian church was an envelope shutting out a secular world and enclosing a sacred world, and the exterior of the Romanesque church constituted a fortress protecting the sacred from invasion by hostile forces, the Gothic church exterior in a sense dissolved and became transparent so that it interacted with the surrounding environment. The Gothic church was not a refuge but a central part of a larger whole; it was the center of a society that was basically Christian, a society that had succeeded in implementing a Christian interpretation of classical culture. It was part of a living organism that was grafted onto the local scene. The church represented an existential image of the transcendent, divine order transmitted to the entire community and permeating every aspect of its life in an immanent way. In the Christian tradition, God's presence was symbolized in a special way by light. Gothic transparency brought that light down to earth, and the stained glass transformed it so that it became a mysterious medium that communicated the immanent presence of a transcendent God.

It was not simply a matter of engineering skills that distinguished the Gothic from the early Christian and Romanesque styles. There was continuity in the styles from an engineering point of view, but from a symbolic point of view the Gothic was something new. It was characterized by its ribbed vaulting, flying buttresses, and high piers. The weight and thrust of the vaulting were carried downward with the help of the extended buttresses, thus eliminating the need for the heavy masonry walls common to Romanesque churches. Like the churches of earlier periods, the Gothic churches were based on the theme of longitudinality and centralization, but the growing interaction with the local environment emphasized movement and transition, so that the nave could be understood as the continuing of the town roads, with the church portal functioning as an inviting porch. However, the longitudinal plan of the building was subordinate to the theme of centrality, for the Gothic churches, especially the cathedrals, were centrally placed in the towns. With their lofty volume and slender spires, the Gothic churches were permeated by a dominant verticality that made their status inherent in all the component parts of the structure.

The plan of the Gothic churches was based on the layout of the major Romanesque churches. They generally had a transept and a chancel with an ambulatory and radiating chapels. The parts of the building, however, lost their relative independence. For example, the towers were generally absorbed by the overall verticality of the building. In contrast to Romanesque churches, the nave was relatively shorter, the chancel larger, and the projection of the transept less obvious. Path and center were combined in one synthetic form with the result that pilgrimage was unnecessary because God's presence permeated the whole town; however, that presence was symbolized especially in every element of the church.

Gothic architecture symbolized Western culture in a period that has been described as the great age of Christian faith, for it expressed the human understanding of divine revelation and God's relation to everyday life. Romanesque architecture had created the strongholds people needed to receive God's revelation, but in the Gothic church God came especially close to the people. The church itself became a mirror not only of God, especially as God was present in Christ, his mother, and the saints, but also of the world and its inhabitants. The iconography of the Gothic church, expressed above all through the stained glass windows and numerous sculptures, brought the heavenly and earthly spheres together. It told the tale of the creation, fall, and redemption of the world so that even illiterate people could grasp the history of the world as well as the basic teachings of Christianity; however, one must not conclude that the iconography was meaningful only to the illiterate, for it revealed for all who experienced it nuanced meanings that could not be readily expressed in written texts. The community as a whole and the individuals who comprised it were able to see their place in a totality that was divinely arranged in a hierarchical order descending from God through Christ and the church to the simplest aspects of creation. The Gothic church symbolized God's coming close to people not only to illumine their understanding but also to share the divine life and love with them so they in turn could love one another. From the Gothic church the existential meaning of Christianity moved out to permeate the whole human environment so that the town became the place where God's world was a living reality for the people.

To appreciate the Gothic churches and their art we must be comfortable with a profoundly symbolic imagination, for Gothic architecture and art were produced by people for whom the world and all that is in it were symbolic expressions of a spiritual universe that could not be immediately experienced. They loved the material world as is evidenced by the details of their stained glass windows, their sculpture, and their illuminated manuscripts, but they felt that the beauty of the material universe was simply a foretaste of the divine beauty that they would enjoy in heaven. Appreciating the Gothic world involved seeing it as an icon and a bearer of the divine mystery.[22]

Although the early Christian and Romanesque churches were named after a variety of saints, the Gothic cathedrals were almost always named after Our Lady. The great cathedrals were experienced as offering an overwhelming sense of security and peace. Their dark interiors evoked a sense of being in the womb where Christ himself was nurtured and in which all the members of the church come to birth, since Mary is the mother of the church. From patristic times, the church was called Mother, *Mater Ecclesia*; and Mary, the mother of Jesus and the mother of God, was intimately related to the church building as one of its primary symbols. The images of the *Sedes Sapientiae* of Romanesque art, which had been inspired by Byzantine icons, were transformed into affectionate motherly images.[23]

The theme of security and peace was also evoked by the name given to the central section of the church: the nave. Probably derived from the Latin *navis,* meaning "ship," the term would have resonated with the medieval understanding of life as dangerous. Hence, the church, the place where God was present above all in Christ, provided people with shelter in the storm of life. In fact the flying buttresses often looked like the oars of a great ship propelling people into the future. But the church is not only a place of safety; it is also a place of gestation and birth, where people are to be nurtured and come to life as responsible adults. The baptized were born at the font of life in the church; they were educated by the stories told in the paintings, sculptures, and stained glass windows, but above all they were nurtured by the Bread of Life at the holy altar. The church was, then, a place of transition. "Wombs are secure, but they are not our final home; ships are safe, but they are taking us somewhere."[24]

The symbolism of the Gothic church was expressed in an especially powerful way in darkness and light. As the people entered the church, they came into darkness, reminding them that we are all people who walk in darkness in search of the light. But as they moved through the church they came to an ever greater experience of light, the stained glass windows throwing more and more light into the church. The spiritual lesson was clear: we are sinners who walk in the dark but we progress throughout life to the light that is Christ.[25] A sense of transcendence was evoked also by the verticality of the churches, which were designed not only to impress but also to teach and inspire. Deeply rooted in both the Jewish and Christian traditions is the affirmation that although God has created the world, God is not of this world. God is other. The staggering height of the Gothic churches affirms this mysticism of otherness. God is beyond what we can experience or imagine. To the otherness of God might be added an invitation to strive for God in holy longing. The arches, lines, and towers of the Gothic churches pulled the eyes of the people upward beyond the here and now into a realm attainable only through mystical experience.[26]

Although the architecture of the Gothic church was greatly refined during the high Middle Ages, the interior arrangement of the edifice was quite similar to what it was during the Romanesque period. The bishop and his presbyters were not the symbols of unity in the assembly; they rather took their places on seats to the right and left of the altar, thus signifying that they were primarily ministers of the altar rather than leaders of the Christian assembly. What they performed was a sacred office, the Latin word *officium* being one of the principal terms for the liturgy. Since theirs was a cultic ministry, they were often far removed from the people until the orders of friars, especially the Franciscans and Dominicans, both founded in the thirteenth century, sought to bridge the gap between the clergy and the ordinary laypeople.

The old principle that there should be but one altar symbolizing the one Christ and his church was mainly forgotten during the Middle Ages, as numerous altars were constructed to accommodate the priests who celebrated Mass individually. In the Gothic period, special chapels, each with its own altar, were also constructed for use by various guilds and confraternities.

Although the life of the whole community, including the laity, was generally infused with a deeply religious spirit, Christian piety, especially that of the simple layfolk, was scarcely liturgical in the strict sense. Intelligent participation in the liturgy by ordinary laypeople was exercised to an ever diminishing degree during the later Middle Ages. Their most important obligation was attendance at Mass on Sundays and on the many holy days of obligation. They were expected to pay reverent attention, if possible, to the most important parts of the Mass, especially the consecration. If a sermon was preached, they were to listen. But in many ways their religious spirit was sustained by popular devotions, which developed to a great degree apart from the liturgy.

The church year with its great feasts provided attractive celebrations for the people, while the saints interceded on their behalf in time of trouble and helped to shoulder the burdens of daily life. It was, however, the Blessed Sacrament, reserved and frequently exposed for veneration, that in many ways sustained the faith of the layfolk and many religious, especially women. Since they rarely received Holy Communion because of their sense of God's grandeur and their own unworthiness, special emphasis was placed on gazing at the sacred Host. In that way ocular communion became a substitute for sacramental reception.

Visual experience was especially important throughout the Middle Ages. For example, we have evidence that Christian conversions were often prompted by seeing a crucifix or a painting. Francis of Assisi, Catherine of Siena, Julian of Norwich, Henry Suso, Margery Kemp, and Dante Alighieri all recount powerful visual experiences that changed their lives. In the Middle Ages, an ancient theory of vision would have been retained which maintained that vision occurred when a quasi-physical ray was projected from the eye of the viewer and touched an object so that an impression of the object traveled back along the visual ray, was imprinted on the soul, and then stored in the memory. Hence the viewer was thought to be active both in initiating and completing the act of seeing by storing a memory of the object seen. Understood in that way, the emphasis of medieval worshipers on contact by sight should be looked upon not necessarily as superstitious but as a desire to be in the most immediate contact with the object of devotion. Viewing the consecrated Host, then, was considered equal to or even superior to ingesting it.[27]

To facilitate the experience of seeing the Host, the monstrance was introduced. The feast of Corpus Christi was propagated in the middle of the thirteenth century, and from 1277 onward, the Corpus Christi procession became increasingly popular.[28] It absorbed earlier traditions of festive processions and developed into a parade throughout the streets of all the towns and villages. Miracle and mystery plays were often performed in conjunction with the feast of Corpus Christi, with the result that great emphasis was placed on the earthly life of Christ to be imitated by his disciples.[29] Unfortunately, this emphasis on the historical Jesus often overshadowed the presence of the resurrected Christ in the liturgy and the divine indwelling in the life of Christian persons through the power of the Holy Spirit.

This popular piety was deeply entrenched in the hearts of the people, but it lived in many ways on the surface of the Christian mysteries; hence it frequently degenerated into superstitions associated with relics, punctilious performance of devotional acts, and the gaining of indulgences. The tendency to concentrate on the peripheral aspects of the Christian life appeared especially in devotions to the Mother of God, a devotion expressed especially in terms of sympathy with her as the Mother of Sorrows. In the twelfth, thirteenth, and fourteenth centuries fascination with the emotional quality of the events in the life of Christ, his mother, and the saints was prominent.[30]

In the fourteenth century, much money was spent on paintings for churches. Large bequests from people who died from the black death gave religious orders and churches much money to spend on paintings and frescoes. By the end of the fourteenth century, many of the walls in churches were covered with frescoes, and church buildings were often modified and newly designed to ensure sufficient lighting on the frescoes. The pulpits were often highly carved. Freestanding sculptures and painted panels were also placed in the churches. A large painting was often placed above the high altar, while a large crucifix was suspended from the ceiling over the altar. These images inspired devotion, and by engaging the emotions they were thought to affect the will.

By the beginning of the fourteenth century, devotion to the Blessed Virgin was at its height in central Europe. She was extolled in such well-loved hymns as "Regina Caeli," "Ave Maria Caelorum," and "Salve Regina." In the twelfth and thirteenth centuries she was regularly depicted as the Queen of Heaven and the Bride of Christ; in the fourteenth century events in her life, such as her birth, the stages of her growth, her marriage, and her death were regularly portrayed. Fascination with the emotional quality of the events was prominent. In this way Mary became a model for Christian life and participation in the life of Christ.

The visual experience of Christians was reinforced by the vivid style of preaching in the fourteenth century, which imitated the emotional intensity of the paintings and sculpture. Although the experience of the late medieval liturgy by ordinary laypeople was especially a visual experience, it was also auditory because of the popular preaching of the mendicant orders, especially the Franciscans.

GOTHIC ART

In Gothic art there is a clear expression that humanity has been renewed in Jesus Christ, for people are no longer simply weighed down by sin and guilt but are free to express beauty, vitality, and joy. In particular the Gothic representation of the human body took on a beautiful aspect. As the tympanums indicate, Gothic art was, like the art of the Romanesque period, still didactic; there was no doubt that punishment awaited the unrepentant sinners whereas salvation and happiness were in store for the good. In the scenes of the last judgment, the major concern was for the redemption of all, and the virtues were as important as the vices. But human flesh was not unholy; it was bathed in light and beauty. Consequently, a new naturalism permeated Gothic culture, so that the human element was pervasive. This humanism only gradually became dominant in northern Europe, but it was clearly evident in Florence at the time of Donatello (ca. 1385/6–1466), Brunelleschi (1377–1446), and Masaccio (1401–1428).

The Gothic style of sculpture was born about 1150 in the Île-de-France and spread across Europe, gradually transforming Romanesque, from which it differed in degree of naturalism, in the scope of the iconographic composition, and the organization of the facade and portals of the churches. Clearly delineated drapery patterns helped to define the shape of the human body. Certainly the sophistication of the iconographic program reflected the rigor of classical culture and its expression in scholasticism, above all in its logic and mathematical precision.

Painting in the Gothic period did not appear until the early part of the thirteenth century. It took four principal forms: frescoes, panel paintings, manuscript illuminations, and stained glass. In the southern part of Europe, the great cycles of wall paintings continued to be put in place because the dematerialized walls of the northern Gothic never found favor there. In the north, especially in France, stained glass became the principal vehicle for pictorial narratives and remained so until the fifteenth century. Painting in its various forms developed pictorial narratives and depicted both historical and typological events. Images were derived from the written commentaries on the Bible, so that scenes from both the Old and New Testaments were placed alongside representations of events from the lives of the saints and even images derived from extrabiblical literature.

Altarpieces became increasingly complex in the fourteenth and fifteenth centuries. Diptychs, triptychs, and polytychs with hinged wings provided ample space for artistic expression. For example, the Isenheim Altarpiece by Matthias Grünewald, with two pairs of wings that fold over each other and cover a sculpture by Nikolaus von Haguenau, presents three ensembles of paintings that were intended to be displayed on specific liturgical days and seasons.

Of special significance in the great Gothic churches are the famous rose windows, for they embody in a special way what the medieval Scholastics took to be the fundamental characteristics of the beautiful: wholeness (*integritas*), harmony (*consonantia*), and radiance (*claritas*). The special beauty of the rose windows was meant to be a prelude or even a sacrament of the beatific vision of God the all-beautiful One. In the classical tradition, medieval philosophers thought that in order for a thing to be considered beautiful, it had to be seen in its entirety, be marked by a harmonious arrangement of part against part, and shine. Theologians thought that all earthly beauty is a symbol of the perfect beauty that belongs to God. The extraordinary beauty of the rose windows was interpreted then as a sacrament and an anticipation of the beatific vision of God's beauty in heaven that people would enjoy at the end of time. The theme of beauty is especially well illustrated in the north rose window at Notre Dame in Paris through its use of number symbolism. Surrounding the center of the rose is a circle of eight images, followed in succeeding rows by multiples of eight, sixteen, and thirty-two. In other words the entire window is composed around the number eight, the holy number that stands beyond seven, which is the number of completed time, and stands for that reality that exists beyond time, that is, eternity. The spiritual message of the window is that the fullness of beauty will become visible only when we pass beyond the time of this world and move into the realm of the eternal.

Perhaps more important than the symbolism of the number eight is the fact that at the very center of the rose window is an image of Christ. Mary is in the center also, but it is Christ who sits on her lap. Hence the spiritual message is clear: Christ must be the center of our lives, not money, power, prestige, or pleasure.[31]

Recent scholarship in art history has shed new light on late medieval sacred art in an unlikely place and one that has been neglected in traditional research. Jeffrey F. Hamburger has produced a groundbreaking study of the art of female monasticism.[32] While traveling to Germany in 1992, Hamburger came across a catalogue of *Klosterfrauenarbeiten,* nuns' handwork consisting of devotional objects made by cloistered women for their own religious use. He discovered a reproduction of a devotional drawing that eventually led him to the Benedictine Abbey of St. Walburga in Eichstät, not far from Regensburg in Bavaria.[33] There he found eleven drawings closely related in style and traceable to the hand of an anonymous nun working at the turn of the sixteenth century. The eleven drawings executed by one of the nuns show little regard for the convention of professional scriptoria. Their technique is awkward and the imagery is idiosyncratic. Aesthetically their quality is marginal; they simply have a childlike charm about them. However, from a theological point of view, the content of the drawings is quite extraordinary. With their sophisticated visual rhetoric and subject matter, they display a vivid resourcefulness on the part of the nun who made them and indicate a prayer life that was profound. Contemplation of the drawings by the nuns would have paralleled contemplation of biblical and other texts as a stimulus for that intimate union with God in prayer which is the goal of *lectio divina* in the monastic tradition.[34] Analysis of one of the drawings will clarify this point.

Today the rose is a banal symbol, but during the Middle Ages as a common icon it carried complex connotations. Mary, for example, was the *rosa sine spina*, "the rose without thorns." Christ's sorrow and ecstasy were often symbolized by the rose.[35] Suffering and love, pain and beauty, all conjoined in the image of the rose, are set out in one of the drawings from St. Walburga. It presents the rose as a single blossom set between two buds and resting on pale green, grassy ground. In the center of the rose is a picture of Christ in agony in the garden. Just as the wounds in Christ's body were traditionally portrayed in medieval art as openings from which the sacraments of baptism and eucharist flowed and through which one could come into intimate union with Christ through the power of the Spirit, so the drawing from St. Walburga invites the viewer to penetrate the mystery of Christ through contemplative prayer. Christ's agony in the garden inaugurated his passion; in a sense the image stood, *pars pro toto*, for the whole of Christ's suffering and death.[36]

The drawing provides the viewer with a compact combination of image and text, for beneath the rose is a passage from Mark's Gospel which serves as a caption: *Non quod volo, sed quod tu*, "Not what I will, but what you will." The drawing, however, does not simply illustrate the text, for the rhetoric of the image is far more compelling than the text. The rose is open to reveal Christ kneeling in prayer, but he does not look down or up or ahead; instead, he looks out to meet the eyes of the viewer, thus creating the effect of immediate presence.[37]

The nun holding this drawing would have been called to be one with Christ in his commitment to do God's will. By gazing intently at her, Christ invites the nun to be one with him in submission to the Father. The nun who prayed with this drawing would have seen herself imitating Christ, presented in the drawing, as a model of prayer. The image would have paralleled the text at the bottom of the page and most likely would have had a more profound impact than the text itself.[38]

The nun who sought to imitate Christ in his agony was not, however, meant to seek out suffering as an end in itself. Rather she was to follow the cardinal rule set out by Christ in the Gospel: "Not what I will, but what you will." She was to seek to follow Christ in his obedience, his submissiveness, his patience. It was an abdication of his own will that constituted the central meaning of Christ's redemptive mystery. Hence, the drawing and its accompanying text were in keeping with the fundamental precept of Benedictine monasticism, namely, the primacy of obedience over works. The drawing would have exhorted the nun not so much to imitate Christ's suffering through penitential acts as to emulate the obedience and compassion that characterized his whole life. The text would have tempered any viewer's inclination to understand imitation literally.[39] As Hamburger notes, "to interpret suffering as patience and obedience is entirely in tune with the tenets of monastic reform as it was preached in convents. Spiritual advisers condemned and sought to control, what they regarded as nuns' extravagant, even excessive acts of self-mortification in imitation of the passion."[40]

In concluding his careful analysis of the drawings from St. Walburga, Hamburger observes that medieval nuns developed their distinctive visual culture within constraints that severely limited their activity. Nevertheless, they and their images exemplify that practical and experiential spirituality which established the benchmark for much of the lay spirituality during the later Middle Ages.[41] They certainly stand as a challenge to much of what has been considered an incontestable theological tradition.

The growing secularization of life that was occasioned by the growth of large cities, the foundation of the universities, the flourishing of trade, and the general expansion of the bourgeois class eventually widened the scope and patronage of the arts. Certainly the increased literacy among the new class and the growing body of secular literature prepared the way for the Renaissance.

What the history of art and theology in both the Romanesque and Gothic periods shows us is that each age tends to produce the images of God that it wants and needs. In faith, Christians believe that Jesus Christ is indeed the image of the invisible God. Throughout the Christian era, the literary and artistic challenge has been to produce images of Jesus that are true to the Christian teaching that the eternal Word of God did in fact become incarnate in the humanity of Jesus.

In faith we believe that the essential Christ of Christianity is the resurrected Christ who triumphed over sin and death, and shares the Holy Spirit with all those who open their lives in faith to that wonderful gift. Resurrection was possible, however, only because the Son of God became incarnate, was born of the Virgin Mary, grew to adulthood in Nazareth, and then ministered for three years as a teacher and healer of his disciples until he was put to death for the sins of the world. As the history of art shows, different aspects of the one paschal mystery of Christ, such as the crucifixion, have been emphasized at different periods. Human needs and wants on the religious level, as well as cultural and theological needs, have inspired this art. But the art has also inspired and made people conscious of their theological and human needs.

6

Renaissance, Baroque, and Reformation Periods

THE FULL DEVELOPMENT OF HUMANISM, WHICH HAD ITS origins in the high Gothic period, was achieved in the succeeding epoch called the Italian Renaissance. It extended approximately from the beginning of the fifteenth century to the end of the sixteenth and was characterized by a rebirth of classical culture, based on careful analysis of the ancient Greek and Roman world, its writings, and its ruins.[1] The Renaissance spirit concentrated on the world here and now; it valued above all the work of human individuality and personality. It was interested in all aspects of human life—mind, body, social relationships, economic conditions, political affairs, and religious experience and commitments. In many ways the Renaissance was a whole way of life that changed and molded the human outlook and attitude that people had toward themselves, one another, and God. Because of the complexity of the Renaissance, there have been diverse interpretations of its cultural spirit and fabrics, some of which have been complementary, others contradictory. Much of modern historiography, especially that rooted in nineteenth-century scholarship, asserted that the Renaissance, which established a new concept of humanity, art, literature, and scholarly life, arose in opposition to the Christian religion; other scholars today, however, maintain that it developed out of the full vitality of a deeply religious spirit that was characteristic of the Gothic period.[2]

The medieval order began to collapse in the fourteenth century. It should not be surprising, then, that Italy was the birthplace of the Renaissance, because the Gothic spirit was never firmly rooted there. In fact the classical tradition never died out in Italy, since there were too many surviving examples of the architecture and sculpture of the classical past for the style to be entirely lost. The beginnings of a new vision of life occurred

148

toward the end of the thirteenth century, when the powerful Byzantine formalism that was manifested in the distinguished mosaics in Ravenna gave way to a more spontaneous treatment of human figures and a naturalism which existed in early Roman art. Spurred on by new scientific and territorial discoveries, the spirit of inquiry, criticism, and humanism developed rapidly. It has been asserted that the theocentric view of the universe and the sense of awe and wonder at the transcendent were displaced by a philosophy in which the human person rather than God became the focal point of the universe.

Recent historians of the Renaissance, however, have interpreted this supposed naturalism more sensitively and profoundly. They see much of the culture as embodying an authentic incarnational theology and many of its artistic representations as genuine expressions of that theology. There is no doubt, however, that during the period modern culture replaced classical culture in many areas of human life. The authority of the individual began to rival that of the community, including both the state and the church; emphasis was placed on personal freedom and responsibility; and the scientific method of investigation displaced deductive reasoning. In art, architecture, and literature there was often a mingling of pagan motifs and Christian traditions. The medieval commitment to asceticism was often overshadowed by a preoccupation with the beauty and care of the human body, which, in the minds of many people, was more important than the human soul.

The spirit of the age was reflected especially in the art and architecture of the period. With the emergence of geniuses like Dante (1265–1321), Petrarch (1304–1374), and Giotto (1266/7–1337) in the fourteenth century, Europe entered a new period of civilized enlightenment. In stark but simplistic terms, the Gothic period has been contrasted with the Renaissance as the idealistic versus the naturalistic, the religious versus the secular, the authoritarian versus the empirical, the institutional versus the individualistic, and the feudal versus the bourgeois. One of the most determining factors in the development of the Renaissance was the change in the status of men and women in society and their relation to visible nature. Individuals were in many ways free to cultivate their own personalities; in some sense they felt free from the dominating authority of both the pope and the emperor.

The spirit of the reform probably began with St. Francis of Assisi (1181/2–1226), but it was developed considerably by the writings of Erasmus (1466/9–1536) and Melanchthon (1497–1560) as well as by the great Dominican preacher Savonarola (1452–1498). However, the spirit of the

Renaissance was not so much one of reform as one of tolerance and compassion. St. Thomas Aquinas (ca. 1225–1274) had developed in his writings a positive appreciation of nature, and St. Francis of Assisi articulated his high regard for everything God had created. The nominalist philosophers, especially William of Ockham (ca. 1285–1347), had laid the groundwork for an exploration of particular natural objects and events and displaced the medieval preoccupation with universals. St. Thomas sought to understand and illuminate faith by using human reason; he sought to harmonize the natural with the supernatural and stressed that divine revelation is above but not contrary to human reason. While some of the positive philosophical foundations for the Renaissance came from St. Thomas, the more mystical and personal elements came from St. Francis of Assisi, who discerned the goodness of the earth by looking at it with spiritual eyes.

The beginnings of a change in artistic style and emphasis came in the thirteenth century with the Florentine Cimabue (ca. 1240–1302?) and the Sienese Duccio (ca. 1255/60–1315/18?), both of whom produced large altarpieces quite different from those inspired by the Byzantine tradition.

RENAISSANCE ARCHITECTURE

The painter Masaccio (1401–1428) and the sculptor Donatello (ca. 1385/6–1466) join the architect Filippo Brunelleschi (1377–1446) as the distinguished fathers of the Renaissance style, but it was probably the latter's work that was most influential. Born in Florence, he was the first important protagonist of a new style of architecture, and he was undoubtedly the most important architect of his time. His first known work is a relief of the "Sacrifice of Abraham," which he entered in a competition in 1401 for the baptistery doors in Florence; the winner, however, was Ghiberti. Brunelleschi worked initially as a goldsmith and a military designer, but he went to Rome and studied the construction methods of the early Romans so as to compete for the job of designing the dome of the Florence cathedral. He won the competition for the design and execution of the dome, made the first projects for this commission in 1417, and brought the work to completion in 1436.[3] The new style was especially obvious in his first completed major work, the Sagrestia Vecchia of S. Lorenzo in Florence (1420–1429). There three important characteristics can be noted: an intentional reintroduction of anthropomorphic, classical elements, such as Corinthian pilasters and Ionic colonnades; the exclusive use of elementary geometrical relationships; and stress on spatial centralization. The hierarchical, integrated patterns of Gothic architecture were replaced by relatively independent elements to form a self-contained whole. Above all, a preoccupation with perfection motivated the architect.

In architecture the Roman Pantheon provided Brunelleschi with an amazing model which had not been duplicated in many years. In their competition with each other to become the new Rome, the cities of Orvieto, Siena, Bologna, Milan, Naples, Venice, and Florence sought to outdo one another in their building projects. Florence already had a cathedral designed by Arnolfo de Cambio, but, like its other buildings, the cathedral seemed inadequate when compared with the churches at Pisa, Siena, and Orvieto. So a competition was held for a new design of a dome for the structure. Brunelleschi, intrigued by the design of the Pantheon, discovered a way to get a dome of great weight over a large space without limiting the ground space and the space for windows. His design called for a double dome with an inner dome supporting an outer dome which in turn held up the inner one in precarious balance. Hence, the dome of the cathedral of Florence became a model of countless other domed churches throughout the world. In a sense it was a metaphor for the relationship between the church and God. The perfect geometric forms of square and circle, depicting since the time of Pythagorus the realms of earth and sky, became in the Renaissance a three-dimensional structure that praised God and transformed the people. The dome weds heaven and earth. The Lord Jesus comes off his heavenly throne, comes down from his cross and enters into the human imagination in stories and events so that the world of the heavenly kingdom becomes a reality on earth. There was no doubt that Brunelleschi's achievement was an engineering feat that involved a marriage between Gothic vaulting and the Roman form of the dome. Brunelleschi's structures were based on simple mathematical relationships, but his actual shapes and decorations were derived from the early Christian basilicas. He also planned S. Maria degli Angeli in Florence with a central octagonal design rather than cruciform and an eight-sided shape that recalled the Temple of Minerva in Rome. Once again there was reference to Roman antiquity; Brunelleschi actually revived the two main types of early Christian worship spaces—the large basilica, suitable for parishes, and the smaller, centrally planned structure that in early Christianity was reserved for baptistries and *martyria*.

The spiritualized understanding of space so significant in the Gothic period gave way in the Renaissance to a conception of space as a concrete container. This represented a return to the classical, especially Roman, world. Renaissance architecture sought to shape spaces characterized by homogeneity, geometric order, concretization, harmony, and perfection. These intentions manifested themselves in all styles of building, both ecclesiastical and secular. Renaissance men and women were in line with their medieval predecessors, however, in that they believed in an ordered cosmos, but their interpretations of the meaning of order were different. Rather than achieving existential security by taking their place within the hierarchically arranged kingdom of God, they imagined the world more in terms of numbers. Hence, architecture was regarded as a mathematical science entrusted with making the cosmic order visible. Perspective was stressed as a means of describing space, and proportion was given special importance as a way of relating the building to the human body. In this way architecture was experienced as both cosmic and human. Naturally it departed from and in fact rejected the Gothic emphasis on verticality.[4]

The new concept of space manifested itself perhaps above all on the geographical level, and in particular in the notion of the ideal city. The Gothic city was ideal inasmuch as it was meant to be a concrete expression of the *Civitas Dei*, but the Renaissance city was ideal inasmuch as it was meant to be an expression of ideal form. It was Leone Battista Alberti (1404–1472) who laid down the theoretical foundations for the ideal city in his work *De re aedificatoria*, written between 1444 and 1452. Unlike the Gothic town, which expressed a communal form of life, the Renaissance city formed the center of a small autocratic state; at the center of the city stood not the church but the palace of the *signore* facing out on a large piazza. As a residence of an autocratic ruler, the palace constituted a new center of meaning for the residents of the city. In Renaissance architecture, the design of urban space was aimed at creating an ideal of formal perfection rather than a vital integrated organism.

In general, then, Renaissance architecture was an expression of urban civilization. The church was still important in the life of the city, but as an institution it often adapted to its surrounding secular culture. Hence, the churches constructed during the period were often modeled on pagan temples in that they followed a centralized plan and contained various side chapels in place of aisles. In other instances the actual shape as well as the decorative forms used in the churches were derived from the early Christian basilicas, but the architecture itself was based on simple mathematical relationships. The content of the decorative forms, however, was often more pagan than specifically Christian. It was fashionable to use the mythology of the Greco-Roman era as a literary and artistic medium. The Renaissance was an age when artists could paint a Bacchus and a St. John or a Venus and a Blessed Virgin that were almost indistinguishable from each other. What was most unfortunate from a Christian point of view was the oblivion of biblical imagery from the minds of ordinary people. Certainly the Christian mysteries had been expressed and celebrated in biblical terms during the early Christian and medieval periods. During the Renaissance the world of Christian types and symbols was often displaced by pagan figures that were entirely foreign to the rites of the liturgy.[5]

RENAISSANCE ART AND SCULPTURE

A distinctively Renaissance style of art developed in the fourteenth century with innovations introduced by Giotto di Bondone, the Florentine painter who broke with the traditional practice of imitating the flat two-dimensional figures of the Romanesque and Byzantine styles and used instead sculptures as his models, thus giving his figures a three-dimensional substance and enlarging the dramatic content of the episodes he painted. It was Giotto who created the liveliness that combined harmonious forms and dramatic action. This is especially exemplified in *The Kiss of Judas*, where the faces of both Judas and Jesus express strong emotion. He also created realistic landscapes as background for the episodes, thus departing from the Byzantine practice of regularly painting gold backgrounds.[6]

It was Masaccio who drew out the implications of Giotto's naturalism. His frescoes manifest sharper figures that are realistic but not too detailed. His works manifest a deep knowledge of human anatomy as well as appreciation for perspective and color. His backgrounds appear distant so that the main figures in the front of his pictures are more prominent. He carefully placed his work in architectural settings that served to frame them effectively, as is evident in his *Tribute Money* and *The Holy Family with the Virgin and St. John.*[7]

The Dominican Fra Angelico (ca. 1387–ca. 1455) is especially remembered for his extraordinary frescoes, with which he covered the walls of the convent of San Marco in Florence and also the high altarpiece in the church. Portraying scenes from the lives of Jesus and St. Dominic, the works manifest great narrative power and the use of brilliant color; they come across as the work of a deeply spiritual artist.[8]

Donatello (ca. 1385/6–1466) was undoubtedly the greatest Florentine sculptor before Michelangelo. It was he who developed a dramatic style based on Christian tenderness and sympathy combined with a use of classical Roman forms. His work often reveals a tremendous sense of energy, inducing in the spectator a sense of fear and tragic catharsis. His figures of

John the Baptist and Mary Magdalene manifest depth of character while his sculptures of the youthful David and the *Madonna of the Annunciation* combine forcefulness and gentleness.[9]

Another important figure, Sandro Botticelli (ca. 1444–1510), fluctuated between an expression of the piety of the lower classes of society and the paganism of his Medici patrons. He often expressed his sadness over the uneasiness of life in fifteenth-century Florence. His *Adoration of the Magi* reflects his gentleness, but the figures of Mary and the Child are subordinated to the painter's desire for perspective.[10]

The Renaissance popes were tolerant of experimentation in the arts and were often dazzled by the brilliance of the humanist scholars of the period who espoused Neoplatonic ideas and were supported especially by the great Florentine families. It was in this context that three of the greatest artistic masters of the period emerged: Leonardo da Vinci (1452–1519), Michelangelo Buonarroti (1475–1564), and Raphael (1483–1520). Leonardo painted but a small number of pictures, yet his influence was fundamental. In many ways he was a universal genius. His early paintings, for example, an unfinished *Adoration of the Kings* and *Virgin of the Rocks*, manifest a powerful dramatic current and a mysterious atmosphere flowing among his figures. His most famous work, *The Last Supper*, is a profound psychological study of Christ and his disciples. The image of Christ is unforgettable in his sense of beauty, serenity, and sensitiveness. He spreads calm in the midst of the psychological confusion, distress, and incomprehension among the disciples, who are struggling with the question, "Is it I, Lord, who will betray you?" Judas, the traitor, whose face is the only one completely shadowed, is shown clutching his bag of coins. The apostles are grouped in threes but they are united by their varied reactions to Christ's prophecy. Emotions are very strong in the picture, manifesting the artist's great ability to portray both intellectual and psychological depth.[11]

The other field in which Leonardo's influence was very creative was architecture, but no buildings can definitely be ascribed to him. It has been asked whether Leonardo's work was indeed motivated by Christian faith. Though that question cannot be answered, there is no doubt that his images of the Virgin and the Last Supper had deeper religious impact than the works of many of the other artists of his time.[12]

Michelangelo Buonarroti acquired a reputation as the most brilliant sculptor of his day at the age of twenty-five by his execution of the *Pietà* in St. Peter's. In an extraordinarily imaginative way, he placed the dead body of Jesus across the knees of his mother by converting her draperies into a podium to support the body. Following that success he was employed in his native Florence to carve the gigantic *David* and the roughly carved *St. Matthew* as the first of a series of apostles for the cathedral, but he never finished. The most outstanding painting of his early life is the vault of the Sistine Chapel in the Vatican, where he set out in powerful images the history of the world from the creation to the sacrifice of Noah following the flood along with vivid figures of seven prophets and five Sibyls who foretold the coming of the Messiah. Around the frames of his panels he painted nude athletes, whose role in the project has been variously interpreted. Below the ceiling proper are representations of events in the lives of the ancestors of Christ, including David and Goliath, Moses and the brazen serpent, Esther's plea for her people, and Judith's victory over Holofernes. The recent cleaning of the ceiling has revealed the startlingly rich colors of the work and has emphasized the amplitude and grandeur that characterized Michelangelo's style.

Many years later, Michelangelo was given the commission to paint the altar wall with a huge representation of the last judgment, which manifests a marked change in the style of his work from his earlier *Pietà* and *David*. In the *Last Judgment* he was no longer concerned simply with pure beauty of form but employed the human nude to express what many commentators describe as profound spiritual experience. The angels summon the dead to new life, and they swirl toward judgment before Christ who is surrounded by the martyred saints who cry out for justice as they hold the instruments of their own deaths. The just are welcomed among the elect, while the unjust spiral downward toward the devils, who pull them into hell. When he painted this masterpiece, Michelangelo was in his sixties; the tragedies that had befallen Rome and Florence had made him pessimistic and disillusioned—characteristics that are expressed in the *Last Judgment*. Although the work was acclaimed as a masterpiece, it was also bitterly denounced by influential religious reformers, who objected strongly to the number and character of the nudes the work contained. Responding to the complaints, successive popes were urged either to destroy the work or at least to clothe the nude figures. The repainting of parts of Michelangelo's work was left until after his death, but with the recent cleaning, most of the offending loincloths have been removed. His last works, two frescoes in Pope Paul III's private chapel in the Vatican, the *Crucifixion of St. Peter* and the *Conversion of St. Paul,* both contain massive figures in urgent movement such as he had used in the *Last Judgment,* but there is increased emphasis on shock, horror, and dread.[13]

Michelangelo's architectural work culminated in his contribution to St. Peter's, a project he worked on for seventeen years until his death in 1564.

He was adamant in demanding a central plan as the only one that could express authentically the oneness and perfection of God. His great architectural contribution to the design of St. Peter's consisted in his grasp that enclosing huge ground spaces demanded equally grand and bold structural elements. Recent research has indicated that he was in fact extremely wealthy, but it has been traditionally held that he worked for nothing, giving his services to the church and the pope until old age prevented him from visiting the site. He was fortunate that successive popes acknowledged his ability, his devotion to the task, and his vision for the project and so supported him in his efforts.

Raphael, along with Leonardo and Michelangelo, was one of the creators of the high Renaissance, but both temperamentally and artistically he was quite different from his gifted contemporaries. In his early years he produced paintings that were quiet and well mannered, but eventually he was influenced by Leonardo's vision, with the result that he produced a series of small madonna-and-child pictures that combined intensely human emotion with deep religious devotion. In 1509 he moved from Florence to Rome, where he undertook work under Popes Julius II and Leo X. He painted a series of rooms in the Vatican known as the *stanze*. They contain, in addition to the celebration of pagan philosophy as taught in the school of Athens, portrayals of major theological themes concerning the eucharist and the church. Raphael also executed three major altarpieces, which are superb examples of his ability to paint figures with grandeur and power. His *Madonna di Foligno* and the *Sistine Madonna* have become over the years ideal types for the representation of Mary and the child Jesus. He was certainly a major creator of devotional works.[14]

In many ways, Renaissance culture was a synthesis of Platonic and Christian themes. During the Gothic period, God was envisioned as being very close to the people. Because they had such an exalted understanding of the incarnation, Gothic people could readily think of God in terms of the humanity of Jesus Christ. It was but a minor change in understanding for Renaissance people to think of God as the divine human being. It was easy to replace the supernatural with the superhuman. In the Renaissance, divine perfection was to be found not so much in transcending nature as in nature itself. Natural beauty was looked upon as an expression of God's own beauty, and human creativity was seen as a share in God's own creative power. Certainly the self-assurance implicit in this interpretation of Christian anthropology brought about an enormous outburst of creative activity among the people of the period. The most exalted achievement in life was thought to be the creation of beauty, for it was in this expression that human persons were thought to realize their highest potential.

Perhaps the most basic characteristic of the Renaissance was its unsurpassed longing for life, especially on the sensual and intellectual levels. This hunger stood in marked contrast to the Gothic concern for sobriety and discipline, both traditional characteristics of the Christian liturgy. This drive was manifested especially in the sculpture of the period, which was often enormous in bulk and powerful in gesticulation, reflected in the works of Michelangelo, especially his statue of David, and later in Bernini's well-known baroque sculpture of *Saint Teresa in Ecstasy*.[15]

Although the outward form and decoration of churches during the Renaissance achieved a high level of technical and artistic excellence, the arrangement of the church interiors was not much different from what it was in the Gothic era. With the spread of the mendicant orders throughout Europe in the late Gothic and Renaissance periods, the pulpit was erected in the nave of the church so as to stand in close proximity to the people. The subject matter of the sermon, however, was often quite unrelated to the liturgy itself. The friars celebrated the divine office and conventual Mass just as earlier monks and canons had done, but they removed the rood screen, which obstructed the people's view of the main altar and the liturgy celebrated there. Although the people could then see and hear what was going on, most of them had little or no understanding of the language being used or the theological meaning of the rites being executed.

During the fifteenth century many devotional additions were made to the interior of the churches in the form of shrines. Especially in Germany, the churches were crowded with statues, which often conveyed the impression that Christianity was above all a depressing religion expressed in suffering and tears. Many realistic representations of Christ on the cross and his sorrowful mother date from this period.

There was a marked shift in Marian piety in the sixteenth and early seventeenth centuries. Preachers tended to downplay her role as the physical mother of Jesus and emphasize her role as spiritual mother of Christ, united to him by shared will and affection rather than by flesh. She began to be portrayed as the obedient, prayerful, silent, distant queen of heaven rather than the active, compassionate, and vocal spokesperson for Christians in need. As European religious life moved away from external devotions and attention to material objects such as relics and images, a new spirituality emerged which stressed inner states and mental prayer with special attention to affections centered on the heart as the seat of the will and emotions.[16]

In the Middle Ages, Mary was not seen as a representative woman but was appreciated simply because she bore the body of Christ. Medieval women identified more closely with Christ than with Mary. They found in Mary's motherhood a positive inspiration to emulate the sufferings of Jesus in their own lives, joining themselves, as Mary had done, with the paschal mystery of Christ. During the sixteenth and seventeenth centuries, the tendency to exalt Mary's inner life and passive virtues coincided with a general post-Tridentine suspicion of the body, especially women's bodies. After the sixteenth century, Mary's role was largely limited to that of intercessor and mediatrix, as is reflected in the various portrayals of Mary in apparitions such as those at Lourdes, Fatima, and La Salette. As part of the cult of the Holy Family, which developed in the seventeenth century, Mary appeared as the ideal mother—humble, quiet, caring, and submissive—to Joseph as well as to God. She found her proper place in a patriarchal structure; her response to that structure was one of simple obedience. In fact, one of the most popular features of Marian piety in the seventeenth century was devotion to her Immaculate Heart. To some extent that emphasis on the heart counteracted the rationalism of the scientific revolution and the Enlightenment.[17]

As the Renaissance moved north of the Alps, there developed a marked difference between artistic presentations in the Franco-Flemish and German areas and those in Italy.[18] The difference lay not so much in subject matter as in the artistic expression of the significant difference between the Augustinian and Artistotelian understanding of human nature and the world. Northerners were inclined toward an Augustinian view, whereas the Italians were much more Aristotelian in their outlook. Augustine had insisted that faith precedes and makes understanding possible; he stressed personal existence and analyzed the psychological processes of memory and perception. Aristotle approached life much more logically, objectively, and abstractly. Consequently, for the northern artists light was the chief symbol of divine presence and illumination. That emphasis, rather than preoccupation with clear doctrinal positions, is revealed in the central panel of the Ghent Altarpiece, known as the *Adoration of the Lamb* (1432).

There are two names attached to the painting, Hubert and Jan van Eyck. The two brothers lived and worked in the Netherlands between 1422 and 1441. It seems the painting was begun by Hubert and completed by his brother Jan. The altarpiece consists of three parts: a large central area and two wings that close over it, each wing painted on both sides. In all there are twenty panels. In the upper panel is a representation of Christ the King crowned with the papal crown as king of heaven; he is flanked by the Virgin Mary crowned as queen and by John the Baptist wearing a jeweled robe over his traditional animal-skin clothing. This is a representation of the heavenly throne described in the Book of Revelation and in Augustine's *De Civitate Dei*. The lower part of the piece consists of the heavenly personages adoring the Lamb. The central scene takes place in paradise, a meadow filled with flowers and shrubs. On an altar stands the Lamb, with blood spurting from his breast into a chalice.

Rogier van der Weyden (1399/1400–1464) was one of the central figures of early Netherlandish painting. His sophisticated painting combined a concern for naturalistic detail with expressive composition and often concentrated on deeply Christian themes. Two of his paintings especially deserve comment. The earliest painting that can be ascribed to Rogier with any degree of certainty is his *Deposition* (ca. 1435–1440). It was intended as an altarpiece for the chapel of the Confraternity of the Archers of Louvain. Ten figures cover the painted surface. The group is placed in a painted altar niche; Golgotha is suggested only by a skull and cross bones on the strip of stone floor. The figures are not static sculptures but live human beings. The limp body of Jesus has already been removed from the cross and is received by Joseph of Arimathea and Nicodemus. It inspires deep reverence in the viewer and would have been the background against which the faithful would have looked at the elevated Host during the celebration of Mass. The identification of the Host with the crucified body of Jesus would have been clear. Christ's body, not disfigured by the scourging, is almost radiant.[19]

The other main figure in the painting is Mary. She sinks to the ground as if almost dead; in this way she forms a parallel to the dead body of Christ, thus illustrating the important theological theme of the period that Mary's compassionate suffering was a share in Christ's own act of redemption. Mary Magdalene stands at the right of the painting, attired in worldly garments indicating that she is a great sinner who has abandoned her former life and turned to Christ in repentance. All the figures in the painting express deep grief, but they also bear a sense of nobility and dignified gravity. Yet each figure grieves in his or her own distinctive way, thus calling on each viewer to respond uniquely to the event.[20]

Rogier was involved also in the execution of a large-scale work, *Seven Sacraments*, commissioned by the bishop of Tournai. Rogier's task was to present both the seven sacraments and the crucifixion. He responded to the challenge by placing the different actions in a church with three naves. The side aisles accommodate six of the sacraments, while the eucharist takes place in the central nave at the rood screen altar. The crucifixion is set at the front of the main nave and is portrayed in much larger proportions than the other liturgical rites. The left-hand aisle shows the sacraments of baptism, confirmation, and penance, while the right-hand aisle shows ordination, matrimony, and extreme unction. Angels hover over the celebrations, wearing appropriate liturgical colors and carrying scrolls explaining the significance of each of the sacraments.[21] Rogier's paintings left such a mark on other artists that he has been described as the most influential painter of the fifteenth century.

Jan Gossaert (ca. 1478–ca. 1533) was a fellow countryman of both Van Eyck and Rogier. His great masterpiece is the *Adoration of the Kings*.[22] It was painted around 1510, probably for the Lady Chapel in the church of a Benedictine abbey in Geraardsbergen in East Flanders. It was meant to serve as the focus of attention during the eucharist. The painting is an attempt to demonstrate the Christ child's divinity. There is no crucifix, only a dense nativity scene that brings together interpretations of a variety of texts from the Gospels of Luke and Matthew. There are impossibilities and improbabilities in the painting, but nothing is accidental. The scene takes place in imposing ruins, which certainly would offer the newly born child and his mother no shelter. The ox and ass peer out from among the ruins but certainly were never there. No humble carpenter's wife would be dressed so luxuriously in a brilliant blue dress and mantle. The mother and child are at the center of the painting, while Joseph, an elderly man leaning on a cane, looks on the scene from behind a pillar. The three kings, whose names are inscribed either on their clothing or on their gifts, are elegantly dressed. Gaspar kneels in adoration in front of the child; Balthazar, the black king, stands to the left; and Melchior to the right. Their gifts resemble liturgical objects that would have been used at the time Gossaert painted the picture. For example, Gaspar's goblet, which he has given to the child's mother, looks like a ciborium in which the consecrated eucharist is reserved. In the painting it holds gold coins, one of which the child Jesus gives back to the king. The gesture certainly resembles a priest giving a consecrated Host to a communicant. There are angels in the painting, which is not surprising, but descending from the miraculous star is a dove hovering over the mother and child. Certainly the events that are pictured in the painting took place at different times. The shepherds, who came to the stable on the night Jesus was born, are still there when the three kings arrive; an angel is shown announcing the good news to them before they set off for the stable.

Gossaert's painting shows that creating an image of the God-made-man is a tricky business. His painting neither simply illustrates a religious event nor interprets it according to the artist's own whims. Rather he has attempted to create a pictorial theology, a distillation of the church's doctrine on the dual nature of Jesus Christ. He has provided his contemporaries and us with a meditation on the theological meaning of Christ's birth and what it means and why it matters to all generations. The painting, placed behind the altar, would have been an effective interpretation of the purpose of the Mass, namely, to nourish the lives of the faithful, just as the infant seems to be giving the bread of life to one of the kings.

Gossaert's painting is markedly different from Pieter Bruegel's (ca. 1525–1569) *Adoration of the Kings*; they hang opposite each other in London's National Gallery. Bruegel painted his *Adoration* in 1564. The rich, exotic attire of the kings in Goessart's painting is entirely missing from Bruegel's work, where the figures crowd the canvas; there is no hint of surrounding countryside, just an oppressive mob by the wooden shed where the kings offer their gifts. Curiously, soldiers are prominent as well as civilian onlookers. They all simply gawk at the scene. Except for the mother and child, all the figures in the painting are exceptionally ugly; they seem to be caricatures of fallen humanity. The soldiers and the civilians have eyes only for the treasures offered to the child; the impression is given that even Joseph is assessing their material worth. The kings do not in any way appear to have humbled themselves before the child; rather they are grotesque examples of worldly pomp in need of soldiers for protection. The open container offered to the child by the oldest of the kings seems to hold granules of myrrh used for anointing the dead. Whereas Gossaert's child is Christ the King, Bruegel's child is born to die. The myrrh indicates the future from which the child naturally recoils as he shrinks back in the protective arms of his mother.[23]

Bruegel located Christ's birth in the Low Countries of his own time and used the painting to paraphrase the travails of his own land. The Christ child does not welcome the kings; rather there seems to be strong opposition portrayed in the child's actions. The painting is, in fact, profoundly subversive and refers to the tragic death that would befall the Christ child. Bruegel used his painting to explore the meaning not only of Christ's humanity but also of the world's inhumanity and inability to recognize what is truly important in human life.[24] Two years after Bruegel painted his *Adoration*, groups of Protestants broke into churches and convents and destroyed many paintings and statues.

PROTESTANT AND CATHOLIC REFORMS

Although the sixteenth century saw the culmination of the Renaissance, it also witnessed the assertion of older traditions and allegiances. No single source of reform can readily be specified. Several factors were knotted together, including sincere religious motivation, civil opportunism, and cultural determinants; they coalesced to produce radical changes in both society and the church. However, three movements contributed in a special way to the critique of the religious arrogance and corruption that had developed in recent centuries: conciliarism in matters of ecclesiology, nominalism in academic thought, and humanistic scholarship as a basis for religious piety. These three movements set the stage for the complex development of Luther's dramatic reform measures.

Conciliarism sought to vest the ultimate authority of the church in a general council, rather than in the pope. As a theory it developed in opposition to the rise of papal power but grew especially during the Great Western Schism. The Council of Constance (1414–1417) attempted to end the schism, but in the process the fathers decreed reforms that required periodic general councils to settle major ecclesiastical affairs. In 1460, Pius II prohibited all appeals from papal decrees to general councils.[25]

Nominalism was a critique directed at the arrogance of reason in matters of faith. William of Ockham (1285–1347) emphasized that we can know only particulars in the empirical world and that without divine revelation we can never know the intrinsic link between creation and God. His hostility was directed toward all those who assumed clear knowledge of the divine plan for the world. His philosophical assertions were meant to preserve the sovereignty of God's free action from any and all contrary claims by either Scholastics or politicians.[26]

Medieval piety stressed the accumulation of merit in the sight of God as well as passive participation in sacramental rituals. It was severely criticized by those who stressed mystical religious experience, by those who were committed to the *devotio moderna*, and also by biblical and historical scholars. Mystics such as Meister Eckhart (1260–1327) promoted an ascetical life in which men and women would be utterly selfless, without possessions, separated from the false idols of self and world. Along with others, like John Tauler (ca. 1300–1361) and Henry Suso (ca. 1295–1366), he preached a return to interiorized religious experience.[27]

Eckhart's doctrine was further supported by the development of a lay-centered piety founded by Gerhard Groote (1340–1384). His personal conversion inspired him to follow an intensely religious life, with an emphasis on penance. In the spirituality he preached, he combined three elements: knowledge of the Bible, knowledge of the great thirteenth- and fourteenth-century mystics, and the need to interiorize religious experience. His devotion spoke to the affective dimension of the human person. The Brethren of the Common Life and Sisters of the Common Life developed out of such a context. They earned their living as printers and teachers, took no vows, but shared a simple monastic life in common in the Netherlands, but they had significant influence on various reformers such as Pope Hadrian VI, Gabriel Biel, and Nicholas of Cusa. The brother who probably had the greatest impact was Thomas à Kempis (1380–1471), whose small work *The Imitation of Christ* has taught countless Christians how to seek perfection by modeling their lives after Christ. The brothers and sisters were suspected and persecuted but spread from the Netherlands to northern Germany and the Rhineland.[28]

It was from these religious circles that humanist scholars such as Desiderius Erasmus (ca. 1469–1536) emerged. Erasmus was truly an international scholar, teaching first in Paris, then in Louvain, and finally settling in Basel. He provided the Western church with its first critical edition of the Greek New Testament and in general stressed the importance of returning to the authentic sources of Christian life. While living with Thomas More in England, Erasmus wrote *In Praise of Folly*, a sharp criticism of civil and ecclesiastical abuses. Despite his sharp criticisms of religious indifference and institutional errors, he never envisioned a separation from the church.[29]

The severe criticism of the church from within should have provided an impetus for genuine revitalization. Although there were honest critics, such as John Gerson (1363–1429), a distinguished theologian, champion of reform, and chancellor of the University of Paris, other church leaders were lacking in both vision and courage. The result of this complex mixture of ecclesiastical and political factors was eventually the Protestant Reformation, which surfaced mainly because of the charismatic and prophetic appearance of three distinguished church leaders: Martin Luther (1483–1546), Ulrich Zwingli (1484–1531), and John Calvin (1509–1664).

Martin Luther's prophetic questions emerged in the context of his own struggles with the absolute gratuity of God's love over all attempts of human beings to merit justification themselves. Luther was adamant that no one can merit or earn God's grace. In three important treatises issued in 1520, *To the German Princes, On the Babylonian Captivity of the Church*, and *Concerning the Freedom of Christians*, Luther urged the civic authorities to take church reform into their own hands by forbidding taxation by Rome, by abolishing celibacy of the clergy, by disallowing the exemption of religious orders from local rule, and by reforming the religious practices of worship and morality. Luther felt that all religious answers were to conform to the norm of the Word of God as found in the scriptures.[30]

Ulrich Zwingli carried the reform measures much further. He stressed that all concrete manifestations of the church, whether sacramental, institutional, ascetical, or artistic, were irrelevant to the inner life of the believer. Hence he was intensely iconoclastic and even limited the celebration of the eucharist to several times a year.[31]

John Calvin sought to reconstitute Christianity by imitating what he thought were the practices and structures of the early church. His *Institutes of the Christian Religion* developed from a small catechism into a large Protestant *summa*, a theological synthesis based on God's sovereignty, wisdom, and love, inviting human beings to share to some extent in the divine glory. In this way he carefully institutionalized what he thought was the authentic Christian tradition.[32]

With the Protestant Reformation, the spirit of independent thought that was active in art, letters, and architecture was expressed in theology and liturgy as well. The Protestant and Catholic reforms of the sixteenth century introduced fundamental changes in the worship patterns of many European Christians. Easy generalizations must be avoided because they would disregard the variety of local practices and exaggerate the rapidity with which changes were introduced. In a sense it was the imbalance between engagement of the visual and auditory senses that became a focus of both Protestant and Catholic reform measures. Although both recognized the need to improve the auditory aspects of the liturgy as well as religious instruction, they responded very differently to the problem of the relation of word and images in Christian worship.

The religious situation in England was quite different from what it was on the Continent. Discerning the difference, Eamon Duffy has discussed at length traditional religion in England from about 1400 to 1580.[33] He reconstructed the traditional English religion of Becket, Chaucer, and More and then told the story of its deconstruction at the hands of the official reformers. Catholicism in England constituted a tradition; it was a body of beliefs and practices received, preserved, and transmitted by the community itself, including both priests and people. It was a religion of the people, different from religion of the intellectuals and different from religion simply organized by the official Catholic hierarchy in the country. In England there were no barriers between the religion of the elite and the religion of the masses. If the religion of the people was marked by credulity, superstition, and mechanical devotions, so too was the religion of the elite. Duffy emphasized that one cannot write off prayers, pilgrimages, and processions as deviations or extravagances of an ignorant multitude. The common people simply put into effect the religious teachings endorsed by their social and ecclesiastical superiors.

The culture of late medieval Catholics in England was predominantly oral and visual. Beliefs, values, and practices were transmitted not by schoolmasters but by the community itself. The available media were not restricted to catechetical handbooks and sermons but included liturgical and devotional ceremonies, paintings, engravings, reliefs, statues, stained glass windows, plays, processions, ballads, and carols. The imaginative dramatic cycles of cities like Coventry and York set out the Christian faith in a way that not only had immediate emotional impact but left a lasting impression on the tenacious memories of people steeped in an oral culture. The period covered by Duffy was an age of great faith, despite the insecurity caused by infant mortality, epidemic diseases, and economic hardships. Even the secular aspects of the country were infused with a religious sense, and social projects were undertaken out of a sense of faith. Prayer was simply part of daily life.

Duffy maintains that in late medieval England, Catholicism was not corrupt but was a coherent, popular, and profoundly rooted religion. He paints a picture of a religious culture that was secure, serene, and self-confident. He claims that it was the Reformation, imposed from above, that destroyed the traditional religion of England, not the collapse of traditional religion that caused the Reformation. In fact, the Catholic religion was responding positively to social change. New needs and opportunities were being met by the friars and confraternities, which often transcended the parish boundaries. New opportunities offered by the growth in literacy and the birth of printing were taken advantage of by both clergy and laity. Duffy himself does not ascribe the English Reformation to any particular cause, but one is inclined to believe that it was imposed by the English nobility to satisfy their own needs and desires.

The traditional explanation of the Reformation was that it was either a response to the abuses, decadence, and corruption of the late medieval Catholic Church or that it was a response to the needs of an evolving society trying to cope with the development of urbanization and the emergence of a capitalist economic system characterized by the growing influence of bourgeoisie or petty members of the nobility. In some circles it was said that Catholicism was a religion for a rural world, not meant for the hustle of the new cities.

Once the Reformation took hold in England, the liturgy of the Church of England was reformed by the Archbishop of Canterbury, Thomas Cranmer (1489–1556), who chaired a committee that prepared two editions of the Book of Common Prayer under King Edward VI in 1549 and 1552. Cranmer's first version of the eucharist retained much of the medieval order and supplied much of the wording of the Prayerbook of 1662, which was the standard of the English Church and shaped the worship of the worldwide Anglican Communion for about four hundred years. Anglican worship took the human community seriously, for it was believed to be the medium through which the presence of God was communicated. The very structure of the Anglican pattern of worship was designed to consecrate the whole of human life to God.[34] Like Roman Catholics, who followed a uniform Latin missal promulgated through the worldwide church under Pope Pius V in 1570, the Anglicans followed an ordered rite that enabled them to approach God as a united community.[35]

The Book of Common Prayer conveyed a deep sense that the whole English nation was at prayer, united by the prayerbook not only within England but also with all those in English enclaves throughout the world. In Cranmer's mind, the church and nation were coextensive. The eucharistic rite, translated into English, united the priest and people in prayer forms that created a fresh sense of national solidarity. Likewise, the dialogical structure of Anglican worship rendered less rigid the distinction between clergy and laity and enabled both to carry religious values into the daily life of the English nation, a fact that profoundly shaped English history in succeeding generations.[36]

During the 1550s, in some of the English churches the altars were replaced by tables set up endwise in the choir to strengthen and symbolize the sense of community gathered at the one table. Fathers of families were expected to lead prayer in their own homes modeled after the worship forms in the prayerbook. A deep note of gratitude for the newly experienced sense of community sounds throughout Cranmer's prayerbook.[37]

Cranmer himself was not a trained liturgical scholar; however, there is no doubt that he was the finest writer of liturgical texts in the sixteenth century and also one of the greatest in the history of Christianity. He was well trained in Greek, Latin, and Hebrew and used those tools of textual criticism to draw out the true spirit of the liturgy from the medieval service books so that the English texts could speak powerfully to the men and women of his age. He was convinced of the power of liturgical language to move the emotions of a congregation and to stimulate them to action in the world. His extraordinary ability as a liturgical writer with a classical background was certainly a great gift to the Anglican Church. It was providential that he was able to use his gifts at just the right time. If he had been born earlier he would not have found an outlet for his talents; had he been born later, he would have encountered Protestant activists in England who would have rejected his traditional approach to an ordered worship service and style of celebration.

Cranmer created a style of vernacular liturgical prose that was dignified, sonorous, and beautifully suited to shaping the imagination and habits of a whole people, all contained in a single prayerbook. His idea of combining "prayer," "common," and "book" was quite revolutionary in that it gave Anglicans a very distinctive biblical spirituality, a religious identity, and an effective vehicle for relating worship and everyday life. His prayers were open to various interpretations and meanings in that they balanced the needs of individuals with the needs and aims of the larger community. Cranmer made available devotional forms that could establish and maintain links between basic theological values and the needs and concerns of the English nation. As the archbishop of Canterbury, he stressed the essential relationship between public virtues, such as justice, courage, and practical wisdom, and the education and participation in the life of God made available to persons and communities in the celebration of the eucharist. In other words, he clearly saw the intimate link between prayer and work. In all of this he had a keen sense of balance and moderation, never encouraging extremism or fanatical martyrdom. It is ironic, then, that of all the reformers, it was Thomas Cranmer who was burned at the stake in 1556 for the crime of heresy.[38]

In the second half of the sixteenth century in England there arose a strong group of English Protestants who sought a further purification of the church from all its nonscriptural forms. They became known as Puritans. Although powerful in their own right, they never became a majority. They demanded a biblical warrant for all the details of public worship, believing that all other forms were simply popish superstitions that were idolatrous and anti-Christian. They attacked church ornaments, vestments, organs, and gestures such as the sign of the cross. They put emphasis on preaching, observance of Sunday, and the table-form of the altar. They also attacked the episcopacy as unwarranted in scripture.[39]

The Congregationalists were an offshoot of the Puritans. They stressed the autonomy and independence of each local church and the principle of democracy in church government. They maintained that Christ is the sole head of the church and that all members of the church are priests. Those who urged complete separation from the Church of England were for a time exiled to Holland; many, along with their Puritan brothers and sisters, eventually made their way to America and settled in Massachusetts.[40]

In response to the prophetic and apocalyptic visionaries who had largely separated themselves from traditional ecclesiastical authority, the Catholic Church, urged on by the growing external calls for reform and prompted by some of its own loyal leaders, realized that only a general council could revive the church. Hence, Pope Paul III called for a meeting of theologians, bishops, cardinals, and national representatives in December 1545. The council began at Trent and lasted for eighteen years of intensive, if rather sporadic, work involving three major sessions and the leadership of five popes.[41]

The final results were of mixed quality, but they were doubtlessly in the reforming tradition. On the negative side, the council did not in any way attempt reunion with the Protestants. Consequently, many of its decrees and canons were so critical of the Protestant Reformers' positions that they ensured that the division would be irreparable. On the positive side, there were remarkable men such as Gasparo Contarini, Jerome Seripando, and Reginald Pole who led the council in its earlier sessions and achieved impressive gains. In the last session, Charles Borromeo (1538–1584), a man of considerable intelligence and training in scripture, doctrine, and religious education, directed the preparation of the council's carefully worded and lucid statements on a whole range of Catholic disciplinary and doctrinal questions. The council formulated a doctrine of justification by faith that asserted God's prior word of love before, during, and after our human choice to love God in return, but it did so in the context of a scripturally based understanding of human development. The fathers asserted that we are saved by and in Christ, but it affirmed the human responsibility to respond to God's love in such a way that both Luther's tendency to deny human choice and Pelagius's tendency to exalt self-salvation were clearly rejected.

In addition, the council formulated practical reform measures. Whereas the Protestant Reformers focused attention on the religious literacy of ordinary Christians, Trent gave its attention to the reform of clerics and religious. Seminaries were to be established to ensure the proper formation of future priests and bishops. The importance of biblical education was stressed as well as the duties of preachers. Clerical celibacy was maintained. Eventually these practical directives were incorporated into a catechism, and a revised missal, breviary, and sacramental ritual were prepared. Doctrinal decrees on the sacraments, the meaning of the presence of Christ in the eucharist, original sin, marriage, ordination, the authority of the Bible, and penance were issued. It was the formation of this stable and uniform ecclesiastical culture that provided the energy and boldness that were manifested in several extraordinary movements within the Roman Catholic Church in the sixteenth century: the rise of mystical theologians and reformers in Spain, the emergence of the Jesuits as prophetic soldiers of God and the pope; and an academic strengthening of Catholicism in the seventeenth and eighteenth centuries. In many ways, the Council of Trent was a classical response to the emerging modern or scientific culture spreading more and more over the Western world.

Concerning the matter of the cult of images, the Council of Trent solemnly reaffirmed the traditional teaching of the Catholic Church. In the thirteenth century, Thomas Aquinas had set out an explanation of the cult of images based in christology.[42] Building on his teaching, Trent took up the question at the very end of the council on December 2 and 3, 1563. The resulting decree was intended both to affirm the traditional teaching and to correct abuses. The council, in its concise teaching, reflects scholastic rather than patristic theology, but it was very careful not to use the word "adoration" in regard to images: only Christ himself is adored, the saints are venerated, and images are honored. Less than a year after Trent, Pope Pius IX issued a profession of faith, taking up the terms of the first phrase of the Tridentine decree: "I firmly assert that images of Christ, of the Mother of God ever Virgin, and of the other saints should be owned and kept, and that due honor and veneration should be given to them."[43] The Tridentine formula was again repeated in 1642 in the profession of faith asked of Eastern Christians by Pope Urban VII and so passed into the official and widespread teaching of the Catholic Church.[44]

In the fourteenth century the German Dominican Meister Eckhart had questioned the emphasis placed on the visual in the liturgy and devotions by his contemporaries because he felt that seeing was associated with activity, whereas hearing implied passive receptivity and availability to God's saving word.[45] In the same vein, Martin Luther and the other leaders of the Protestant Reformation stressed the importance of receptivity on the part of Christians in worship, since, as they claimed, salvation is totally dependent on God.[46] Luther himself was certainly not a violent iconoclast; he saw images not as dangerous but as simply ineffectual.[47] In contrast, Zwingli clearly encouraged and supported iconoclasm. In 1524 all the art from the Grossmünster, the church in Zurich where he was pastor, was removed and destroyed; likewise walls were whitewashed so that no traces of the old appointments were seen.[48] His action became a model for icon-oclasm in the Protestant areas of German-speaking Switzerland and south-ern Germany.[49] However, the iconoclastic spirit did not reach into all sectors of Protestantism; wall paintings from the period are visible in cer-tain Scandinavian churches to this day. In fact, some of the most splendid Gothic churches were built in England during the reigns of Henry VII (1457–1509) and Henry VIII (1491–1547).[50]

The two Protestant charges against the representation of God and the saints were blasphemy and idolatry. Claims were made that it was blas-phemy to represent God anthropomorphically, though it could be argued that God had become incarnate in Jesus and that in Jesus were to be found a truly authentic icon of the invisible God and consequently a justification for making copies of the true image. The charge of idolatry seemed more reasonable, since it was based on the fact that God alone deserved the honor that Catholics traditionally gave to the saints.[51] Catholics, however, defended the reproduction of images of the saints by maintaining that the saints were imitators of God and hence reminders of the holiness that human beings could attain by responding to the divine gifts of grace.

It is erroneous to claim that Protestantism killed artistic creation. John Calvin, who disapproved of religious images, recognized that the ability to paint and sculpt were special gifts of God.[52] Certainly various artists were highly respected in the Protestant tradition, including Rembrandt, Dürer, Grünewald, Holbein, and Jordaens. Lucas Cranach was a special friend of Martin Luther. Though these artists produced religiously inspired art based on biblical texts, they did not have as their main concern the production of religious art that would be used in worship. They tended to confine them-selves to illustrating biblical scenes, recounting events from church history, or illustrating the work of God in creation.

A number of positive reasons have been set forth to account for the Protestant attitude toward sacred art. First, Protestants were committed to the primacy of the Word of God and the human responsibility to listen whenever God speaks. They felt that the relationship between God and human beings should be as pure as possible and should be distanced from anything or anybody that might hinder or add to that essential relation-ship. The primary means by which God's Word comes to people is by preaching and the sacraments. They felt that the production of sacred images was the result of inadequate preaching. Calvin maintained that images were dangerous intermediaries and that behind the images were potential idols; he was so insistent on this point that he proscribed images.[53] Because of the emphasis on preaching the Word, pulpits were given a prominent place in Protestant churches; the people were gathered around the preacher, whose sermon was meant to bring the faithful together through the power of the Word and so build up the church.

A second reason for the Protestant attitude toward sacred images was their conviction that God's presence was not to be found in either monuments or images. Between the utter transcendence of God and the immanence of the world they held that there was an abyss that only God could bridge in order to approach humanity. It was a serious error on the part of humanity to attempt, through monuments, images, or other material things, to try to enter into a direct relationship with God. Certainly Luther fought passionately against any human effort to contain the divine within any persons, places, or things. For him, God was not located in a church or temple any more than in any other place. Every reification of divine grace, even if that reification would be in the eucharistic species, or any claim that God's presence could exist outside of the life-giving action of the Holy Spirit was condemned as a form of idolatry. Consequently, it was emphasized that art, even sacred art, does not contain in itself an immanent presence of the divine.

The third reason for rejecting sacred images was the conviction that preaching was the most suitable means to fulfill the church's prophetic mission. The Protestant Reformers emphasized the prophetic aspect of Christianity. They felt that God did not take up a dwelling in the world. The kingdom of God has come into the world but was not meant to remain there or to be immobilized. The church can only proclaim the kingdom as a reality that is still to come, even though it has already begun and is already manifested. The "already" is a sign of the "not yet." They maintained that preaching is the best instrument to fulfill this prophetic mission. The plastic arts were thought to be the least suited to express the tension between the present and the future, since architecture, painting, and sculpture produced works that were static, whereas speech and music were more mobile. Speaking and preaching were capable of breaking the bonds of a static universe.[54]

In the Reformed churches in Austria, Switzerland, the Netherlands, and Scotland, the changes in the medieval churches were often quite radical. For example, the chancel was often abandoned completely, so that the nave, as the place for hearing the Word of God, was looked upon as the only place necessary for worship. Choirs and organs were completely eliminated. A small table was placed at the head of the central aisle in the nave for the celebration of Holy Communion, which was distributed to the people sitting in their places. In Scotland the people sat around tables placed in the church aisles.[55]

The Reformation inevitably marked a watershed in the design and decoration of church buildings, since the Protestants generally had their own ideas, which differed radically from those embodied in the Romanesque and Gothic buildings. Among Roman Catholics there was no such break with the immediate past.[56] Out of the Renaissance grew the baroque, an exuberant proclamation among Roman Catholics of traditional Roman Catholic beliefs. The prototype was no longer the temple, as had been the case during the Renaissance, but rather the theater, which through the opera became a cultural focal point for the people, at least for those who were better off economically. For Roman Catholics, the focus of their worship was not so much the celebration of the Mass as the exposition of the Blessed Sacrament, which was reserved on the main altar. In the presence of the Sacrament a kind of grand opera was performed, with the high altar, profusely decorated with candles and flowers, as the centerpiece.[57]

In the baroque churches, however, emphasis was not only on visual experience but also on hearing.[58] Worshipers were concentrated in the large central areas of the churches, made possible by the width of the nave; there they could both see and hear. Pulpits were usually placed a third to halfway down the nave, where the preacher's voice could be better projected among the people. The choir, which traditionally separated the clergy from the other worshipers, was placed in another part of the church, often in galleries when they became available.

The Church of the Gesù in Rome, begun in 1568 and completed in 1584, was the mother church of all Jesuits; it became a model for Jesuit churches all over the world. The Jesuits had no need of choir space, since they did not celebrate the liturgy of the hours in common. They placed great emphasis on preaching, which was done from a pulpit that stood high in the middle of the north wall of the nave, and devotion to the eucharist, which was reserved in a tabernacle placed on the high altar situated in the apse. There were no barriers such as choir screens that would block the congregation's view of the altar. Hence, the Gesù is a great hall for preaching, lavishly decorated because, although the Jesuits valued poverty, they also were educators and hence valued images and their ability to form religious sensibilities.[59]

In the liturgy of the baroque church, words, spoken and heard, were meant to balance the visual symbols, so that auditory participation relieved any sense of visual overload. The function of the liturgical ministers was to embody, to act out, and to link, through word and gesture, the worshipers with the sacred world set out in the ceiling and wall paintings of whirling scenes of heavenly bliss. Angels, scriptural figures, and saints overpowered the worshipers so that they must have felt lost and insignificant in the midst of the strong beauty and timelessness of the spiritual world. That spiritual world, rendered visible in baroque churches, was not a chaotic world but an ordered world involving hierarchies indicating the steps by which one could reach the heights of spiritual power.

Certainly Roman Catholic churches contrasted markedly with the Protestant churches after the Reformation. Many of the Protestants eventually rejected the traditional sacrificial interpretation of the Mass as it was defended by the Council of Trent. Wars and religious strife at the time generally precluded any large-scale building programs among Protestants, who generally reordered the existing medieval churches they had taken over.

The basic problem that Protestants had with the late medieval church buildings was that they did not gather the congregation but rather divided it. The typical medieval church had several rooms in which various activities were carried out by different groups within the one body of Christ. Not only were there the nave and the chancel, often separated by a rood screen, but there were also numerous bays and chapels where additional altars were erected for the celebration of private Masses. The typical late-medieval churches were a series of compartments of more or less self-contained rooms intended to accommodate the different needs of the clergy, canons, monks, guilds, noble families, and the laypeople in general. The buildings tended toward longevity; hence when medieval churches were taken over by the Protestants they had to experiment with the space to make it work for their renewed understanding of the church and its liturgy.

Lutheran architecture initially reflected the noniconoclastic character of the conservative Reformation; hence altars, candles, crucifixes, vestments, and organs were generally retained. In his *Deutsche Messe* of 1526, Luther recommended that the priest should always face the people when celebrating the eucharist in imitation of Christ's position at the Last Supper.[60] In some places the altars were placed in the middle of the chancel and were sometimes adorned with carved reredoses and surrounded by a low circular fence. The numerous side altars were destroyed so that there would be only one altar in each church. The medieval side chapels were often turned into burial rooms for members of the royal families.

Because sacred images threatened to become idols, they were generally eliminated in order to suppress idols. Nevertheless, windows were often adorned with stained glass containing images. Likewise pictorial decorations appeared on interior walls, sometimes representing biblical personages. The cross often found a central place in the church, and the pulpit was frequently adorned with symbols such as the Alpha and Omega, the monogram of Christ, as well as figures of the Good Shepherd, the prophets, and the apostles. Candles were burned during advent to symbolize the coming of Christ the Light. Thus, sight, and not only hearing, had a place in Protestant worship.

Intense efforts were made by both Protestant and Catholic reformers to educate the common people, both adults and youth. Following the Protestant Reformation, education concentrated on the effective use of language, in contrast to the earlier and traditional education of children in the home as well as in monastic and cathedral schools. Earlier methods of educating children stressed the importance of pictures of saintly children to be imitated. By contrast, Protestant Reformers stressed the importance of teaching the catechism to children. Verbal instruction was communicated in a variety of media: preaching, pastoral instruction, catechetical examination, written treatises, and perhaps above all the new printed mass medium in the form of pamphlets, which replaced the traditional notice boards on the church doors. More than ten thousand different pamphlets appeared in the first half of the sixteenth century. Apparently literacy was more widespread in Germany at that time than is usually recognized. However, printed images were not absent from pamphlets and other publications. Luther encouraged the inclusion of illustrative images in his German Bible, published in 1534. It was maintained that printed images were not as dangerous to the faith as painted images, since they did not encourage devotional adoration, were not part of the liturgy, and were carefully labeled so that personal interpretation was kept to a minimum. Likewise the newly developed techniques of woodcutting and engraving enabled printed images to be mass-produced; furthermore, they were not vividly sensuous, as was often the case with oil paintings.

In general, the Protestant Reformers were keen to use images to accompany, illustrate, and reinforce verbal education. Certainly the images were to be balanced by verbal instruction, a role that artists who were associated with the Protestant Reformation seemed to understand. Although the advent of Protestantism did not put an end to the development of the arts in Protestant territories, the immediate effect was to curtail the quantity of religious images and the media through which they were presented. The educational efforts of pastors and parish visitors were quite successful in establishing an authoritative verbal culture and commitment to basic Protestant beliefs.[61]

After the Council of Trent, Catholic educational reform came slowly, and in the sixteenth century there was no effort to concentrate on the masses but rather to educate the clergy. In general, there was an effort to balance the aural and visual aspects of Catholic life and worship rather than intensify one to the exclusion of the other. New uses of images for the purpose of education, however, were both imaginative and effective. Sanctuary art, including paintings and sculpture, as well as other forms of devotional images and inspirational art, appeared in the second half of the sixteenth century and throughout the seventeenth.[62] The images usually exhibited a fresh intensification of feelings. Painted and sculpted figures in ecstasy were prominent, as were representations of saints meditating on death, possibly inspired by Ignatius Loyola's meditations on death in his *Spiritual Exercises*. The powerful stimulus of visual images for prayerful meditation was acknowledged by church leaders, and images were therefore incorporated both in public churches and in private homes and religious houses. In many ways the use and popularity of religious images among Catholics affirmed those aspects of traditional piety and belief that were severely criticized and rejected by Protestants. There was an air of triumphalism about the way Catholics used religious images. Certainly the existence of purgatory, the veneration of the Blessed Virgin, and the imitation of saints and martyrs were all strongly affirmed in visual images.

The radical difference between Protestant Reformers and Catholic Reformers might be effectively illustrated by a consideration of the works of three distinguished artists from the sixteenth century: Rembrandt van Rijn (1606–1669), Michelangelo Caravaggio (1571–1610), and El Greco (1541–1614).

Rembrandt van Rijn was certainly one of the greatest religious painters in the Protestant tradition. He came from a Dutch Calvinist or possibly Mennonite background. He produced prodigiously—about six hundred paintings, three hundred etchings, and sixteen hundred drawings. In the early decades of his artistic career he prospered primarily as a painter of portraits, though he also painted religious subjects, including a group of passion scenes and various Old Testament scenes treated in typical exuberant baroque fashion, including *Belshazzar's Feast* and the horrific *Blinding of Samson*. Some of his early etchings also combine the baroque sense of drama with an effective use of light and shadow, exemplified in his *Raising of Lazarus*, his *Descent from the Cross*, and especially his *Christ Healing the Sick*. After the death of his wife, Saskia, he painted and etched with a quieter, less theatrical feeling, in a manner that was more appropriate in a Protestant environment. His painting *Peter Denying Christ* and especially his *Return of the Prodigal Son* are works of utmost tenderness and emotional depth. He is universally recognized as one of the greatest etchers in history, a reputation gained for works like *The Three Crosses,* in which he produced one of the most awesome images of Christ's passion. In the Protestant tradition, he generally confined the subjects of his religious paintings and etchings to events and personages in the Bible.[63]

Michelangelo Caravaggio (1571–1610) was probably the most original and influential Italian painter of the late sixteenth and early seventeenth century, distinguished above all because of his religious paintings. His earliest religious work, *Flight into Egypt,* is a tender presentation of Joseph holding the music for an angelic violinist playing a lullaby for a tired Madonna nodding over her sleeping Infant.

Caravaggio's subjects are often portrayed crudely in down-to-earth settings, always dressed in the clothes of his own time, in a way that paralleled the Roman Catholic preaching of the time, especially that of St. Philip Neri, a contemporary who preached the gospel in the everyday images of the poor and humble people who followed him around the streets of Rome. Caravaggio was bitterly attacked for his blatant realism, for the dirty feet and fingernails and the patched clothes of the poor people portrayed in his paintings, for example, the shepherds shown kneeling before the Madonna carrying a heavy Christ child in the *Madonna di Loreto.* One of his greatest works, the *Decollation of St. John the Baptist,* encapsulates most of his artistic gifts. There is the realism of the brutal execution, the indifference of the prison guards, the horror of the old woman who looks on at the scene, the passive obedience of the poor maidservant who has been sent to collect the trophy, and the eager curiosity of the other prisoners peering from their prison bars, all depicted in light falling from a high unseen window. Caravaggio's subjects included not only scenes and personages from the Bible but also saints and events from the history of the church, something that was generally not acceptable in Protestant circles. His influence was immense, especially outside Italy.[64]

The artist whose work was most explicitly both Roman Catholic and doctrinal was Domenikos Theotocopoulos, better known as El Greco (1541–1614), for he was in truth a Greek, having been born in Crete. Early in his career he moved to Venice, where he was influenced by Titian and Tintoretto.[65] It was there that he produced his first version of the *Purification of the Temple,* a painting rich in color but lacking precision in perspective, composition, gesture, anatomy, and movement. In 1570 he moved to Rome, where he was influenced by Michelangelo, especially in his philosophy of art, which extolled the primacy of imagination over imitation.[66] By 1577, he had moved to Toledo, where he remained until his death. It

was there that his style matured and found expression in his elongated figures painted in cold, sometimes eerie, bluish colors manifesting the artist's
own intense religious feeling. He produced huge altarpieces, sharp and
almost violent in color, reflecting passionate and ecstatic emotions. He was
formed by his early training in Venice, by his own deeply religious temperament, and by the strong influence of the *Spiritual Exercises* of Ignatius
of Loyola, which encourage retreatants to enter deeply into the experience
of the passion and death of Christ, an experience manifested so clearly in
many of El Greco's paintings.

Almost all of his major works in Toledo were executed for churchmen
and have rich theological meaning. He was encouraged to create multi-
leveled works that distill Catholic doctrine. Though he himself was not a
theologian, he had close friends who were. He was committed in principle
to a non-naturalistic style that seemed ideal for setting out Catholic beliefs
and doctrines rather than events.

Doctrinal matters were of great concern to the archbishop of Toledo,
the primatial see of Spain, and he surrounded himself with able theologians, who befriended El Greco. These men were not mystics, and in fact
were probably hostile to the mystical trends prevalent in Spain in the sixteenth century. They did, however, have a vested interest in salvation and
eternal life achieved by the death and resurrection of Christ. El Greco lived
at a time when the Catholic Church was undergoing a period of intense
self-examination and reform. A great part of his genius lay in his ability to
portray in profound pictorial language the articles of faith and to arouse in
others, especially those who were more theologically astute, an affirmation
of that faith. He emulated the popular preachers of his day, especially those
who sought to stir up the spirit of the faithful as they traveled on their own
distinctive ways to the eternal life won for them by the death and resurrection of Christ.[67]

This survey of the reformation of the Protestant and Catholic Churches
and their liturgies leads us to conclude that there were major adjustments
in the roles of vision and hearing in both worship and religious education.
Protestant worship tended to emphasize what might be called the spiritual
equality of all Christians, with each baptized person equidistant from God.
The whitewashed churches and lecture halls of the Protestant communities
did not so much imply a rejection of visual participation as provide a radically different expression and experience of a nonhierarchically ordered
church and universe as a setting for Christian worship and life. For those
who were not educated to understand the ecclesiological implications of
the newly ordered churches, the new visual experience must have been one

of distaste or even ugliness, but for the well informed who saw it as a spiritual cleansing of triumphalism and the elimination of class distinctions in the Christian community, the experience must have been liberating. The Protestant Reformation was successful in communicating the visual message of basic equality among all Christians. The leaders of the reform did not intend that the visual experience should communicate political and social equality, but that was in fact the message received by many among the Protestant masses.[68]

The ultimate success of the Protestant Reformation was dependent on the emergence of a word-ordered religion and culture. As the people were gradually educated to attend more and more closely to words rather than to visual images, and as they became used to worshiping in churches devoid of visual images which emphasized the hierarchical nature of the church, a distinctively Protestant culture developed. Furthermore, the invention and use of the printing press resulted in the use of the reading eye as ancillary to the hearing ear. Vision thus lost its central role in Protestant religion and in worship. The medieval use of visual images to communicate a sense of self-identity, community identity, and an understanding of both the universe and God was replaced by linguistic symbols, metaphors, and stories. The Protestant understanding of the self, the community, the church, the universe, and God was imparted verbally through preaching, private and public reading of scripture, and doctrinal pamphlets.[69]

The Protestant reform also had a major effect on the education of church ministers, who were expected to be competent biblical exegetes and interpreters; they maintained that sermons were not to be simple moral exhortations. In all of this, Protestants were being trained to use their ears; if they used their eyes it was primarily for the purpose of reading.[70]

The Catholic reform did not undertake a transformation of society as a whole but rather concentrated on the education of the clergy, including the bishops. In baroque churches, a spiritual world was set out in visual images that were meant to project the real world in which Catholics not only worshiped but also lived their daily lives. Architecture, sculpture, and painting communicated a strong message about Catholic identity and the world in which Catholics were meant to live. That world was a hierarchically arranged world, both in heaven and on earth. The basic doctrines of the Catholic Church were clearly imprinted on the church environment; these included belief in purgatory, devotion to Mary and the saints, and the role of penance and suffering to be endured on the Catholic's journey to heaven. These reform measures were carried out not only by strong bishops but perhaps especially by the various religious institutes and confraternities established in the post-Reformation period, notably by the Jesuits. Although there were major doctrinal differences between the Protestants and Catholics after the reform movements, a crucial difference in the two groups was in the way they perceived reality. The message received by Catholics in their churches reinforced their traditional hierarchical understanding of the church and consequently their understanding of the social order.[71]

7

Seventeenth, Eighteenth, and Nineteenth Centuries

THE SEVENTEENTH CENTURY WAS AN ERA OF MUCH intellectual ferment and scientific discovery; consequently, religion was more or less marginalized and so settled itself quite comfortably into Protestant and Catholic camps, each intensely antagonistic to the other. Toward the end of the century, orthodox Christianity was challenged by pietism, a personalized "religion of the heart," as well as by the spirit of rationalism. It was inevitable that the various scientific discoveries would raise serious questions about the reliability of the Bible, that a much more positive understanding of the human person would champion free will over predestination, and that a new natural theology would be developed on the foundation of a new understanding of the cosmos. The clergy who were influenced by rationalism found the traditional worship books and sacramental practices objectionable, since they had no sympathy for any worship based on a faith they no longer embraced. The worship books of Roman Catholics and Anglicans were in general not affected by rationalism, but the Reformed and free churches were more vulnerable because they depended often on outlines of worship developed by the minister rather than formally approved rituals.[1]

During the seventeenth century, many new churches were built in a variety of styles—Georgian or Palladian in England, classical in France, and rococo in the rest of Europe. The ideal of the church as a eucharistic community was lost in much of Protestantism. In the post-Reformation period, the eucharistic ideal never came to mean for Lutherans, Calvinists, and Anglicans what it should have meant. It has been estimated that, in the seventeenth and eighteenth centuries, most Lutherans received Communion only twice a year, contrary to Luther's recommendation in his *Large Cate-*

chism that people should receive "often." The preaching of the Word became the general focus of Lutheran worship. The clergy and laity alike regarded Holy Communion as a rite to be dispatched as quickly as possible so as to get to the sermon, which was the chief focus of the Sunday liturgy.[2]

Among Calvinists, celebration of a weekly eucharist never established itself as normal practice. The first Sundays of March, June, September, and December were established as days for the Lord's Supper. Consequently, the meaning of the liturgical year was, for all practical purposes, lost in Calvinist churches as the sermon became increasingly important and dominated Sunday worship. When the eucharist was celebrated, it became an individualistic rite, surrounded by a dark penitential sense of unworthiness; hence it lost its communal and social dimensions.[3]

In the Anglican service, the eucharist also lost its place as the central rite of the liturgy. It was treated with less and less reverence and regularly became a mere appendage to morning prayer. The developing glories of the musical tradition in the Anglican cathedrals were lavished on morning and evening prayer, rather than on the eucharist. Following the English Restoration of the monarchy in the 1660s, some attempt was made to maintain a daily eucharist in certain cathedrals and London parish churches, but these were exceptions. In general, most Anglican churches celebrated the eucharist three or four times a year.[4] In all of these Protestant churches—Lutheran, Calvinist, and Anglican—the role of the laity in worship became one of "hearing."

The need developed in the seventeenth century not only to adapt medieval church buildings but also to construct new buildings for both Protestant and Catholic use as a result of the destruction of churches during the Thirty Years' War or by fire. Likewise the growth of urban areas and the relocation of large segments of the population, for example, to America, created a need for new structures. Lutherans quite readily adopted the new baroque external form but were sure to arrange the interiors of their buildings to reflect and facilitate the requirements of evangelical worship, which was often not possible when existing medieval church buildings were adapted. In many Lutheran churches the altar and pulpit were brought into close relationship. In Germany this often meant that the pulpit was placed directly behind and above the altar so it functioned like a canopy. The altar itself was still dressed with coverings and adorned with a crucifix and candles and was regularly placed at the end of a long central aisle. In some of the Scandinavian churches, the altar continued to be placed in a shallow apse, and the pulpit was placed to its right facing out into the nave. The baptismal font was translated from its traditional place near the entrance and was placed in the front of the church so that the people could witness the baptismal rite. Galleries were constructed, sometimes multitiered as in opera houses and theaters, so that the people could both hear and see the preacher. The usual place for the organ and choir in Lutheran churches was in a gallery at the opposite end of the church from the altar and pulpit. In this position the organist and choir could support congregational singing and execute church music such as cantatas without either disturbing or distracting the rest of the congregation.[5]

Lutheran and Reformed churches were somewhat similar in their designs; however, the Reformed churches usually did without organs, choirs, and other instrumentalists. They regularly had galleries in order to accommodate those who came to church to hear the preaching. Among the Reformed Christians, the altar was not a principal liturgical appointment, since Holy Communion was celebrated only four times during the year. Usually a simple table was brought in when needed and placed at the head of one of the aisles. Since preaching was the central activity of the service, the church buildings were usually designed in such a way that the people could be brought quite close to the preacher. At times the pulpit was placed in the center of one of the long walls rather than at the head of the longitudinal axis of the church.[6]

The Anglicans had to adapt their medieval churches for their own distinctive type of worship. This process has been defined as "taking the communicants into the chancel for eucharist, so that they can be within sight and hearing of the priest at the altar; and of bringing down the priest from the chancel into the nave so that he could be amongst his people for Morning and Evening Prayer."[7] In the Reformation and post-Reformation Protestant churches the rood screen became a slight partition that distinguished two liturgical centers, one for prayer and the sermon, and the other for the communion service; hence, the screen did not separate clergy and laypeople since they were together in the nave for morning and evening prayer and together in the chancel for Holy Communion. There was, of course, a third liturgical focus, that of the baptismal font, which was placed immediately inside the west door.[8]

Various experiments were carried out in Anglican churches to ensure that the liturgy, translated into the vernacular after the Protestant Reformation, would be heard, seen, and understood by the laypeople.[9] In place of paintings and sculpture in the churches, the Ten Commandments were set up at the east end of every church and chapel. Frequently they were framed in a triptych with the Lord's Prayer and the creed on either side. Though the latter were not required, it was felt that they conveniently summarized the Christian way of life, since they contained the essentials of Christian belief, prayer, and morality. Placement of the royal coat of arms, either painted or carved, also became a requirement in churches after the restoration of the monarchy in 1660. This was to emphasize that the sovereign of England was the supreme governor of the Church of England. The placement of the royal arms in churches was also customary in many French and Spanish churches in the seventeenth century.[10]

In 1666 a fire spread throughout a major part of the city of London, destroying St. Paul's Cathedral and eighty-four other city churches. This catastrophe had major effects on the Anglican Church and the future design of its church buildings. Christopher Wren (1632–1723), one of the greatest architects of the period, was chosen as the architect for fifty-two of the new parish church buildings, as well as the cathedral. In 1663 he designed a chapel for Pembroke College in Cambridge and the following year the Sheldonian Theater in Oxford, commissions that established his reputation as a superior architect. He designed churches specifically for the Anglican rite. In a memorandum on church building (1708), he explained that for Roman Catholics "it is enough if they hear the murmur of the Mass and see the elevating of the host, but our churches ought to be fitted for auditories," allowing "all to hear the Service, and both to hear distinctly, and see the preacher."[11]

In his design for churches, Wren combined his interest in the ancient Roman basilicas with the strong English preference for the Gothic, and so brought both styles to bear on the design of a space meant to facilitate worship according to the Book of Common Prayer. He was, however, very discreet in what he adopted from Gothic architecture, for he felt that it was a style of architecture suitable for a type of worship that was to be seen but not heard and in which ordinary worshipers were mere spectators rather than participants. If the Gothic style was characterized by aggregation, by the mere addition of further facilities when they became necessary, such as a Lady Chapel and other side chapels for private Masses, Wren's buildings adopted the classic principle of planning by subdivision in which the individual parts were clearly subordinated to the design of the whole building in the interest of aesthetic composition. Wren referred to his churches as "auditories."

St. Paul's Cathedral (1675–1716) was at the time of its construction the largest Protestant worship space in the world. It was superficially baroque

but was restrained and quite sober in its decoration, especially when compared with Catholic baroque churches such as St. Peter's and the Jesuit
churches in Rome. As a cathedral, the building required spaces for the
choir to sing the daily offices; the choristers, however, did not dominate
the space. The cathedral was designed so as to give the clear impression that
the whole congregation was gathered together under the immense dome as
joint ministers of the service. Neither St. Paul's nor the other Wren
churches come across as temples or houses of God; they are meeting places
for the Christian assembly. They were designed as simple one-room meeting halls. Wren's primary concern was that all who gathered could both
hear and see distinctly. He designed his churches in such a way that the congregation would remain passive and stationary in their pews and galleries
throughout the Anglican rite.[12] The stress on preaching required seats for
the congregation. The benches that were installed were usually enclosed by
high backs or even in boxes with doors.[13]

Archbishop William Laud (1573–1645), the archbishop of Canterbury,
opposed Calvinist theology and sought to restore something of the pre-
Reformation liturgical practice to the Church of England.[14] He aroused the
intense hostility of the Puritans, since he made the communion table rather
than the pulpit the center of the church. In that tradition, Wren's churches
generally had the altar tables placed in their east wall position enclosed by
altar rails on three sides at which the communicants knelt to receive the
eucharist. The pulpit was usually located to the north of the altar with the
reading desk to the south, both in close proximity to the congregation but
not in such a way as to suggest a separate chancel for the clergy. His pulpits
often had three levels with sounding boards in prominent places. They
were usually placed toward the middle of the nave against either one of the
pillars or on the north or south wall of the church. In his larger churches,
the three-tiered pulpits were often placed in the central aisle in front of the
altar, with the result that the minister had his back to the altar during the
service. Baptismal fonts were, as was the custom, placed at the entrance of
the church. Hence, although there was but one room in the church, there
were different foci—for baptism, for the liturgical offices, for the liturgy of
the Word, and for the celebration of Holy Communion. In contrast to
Roman Catholic baroque churches, where the altar was the main focus in
the church and was designed in such a way that it appeared to be a throne
for Christ the King reserved in the tabernacle on the altar, the altars in
Wren's churches were not intended to dominate the space. They were the
focus of attention only when the communicants gathered around them to
receive the sacrament. Many of Wrens's churches were in fact altered dur-

ing the Victorian era to reflect the concerns of the ecclesiological movement; high altars were put in place and much more prominence was given to the choir.[15]

In Wren's churches and those inspired by his designs, Gothic-type steeples held bells that summoned the people to worship. Large domes and curved ceilings assembled the congregation in an open room, where amplified acoustics enabled them to hear the word proclaimed and preached. Tall glass windows let in natural light so the people could read their Bibles and prayer books. Wren's churches stand as the glory of Protestant church architecture and became models for most Anglican churches in both Britain and America until the middle of the nineteenth century. The style is generally called Georgian, because England was ruled from 1714 to 1830 by four successive kings named George.[16]

Throughout the period of rationalism there were strong voices raised objecting to the direction being taken in both theology and worship, the strongest of which was probably that of the great awakenings first in Great Britain and then in America. Among the most influential voices were those of John (1703–1791) and Charles (1707–1788) Wesley. John Wesley's early formation conditioned him to follow an antirationalist direction. Born into the family of a high church Anglican parson, he was convinced of the need for inward holiness. At Oxford he was exposed to the beginnings of a high church movement that stressed a disciplined devotional life, frequent reception of Holy Communion, and a strong commitment to pastoral works of charity, especially among the poor, the imprisoned, and the illiterate.[17] On a journey to Georgia in the United States in 1735, John Wesley encountered the devout piety of the Moravians, which affected his overall approach to both theology and worship. The end result was the development of Methodist worship, which proved to be a strong countercultural movement in the midst of British enlightenment. It was countercultural in that it was enthusiastic and emotional, a characteristic frowned upon by traditional Anglicans. It reached out to the poor, especially those affected by the industrial revolution. It was Charles Wesley who provided the Methodist meetings with numerous hymn texts, which were sung not only at the preaching services but also during the celebration of Holy Communion. The eucharistic hymns give a clear indication of Wesleyan piety, because they emphasize the eucharistic sacrifice, the important role of the Holy Spirit in the celebration, and the eucharistic meal as a foretaste of the heavenly banquet.[18]

Methodist worship was countercultural also because it was deeply sacramental, emphasizing baptism, the Lord's Supper, and prayer as channels of divine grace. John Wesley believed that only an ordained minister should preside at the Lord's Supper, so his emphasis on lay preaching at meetings did not extend to the eucharist.[19] Because ordained ministers were not always available, especially in America, Holy Communion was celebrated less frequently, which led to the development of the Love Feast presided over by a deacon. Methodism in America was deeply affected by the individualistic piety prevalent on the frontier and by the enormous distances to be traveled by the ministers so that frontier revivalism replaced the liturgical life of the early Methodist societies.[20]

It is only in the eighteenth century that one can accurately distinguish a typically dissenting style of church architecture. Before that time Puritans and Nonconformists generally used temporary buildings with the hope that the established church would eventually come to understand them enough to accommodate their needs. These temporary buildings were simply cottages or larger private dwellings. Only the Quakers and the Baptists built their own worship spaces in the seventeenth century. Neither group had ordained ministers, and both detested any ostentation in worship as unworthy of authentic Christian religion. Their buildings were like well-scrubbed farmhouses with stone floors, white-washed walls, windows of clear glass, and open seats. There were no pulpits in either early Quaker or Baptist houses of worship.

When the Nonconformists built their own churches, they showed a marked departure from the medieval type of church structure. They were rectangular rather than cruciform and were designed as essentially auditory structures, designed for the preaching and hearing of the sermon and the prayers. They avoided all the Renaissance motifs in carving that often characterized Georgian established churches. Any ornamentation was thought to be contrary to the simplicity and spirituality of evangelical worship. Dissenters felt that worship was most fitting when it was freed from all earthly associations, and so considered any Anglican appeals to beauty, mystery, or symbolism as unworthy attempts to reintroduce the sensuous aspects of Christianity for which the Protestant martyrs had given their lives.[21]

The exteriors of the meetinghouses were just as devoid of ornamentation as the interiors; they looked like modest country houses built of good brick. Occasionally there would be a sundial on the south wall bearing a biblical inscription or the text *Memento mori*. Unlike the worship spaces of the established churches, which were dominated by the pulpit, the central position in the meetinghouse was reserved for the Communion table. This was a unique feature of the Dissenting meetinghouses. This followed from the fact that they were descendants of Calvin, who replaced the Mass with

what he and the Puritans called the "Lord's Supper." The Dissenters celebrated the Holy Sacrament not at a remote altar placed at the east end of
the church but at a table in the midst of the congregation. In fact the earliest arrangement for Calvinists at the "Lord's Supper" was to sit at the
Lord's table. As was customary in the Georgian churches of the establishment, the pulpit was lofty, to which the minister ascended to the third tier
for the sermon; on the second tier he led the prayers and the lessons; on the
first level, the clerk presided at his desk, from which he gave out the met-
rical psalms or hymns line by line.[22]

The general impression of the meetinghouse was that it was a very
dreary place. On each side of the pulpit there was a large window, but the
light would have been blocked from entering the other three walls because
of the galleries. The gloomy interior would have accented the black gown
of the preacher and the customary Sunday black clothes of the congregation. The heirs of the Puritans rejected all symbols in stained glass, wood
carving, and sculpture because they were committed to keeping the second
commandment; they did not dislike beauty, but they admired biblical
fidelity more.[23]

In the Roman Catholic Church of the seventeenth and eighteenth centuries, worshipers were concerned with their obligation to "hear Mass,"
but did not feel obliged to receive Communion. In practice, the Mass was
the priest's Mass; hence, the reception of Communion by the people had
nothing essential to do with the thanksgiving and praise of the eucharistic
celebration. The lay worshipers did not have an active voice in the Mass
prayers, since altar servers and choirs took over all the people's dialogical
parts. Hence, the congregation's participation was not considered essential
to the celebrant's actions. The altar was not so much the table for the sacrificial meal as a pedestal for the eucharist reserved and venerated in the
tabernacle.

In the second half of the seventeenth century, the temporal power of the
papacy declined and with it Rome's important role in artistic patronage. In
Italy, the cities of Venice, Genoa, the Piedmont, and Naples became important artistic centers. As the Catholic Church in Italy moved into the eighteenth century, two stylistic currents affected the design of church
buildings: one was the continuation of the late baroque style, the other a
freer rococo style emphasizing a skeletal structure, verticality, spatial
unity, and abundant light.

In France, the principal architecture of the seventeenth and eighteenth
centuries is called "classic" because of its dependence on the principles of
the high Renaissance. It developed at the time of the Enlightenment and

was characterized by a renewed interest in and a close study of the arts of antiquity. Baroque classicism is rational, reserved, and a distinctively French phenomenon that influenced most of northern Europe. In Flanders and Spain, church architecture was more fluid and sensuous than in France and less dependent on the high Renaissance.

A fully developed baroque style with an Italian flavor appeared in central Europe after 1680 because of the unstable political situation created by the Thirty Years' War and the expanding Ottoman empire. It was not until the eighteenth century that any independent work was produced. Especially important was the work of Jacob Prandtauer (1660–1726), whose commissions were primarily for monastic churches, most notably the abbey church at Melk (1702) and the abbey church at Weingarten in Germany, built between 1715 and 1723. The latter was the largest religious structure of the baroque in Germany.

The rococo style produced a general lightening of the baroque. The church buildings constructed in the style were airy, light, and decorative; they were rather fluid in form. Spread across Germany and Austria in particular, they were, from an architectural point of view, more secular than religious. Certainly the era of the rococo was not an age of great religious building. The various projects entertained one's aesthetic sensibilities but rarely edified or induced profound religious sentiments.[24]

The French Revolution of 1789 marked a significant change in the relationship between the church and secular society. France became a secular state wholly separated from the church. This arrangement was soon followed in many other European and American countries. Since the late eighteenth century, throughout the Western world, the state was increasingly conceived of as an independent institution, needing no religious sanction for the exercise of its authority or public forms of worship to express this authorization.[25]

Following the defeat of Napoleon at Waterloo in 1815, a strong political reaction was set in motion across Europe. Governments were determined to return to earlier forms, but they were inattentive to the need to control the economic changes that were taking place because of the industrial revolution. Wealth and power were quickly passing from the hands of the landed aristocracy into the hands of the large-scale employers in industry who put to work countless peasants displaced from their farms and herded together in crowded cities in search of employment. The squalor resulting from industrialization and urbanization was powerfully depicted in the novels of Charles Dickens, whose indignation at the social conditions of the poor was shared by John Ruskin (1819–1900), the Slade Professor of Fine Art at Oxford. He abandoned art criticism in order to champion the poor and denounce the ills of Victorian industry and commerce. In his *The Stones of Venice,* Ruskin extolled the architecture of the Gothic period and praised the society that was able to produce such impressive buildings. He explained that Gothic architecture was the result of free, intelligent, and creative workers, the kind of people whose creative powers were enslaved by industrialists in the nineteenth century.[26] Ruskin urged a Gothic revival, a call that was supported by the novels of Walter Scott, who nurtured in England a sense of nostalgia for the lost era of chivalry.[27]

The age of romanticism was rooted in a yearning after an ideal golden period of the past, whether it was to be found in ancient Greece, the high Middle Ages, or the sixteenth-century Reformation. It was a time when an effort was made to bring the resources of one age to the rescue of another. At times it was a mythical age that was invoked in order to reform the present. The suppression of the peasant style of life and the consequent depletion of rural communities caused by the industrial revolution inspired an interest in folk culture as well as village arts and crafts. All of this affected the worship of the church, for there were efforts to retrieve historical liturgies, music, architecture, vestments, and ceremonies as well as efforts to inspire a deeper spiritual life, recover clear doctrinal statements, and instill moral practices. The age of reason extolled the past and its diverse forms, but, as often happens, old forms were retrieved on a superficial level without the internalization of values and meanings.[28]

Although European architecture at the end of the eighteenth century was predominantly classical, the architecture of the nineteenth century itself, including that of the churches, was one of unbridled eclecticism. For example, classicism produced the Church of the Madeleine in Paris, built between 1806–1842. It was originally intended to be a secular temple but was later converted into a church by Napoleon. The classical influence was also expressed in England in the building of St. Pancras in London between 1819 and 1822, and in the United States in the building of the Basilica of the Assumption in Baltimore between 1805 and 1821, designed by Benjamin Latrobe.[29]

Toward the end of the eighteenth century there was a revival of interest in Romanesque and Gothic architecture, promoted especially by antiquarians. In the nineteenth century that interest was allied with the romantic movement. Cultural romanticism accompanied the democratic age and threatened the classical tradition; hence, a preoccupation with the medieval past increasingly informed art and architecture. The Gothic revival received a significant impetus in England from the writings and designs of

Augustus Welby Pugin (1812–1852) and was identified with social protest.[30] Pugin became a Roman Catholic at the age of twenty-three because he believed that the Catholic Church was the only true church and the only one in which the noble and sublime style of architecture would be restored, a style he identified with the fourteenth-century decorated period of English church architecture. He felt that style was a visible expression of the ideal church in the ideal period of its history. He urged a return to the Catholic faith and its expression in Gothic architecture which he felt was the last valid expression of Christian society before the Protestant Reformation. He was convinced that the return of Christians to the Catholic faith would set the Western world on the right track once again, and that medieval architecture was the expression of an integrated society where the worth of individual persons and the social fabric were not blighted by the industrial revolution.[31]

Commentators have maintained that Pugin was committed not primarily to a style but rather to an understanding of the church that underlay the style. The Gothic style which he spread across nineteenth-century England was essentially English in its roots, since Pugin's research into the Middle Ages was mainly confined to England. His style, however, was quite removed from the style of ordinary Catholic Church life in England during the first half of the nineteenth century, for the church was still suffering from penal times; its worship spaces were mainly chapels rather than churches; and it was beginning to be populated by many poor Irish immigrants.[32]

Pugin's theory was never seriously tried, but his writings and his architectural designs prompted a strong revival of Gothic architecture in England and also in Germany and France. His success was due to his native genius and very hard work, and also the patronage of wealthy Catholics and successful collaborators. He was described as a lone romantic figure working himself to death in his Gothic house in Ramsgate in an attempt to change the face of architecture and design. He dominated Catholic architecture for a brief time in England but was not without severe critics, including John Henry Newman, who felt that the whole Gothic revival was a form of escapism.

Pugin's understanding of the eucharist is reflected in his strong defense of rood screens, which he felt rightly expressed the great divide between the sacrifice of the Mass and the worshipers, and between the priest and the people. In spite of Newman's reservations, the Gothic style was in fact picked up by followers of the Tractarian movement in England, which emphasized the importance of the altar in a church and the legitimacy of symbolism. For the so-called ecclesiologists of the nineteenth century, a church was not an auditory edifice as it was for Wren but a sacred place for an altar which was placed at the end of the chancel. The altar was emphasized by elevating the chancel above the nave, thus also stressing the significance of the ordained clergy as successors of the apostles.

The Gothic style of architecture was naturally adaptable to church building. Through Pugin's influence, it firmly lodged itself as an ecclesiastical style in English-speaking countries, where it was supported by revivals in both the Anglican and Roman Catholic churches.[33] He built about sixty-five churches in the United Kingdom.

John Ruskin was interested not only in Gothic architecture and social reform but also in Pugin's ideas, which made a link between morality and art.[34] Ruskin emphasized the idea of worthiness as an essential ingredient in both church art and those who created it.[35] He condemned capitalist industrialism and sought to give practical shape to his ideas concerning the work ethic of the individual and production methods by founding in 1871 the Guild of St. George, with himself as the master. Members were expected to live and work in accord with Ruskin's moral and religious principles and to contribute to common guild funds; in return they received a just wage and enjoyed healthy working conditions and shared in community-owned farms and small industries. Ruskin's project attracted little response but it provided an impetus for later craft guilds.

Ruskin's lectures in London, Oxford, and other British cities attracted large audiences, and his writings were widely read and appreciated both in Britain and the United States, but it was William Morris (1834–1896), who was the founder of the Arts and Crafts movement in England. He, along with C. R. Ashbee and W. R. Lethaby, hoped for a return to a form of medieval society that would destroy the industrialized society of their own day. They were trained as architects but strove to bring about unity in the arts and crafts, since they felt that all creative efforts were to be revered. They wanted to reform design methods and restore quality to the work process itself as a reaction to the industrial revolution, which had devalued the work of craftspersons and turned them into mere cogs on the wheels of machines. The goal of the Arts and Crafts reformers was to restore harmony between architects, designers, and craftspersons and to bring well-crafted objects within the price range of ordinary people. Morris claimed that art should be not only by the people but also for the people.

Morris's assertions were directed mainly against the standards and designs shown at the Great Exhibition of London in 1851, Paris in 1855, London in 1862, and Paris in 1867. He started a firm that produced decorative articles and so had significant influence on English industrial design and interior decoration during the latter part of the nineteenth century. However, if one refuses to use any machinery, objects cannot be produced cheaply. Much of what Morris's firm produced was in fact expensive and could not be purchased by ordinary working class people. He succeeded, however, in inspiring young painters and architects in Britain and beyond and made them sensitive to the quality of the everyday life of many people. Unlike some of his disciples, Morris was not entirely opposed to the use of modern machinery, which he realized could relieve hard drudgery, but he criticized the machine when it displaced genuine artisans—people skilled in the arts and crafts.[36]

The movement, however, was not simply a sudden reaction to the ugliness of industrial society. It evolved out of the design morality of the Gothic revival in early Victorian Britain and was supported by a number of theorists and practitioners, including A. W. N. Pugin, whose books provided the theoretical foundation from which the moral aesthetes of the Arts and Crafts movement evolved.

In 1891, W. R. Lethaby wrote a short book entitled *Architecture, Mysticism, and Myth*. He summarized the idealistic nature of the Arts and Crafts movement at a time when it was in fact a major professional design force in Britain.[37] In England, the enthusiasts of the Arts and Crafts movement took to socialism as a way of life and moved to the Cotswolds, northeast of Bath, where they founded guilds and revived rural crafts. Continental visitors took the model home with them, which resulted in similar projects in Germany, Austria, Switzerland, and Sweden. In the United States, the movement was imported to California about 1900, where it called for a return to a preindustrial vernacular in both art and architecture. Hence, homes were to be built by skilled carpenters, not machine technologists. The movement venerated handcrafts, particularly objects designed by craftspersons dedicated to producing work that was both functional and beautiful. Buildings and their furnishings were to be concerned with a general composition and color scheme that would ensure continuity in tone, texture, form, and character. They were also to harmonize with the larger natural environment and to fit into the landscape as an integral part of an existing whole. Visual interest was meant to come from the design and craftsmanship of the structural elements themselves—exposed rafters, roof timbers, and modular wood framing.

One of the ideas that was central to the Arts and Crafts movement was that each country should have a distinctive architecture reflecting its history, geography, and climate. Embracing the principles of Ruskin and

Morris, American architects in the Arts and Crafts tradition condemned as artificial the symmetry and proportion characteristic of classical architecture. They rejected as flamboyant the style developed for large public buildings and encouraged a more domestic style of building designed simply to provide an enclosure for ordinary human life.

In the United States, the Gothic was looked upon as especially appropriate for church buildings. When Bertram Grosvenor Goodhue (1869–1928) joined the Boston architectural firm of Cram and Ferguson in 1891, they became the most important practitioners of the neo-Gothic style in the United States. Ralph Adams Cram (1863–1942) was a convert to high Anglicanism and a staunch follower of the Anglo-Catholic Oxford movement, which included the idea that Gothic churches were the most appropriate settings for Catholic rituals.[38] Goodhue was not so religiously motivated. He was, however, an Anglophile who had deep admiration for W. R. Lethaby's architecture.[39] The Boston firm was responsible for many commissions, ranging from the modestly scaled St. John's Church in West Hartford, Connecticut (1907–1909) to the grand St. Thomas Church in New York City (1905–1913), for which Goodhue designed an enormous reredos. In general Cram and Goodhue adopted the fifteenth-century perpendicular style, which was lighter than the Gothic style revived in Victorian England.

Goodhue and Cram helped to found the Society of Arts and Crafts in 1897. Modeled after the Arts and Crafts Exhibition Society in London, the Boston group promoted excellence in craft design and execution through exhibitions and sales. Goodhue and Cram regularly used the products of the society in the interior decoration of their churches, which exhibited superb wood carving, ironwork, silver plate, and stained glass. Cram had a close working relationship with Charles Cornish (1875–1945), whose studio produced some of the best stained glass in America. He was also a prolific writer, whose publications indicate a disdain for the modern world and its materialist bent; he attacked modern civilization and exalted the medieval world.

There is no doubt that the Arts and Crafts movement produced worthy trappings for both Anglican and Roman Catholic worship. To some degree it taught the churches to appreciate handsome, well-made furnishings. Unfortunately the churches failed to make much use of the most gifted exponents of the movement. As a result, a wide gap developed between the churches and the leading artists and designers. The artists suspected that science was replacing religion, and the churchmen were suspicious of the beliefs and morals of the artists. Consequently church goods were regularly bought from church furnishing shops, which carried wares that were dull, pious, and inferior in quality.[40]

RECOVERING THE PEOPLE'S WORSHIP

The ideas behind the Enlightenment and the age of reason certainly supported and influenced the spirit of political revolution that occurred first in America and then in France at the end of the eighteenth century. The French Revolution transformed life not only in France but also in much of the Western world. The privileges of the feudal system were abolished; human rights were championed; and the church was secularized.

A rebirth of liturgical community and a renewal of eucharistic worship among Lutherans, Anglicans, and Roman Catholics began in the nineteenth century as part of a response to the industrial revolution. A number of significant theologians and pastors found ways in which to relate an ordered worship of God to human beings as they struggled for a dignified existence in the midst of the dehumanizing conditions of an increasingly industrialized society. A number of Christian theologians sensed the marked alienation of spirit from matter and of the individual person from the community as the industrial revolution took a stronger and stronger hold on the Western world. Essentially the industrial revolution replaced human and animal work with machines, and organized much of the machine work into the factory system. Patterns of human life were radically changed for most people.[41]

Materialism was the basic philosophy of the industrial revolution; consequently, life in the Spirit was distant from the industrial world. Materialism manifested itself in a variety of ways: in the displacement of natural materials by machine-made goods, including steel, concrete, and glass; in the construction of new buildings; and in the impersonalism and indifference of workers, who often felt like mere cogs in a machine. Religion was looked upon as a purely private affair to be kept to oneself; it had nothing to offer in terms of the value of the human person and the human condition.[42]

The experience of community also declined steadily in the industrialized world. The long hours of hard work in the factories removed workers from their families and their rural communities. In the large cities like London, the churches could not begin to accommodate the newly transplanted population. Workers naturally complained that they were like slaves working for unknown millionaires who alone benefitted from the new inventions of the industrial age.

Among the most distinguished ecclesiastical voices to be raised in opposition to the inhuman conditions of the working class in England were those of John Keble (1792–1866), Edwin B. Pusey (1800–1882), and John Henry Newman (1801–1890), all part of what came to be known as the Oxford movement (1833–1845). The Oxford movement has sometimes been interpreted as having a primary concern for adopting Roman ritual forms, but, as a matter of fact, the principal Tractarians, Keble, Pusey, and Newman, were not at all concerned about rubrical details and elegant ceremonies. Their own liturgical style was more akin to a careful observance of the rubrics of the Book of Common Prayer. They were more concerned that the eucharist be celebrated frequently than that it be celebrated ostentatiously.

It was under the influence of the Cambridge Ecclesiological Society, and particularly under the leadership of John Mason Neale (1818–1866), that the external aspects of the liturgy became major concerns. The Cambridge Society was above all preoccupied with church architecture and Christian aesthetics in the face of the construction of many new churches in the early nineteenth century.[43] Neale, a founder of the society and a distinguished translator of early Greek and Latin hymns, linked the recovery of the Gothic architecture with the awareness of the poverty of church vestments. At that time the ordinary vesture for the clergy probably included a cassock and surplice with scarf, since the cope, chasuble, and stole had long since disappeared from Anglican usage. The ritualists were responsible for the retrieval of the cope and stole for solemn celebrations, along with the miter and crozier for bishops, as well as the chasuble and stole for the celebrations of the eucharist. Instead of taking over the short surplices and fiddleback vestments common in baroque Catholicism, the Anglicans adopted full and ample Gothic-style vestments. Since the new churches included chancels with choir stalls, surpliced choirs were developed that took on responsibility for singing the choral services on Sundays and major feasts. These well-trained choirs displaced the amateur singers and instrumentalists who formerly performed from the west galleries in Anglican parishes.[44]

These aesthetic and musical concerns, however, were not uppermost in the minds of the leaders of the Oxford movement. In the face of disapproval from the evangelicals, who stressed salvation by faith alone, and contempt from the English rationalists, among whom the liturgical life had simply fallen into total neglect, the leaders of the Oxford movement proclaimed that religion that was not nourished by a visible church with a vibrant sacramental system could not possibly sustain a vital spiritual life for people in an age of materialistic secularism. On July 14, 1833, John Keble, a high church divine at Oxford, preached a sermon denouncing what he called the "national apostasy" rampant in England. He stressed that a visible church is essential for the survival of Christianity and that bishops are necessary in every Christian church. He emphasized that the church of Jesus Christ is a spiritual organism deriving its authority from Jesus Christ and his successors, not from the British crown, the laws of Parliament, or the actions of sixteenth-century Reformers. He argued that the Church of England was not the *Protestant* Church *of* England, but the *Catholic* Church *in* England. In other words, the Oxford movement was aimed at returning the Church of England to a character reflecting the best in its Catholic past tradition.[45]

From September 1833 to 1841, John Henry Newman, a fellow of Oriel College in Oxford, wrote the Oxford movement's *Tracts for the Times* in an effort to stimulate a second reformation. He stressed that the Church of England was a divine or ecclesial institution with a social mission to the people of England and that Christ had established his church as a collective body; men and women were meant to assemble together, since it was in the context of community that God's life and grace were shared with individual persons.

After September 1833, Pusey strove to recover the communal dimension of the Church of England through a revival of eucharistic liturgy and piety and campaigned for the building of parish churches in the recently developed industrial towns in England. Previously the established church had achieved its privileges and prestige from a close association with the country gentry. Pusey himself had been reared among the landed aristocracy and was appointed Regius Professor of Hebrew at Oxford in 1828 by the Tory Duke of Wellington. But as a Tory he advocated the construction of a parish church in all the mill towns, where there were appalling social conditions. In his sermons he described the emergence of a new dehumanized economic individual cut adrift from all that contributed to a safe, healthy, and happy livelihood. He attributed this loss of community in English life to the growing chasm between the rich and the poor and the cruel conditions in which factory workers eked out their existence.[46]

By revising parish worship and promoting the construction of churches in factory districts and slums, Pusey reminded the working classes that they were in fact supported by the community of God's people and were embraced by God. He insisted that visible communities of faith and loving care were essential if there was to be a breach in the dehumanizing conditions in which so many people lived and worked. He was convinced that a revival of the eucharist as an essential component of Christian life could go a long way in helping the poor reclaim their dignity, and that a liturgy worthily celebrated could dramatize vividly the true Christian understanding of what it means to be a child of God.[47]

Pusey's strong conviction that the Church of England needed eucharistic communities in order to nurture its faith was encouraged by lectures and articles by the Berlin Protestant church historian Johann Augustus Neander (1789–1850), whose theology was grounded in the incarnational teaching of the church fathers.[48] The intense sense of human community articulated in the writings of the fathers, the conviction that community is expressed and constituted in the celebration of the eucharist, and the clear statement that the church must often stand in opposition to secular society were all lessons that Neander gave to Pusey. Pusey and his followers were convinced that active participation in the liturgy through ritual action and words, singing hymns, participating in processions, and frequent reception of the eucharist were the primary ways in which parishes and their congregations could bear authentic witness to Jesus Christ in the industrialized areas of England.[49] They felt that Puritan spirituality had deprecated the human body and condemned any material signs of religious experience as hypocritical; in contrast, Pusey and his followers espoused a sacramental church, which they felt could liberate Victorian society from its economic, political, and sexual oppression.[50]

For Pusey and his followers, there was a close relationship between the eucharistic liturgy and the Christian commitment to social justice. Funds for workers' compensation and for dignified burials as well as distribution centers for food and clothing were established. Likewise, the eucharistic bread and wine were shared equally with all members of the church regardless of class; baptism was administered to all with great dignity, even to the poorest of the poor; and all were welcomed to participate in the pomp and glory of all the liturgical celebrations. Certainly Pusey and his followers left a strong mark on nineteenth-century English parish life, a tradition that was continued by the revived Anglican religious orders, which effectively paired worthy liturgical celebrations with social protest and care for the poor.[51]

The Oxford movement had its counterparts in other religious denominations and other countries; especially noteworthy was the effort of the Danish Lutheran bishop Nikolai Grundtvig (1783–1872). As a young man he was influenced by the ideas and currents operating in the early nine-teenth century, including the Enlightenment, the French Revolution, and the early romantic movement. In the 1820s he experienced a pietistic con-version that drew him away from rationalism and toward more traditional Lutheran theology. Grundtvig's career as a churchman was turbulent, so it was not until 1839 that, at the age of fifty-six, he was appointed pastor at the Vartov home for the aged in Copenhagen, a post he held for the next thirty-three years. There he founded a movement in the Danish church similar to the Tractarian movement in England, with a high ecclesiology and stress on the place of the sacraments in Christian life; however, his pietist background eschewed any preferential treatment of the clergy. At Vartov he gathered about him a congregation of disciples who eventually formed the nucleus of the Grundtvigian Party, committed to their convic-tion that the incarnate Lord Jesus was encountered in baptism and the Lord's Supper. They worked for the spiritual and intellectual development of Danish artisans and small farmers and encouraged folk arts and crafts, including weaving, folk dancing, and storytelling, so that Danes might avoid the ill effects of industrialization and might live lives of simplicity and authenticity, close to the rhythms of the earth. Grundtvig was appalled by the intense individualism he discovered all over Europe and so sought to respond to the human need for community.[52] His emphasis on public worship was new at the time in Denmark, where the Lutheran Church was dominated by individuals and parties who had little time for worship. The Danish philosopher Søren Kierkegaard had stressed that the marks of the Christian life are found only in a strong personal and ethical commitment grounded in the teachings of Jesus. By contrast, the congregation was cen-tral to Grundtvig's understanding of his Christian faith; in fact, like Luther, he used the term "congregation" rather than "church" to describe God's people. He reminded his Lutheran confreres of the centrality of the Lord's Supper celebrated by the whole community, a practice that many of the Danish Lutheran churches had abandoned.

Through Grundtvig's efforts, the eucharist once again became the regu-lar form of worship in the Danish church, celebrated twice every Sunday and on festivals. He successfully integrated the products of the folk arts and crafts into the worship of the people by incorporating their weavings and carvings into the worship space, and he enlivened the services by including songs and dances. He also revived the liturgical year and wrote hymns for almost every day of the church year. He was convinced of the power of community singing to forge a strong sense of joy and unity among the participants. The hymns, however, were so new that they aroused great opposition among Grundtvig's enemies. Kierkegaard, for example, derided Grundtvig as "a noisemaker who will be unpleasant to me even in eternity."[53] However, it is perhaps above all as a hymn writer that Grundtvig is remembered by Protestants today, for his texts appear in numerous contemporary hymnals.[54]

THE ROMAN CATHOLIC CHURCH IN FRANCE, GERMANY, AND BELGIUM

By the time the Gothic revival began to influence the architecture of Roman Catholic churches, attempts were being made to reform liturgical practice. During the eighteenth and early nineteenth centuries isolated efforts were made to lay the theological foundations for a recovery of a sound biblical ecclesiology and vibrant sacramental practice, especially in Germany.[55] Pastoral efforts to bring the liturgy closer to the people, however, especially in the early part of the nineteenth century, were officially rejected.[56] More successful attempts at liturgical reform were initiated and consolidated by Abbot Prosper Guéranger (1805–1875), who refounded the French monastery of Solesmes in 1833. For French and German Benedictines, the reform of the liturgy began first of all in the monasteries. This revival has been the subject of diverse interpretations, not all of them positive. For example, Louis Bouyer pointed out the uncritical way in which the liturgical reformers of the romantic period adopted a great many of the most serious errors of the baroque. He felt that the worship of the monasteries was an antiquarian reconstruction and one of very doubtful authenticity on many cardinal points. The primary weakness lay in the scholarship underlying the reform movement. He criticized Guéranger for his efforts to exalt the Roman liturgy as if it were the most perfect and most catholic of all Christian liturgies.[57]

Other interpreters have been more sympathetic to Guéranger's efforts. He was deeply committed to sacred scripture and its interpretation by the fathers of the church, as well as to the value of tradition and its expression in the ordinary magisterium of the church. He was a keen apostle of the primacy of Rome and the superiority of Roman practices over all other liturgical rites. He favored centralized discipline rather than episcopal independence in liturgical matters. His monastery developed into a center for educating the laity in proper liturgical practice and for the reform of liturgical music in the Gregorian chant tradition. The abbey church was restored, however, in the Gothic style, rather than according to an early Roman model.[58]

The early efforts at liturgical reform in the nineteenth century were limited because of the lack of the academic resources needed for the project. The Roman Catholic Church was in various ways intellectually weak owing to the suppression of many of the great European universities during the French Revolution. Furthermore, the conservative traditionalism that had characterized the Roman Catholic reform in the seventeenth century developed by the nineteenth century into what might be described as a full-blown philosophy of Catholicism that was not open to critical evaluation and was irrelevant to history. There is no doubt that the monastic liturgy of the romantic era, such as was to be found at Solesmes with its restored Gregorian chant, a careful observance of prescribed rubrics, and an austere architectural and artistic environment cleansed of theatricalism, was impressive, but it was quite removed from the secular concerns of the world in which it was celebrated.[59]

In 1862–1863 Maurus and Placid Wolter, two brothers who had founded the Benedictine monastery at Beuron in Germany, went to Solesmes to experience the monastic and liturgical life there. They took much of the Solesmes spirit back with them to their monastery and eventually enabled it to spread to Beuronese foundations in various parts of Germany. In Germany, special account was taken of the pastoral aspects of the liturgy and its availability to ordinary people through the publication in 1884 of a popular hand missal, the *Messbuch der heiligen Kirche*, frequently designated by the name "Schott," after its original compiler.[60] In 1872, the monks of Beuron founded the monastery of Maredsous in Belgium, and so eventually the Belgian congregation also inherited the Solesmes spirit.

During the latter part of the nineteenth century, attempts were made to depart from the Gothic tradition in church ornament and art. A special effort was made by the monks of Beuron to develop a new and independent style of church art. Beginning in 1864, Desiderius Lenz, a sculptor and architect, developed his concepts in theoretical monographs, sketches, and art projects. He aimed at what he thought was a liturgically inspired art. He rejected the naturalism that was so prominent in both secular and sacred art at the time and reverted to primitive Christian, early Greek, and especially Egyptian art for his inspiration in the hope of creating a religious style that was ordered, serene, and hieratic in conception and style. After the decoration of the crypt church at Monte Cassino in Italy in 1913, the style steadily declined. In many ways the Beuronese efforts were unsuccessful because they were cut off from vital sources of inspiration.[61]

TRANSFORMATION OF PROTESTANT ARCHITECTURE
IN AMERICA

For approximately eighteen centuries, two basic spatial plans dominated Christian architecture: the basilical plan, which was more or less hierarchical, and the central plan, which was more egalitarian. In the 1880s in the United States, the profound social, economic, and technological changes taking place in the Western world contributed to the displacement of these traditions among Protestants in favor of the development of a worship space that was simply an auditorium. In the latter part of the nineteenth century, evangelical Protestant churches took the form of theaters or auditoriums as a result of certain changes in worship style and religious mission.[62]

In the early years of the nineteenth century, Protestants churches in America followed a typical form. The exterior featured classical Greek and Roman elements, typical of Christopher Wren's churches in England. Protestant churches were rectangular buildings oriented on an east–west axis. Unlike earlier Protestant meetinghouses, which were oriented horizontally toward a pulpit centered on a long wall, later Protestant churches, such as First Church of Christ in New Haven, designed by Ithiel Town, oriented the rectangular space on the longitudinal axis, centering the main door on the east wall and the pulpit opposite it on the west wall. The pulpit dominated the room, since it was elevated several feet above the main floor. A large west window behind the pulpit provided the minister with sufficient light to read the scripture and his sermon. Box pews filled both the main floor and the galleries, which were supported by Ionic columns running the length of the building on both sides. The formality of these churches, so different from the sober and unadorned meetinghouses of the Congregationalists and Puritans, indicated a gradual evolution of Protestant church architecture that would continue to shape and transform both the identity and mission of Protestant congregations in this country.[63]

This evolution is indicated in the design of the First Baptist Church of Minneapolis dedicated on December 19, 1896. There the rectangle of the early churches gave way to a square room oriented diagonally toward a corner that held not a pulpit but an elaborate stage elevated three feet above the main floor. A portable lectern served as a pulpit but was dwarfed by the features located behind it—the baptistery, the choir, the grand organ console, and the stenciled organ pipes that rose to the ceiling. The main floor continued the style prevalent in theaters, for the floor sloped upward from the stage to the back of the room. A balcony encircled most of the room, dropping gradually down to the stage level in a series of steps that resembled boxes in an opera house. The exterior of the building shifted from a classical Greek and Roman style, to a medieval one with Gothic and Romanesque characteristics. The overall impression was one of massiveness and solidity.

Early Protestant churches in the United States were certainly austere. Carving was generally limited to the pulpit, but in later nineteenth-century churches ornamentation was often extravagant. Wainscoting lined the walls; inscriptions of biblical verses, often highlighted with gilt, adorned the walls; colors highlighted the ceiling vaults and large gas chandeliers with crystal pendants hung from the center of the ceiling dome. Rich colors appeared in the stained glass windows, carpeting covered the floor, and cushions sat on the pews.

While these changes in Protestant church architecture are significant in themselves, even more significant are the changes in the transformation that would have taken place in the worshipers themselves because of the environment in which they gathered. In the early years of the nineteenth century, Protestants would have gathered on a Sunday morning to hear the minister offer prayer, read scripture, and deliver a long sermon explaining the biblical text. The congregation would have recited a psalm or sung a hymn. After lunch, they would have returned to church to hear more prayers and another sermon. By the late nineteenth century, the evangelical Protestant service had changed remarkably. The sermon was considerably shortened and would have extended beyond mere reflection on scripture to include commentary on social issues, prayers were not given extemporaneously but were often read from a service book, and the congregation engaged in exchanges with the minister by voicing a psalm or a prayer of petition or praise. Music was also a much more important part of the service and included organ solos and renditions by a choir and instrumentalists.[64]

These changes in the worship service were stimulated by and reflected major changes in evangelical Protestantism itself and reflected the broader social and cultural changes taking place in the United States. As Protestants altered their religious beliefs and practices, they also altered their worship patterns and the spaces within which they gathered, for there were indeed serious spiritual and social motivations that inspired changes in both cult and architecture, both of which were strongly influenced by the missionary thrust of evangelical churches in the United States. Their evangelical zeal was derived from their sacralization of the Christian family and resulted in the redefinition of the church building as a proxy home. As Jeanne Kilde has noted, "these new church homes drew heavily on the architectural contexts of the domestic sphere: from kitchen, dining room, and parlor spaces to the decoration of the sanctuary itself, church homes evoked family houses."[65] Protestant congregations developed into agencies for family ministry, offering each family member a variety of organizations and activities as well as spaces in which to pursue personal interests.[66]

Sacred architecture has always been imbued with important meanings and values, for churches form an important link between abstract ideas and concrete expressions, between doctrinal beliefs and the everyday lives of worshipers. Churches connect the transcendent and the immanent, the divine and the human, the human and the social. They are both expressive of reality and also constitutive of reality for those who worship in the buildings. In more religious terms, God, clergy, and laity meet in such a situation that relationships are negotiated and often transformed unwittingly.

The meanings and values associated with church buildings are often rooted in authority and power: the power of God in persons and communities; the power of the congregation within a specific social and political context; and the power of the individual worshipers. Churches are most often associated with the first kind of power—God's power in persons and communities; hence, a church is considered a powerful place because worshipers believe that God's presence is to be found in a special way within its walls. What late-nineteenth-century evangelical churches in the United States clearly demonstrated is the second category of power, namely, the power of the congregation within a specific social and political context.

Throughout history, Christian churches have provided the context in which there have regularly been displays of social power—the power of the clergy; the power of the wealthy, especially benefactors and patrons; and the power of the assembled laity. Since the apostolic era, Christians have gathered in spaces designed not only to accommodate their physical presence but also to facilitate the execution of roles determined by status within the assembly, for example, the ordained sitting in special places and on special seats; laity gathered outside the chancel; women on the left and men on the right; and whites on the main floor, blacks in the gallery. The exteriors of church buildings also proclaimed the social significance of the congregation; for example, a modest storefront church said something different from a grand cathedral sitting on a prominent hill.

Ever since the Reformation, Protestants had been engaged in a search for appropriate worship spaces. Early in their history they minimized the visual nature of Christian worship, especially as it had dominated the celebration of the eucharist in the Middle Ages. Influenced by the development of the printing press and by increased literacy among the masses, Martin Luther and other Reformers emphasized the written and spoken word as the most important medium for divine revelation. Hence, the sermon emerged as the focus of Protestant worship. It linked otherwise diverse Reformation movements and generally displaced the Mass, which was at the time primarily a visual ritual.

Initially the Protestant Reformers concentrated their attention on the furniture within the church, replacing the main altar with the pulpit as the focus of attention. The Protestant pulpits, which loomed high above the main floor of the church, visually communicated a top-down sense of clerical authority and power in the congregation. It was this change in the interior of the church that radically transformed the power relationship between the clergy and the laity. With his power to interpret the Word of God for the congregation, the minister both literally and figuratively transcended the lay assembly.

The floor plan of Reformation churches physically proclaimed clerical power but in a way quite different from Roman Catholic churches. Roman Catholic priests derived their authority through ordination by a bishop, which gave them a direct line to Jesus Christ through the historical episcopate. The holiness, separateness, and mysteriousness of the medieval chancels where the priests presided over the liturgy articulated the distinctiveness of the ordained priests, just as their special power to confect the eucharist gave them the power to reveal and conceal God. The Protestant Reformers rejected the doctrine of apostolic succession; hence they both theologically and visually separated their own authority from that of Jesus Christ. Their power was dependent on their erudition, their ability to proclaim and interpret the scriptures. But such authority was not self-appropriated; it was granted by the congregation, who had to agree that the minister's talent and education warranted his right to occupy the pulpit.

OTHER ARCHITECTURAL DEVELOPMENTS

In the nineteenth century, the concerns of secular and ecclesiastical architecture differed considerably. The absence of city walls and uncontrolled industrial development made way for sprawling agglomerates where factories, slums, and railroads were often most prominent.[67] Urban plans simply called for orthogonal grids divided into similar building lots treated as mere economic commodities; hence, meaningful development was replaced by a coordinating system in which structures were built without any serious account being taken of the environment.[68]

The new situation created by the social, economic, and industrial revolutions stimulated a vast number of building projects. During the nineteenth century, however, the church and the palace lost their importance as central places in the new towns and cities and were replaced by the factory, the office building, the domestic dwelling, the museum, the theater, the exhibition hall, and the monument. In a sense the monument symbolized a desire to return to original archetypal forms; it expressed a longing for eternity. The museum became an aesthetic worship space where human art works could not only manifest creativity but also stimulate aesthetic experience as a replacement for religion. The exhibition hall displayed the economic achievements of the new capitalist society, while the factory and office building represented its productive power. A pluralism of meanings and desires interacted in various ways but clearly replaced the integrated and hierarchical order of life that existed in the past.[69]

Because of fresh developmental tasks, a new spatial image developed after the middle of the nineteenth century. Development of large halls for production, distribution, and exhibition, as well as construction of office buildings and dwellings constituted the primary architectural tasks; they also determined the character of the environment in which most people lived. The hall developed above all in Europe as iron and glass were used to erect large factories, railway stations, department stores, and exhibition buildings. The hall was a unitary space into which other elements could be freely placed. In contrast, the office building was a repetitive, orthogonal edifice that could be extended both horizontally and vertically. It developed as a skeleton construction, thus preparing the way for the skyscraper. The one-family dwelling was the third basic building type of the latter part of the nineteenth century. Influenced especially by Frank Lloyd Wright (1867–1959), it departed from the traditional box to achieve a vital interaction between the interior and exterior space, at least for those who could afford to move out of the slums and into a more humane environment.[70]

The multiplicity of the new building tasks in the nineteenth century stimulated architects to experiment with forms taken from various styles, representing a cultural heritage of diverse meanings. Hence, a style was usually chosen that was thought to be best suited to the project at hand. The museums and universities as museums of knowledge were often built in the classical style, whereas churches were built in the Gothic style.[71]

In general, nineteenth-century architecture attempted to create a sense of open space, a limitless and continuous environment where people could act and move about freely, not for the sake of movement but as an expression of freedom to search for, choose, and create one's own place. This concept was realized in the large halls of iron and steel, in the office buildings, and in human dwellings. The basic goal behind the new image of space was liberation from past confining systems. Men and women of the Enlightenment did not want to be restricted in any way. The slogan "Liberty, equality, fraternity" captured the ideals effectively. The Enlightenment concentrated on sensation, so that the illusive, allegoric image of the baroque was replaced by the natural, authentic image in both science and art. The rationalism and romanticism of the nineteenth century were two different reflections of the same fundamental attitude.[72]

The new architecture of the nineteenth century naturally gave priority to the building tasks associated with work and human dwelling. Understandably it was not accepted by the totalitarian movements of the twentieth century. The new spatial images created in the nineteenth century surely possessed a fundamental symbolic meaning. That meaning, however, was far removed from the harsh reality experienced by most people in the Western world. It is for that reason that the idea of freedom hailed during the nineteenth century was undoubtedly more illusion than fact.[73]

There was also a Romanesque revival parallel to the Gothic revival, which resulted in a style that mixed Byzantine and Renaissance along with Romanesque. The Germans called the revived style *Rundbogenstil* because the round-arched style was implemented throughout Europe. It was also used in the United States, especially by H. H. Richardson (1834–1886), whose best church work is Trinity Church in Boston (1873–1877). A Romanesque-Byzantine style also characterized Paul Adabie's Church of the Sacré Coeur in Paris, begun in 1874 and largely finished by 1900. London's Westminster Roman Catholic Cathedral (1895–1903) by J. F. Bentley is more Byzantine than Romanesque. Perhaps the most extraordinary Gothic-derived church is that of the Sagrada Familia in Barcelona. Designed by Antonio Gaudí (1852–1926) and begun in 1884, it is still unfinished but stands as one of the grandest ecclesiastical monuments produced in the nineteenth century. These various revived styles continued to be implemented well into the twentieth century until they were generally replaced by more modern styles after World War II.

Notes on the Photographs

The contemporary churches and artworks discussed in the book and shown in the following photographs are located in the United States, England, and Ireland because these are the countries that I know best. Because of my own Benedictine background, monastic churches are especially featured in the photographs. The churches have been chosen not because they necessarily illustrate great architecture that facilitates an experience of the transcendent but because they are structures that reflect sound liturgical theology and practice. Christian churches are meant to be sacred places in which the church, the body of Christ, gathers to celebrate the paschal mystery of Jesus Christ through the power of the Holy Spirit. Many of the churches are not new structures but old buildings that have been renovated. The sacred artworks discussed in the text and shown here have been executed by distinguished artists. They have found an appropriate place in churches because they are beautiful, have inspired devotion in the communities that frequent the churches, reflect sound theology, and are carefully related to the sacred mysteries celebrated in churches.

Nos. 1 and 2. Exterior and interior views of the Abbey Church at Mepkin Abbey, Moncks Corner, South Carolina. Architectural team: Theodore Butler and Frank Kacmarcik. The church is consonant with the Cistercian tradition; it is not monumental but is the central building among the other handsome structures that make up the monastic complex. Beauty is found in the lines of the structure and the materials used, in the light and shadows in the space, in the careful design and execution of the altar, ambo, presider's chair, and holy water font, and in the choir stalls. The space is extraordinarily hospitable; it responds carefully to the distinctive roles of the monks in the liturgy but also brings guests into a close relationship with the monks. It is clear that the whole assembly is celebrating the liturgy. Even without an assembly present, the church is not simply an empty shell but proclaims some part of its meaning by its very existence.

No. 3. Cathedral of Saint John the Evangelist, Milwaukee, Wisconsin. The renovation of this cathedral is eminently successful. Richard Vosko served as the architectural/liturgical consultant. The axis of the building has been changed so that the community gathers around the altar. The rich stained glass windows have been retained and the original color scheme has been restored. There are excellent sculptures in the space, but they are discreetly placed so as not to distract from the celebration of the liturgy. The worship area has been carefully related to the adjacent building housing the archdiocese's social services. Thus, the complex emphasizes the meaning of the eucharist beyond the church building.

No. 4. Church of the Irish Martyrs, Naas, Ireland. Architect: Eamon Hedderman. This is a new construction. In this original design, the assembly gathers on both sides of the altar, ambo and presider's chair facing each other. There is a sense of transcendence in the space accompanied by an honest use of materials. Light is diffused throughout the building from the ceiling and the stained glass windows.

No. 5. Our Lady of the Wayside, Jenkinstown, Ireland. Architect: Rooney and

McConville. In this church the assembly gathers in an antiphonal form surrounding the altar, ambo, and presider's chair. Circular altars are not common in the United States, but they are not unusual in Ireland and England. In Our Lady of the Wayside, the strong circular altar functions as a mandala symbolizing completeness and perfection.

No. 6. Cathedral of Saint James, Seattle, Washington. In this renovated space, the strong altar is surrounded by the bishop's cathedra, the ambo, and the presider's chair. Every effort was made to bring the assembly into close relationship with the actions taking place in the central area of the space.

No. 7. Chapel of the Sacred Heart, Saint Benedict's Monastery, Saint Joseph, Minnesota. Architectural team: Theodore Butler and Frank Kacmarcik. In this original renovation project, special effort was made to include as much of the old chapel as possible, so that the Benedictine Sisters would sense a continuity between the old and the new. The fact that the assembly gathers on four sides of the altar makes effective preaching and presiding a challenge.

No. 8. Saint Peter's Lutheran Church, New York City. Architect: Hugh A. Stubbins, Jr.; Designers: Vignelli Associates. This well-known building facilitates a variety of celebrations because all the appointments, including the various platforms, are portable.

No. 9. Worth Abbey Church, Crawley, West Sussex, England. A large parish and school are served from the abbey. The church, designed to accommodate assemblies of a thousand, is the largest church in the local Roman Catholic diocese; hence it serves the local community well. When the monks celebrate the liturgy of the hours, guests join them in the choir area. The overall space easily contracts and expands by controlled lighting, so that it serves well both for liturgical celebrations and for personal prayer.

No. 10. Saint Meinrad Archabbey Church, St. Meinrad, Indiana. Great care was taken in planning the renovation of this church, so that the altar, ambo, and presider's chair are all in themselves distinctive works of art, as is the floor. The organ pipes effectively frame the strong figure of Christ in the apse.

Nos. 11, 12, 13, and 14. Almost all Roman Catholic churches and many Anglican/Episcopal churches have an image of Mary, the Mother of Jesus. These images of the Mother and Child shown here reflect the diverse cultures from which the sculptors have come. For about fifteen centuries Mary was always identified as the mother of God, and she was regularly portrayed in art in close association with her Son. In the representations of modern apparitions, she is frequently shown without the child. That latter representation runs the risk of encouraging sound mariology to degenerate into mariolatry. Mary is not only the Queen of Heaven; she is above all the Mother of God and our mother. No. 11. The bronze sculpture of Mary Seat of Wisdom in Mepkin Abbey Church is the work of the Jewish artist Alexander Tylevich. No. 12. The print of Mother and Child is the work of the distinguished Japanese print maker Sadao Watanabe. No. 13. This moving sculpture of the Pregnant Mary is the work of the Australian Aboriginal artist George Mung.

It portrays Mary as the living Bible, bearing the eternal Word written in both her heart and her womb. No. 14. This simple but lovely Madonna and Child in Christ Church Cathedral, Dublin, Ireland, is the work of Imogen Stuart, a well-known German artist who has resided in Ireland for many years.

No. 15. The Walking Madonna by Elizabeth Frink stands outside Salisbury Cathedral in England. A strong figure, she walks with purposeful compassion as a member of the Christian community to bring the love of her Son Jesus Christ to the area surrounding the cathedral.

No. 16. This is the thirteenth station of the cross, "Jesus is taken down from the cross," by Imogen Stuart. The figures communicate a deep sense of power and pathos. The stations are in the parish of Firhouse Church of Our Lady of Mount Carmel in Ireland.

No. 17. The figure of the Christus by Peter Eugene Ball hangs in the Anglican Cathedral in Portsmouth, England. It has been carved from a single piece of driftwood.

No. 18. The bronze statue of St. John the Baptist overlooks the baptistery in Saint John's Abbey Church in Collegeville, Minnesota. John points away from himself to the waters of baptism and ultimately down the church isle to the altar, where the final stage of Christian initiation is celebrated.

No. 19. This sculpture of St. Anselm of Canterbury is the work of the English artist Peter Watts. It hangs in a small chapel beneath Saint John's Abbey Church in Collegeville, Minnesota. Carved from Bath stone, which is beautiful in texture, the figures are caught in the middle of the rite as Augustine baptizes King Ethelbert of Kent.

No. 20. The baptistery in the Cathedral of Our Lady of the Angels in Los Angeles was designed by Richard Vosko. It occupies an autonomous space so that the assembly can easily gather around it for baptism and other rites. The design allows for baptism by immersion and is planned carefully so that there is no danger of anyone falling into the baptismal pool.

No. 21. This altar, designed by Frank Kacmarcik, stands in the church of New Melleray Abbey in Peosta, Iowa. It derives its strength not because of its grand size but because of its clear lines, the texture of the granite, and its rich color.

No. 22. This design for the reservation of the Blessed Sacrament in Saint Mary's Oratory at Saint Patrick's College in Maynooth, Ireland, is the work of Richard Hurley. The enameled copper tabernacle is the work of Benedict Tutty, O.S.B.; the oil on canvas surrounding the tabernacle is the work of the Dominican artist Kim En Joong; and the brass-on-stone tabernacle lamp is the work of the Irish architect Richard Hurley.

1. Exterior of the Abbey Church at Mepkin Abbey, Moncks Corner, South Carolina

2. Interior of the Abbey Church at Mepkin Abbey, Moncks Corner, South Carolina

3. Cathedral of Saint John the Evangelist, Milwaukee, Wisconsin

4. Church of the Irish Martyrs, Naas, Ireland

5. Our Lady of the Wayside,
Jenkinstown, Ireland

6. Cathedral of Saint James, Seattle, Washington

7. Chapel of the Sacred Heart, Saint Benedict's Monastery, St. Joseph, Minnesota

8. Saint Peter's Lutheran
Church, New York,
New York

9. Worth Abbey Church, Crawley, West Sussex, England

10. Saint Meinrad Archabbey Church, St. Meinrad, Indiana

11. Mary Seat of Wisdom, Mepkin
    Abbey Church, Moncks
    Corner, South Carolina.
    Sculptor: Alexander Tylevich

12. Mother and Child.
    Print by Sadao Watanabe

13. The Pregnant Mary, Turkey
    Creek in East Kimberley
    region of Western Australia.
    Sculptor: George Mung

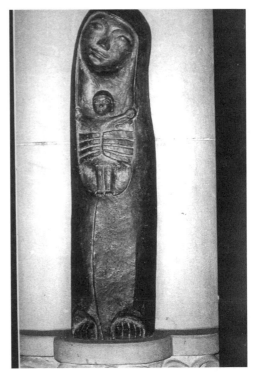

14. Madonna and Child, Christ
    Church Cathedral, Dublin,
    Ireland.
    Sculptor: Imogen Stuart

15. The Walking Madonna,
    Salisbury Cathedral, England.
    Sculptor: Elizabeth Frink

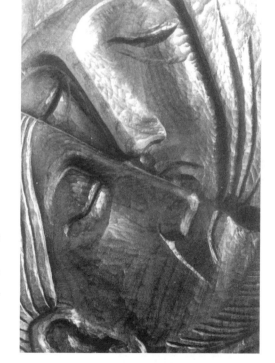

16. Jesus is taken down from the
    cross. Firhouse Church of
    Our Lady of Mount Carmel,
    Ireland. Thirteenth station.
    Sculptor: Imogen Stuart

17. Christus, Anglican Cathedral in Portsmouth, England. Sculptor: Peter Eugene Ball

18. Bronze statue of Saint John the Baptist in Saint John's Abbey Church, Collegeville, Minnesota. Sculptor: Doris Cesar

19. Saint Anselm of
    Canterbury in Saint
    John's Abbey Church,
    Collegeville, Minnesota.
    Sculptor: Peter Watts

20. Baptistery in the Cathedral of Our Lady of the Angels in Los Angeles,
    California. Designed by Richard Vosko

21. Granite altar in the church in New Melleray Abbey, Peosta, Iowa. Designed by Frank Kacmarcik

22. Reservation of the Blessed Sacrament in Saint Mary's Oratory at Saint Patrick's College in Maynooth, Ireland. Designed by Richard Hurley

8

Architectural and Liturgical Reforms in the Twentieth Century

ALTHOUGH THERE WAS AN INTRUSIVE THRUST OF MODERNISM into the arts following the First World War, nineteenth-century romanticism survived in various forms among distinguished artists. For example, in music, romanticists such as Claude Debussy, Anton Bruckner, and Serge Rachmaninoff flourished at the same time as modernists Igor Stravinsky and Arnold Schoenberg. In the realm of poetry, Robert Frost and William Butler Yeats were taken just as seriously as Ezra Pound and T. S. Eliot. However, the modernists in art, architecture, music, and literature seemed to be radical because they tended to probe the inner meaning of reality. Some of them indeed appeared to be rather violently antiromantic. Nevertheless, gifted artists like Walter Gropius in architecture, Pablo Picasso and Henri Matisse in painting, Igor Stravinsky in music, and James Joyce in literature were not disinterested in tradition; in fact some of them were described as primitivists. The cultural upheavals of the twentieth century caused by world wars, Communist revolutions, totalitarian governments, amazing technological progress, and extraordinary developments in the communications media seemed to have two alternative results. On the one hand, they encouraged nostalgia for an imagined past with its simple, uncomplicated lifestyle, and on the other fostered primitivism as a reflection of the cultural situation into which the modern Western world was moving.[1]

Rethinking the past and the sense of tradition also had its significant effects in theology, perhaps especially in the study of the Bible. For example, Rudolf Bultmann proposed "demythologizing" the New Testament, while church historians and liturgists engaged in a critical analysis of texts and practices. The goal was to get at what was thought to be the original meaning of texts and the original intentions of the authors by peeling away the layers of interpretation that had obfuscated the original core meaning. This all led to the development of neo-orthodox systems of theology, exemplified by the great dogmatic syntheses produced by Karl Barth, Paul Tillich, Karl Rahner, Edward Schillebeeckx, and Hans Urs von Balthasar. Theologians applied the historical-critical method of interpretation to the earlier syntheses produced by the great theologians of the past, including Thomas Aquinas, Martin Luther, and John Calvin, as well as to historical creeds and documents of the ecumenical councils. It is significant that some of the most important liturgical scholars of the twentieth century were in fact historians, including Josef Jungmann (Catholic), Gregory Dix (Anglican), Luther Reed (Lutheran), and William Maxwell (Presbyterian).[2]

Romanticism was at times severely criticized by liturgical scholars such as Louis Bouyer.[3] But use of the historical-critical method often led to the idealization of the patristic period as the golden age of the church's liturgy.[4] Dom Guéranger looked upon the Middle Ages as the ideal period in liturgical celebration, but a hundred years after him, the abbot of Maria Laach, Ildefons Herwegen, showed that the liturgy in the Middle Ages was already overburdened with allegorical interpretations and devotional elements that were foreign to the biblical and patristic roots of the liturgy. Many liturgists, then, looked for a clear apostolic model on which all liturgical celebrations should be based, but what was often assumed to be the original ritual and textual form has recently been questioned.[5] Liturgical studies in the last century went hand in hand with patristic studies, since the texts of the fathers were made available in both critical editions and careful translations, in series such as *Sources chrétiennes* and *Ancient Christian Writers.* The study of the early sources revealed earlier practices that liturgists thought could well be incorporated into contemporary celebrations, such as Mass facing the people, emphasis on the epiclesis in the eucharistic prayer, a wider use of biblical pericopes, the public and communal celebration of the rites of Christian initiation, and the celebration of the liturgy of the hours by the whole community, rather than simply by clergy and religious. This emphasis on the community as the true subject of liturgical celebration was thought to be a sound pastoral response to the intense individualism and pragmatism of much of Western society.[6]

As we shall see, many of the aspirations of those involved in the modern liturgical movement not only had spiritual affinities with the hopes of the Protestant Reformers but also with earlier post-Tridentine developments in the Catholic Church. Leaders of the modern movement would disclaim any links with Jansenism, Roman Catholic modernism, or the *Aufklärung*. There is no doubt, however, that a movement which embraced reforms of a surprisingly similar nature to those of the modern liturgical movement was Jansenism, especially as it was promoted by Abbé Jube d'Asnières and the Synod of Pistoia, whose acts were condemned in 1786 by Pius VI. Among the positive hopes for reform that the synod proposed were a return to an emphasis on the Bible, a return to the liturgical practices of the early church and the writings of the fathers, and translation of the liturgy into the vernacular languages. The twentieth-century focus on the community as the primary celebrant of the liturgy naturally raised questions about the buildings in which the liturgy was customarily celebrated, and developments in contemporary architecture were brought into the discussions of the liturgy.

ARCHITECTURAL DEVELOPMENTS
IN THE TWENTIETH CENTURY

Since the middle of the eighteenth century there have been recurring efforts to develop a dominant style in architecture such as existed in earlier periods. The chief attempts were the classical and Gothic revivals, but in the long run both failed to respond effectively to new needs and new methods of construction made available through progress in industry and engineering. The diverse styles that were produced in the nineteenth century were in many ways simply decorative additions to architecture; the overall impression was one of rather chaotic eclecticism.[7]

It was between the First and Second World Wars that a clearly defined new style emerged, known as the international style. The variety and confusion of the nineteenth century gave way to a uniform and readily recognizable approach to architectural design. The buildings of that interim period were usually derived from simple stereometric shapes; they appeared to be unitary volumes enveloped by a thin, weightless skin of glass and plaster; they were austere and severe, usually lacking in obtrusive material texture and articulate detail. The distinguished architects of the period developed buildings that were transparent structures, designed in such a way that each component merged naturally into the comprehensive volume of the whole.[8] The structures furthered the concepts of spatial continuity and transparency, but they also recalled the elementary shapes and geometric relationships that had been introduced into architecture in the late eighteenth century.[9]

The period between the two world wars was characterized by a search for sound architectural principles. The availability of the steel frame, reinforced concrete, and environmental engineering challenged architects to design buildings that combined them in new forms. Louis Sullivan (1856–1924) perfected structures in glass and steel, but it was above all Frank Lloyd Wright (1867–1959) who grasped the new opportunities in the use of frame, cantilever, and slab. In the early years of his career he was largely ignored in the United States. He experimented with concrete, which he used in developing his "prairie style" houses, characterized by a spatial flow combining internal environments that were continuous and blended with the exterior. He revolutionized the design of the private house and was a seminal influence on European architecture of the international style after 1918. His basic work was published in Germany in 1910, where it exercised a decisive influence on architects who were convinced that the new architecture was the logical product of the international character of the age and its technical advances. In 1928 the Congrès internationaux d'architecture moderne was established; it coordinated the search for principles capable of dealing effectively with practical tasks. "Functionalism" was the name used to describe the architecture designed to serve what was thought to be a well-ordered society. This does not mean, however, that the architecture was lacking in artistic value. Le Corbusier, one of the greatest proponents of the new style, regularly affirmed the human need for beauty, which he felt resulted from the effective use of elementary forms and proportional geometry. He was convinced that when things truly respond to human needs, they are essentially beautiful.[10]

Functionalism was deeply concerned with the human condition; hence it gave serious attention to landscape, environment, and human settlements. The architects planned whole urban areas with the hope of solving human problems of relationships, especially those created by the inhuman conditions of nineteenth-century industrial areas. While preserving some of the properties of the traditional village, they hoped to restore sunlight, space, and greenness to the lives of ordinary people. Towns were regarded as biological phenomena with hearts, organs, and limbs, all indispensable to their functions of living, working, relating, and circulating. The architects became sensitive to the different velocities in the city, such as those produced by motor traffic and pedestrians, and the different kinds of resultant rhythms requiring different kinds of space.

The four leading functionalists were Swiss-born Charles Edouard Jeanneret, better known as Le Corbusier (1887–1965), Dutch-born J. J. P. Oud (1890–1963), and the two Germans, Walter Gropius (1883–1969) and Ludwig Mies van der Rohe (1888–1965). The theoretical writings of Oud and Gropius, and to some extent those of Corbusier, together with the publication of their projects, established and promoted the principles of the new style.[11]

The first principle concerned architecture as volume. The functionalist method of construction provided a cage or skeleton, which appeared before the building was enclosed. Whether the supports were of reinforced concrete or metal, the impression was that of a grille of vertical and horizontal limbs. In earlier architecture the walls formed the supports, whereas in the new style the walls were subordinate elements that were fitted like screens between the supports and formed a continuous outside covering. In the new style the supporting piers were so light in section that they created no serious obstruction. Occasionally supports could be omitted, with their burden being carried by cantilevering. Hence, the effect of mass and static solidity, traditionally the principal quality of architecture, more or less disappeared and was replaced by plane surfaces bounding a volume. An open box rather than a dense block became the primary architectural symbol. The architects in the international style sought to display the real character of their buildings and to express their provision for function.

Flat roofs were normal in the international style, for they appeared to be less massive and simpler than the gabled roofs of the past. The building surfaces tightly stretched over the supporting skeleton created the impression of an immaterial, weightless space. Windows constituted an important element in the international style. Together with the materials used to surface the buildings, they often determined the aesthetic effectiveness of the structures. Stucco was frequently used on the surfaces because it had the advantage of forming a continuous, even covering. Stone, granite, and marble were also used.[12]

The second principle of the international style was regularity. The supports in skeleton construction were normally placed at equal distances in order that the strain might be equalized, resulting in an underlying regular rhythm that was clearly evident before the outside surfaces were applied.[13]

The third principle concerned the avoidance of applied decoration or ornament. Since the middle of the eighteenth century, the quality of the ornament had steadily declined, although there was a renaissance of craftsmanship during the nineteenth century, due in large part to the efforts of William Morris and the Arts and Crafts movement. Decoration, however, comes not only from applied ornament but also from the incidental features of design, which contribute interest and variety to the whole. It was architectural detail that provided the decoration in the international style.

The fact that there was so little architectural detail in the functionalist buildings increased the decorative effect of what was in fact there. Hence, the details of fenestration were extremely important. In general the style set a very high but not impossible standard in regard to color. In the early days of the style, white stucco was very prominent. Then in Holland and Germany bright elementary colors were used in small areas; in France large areas of more neutral shades appeared. Usage was influenced by the abstract painters Piet Mondrian and Amedee Ozenfant. In general, however, it was felt that light neutral tones blending with those of nature were usually more satisfactory.

Trees and vines were often used as a means of decoration in the international style; they provided natural surroundings that both contrasted with and emphasized the buildings. Hence choice of sites and the placement of the structures on the sites were important concerns. The elaborate formal gardens of earlier periods had no place among the functionalist architects. As much as possible, the original natural beauties of the environment were preserved.[14]

In many ways the international style was epitomized by the Bauhaus, or more properly Das Staatliche Bauhaus, a school of art founded in 1919 at Weimar in Germany by Walter Gropius for the purpose of training commercial and industrial designers and liberating art and architecture from the historicism and aestheticism taught in the academies. It sought to integrate art and industry by relating the worlds of the artists and craftspersons. In this regard its aims were similar to those of the Arts and Crafts movement in nineteenth-century England. It rejected as artificial the distinction between fine and applied art and favored a rationalist approach to both in which collaboration was emphasized. Architecture became the master art governing and unifying the others. Aesthetic judgments that were based on individual sensibilities were replaced by judgments of logic and efficiency. Sound engineering and honest use of materials determined good design. In the early years, the functionalist conception of art failed to provide sufficient scope for the painter until greater concern was shown for the social and psychological aspects of human life.

In 1925 the school moved into new quarters at Dessau, designed by Gropius himself. The extraordinary impact of the institute was partly due to the very talented faculty, including Paul Klee, Wassily Kandinsky, Lyonel Feininger, Laslo Noholy-Nagy, Marcel Breuer, Ludwig Mies van der Rohe, and Josef Albers. When the Nazis closed the school in 1933, many of those distinguished men emigrated to the United States, where they taught the Bauhaus principles in the prestigious architectural schools at Harvard, Yale, M.I.T., and the New Bauhaus in Chicago.

To understand the Bauhaus, the international style, and functionalism one must remember that, for Gropius, the architect was more a coordinator than an artist in the traditional sense, for artistic freedom and expression meant not the right to lay out one's personal meanings or manifest arbitrary caprice but rather the power to use creatively the results of scientific investigation and technological progress. Likewise, architectural order meant the achievement of clearly established standards, which could be varied creatively. In a sense the Bauhaus stood for a method of building rather than a style.[15]

Certainly the scientific approach to architecture did not impede the creation of expressive, aesthetically pleasing buildings. They resulted from the establishment of unity between form and function and the recovery of a basic sense of meaning in the buildings. In the hands of second-rate architects, functionalism degenerated into machine-like juxtaposition of separate entities, but in the hands of truly creative architects the results were impressive. In retrospect, however, the style has been criticized for failing to attend sufficiently to topological concerns. Elementary enclosures and environmental warmth were often lacking. In the past these values were frequently expressed through urban squares and streets, through intimate interior spaces and through varied building types. In a sense, functionalism failed to design buildings that responded to the human needs for boundaries, intimacy, and warmth. It did, however, represent an important step toward the creation of fully satisfactory human environments. Furthermore, successful developments toward those goals did in fact grow out of the international style.

The functionalist emphasis on the essentials of human life in the world influenced many fields of activity following the First World War. In painting and sculpture it manifested itself in various purist currents, especially in the art of Piet Mondrian and the other members of the De Stijl group in Holland, the constructivism of Antoine Pevsner, Naum Gabo, and Kazimer Malevich, the sculpture of Le Corbusier and Ozenfant, and above all the work of Constantin Brancusi. As a simple synthetic form Brancusi's *Bird* is a true archetype, expressing the bird's efforts to conquer the vertical. Paul Klee, in his own irrational way, tried to develop a systematic *Gestaltungslehre*. In music it was Arnold Schoenberg who developed the first truly open organization of symbolic forms. In philosophy it was Ludwig Wittgenstein and Rudolf Carnap who emphasized the importance of searching for essentials and the need for a logical method. They stressed the importance of continuity between structure and the reality behind the structure. This was also the basic functionalist thesis. But as contemporary theorists are quick to point out, symbols can never fully express the reality behind them; they partly reveal and partly conceal what is simultaneously expressed and hidden in the symbolic structures themselves. Symbols are always ambiguous. It should not be surprising, then, that functionalism could not account for all aspects of human existence. It turned out to be but a transitory stage in the modern movement in architecture. To assert, however, that functionalism was concerned only with efficiency is to misunderstand the method. It was concerned above all with human meanings; its goal was to enable human beings to graft themselves onto this world as an essential part of nature in such a way that they would have a sense of belonging and be able to relate to the world, themselves, and one another in human ways.

As we shall see, the insights and values of the international style were slow to be accepted among the builders of churches, but the architects who did accept them appropriated them in their designs and moved beyond them in their own projects. They were able to produce sacred spaces that have been recognized as places of profound spirituality, structures in which communities have been able to worship in accord with the best tenets of the Christian liturgy.

LITURGY IN THE FIRST HALF
OF THE TWENTIETH CENTURY

The liturgical movement, which had begun in the nineteenth century, gathered momentum in the early twentieth. In 1903 Pope Pius X issued his *Motu proprio* on sacred music, *Tra le Sollecitudini;* however, he did not limit his remarks to music alone but rather pleaded for a general return to the liturgy as the center of Christian life.[16] In regard to church architecture he noted,

> [I]t being our desire to see the true Christian spirit restored in every respect and be preserved by all the faithful, we deem it necessary to provide before everything else for the sanctity and dignity of the temple, in which the faithful assemble for the object of acquiring this spirit from its foremost and indispensable fount, which is the active participation in the holy mysteries and in the public and solemn prayer of the Church.[17]

This papal document was followed shortly by a decree of the Sacred Consistorial Congregation on frequent Communion.[18] For Roman Catholics, these official texts were important steps in the right direction, but it would be years before they would be fully implemented.

It was above all Dom Lambert Beauduin (1873–1960) who exercised the most decisive role in promoting the liturgical movement in the twentieth century. He understood the impact of Pius X's exhortation on the liturgy and church music. As a priest in the Belgian diocese of Liège, he had parochial experience for eight years and was quite active as a chaplain to workers, appointed to assist in the application of the encyclical letter of Pope Leo XIII on economic justice, *Rerum novarum*. In 1906 at the age of thirty-three he entered the Benedictine monastery of Mont César at Louvain, a foundation made from Maredsous in 1899. In the monastery he was assigned to teach theology to the young monks; to this task he brought a wide experience in pastoral work, a genuine zeal for the laity, a profound piety, and a keen interest in Christian doctrine. It was this background that helped Beauduin realize that the liturgy is meant to be the framework for all Christian life, not only for a select few but for all God's people.[19] He was to a certain degree the heir to Guéranger's liturgical legacy, but he was able to set aside what was obsolete and meaningless because he realized that the true object of the liturgical movement must be not to create an artificial community to take part in an antiquarian liturgy but rather to prepare the real communities of the church to take part in a genuinely traditional liturgy rightly understood.

The decisive step in the Belgian liturgical movement was taken in 1909 at a Catholic conference in Malines when Beauduin proposed a practical program for liturgical renewal. With the approval of Cardinal Mercier, he advocated the translation of the Roman missal into the vernacular, the development of a liturgical spirituality based on the Mass and the prayer of the divine office, the promotion of Gregorian chant, and the liturgical formation of choirs through special retreats in liturgical centers such as Benedictine monasteries. Following the conference, Mont César became a major center for carrying out Beauduin's program, along with two other Belgian monasteries, Maredsous and St. André. Special attention was given to the formation of priests through the publication of a new review, *Bulletin liturgique et paroissial*, eventually known as *Questions liturgiques et paroissiales*, and through liturgical conferences, *Semaines liturgiques*.

In Germany the center of the liturgical movement shifted from Beuron to the Abbey of Maria Laach. There the first liturgical week for laypeople was held during Holy Week in 1914; this was the first effort to reach out

directly to laypeople. It was there that the dialogue Mass was first introduced in Germany. The leader of this center was Abbot Ildefons Herwegen
(1874–1946).

There is no doubt that the Benedictine communities were key leaders in
the modern liturgical movement. They were religious groups primarily
committed to the celebration of the liturgy; they enjoyed a certain amount
of autonomy and exemption from diocesan authorities, and they had the
trained personnel. Already in the nineteenth century at Meredsous the first
complete translation of the Roman missal for the use of the laity was made
available—obviously in the midst of much controversy, since in 1661 Pope
Alexander VII had condemned vernacular translations of the Roman
missal.[20] One of the monks, Dom Gérard van Caloen, had caused controversy at a liturgical congress held in Liège in 1883 by advocating that Communion should be received during Mass—it was often received before or
after Mass but not during Mass itself. Shortly after, van Caloen founded *Le
Messager des fidèles*, a liturgical review that developed into the scholarly
journal *La Revue bénédictine* under the editorship of the learned Dom
Germain Morin.

Following the First World War, the Belgian liturgical movement continued to develop with a strong pastoral emphasis. Meanwhile further
important advances took place in Germany. Through the efforts of
Romano Guardini (1885–1968), Abbot Herwegen (1874–1946), and Dom
Odo Casel (1886–1948), the movement took on a sound scientific, specula-
tive character that established a firm theological foundation for the centrality of the liturgy in Christian life. With research into patristic liturgy
and the development of the theory of the *Kultmysterium,* the abbey
founded the monograph series *Ecclesia orans* in 1918 as well as an academy
of patristic studies and a center for sacred art. The first published book was
Guardini's *Vom Geist der Liturgie (The Spirit of the Liturgy).*[21] Herwegen
also established the annual, *Jahrbuch für Liturgiewissenschaft* (first published
in 1921).[22] His great contribution was to show, contrary to Guéranger's
assertion, that the Middle Ages was not the high point in the history of the
liturgy but that during that time the liturgy had been compromised by the
introduction of various subjective and dramatic characteristics inspired by
allegorical interpretations that were foreign to the patristic development of
the liturgy. He demonstrated that the medieval period, though superior to
the baroque in its liturgical practices, had already begun to interpolate the
liturgy with poetic developments quite foreign to its nature. He claimed
that, far from manifesting an ideal practice and understanding of the
liturgy, the medieval period prepared the way for the abandonment of the

liturgy by many Protestants and the neglect of the liturgy by much of Catholicism in the post-Tridentine period. Herwegen's ideas in this regard shocked most of the early readers, but contemporary research tends to support his basic assertions.

Herwegen and his followers maintained that the fundamental error of the Middle Ages, when that era is compared with early Christianity, was its turning from an objective to a subjective kind of piety. They held that the authentic spirit of the liturgy lies in its objectivity, whereas the piety of the Middle Ages and subsequent periods tended more and more to subjectivism. In short, there was a shift from an emphasis on the union of the whole church with God to the union of the individual with God. That was the substance of Herwegen's little book *Kirche und Seele*,[23] in which he seemed to propose an opposition between the church's piety and the piety of the individual Christian. His opponents immediately accused the Maria Laach school of lacking any genuine interest in personal devotion and therefore of tending to foster a brand of religious piety that would not be a valid piety at all, since it would be based on an indifference to the religious life of individuals. It was in the *Jahrbuch* and especially in his *Christliche Kultmysterium* (1932) that Casel set out his perspectives on the theological understanding of the liturgy based on the church fathers and the history of religions. Both Herwegen's views and those of Casel have been considerably refined and in a sense corrected by more recent and more balanced liturgical scholarship.[24]

The German movement took a more pastoral turn under the leadership of men such as Johannes Pinsk (1891–1975), who was a chaplain to Berlin students. Although he never had an academic post, he exercised extraordinary influence on Berlin Catholics, especially in academic circles. He stressed the importance of the Easter mystery and the triumph of Christ over sin and death, the experience of the church as a worshiping community, and the transformation of the world through sacramental celebrations. He edited *Liturgische Zeitschrift* (1929–1933) and in 1934 started the publication of *Liturgisches Leben,* which at the time was the most outspoken journal of its kind in Germany. It dealt with the vital questions of liturgical piety, the Mystical Body, and the ecclesial dimensions of the sacraments. The Oratorians at Leipzig also took a sound pastoral approach in their parish.[25]

This activity naturally brought attention to the liturgical movement along with both support and opposition. The historical research carried on at Maria Laach, especially investigation of the patristic period, precipitated a heated debate over the relative merits of liturgy as the official prayer of the church, on the one hand, and the various spiritual and devotional exercises, on the other. For example, the bishop of Linz in the province of Vienna issued a strong statement condemning the celebration of Mass facing the people, the removal of the tabernacle from the main altar, disparagement of Marian devotions, and the suppression of the long-standing custom of reciting the rosary during Mass. To resolve some of the tensions associated with the liturgical movement, the bishop of Passau organized a liturgical committee in 1939 with such men as Jungmann and Guardini among its members. In 1940 the German hierarchy took over the leadership of the movement and appointed Bishop Simon Landersdorfer, O.S.B., of Passau and Bishop Albert Stohr of Mainz as the advisors on liturgical matters to the Bishops' Conference of Fulda. These two bishops appointed a liturgical commission consisting of the original members of the committee organized in 1939, along with representatives from Maria Laach, Beuron, Klosterneuberg, and the Oratory at Leipzig. The establishment of the commission avoided a sweeping condemnation of the liturgical movement. This commission issued an official guide to the arrangement of parochial liturgical services in 1942. Austria followed the German example and set up its own commission and liturgical offices in the various dioceses.[26]

On April 10, 1943, Cardinal Bertram, the archbishop of Breslau and chairman of the German Bishops' Conference, sent a report to Pope Pius XII on the liturgical movement in Germany and requested a number of indults for the Catholic Church in Germany. He also pleaded for a reform of the breviary and the ritual for the celebration of the sacraments.

Pius XII issued his encyclical letter *Mystici Corporis* on June 29, 1943. Since the liturgy is both expressive and constitutive of the life of the church, this encyclical was an important document in the history of the liturgical movement. On December 24, 1943, Cardinal Maglione, the Papal Secretary of State, sent a letter to Cardinal Bertram informing him that a meeting of the cardinals of the Sacred Congregation of Rites and of the Sacred Congregation for Extraordinary Ecclesiastical Affairs had taken place to discuss the German liturgical movement. Permission for dialogue Mass was granted and the "German Solemn Mass" was kindly tolerated, even though it was not in accord with the existing Roman rubrics, since the faithful were singing in the vernacular during the solemn Mass. Vatican officials, however, were hesitant to approve what they regarded as antiquarianism manifested in efforts to shy away from historical developments in the liturgy, especially those of a devotional nature.[27]

The important work done in Germany was complemented by a sound pastoral approach taken by Pius Parsch (1884–1954) at the monastery of the Augustinian Canons at Klosterneuberg near Vienna in Austria. Combining biblical commentaries with careful attention to the devotional needs of the people, Parsch made his abbey a center of the liturgical movement in Austria. He founded the periodical *Lebe mit der Kirche* (later called *Bibel und Liturgie*), which stressed that a living understanding and practice of the liturgy could be deeply enriched by a greater knowledge of the Bible, a conviction that he disseminated through his "Leaflet Missal" and his five-volume work *Das Jahr des Heiles,* published in 1923 and eventually translated into English as *The Church's Year of Grace.*[28] Parsch attempted to explain the Mass and the breviary on a popular level. Although he had a great love and earnest zeal for the liturgy and for God's people, he was not highly trained in theology; consequently, contemporary liturgical scholars have reservations about many of the statements made in his works.

In 1936 Josef Jungmann, an Austrian Jesuit, published his *Die Frohbotschaft und unsere Glaubensverkündigung,* translated as *The Good News and Our Proclamation of the Faith.*[29] This work exerted an important influence on the development of both catechetical and liturgical movements by providing a scholarly foundation for both reforms.[30]

Liturgically, France seemed for many years like a desert, with Solesmes, the major center for the study of Gregorian chant, as an isolated oasis. Serious scholarly work on the liturgy was done in France in the early part of the twentieth century. For example, the *Dictionnaire d'archéologie chrétienne et de la liturgie* was begun in 1903 by Fernand Cabrol and Henri Leclercq, though its completion was not undertaken by Henri Marrou until 1947. In the course of the century, the great literary works of Paul Claudel and Charles Péguy had given many readers a fresh concept of the Catholic Church and its life, but in general this thought never penetrated the minds of the ordinary French clergy, to say nothing of the ordinary laypeople. In the late 1920s there was some contact with the German and Austrian movements. The French translations of works by Guardini and Parsch left a mark on a limited number of clerical and lay elite; likewise, Casel's theories influenced a limited number of scholars.[31]

It was not, however, until the 1940s that the French took an active role in the liturgical movement. From 1942 on, the distressing religious situation in France received increasing attention, for example, in the book *La France, pays de mission?* by Abbé H. Godin and Père Y. Daniel. At Lyons a series of pamphlets on the liturgy, *La Clarté-Dieu,* was published, and French translations of the important works of Casel, Pinsk, and Parsch were circulated. This culminated in 1943 in the establishment of the Centre de Pastorale Liturgique under the direction of the French Dominicans,

Roguet and Duployé. From the start this center was independent of the French hierarchy, although it has always worked in close collaboration with many of the French bishops. The well-trained members of three religious orders, the Dominicans, the Jesuits, and the Benedictines, cooperated with the diocesan clergy in bringing the liturgy to the masses. In 1945 the Centre began the publication of *La Maison-Dieu,* which from the start has been one of the most important liturgical journals. Also in 1945 the first national French liturgical congress was held at Saint-Fleur to discuss *La messe paroissiale du Dimanche.*

Another figure in the French movement was Paul Doncoeur, a Jesuit who did much to popularize the liturgy among French youth. It is important to note that the French movement gained its strongest adherents from those who realized the necessity for a missionary effort in the dechristianized homes and industrial cities. The movement was pastoral in this sense, but it was not parochial, for some of its most influential leaders felt that the modern parish could no longer be the center of Christian life and worship.

The liturgical movement was very slow in getting started in the British Isles. In the nineteenth and early twentieth centuries considerable research into the origins and the evolution of liturgical rites was carried out by English scholars such as Edmund Bishop, but the practical importance of such work was not always realized at the time. The reason for lack of Roman Catholic interest in the liturgical movement was the fact that the Roman Catholic celebration of Tridentine liturgy in Latin gave Catholics a clear sense of identity over against the Anglicans, who celebrated in the vernacular. Furthermore, the Protestant churches harbored an intense anti-Catholic feeling, which even hindered liturgical renewal among the Catholic wing of the Anglican Church. However, within the Church of England, the Alcuin Club produced impressive studies of the orders of service in the Book of Common Prayer, while the Henry Bradshaw Society published more general but scholarly works on Christian worship.[32]

By the end of World War II the liturgical movement was well on its way in the major Catholic countries of the world. In August 1946, at the Liturgical Congress at Maastricht, a major international congress was planned but was never held because of postwar conditions. At Maastricht, however, contact was established between the French and Dutch liturgists for the first time. On January 18, 1947, the Holy See granted the Belgian hierarchy permission for the celebration of evening Mass on Sundays and holy days. From that date, privileges of this nature were granted more and more frequently. In the same year, the Liturgical Institute at Trier was founded under the direction of Johannes Wagner, secretary of the German Liturgical Commission. Balthasar Fischer was appointed one of the professors at the institute.

In the United States the initiative taken by Pius X to encourage liturgical reform received little attention, apart from the remodeling of several of their churches by the Paulist Fathers. The European efforts at reform were brought to the country in the mid-1920s by Dom Virgil Michel (1890–1938) of St. John's Abbey in Collegeville, Minnesota. Father Virgil was sent by his abbot to study philosophy at Sant' Anselmo in Rome under the direction of Joseph Gredt. He found that experience quite suffocating, but he came to life on liturgical, ecumenical, and pastoral levels through his close association with Dom Lambert Beauduin, the Benedictine from Mont César who taught fundamental theology at Sant' Anselmo. Returning to the United States, Father Virgil brought the European liturgical movement with him, but he gave it a distinctively American character. His theology and pastoral sense were solidly grounded in the doctrine of the Mystical Body of Christ and a firm conviction that the liturgy belongs to the entire church, not simply to clergy and religious but to all laymen and women because through baptism they are all sons and daughters of God and sisters and brothers of Jesus Christ. In 1926 he established the Liturgical Press and began the publication of *Orate Fratres,* which in the early 1950s became known as *Worship.* Father Virgil's horizons were far-reaching. He knew that the liturgical, biblical, social, and educational dimensions of the church's life must be carefully interrelated. He also believed that rural and national political issues must be discussed in a liturgical context, because everything that touches on the life of the Mystical Body of Christ should be of concern to every worshiping Christian.

Although a Liturgical Day was held in Collegeville in 1929, it was Father Michael Ducey, originally a Benedictine of Saint Anselm's Priory in Washington, D.C., who laid the groundwork for the American liturgical weeks. He succeeded in convincing the American Benedictine abbots that some kind of liturgical weeks similar to the Belgian study days should be held in the United States. In 1940 the first American national liturgical week was sponsored under the auspices of the Benedictine Liturgical Conference, which was replaced in 1944 by the National Liturgical Conference.

The period between the First and Second World Wars was a time of special development for American Roman Catholics. Certainly the secular world was struggling to come to terms with modernity. Although the church at large sought to insulate itself from secular forces, an increasing number of Roman Catholics sought an identity that incorporated both their Christian tradition and their experience as American citizens. During the First World War and in the 1920s many had become affluent and had begun to send their children to prestigious Ivy League universities. This resulted in intellectual activity that had an impact on many aspects of Roman Catholic life, including education, politics, theology, social welfare, and liturgy. However, the aesthetic dimensions of their lives were generally left unaffected by the new climate, especially their taste in liturgical art. Most of the Catholic churches had been built before the First World War in accord with the ethnic tastes of European immigrants. They were, as was the custom, furnished by catalogue sale houses that catered to sentimental tastes. Hence, Catholic churches generally displayed mass-produced furnishings and poorly designed vestments, statues, and altarware.

In an effort to improve the quality of church art and furnishings Alexandre Cingria (1897–1945) published his *Decadence de l'art sacré* in 1917; it was translated into German and published as *Der Verfall der kirchlichen Kunst* in 1927. In 1920 Cingria founded the Society of Saint Luke, which brought together forward-looking painters and sculptors who had a deep commitment to the church and who cared deeply about the artistic environment of church buildings.[33] A similar development took place in the United States.

In 1927 fourteen young men gathered at Portsmouth Priory in Rhode Island; they were fledgling architects, draftsmen, and artists, financially secure, well educated, and convinced of the value of Christian tradition. Although they were imbued with romantic medieval nostalgia, optimism, and a longing for identity and status in a society that was dominated by Anglo-Saxon Protestantism, they were ambivalent about the value of modern technology. This group formed the nucleus of what developed into the Liturgical Arts Society, an organization of both lay and clerical people who originally were concerned with the quality of art objects used in public worship but who gradually developed an understanding of the modern liturgical movement and were able to contextualize their artistic concerns within an appropriate liturgical framework. The society met for the first time in December 1930 and began publication of its journal *Liturgical Arts* in 1931. From 1937 until it ceased publication in 1972, the periodical was edited by Maurice Lavanoux (1894–1974), who did so much to improve the state of liturgical art and architecture in the United States. The demise of the periodical, followed shortly by Lavanoux's own death, left the Roman Catholic Church in the United States without a critical voice both championing the efforts of competent professional artists and architects working for the church and denouncing the inferior kitsch that priests and religious regularly purchased from liturgical catalogues.[34]

On September 18, 1947, Pope Pius XII gave an important address to the Benedictine abbots of the world who had gathered in the Basilica of Saint Paul Outside the Walls on the occasion of the fourteenth centennial celebrations in honor of St. Benedict. He warned the abbots that they should not belittle private and popular devotions in their efforts to retrieve the public and communal worship of the early church. His address formed a prelude to the publication of the encyclical *Mediator Dei* on November 20, 1947. Sometimes styled as the Magna Charta of the liturgical movement, the encyclical was the first to be entirely devoted to the liturgy. Although it was generally positive in tone, it contained many statements that reflected the spirit of unrest and mistrust which the liturgical movement had engendered above all in European countries. Looking back, we see that the document did in fact give the liturgical movement a decisive impetus.

On November 28, 1947, a bilingual ritual was approved for use in France. Although the texts were simply translations of the traditional *Rituale Romanum* without any emendations or additions, the publication was a move in a positive direction. Eventually similar rituals were published in the major modern languages for general use throughout the Catholic Church.

In 1948, Father Jungmann published his *Missarum Sollemnia*. Although written during the war years with very limited scholarly resources at hand, the book is still a milestone in the history of liturgical research; it is a work of enormous learning combined with a catechetical and pastoral perspective.[35]

For the next few years progress in the liturgical movement was rather slow. In June 1950 the first national German Liturgical Congress was held dealing with the Sunday celebration of the eucharist. This was the first public conference organized by the Institute at Trier. Of special importance was an address given by Romano Guardini, which eventually led to the resolution that the German bishops should ask the Holy See to transfer the Holy Saturday liturgy to the evening or night. On November 2, 1950, the bishops of Germany, Austria, and France asked for this transfer of the Holy Saturday liturgy. The request was favorably received, and on February 9, 1951, the Holy See granted permission for the evening celebration.

From July 12 to 15, 1951, the first international liturgical study week, organized by the Liturgical Institute at Trier and the Centre de Pastorale Liturgique, met at the abbey of Maria Laach. Some forty scholars, mainly from France, Germany, and Belgium, discussed the "Problems of the *Missale Romanum.*" In 1948 a study was made by the editors of the journal *Ephemerides Liturgicae* to discern which proposed reforms of the Roman liturgy enjoyed widespread support. The first international meeting, therefore, concerned itself mainly with those proposals, which centered on the rite of the Mass and the Easter Vigil celebration. Many of the conclusions from this session, which were passed on to the Sacred Congregation of Rites, were adopted in the *Ordo Sabbati Sancti* and in the decrees that simplified the Roman rubrics.

In the following year a somewhat larger meeting of scholars was held at Sainte-Odile near Strasbourg to follow up on the work done at Maria Laach. These meetings proved to be quite helpful for channeling liturgical investigations; consequently, it was decided that the scope of the sessions should be expanded at a meeting to be held the following year in Lugano. This site was chosen so that the Italians could attend. The national liturgical organizations of Germany, France, Italy, and Switzerland collaborated in planning the Lugano gathering, which was attended by Cardinals Ottaviani, Pro-prefect of the Holy Office, Frings of Cologne, and Lercaro of Bologna, by officials of the Sacred Congregation of Rites, and by bishops, priests, and laypeople from approximately a dozen countries, including the United States and England. The bishops submitted the four major resolutions of the conference to Rome. They included a request for a reform of the entire Holy Week liturgy, permission to extend the format of the "German Solemn Mass" to other countries, permission to have the liturgical readings in the vernacular, and encouragement of more active participation on the part of the laity.

The following year, 1954, the fourth international study meeting was held at the abbey of Mont César in Louvain. The major topics discussed were the system of biblical pericopes used in the Mass and concelebration. No definite resolutions were passed on to the Holy See because the subjects had not yet been sufficiently studied.

Far-reaching changes in the Holy Week liturgy were effected on November 16, 1955, by the decree *Maxima redemptionis nostrae.* On December 25, 1955, Pope Pius XII issued his encyclical *Musicae Sacrae Disciplina.* International congresses on church music had been held in Rome in 1950 and in Vienna in 1954, but neither of these meetings had been pastorally oriented; they were of interest mainly to musicologists and treated such relatively minor matters as orchestral Masses and singing by women during the liturgy. In his encyclical Pius XII sought to expound the true place of sacred music in the liturgy. This theme was taken up and numerous practical points were made in the instruction issued by the Sacred Congregation of Rites on September 3, 1958. This latter instruction also contained important regulations governing the active participation of the laity in the liturgy.

In September 1956, the fifth international study meeting was held at Assisi as a tribute to Pope Pius XII on the occasion of his eightieth birthday. Far-reaching liturgical reform took place during his pontificate, and his encyclicals *Mystici Corporis* and *Mediator Dei* helped to clarify the theological foundations of the liturgy and to give inspiration to liturgical renewal among all the baptized. There were approximately twelve hundred participants at Assisi from all over the world, including a half dozen cardinals and about eight hundred bishops. The congress closed with an allocution by the pope in the course of a papal audience in Rome. Pius XII dealt particularly with the relation between the eucharist and the altar and the problem of concelebration. In general the impression was given that Rome was disturbed by the quickening pace of the liturgical movement and by the far-reaching demands made by the northern European countries. As a result the development of the liturgical movement was delayed for a considerable time following the Assisi meeting.

The advances made by the biblical movement and the liturgical movement were brought together at the Congress of Strasbourg in July 1957. Scholars had come to realize that no true liturgical progress is possible without a sound biblical catechesis, for without the Bible there is no liturgy. It was the biblical movement that gave the liturgical movement the authenticity and profundity that it needed.

Pope John XXIII became pope in October 1958. Shortly after that he announced the forthcoming ecumenical council and established three secretariats and eleven commissions to prepare the council agenda. Unlike the other commissions, the liturgical commission faced issues that had already been quite clearly formulated over the past fifteen years. Four points especially had come to the fore: the pastoral character of the liturgy, its importance in missionary countries, the desire and need for vernacular languages in the liturgy, and the desire for concelebration.

As country after country had come into contact with the liturgical apostolate, the conviction grew that the liturgy is intrinsically pastoral. It was this conviction that inspired the far-reaching reforms of the Second Vatican Council and encouraged Protestant and Anglican churches to evaluate their own liturgical practices.

CHURCH BUILDING DURING THE FIRST HALF
OF THE TWENTIETH CENTURY

It should not be surprising that the modern liturgical movement eventually had a serious effect on the design of church buildings. Developments in form, material, technique, and culture, as well as the modern liturgical movement, all affected to some degree the shape and style of churches constructed in the twentieth century. Whether the modern churches were primarily a result of changes in the understanding of form and materials or of cultural, theological, spiritual, and liturgical developments is an open question. Although some of the leaders of the functionalist movement designed churches, in general they were not called upon to design churches because it was felt that their intense rationalism inhibited their ability to provide worship spaces that would differ in any significant way from meeting halls.[36]

New building materials were used for scaffolding in the construction of churches in the early part of the century; however, it was not until after the First World War that there was a new stylistic use of iron, steel, glass, and concrete in the design and construction of churches themselves. A major breakthrough occurred in 1922 when Auguste Perret (1874–1954) was commissioned to design and build a large war-memorial church at Le Raincy near Paris. Perret was the creator of reinforced concrete architecture, that is, architecture in which all the elements of the reinforced concrete structure remain visible externally and, as far as is feasible, internally as well. In the church of Notre Dame du Raincy, reinforced concrete showed its extraordinary possibilities as a building material. Both internally and externally the church was made of bare concrete. The roof was a thin covering; the slender vertical supports were carefully crafted monoliths; and the walls were a continuous grille of precast segments filled with stained glass. The altar was placed somewhat freely on a raised platform. The overall effect was one of austere beauty which established the possibility of using the new materials not only for secular buildings but also for churches. Perret's church, however, had only a slight effect upon future church-building projects, but then one must remember that there was really no liturgical movement in France before the Second World War.[37]

The renewals in architecture and liturgy were probably first brought together in the Schloss Rothenfels-Main, a castle that served as the headquarters for the Catholic Youth movement, the Quickborn, in Germany between 1917 and the Second World War. The building was remodeled in 1928 under the direction of Romano Guardini, who was already known for his interest in liturgy,[38] and Rudolf Schwarz, who would become one of the most important church designers in Europe. The castle had a regular chapel, but the main hall was also occasionally used for the celebration of the eucharist. It was a large rectangular room with white walls, deep windows, and a stone floor; the space was devoid of any decoration. As remodeled, the only furnishings were a hundred small cuboid black stools. The disposition of the room could be easily changed for different functions. For example, if a discussion, recital, or conference was being held, the stools were arranged as in an auditorium, but if a eucharist was being celebrated, a provisional altar was set up in such a way that the people could gather around it on three sides. The presider closed the circle by facing the community from behind the altar. The liturgy as celebrated in the space was certainly a celebration of the whole assembly; it was expressed with great simplicity and flexibility. Hospitality surely took precedence over monumentality, and the community took precedence over objects. Both the distinguished community that gathered with Guardini and the liturgical space had significant influence in Germany and Switzerland.[39]

Inspired by Perret's church near Paris, Karl Moser (1860–1936) designed a bold structure for the church of St. Antoninus at Basel in Switzerland in 1926–1927. Although it appears to be a somewhat heavy, factory-like structure, its plain rectangular tower, rising free at one corner of the church, was quite successful and was frequently emulated by other architects.[40]

The use of unfinished concrete in churches was further developed by Dominikus Böhm (1880–1955) in Germany. His professional work was mainly confined to the building of churches and other ecclesiastical structures. Although from an architectural point of view his buildings appear to be less innovative than Perret's work, he is recognized as being original in his emotional approach to building and also in his sensitivity to the demands that the modern liturgical movement put on church buildings. His church of Christ the King at Mainz-Bishofsheim, built in 1926, is an early example of the effective use of paraboloid forms, with the concrete barrel vaulting of the nave intersected by lower cross vaults over the bays of the side aisles. The design created a strong expressionist or even Gothic emotional effect.

Böhm was a pioneer of the one-room church plan. The open interior took various geometric shapes, including the circle. One of the best examples of his earlier work is St. Engelbert at Cologne-Riehl (1931–1932). This circular church is also notable for its ingenious roof, which is not a dome but rather eight paraboloid vaults with small circular windows near the apex of each. The result is a rather dark but mysterious interior. Some of his other churches are simple rectangular forms. His liturgical concern was to bring the community into a more active participation in the eucharist; hence, he fulfilled the basic functionalist axiom that "form follows function." He brought the liturgical presider and the rest of the assembly into close proximity to each other around the altar as the focal point of the celebration. He built a church at Ringenberg in 1936, which was the first modern church in which the congregation gathered on three sides of the altar. There he used a transeptual plan with the altar at the center of the crossing and the congregation in the nave and transepts. His work before the Second World War reveals a sense of maturity and power.[41]

From 1933 until the end of World War II, what is generally called "modern architecture" was banned throughout the Third Reich. This restriction tended to stifle Böhm's creativity. Among his best post–World War II churches are St. Elizabeth in Coblenz (1953), done with his son Gottfried, and Maria Königin in Cologne-Marienberg (1954), a church with an enormous south wall of stunning stained glass done with Heinz Bienefeld.[42]

Otto Bartning (1883–1959) designed the first steel church in Cologne in 1928. An evangelical church, it had a steel frame and steel and glass walls. In addition to being a trained architect, Bartning had a doctorate in theology and was keenly interested in the development of Lutheran liturgy.[43]

Rudolf Schwarz (1897–1961) was also an innovative church builder in the years before the Second World War. He has been described as "probably the most profound church architect" of the first half of the twentieth century.[44] For him, religious architecture was not limited to constructing church buildings but was meant to reflect his basic philosophical and theological thinking, which he set out in his book *Vom Bau der Kirche*.[45] Schwarz was a modern functionalist architect who was concerned that form follows function; hence, he too became one of the pioneers of the one-room type of church interior. The prototype of his early churches was the early Christian basilica. One of his most impressive churches is that of Corpus Christi built at Aachen in 1930. It is a simple rectangular hall without aisles; it is rather severe with the altar mounted on a platform visible from any point in the space. Everything that is not directly concerned with the liturgy has been relegated to a porch at the front of the church or to a hall set at right angles to the nave. Outside, the tower is characterized by equally stark simplicity. Overall the building is deeply religious; one experiences a profound sense of transcendence.[46]

In most of these early-twentieth-century churches the design included a large altar elevated usually at the far end of an elongated room. It was placed at a considerable distance from the laity and was monumental in size. The overall impression was that it was the altar rather than the assembly that was meant to be the central focus of the structure. In fact, most of these early churches appeared to be somewhat monumental in the local environment.

An exception was set out in three projects by the German architect Emil Steffan, which were published in 1938 but unfortunately never realized. They included exteriors that consciously avoided monumentality by looking more like ordinary barns or simple dwellings. The plans called for a freestanding altar with the assembly gathered on three sides; they also provided for the other needs of the community in addition to a worship space. During the Second World War, Steffan was able to build a barn-like church at Bust near Thionville.

After 1933 the German initiative passed to Switzerland and was reflected in a series of excellent buildings dating from the early 1930s. One of the earliest Swiss achievements was the church of St. Charles constructed at Lucerne by Fritz Metzger and consecrated in 1933. The church is based on the plan of a horseshoe, with the altar standing in the semicircular apse, raised somewhat above the level of the nave. The pulpit is carefully related to the altar. In the next few years, Metzger and two of Karl Moser's former students, Otto Dreyer and Hermann Baur, built a series of high-quality churches, primarily in Basel, Lucerne, and Zurich. These prewar churches are relatively conventional in that they were based on a simple rectangular plan. It was only after World War II that Baur and Metzger began to explore the possibilities of more complex designs. Before 1945, the concept of the church remained quite traditional; it was primarily the house of God, revealed above all at the altar and to some extent in the pulpit, rather than the house for God's people revealed in the celebrating assembly. It would be several decades before the primacy of the assembly in the design of church buildings would surface as the principal symbol in the edifice, a primacy that is still not always appreciated in the plans for both new and renovated churches.

In general, the trend among the architects who were more in tune with the developments in the liturgical movement accented the essentials of the liturgy and either eliminated or played down the accretions. More positive attention was given to the altar, the baptismal font, and the confessionals. Side altars were either eliminated or relegated to separate chapels; the number of statues in churches was reduced in favor of good art; the stations of the cross were given a less conspicuous place. The church building was conceived as a spatial envelope for the altar which is Christ (*Altare est Christus*), not simply as a static site for the tabernacle.

The church architectural trends in Germany after 1933 were reflected in other parts of Europe. In most of Europe the neo-Gothic style was thought to be the one proper form for church building. Hence, the Catholic cathedral at Cologne, the tower of the Protestant cathedral at Ulm, and the basilicas at Lourdes and Lisieux were all finished in a neo-Gothic style. In 1912 the Catholic archbishop of Cologne decreed that only neo-Romanesque and neo-Gothic structures could be built in the archdiocese. But in 1927 the Association for Christian Art in Cologne spoke against the dominance of the old styles; however, it considered reinforced concrete a building material unsuited for churches. Nevertheless, as the traditional styles lost popularity with the more progressive architects and as the new building materials revealed their positive potentials, reinforced concrete, steel, iron, and glass became more legitimate between 1925 and 1927. Because of financial limitations and the strong place of tradition in Austria, new styles of architecture developed very slowly. Even though the liturgical movement had been promoted since the 1920s by the Augustinian Canons of Klosterneuberg, it had little effect on church architecture until after the Second World War. Italy was even more tradition bound, while in Spain commissions for new churches were offered to modern architects only by religious orders, especially the Franciscans and Dominicans.

It was in the United States that modern architecture was readily accepted by Protestant communities. Frank Lloyd Wright designed the first modern church in the United States in 1906. In designing Unity Temple Church in Chicago, he departed from an axial plan and used nonderivative forms in poured concrete. The First Church of Christ Scientist in Berkeley, California, designed in 1912 by Bernard Maybeck, was avantgarde in the creative use of industrial materials. It was Ralph Adams Cram (1863–1942) who exercised the strongest influence in church building in the United States in the early decades of the twentieth century. He emerged as the leader of the Gothic revival in the country. The son of a Unitarian minister, he rightly believed that architecture should enhance the reality of the liturgy and felt that the Gothic style was the ideal form to do that. His Gothic designs for the West Point Military Academy and St. Thomas Episcopal Church in New York (1907), and his plans to complete the Episcopal Cathedral of St. John the Divine in New York City (1907) established his international reputation and enabled him to get commissions for many cathedrals and churches in the United States, Canada, and Cuba. His designs for Catholic churches included Sacred Heart in Jersey City (1925), St. Mary's of Redford in Detroit (1929), and Holy Rosary in Pittsburgh (1931). He became a professor of architecture at Massachusetts Institute of Technology and wrote several important publications, including *Church*

Building (1901) and *The Catholic Church and Art* (1931). He was the editor of *Christian Art* from 1908 until 1912.

ARCHITECTURAL PLURALISM AND
THE POST–WORLD WAR II PERIOD

In contrast to the period between the two world wars, which was architecturally dominated by the international style with a clearly defined understanding of both ends and means, the decades immediately following World War II showed an ever increasing diversity in architectural styles. The whole architectural scene exploded after World War II, resulting in scattered parts often described as visual chaos. Countless buildings were constructed to replace those destroyed by bombing, to accommodate the rapid increase in world population, and to respond to new cultural, scientific, and technological needs. If any general architectural order existed, it usually consisted of the unimaginative, monotonous repetition of inarticulate components. At no period in human history up to that time was the human environment more problematic, nor had people felt more insecure in their relationship to themselves, one another, and their world. There was, however, a growing conviction that architecture could be a useful but modest instrument in moving some of the environmental problems toward resolution. To some extent, at least in the hands of a number of important architects, the profession developed in the decades after World War II into a flexible tool designed to respond effectively to concrete human and cultural needs.

Pluralism became evident shortly after World War II. It grew out of a desire to develop buildings that had individual characterization. This was to some extent a reaction to the lack of variation in the world of early functionalists. Individual architects sought to take account of differences in regional character, not only in the sense of geographical location but also in the sense of cultural and historical factors. These factors had often been overlooked in the world of the early functionalists, who were so preoccupied with global awareness that they often neglected the need of people to identify psychologically and physically with a local place. One of the major concerns of the past few decades has been to help people find a home in the world without sacrificing their sense of freedom which is such an important value in the modern world. In other words, many of the pluralists want to satisfy the human need for both stability and mobility. They realize that neither the homeless nor the isolated can contribute to the creation of a world in which both communities and persons find a place in which they can find a world within a world. The landscape, the town, and the city may contain mobile elements, and structures may offer freedom in varying degrees, but the world cannot be characterized by overall mobility. If the human environment changes too quickly, human beings become rootless and historical process becomes impossible. Individuals and communities need a relatively stable system of place in order to grow and develop as persons, communities, and cultures.

Since World War II there have been three major generations of significant modern architects. There was the first generation made up of the form givers, whose distinguished careers spanned the period between the two world wars and who continued to exert a strong influence in the decades immediately after World War II. The most distinguished architects in this category would be Walter Gropius, Le Corbusier, Mies van der Rohe, and Frank Lloyd Wright.

They came to architectural maturity in the first third of the twentieth century and shared a conviction that architecture should be a primary force in culture. Because they felt that it should mold and even improve lifestyles, they sought inspiration from outside cultures, as in the case of Wright and his interest in Japan, and from the machine, as in the case of Gropius and Le Corbusier. The new world they sought to create was to eradicate the traces of earlier Western culture from contemporary cities. They sought to destroy the architectural box of earlier periods but in fact often ended up creating a new kind of box. Unlike the architects of the older static boxes, which were divided into smaller boxes by structural walls, these architects wanted to make their buildings something more than mere functional, articulate structures. For example, in the National Gallery in Berlin (1962–1965), Mies van der Rohe sought to give the basic box a strong, articulate structure. Le Corbusier also sought to give his later buildings a clear, symbolic character that could identify the societies for whom they were built. This is surely the case with the monastery he built for the Dominicans of Sainte Marie de la Tourette (1956–1959) at Evreux in France. The heavy concrete walls soar in a white lightness, while inside and out along the prestressed concrete run red, blue, and green painted containers for water, electricity, and gas. In the library, common room, and refectory, windows look out on the countryside. Each friar has a small cell with a balcony, while a promenade on the roof directs one's gaze toward the sky. The variety of curved shapes speaks of the transcendent, while the concrete blocks in bright primary colors speak of life and creativity. Austerity and mysticism are combined in the structure, as are symmetry and subjectivity.[47]

When the project for Le Corbusier's pilgrimage church of Notre Dame du Haut at Ronchamp was published in 1953, it disconcerted adherents to the pluralist movement because it seemed to utilize all the old proscribed forms: plastic mass, a cavelike interior, and sweeping curves. When completed in 1955, the response was enthusiastic and the church was acknowledged as an important religious structure. Located in a high place that had been a center of prayer for centuries, the church was designed as a locus of interior concentration and meditation. It is carefully related to the surrounding landscape. An outdoor altar and pulpit are designed to be used for liturgical celebrations with large groups of pilgrims. The interior is simultaneously a refuge and an embracing open form meant to foster the pilgrim's return to the center of meaning.[48] It is a space more for contemplative prayer rather than for liturgical celebrations.

The second generation of modern architects sought to adjust the forms of the first generation to a less abstract position. They might be described as formalists, refiners, and redefiners. Included here would be Philip Johnson, Eero Saarinen, Paul Rudolph, Louis Kahn, Pier Luigi Nervi, Hans Scharoun, and Alvar Aalto. The economic depression of the 1930s, the Second World War, and the postwar global and urban crises tended to relegate architecture to a less important role in solving the world's problems and in shaping the destiny of the human race. The effort to go beyond the international style resulted in the chaotic eclecticism of the early 1950s. That in turn gave way to two rather well-defined architectural positions. The first was a rigorous, sculpturally active style closely related to the later projects of Le Corbusier and Wright and best exemplified by the work of Paul Rudolph. The second was the bold neoclassicism that relied on the style of Mies van der Rohe, best exemplified in the work of Kevin Roche and the early work of Philip Johnson.

There are several architects belonging to the second generation who have played a very important role in contemporary developments. The Finnish architect Alvar Aalto (1898–1976) certainly developed beyond the international style. His buildings were often rough in texture, and though natural in color, were lyrical rather than strictly ordered in their floor plans and even in the distribution of their structural elements. His work was especially fitting for the limited economic and natural resources of his native Finland. Shortly before World War II he formed the Artet Company, which manufactured and distributed a series of brilliant furniture designs. His work ranged from the creation of stools, vases, and lighting fixtures to the planning of sizable buildings and urban areas. It is generally characterized by thoughtfulness, grace, and poetry, which made him a master of artistic form and intelligent planning. He gave special care to practical details such as handrails, bookshelves, and storage spaces. He represents a simple but honest humanism in the midst of a world often given to pretensions. He designed several remarkable churches for Lutheran congregations, including the Seinajoki Church and the Church of the Three Crosses in Vuoksenniska, Imatra.

The Italian structural engineer and architect Pier Luigi Nervi (1891–1979) was one of the most notable architects working in reinforced concrete. He evolved his own system of structural design, mainly for large buildings, into which he introduced variations in response to specific needs and economic limitations. He often collaborated with other architects. He was basically a structural engineer who was also an artist. Among his most acclaimed projects are the Roman Catholic Cathedral of St. Mary in San Francisco, a project done in collaboration with Pietro Belluschi, and the papal audience hall in Vatican City.

Eero Saarinen (1910–1961), the son of the distinguished architect Eliel Saarinen, was one of the most sculptured architects of his era. He achieved worldwide recognition for winning a competition for the design of the Jefferson National Expansion Memorial in St. Louis, later known as the Gateway Arch. During the last ten years of his life he was especially prolific. Instead of building what could be a personal style with each succeeding design based on its predecessor, he sought to produce singular designs that were distinctly appropriate for each new building. As a result, his designs were fresh, intriguing, and mysterious, providing a creative legacy of originality that has profoundly influenced architects since his early death at the age of fifty-one. Among his most remarkable designs is that for the Dulles Airport outside Washington, D.C., completed after his death.

Mention should also be made of the German architect Hans Scharoun (1893–1972). His early work was a mixture of the international style and expressionism, exemplified by his housing designs, which provided for interior spaces incorporating outlook, comfort, and surprise. He was little concerned about the external appearances of this buildings, which were often not very pleasant. It was not until after the Second World War that he came into his own as the great expressionist of his age, above all through the creation of a housing project in Stuttgart-Zuffenhausen (1954–1959), in which the buildings are almost devoid of right angles and project a curious, even disturbing appearance. His best known work is the Berlin Philharmonie (1956–1963), certainly one of the world's great concert halls, in which parcels of seating surround the orchestra, resulting in an experience of both unity and intimacy. Although the exterior of the building is drab, the concert hall is considered a masterpiece of organic architecture.[49]

The second generation of modern architects exercised strong leadership in the profession both in terms of actual accomplishments and public esteem. Their basic philosophy has been described as exclusive in that they operated within the tradition of the modern architecture that dominated the scene since the 1920s. They sought to create a humanly made world in accord with what they thought were the ideal formal and social images. They dealt with pure and simple shapes but did not generally attend to problem solving.

A third generation of modern architects seeks a redefinition of architecture in terms of the complexity and contradictions of modern life. This generation might well be called reactionary. They agree that modernism died in the 1970s, but they have certainly not succeeded in putting any unified style in its place. The result has been what might be called architectural eclecticism, which often goes by the name postmodernism. There has been no moratorium on building, but, with a number of exceptions, many of the buildings bear no trace of creative imagination. Among the postmodern architects, especially in the United States, there has been a ferment of activity, exploring a great variety of styles. For example, Frank Gehry has worked in the raw materials that were common in the sculpture of the 1960s—plywood, corrugated iron, and asbestos shingles. He has achieved widespread recognition for his stunning design for the Guggenheim Museum in Bilbao, Spain. At the other extreme, Richard Meier and Charles Gathmey both have created clear, carefully modulated voids and surfaces similar to those designed by Le Corbusier. In between these extremes are the glass caverns of Cesar Pelli, the playful historicism of Charles Moore and Robert Stern, the interplay with pop art and history exhibited by Robert Venturi, the sometimes outrageous displays of Stanley Tigerman, and the technological flexibility of Hugh Hardy.

The main thing all these architects have in common is a fascination with architecture as a language. They have no common ideology even though they are commonly described as postmodernists. They cannot trace their styles to a common source, though they all have had a certain awe and devotion to Philip Johnson, who throughout his long career has been a brilliant opportunist capable of adapting to changing tastes and so has traversed the whole range of twentieth-century styles ranging from the international to the postmodern.

One of the most articulate and productive representatives of what has happened in recent decades is Robert Venturi (b. 1925), whose projects and writings attempt to provide critical alternatives to the functionalism of the second generation of architects. His principal books are *Complexity and*

Contradiction in Architecture and *Learning from Las Vegas.*[50] He seeks to observe the requirements of function, program, and activities while creating architectural places that are inherently scaled to human use, comfort, and memories. He has had a remarkable influence on other architects and their commitment to a modest and flexible position in which architecture embodies the values and meanings of the people for whom the buildings are designed and not simply the meanings and values of the architects themselves. They tend to reject prototypical solutions in favor of positive responses to individual cases and needs, and they recognize the dysfunction between a reductive architecture and a complex world of very different cultures. Charles Moore has also influenced the architectural scene through his writing, especially his book *Body, Memory and Architecture,* in which he sets forth, together with Kent C. Bloomer and Robert J. Yudell, his ambitions for a more humanistic mode of building.[51]

Several principles or at least attitudes characterize the work of many contemporary architects. There is the principle of contextualism, which asserts that an individual building is but a fragment of a larger whole; it is not an isolated entity meant to project an image of absolute perfection. Then there is the principle of allusionism, which insists that architecture is meant to be a response to a concrete historical and cultural situation. Finally, there is the principle of ornamentation, which believes that ornament need not be justified in historical or cultural terms but responds to an innate human need for elaboration and serves as an effective articulation of a building's elements in relation to human scale.[52]

Much of the best in contemporary architecture does not concentrate its attention on fixed types or inflexible principles, but rather seeks to understand the total character of the project. The result is an architectural method rather than a style. Meaning and character are once again given primary importance. A buildings is not a mere container housing functions; it is also an expressive presence that is dynamic in the environment. It both anchors people in a place and also gives them a sense of mobility. Buildings then are the products of various natural, social, and historical forces. They have their roots in the past, relate to the present, and reach out to the future.[53]

Among contemporary architects there is a conscious desire to manifest a regional character. For example, Reimi Pietilä, like his Finnish predecessor Alvar Aalto, has concentrated on topological forms and natural materials. James Stirling has produced metal and glass buildings that are quite proper in the English scene, just as Paolo Portoghesi has designed projects that are unmistakably Italian in their sophisticated elegance. The restrained dynamism of Jörn Utzon's work is clearly Danish, and the so-called melting pot architecture of Robert Venturi is overtly American. Venturi's work is especially intriguing in that it retrieves conventional elements from the past that bring a new psychological dimension to architecture in their appeal to memory and association. He manages to express both the richness and the ambiguity of modern experience.[54]

The new architecture of pluralism is still developing. The pluralism of the exclusivists carries with it the danger of being sterile and monotonous, whereas that of the inclusivists runs the risk of degenerating into environmental chaos. Awareness must be developed through education. The very term "pluralism," used to describe contemporary architecture, certainly suggests that architects and their patrons have abandoned an absolutist approach to the world and absolute solutions to the world's problems. There are those who do maintain an absolutist attitude toward life and take a nonhistorical approach to all of life's problems, but absolutism seems to be spiritually dead. Like all people, architects have to make choices, but those choices should be made not only in light of abstract principles but in light of the concrete environment, hopes, and needs of contemporary persons and communities. People are their histories, but those histories are not limited to past experiences. There are present realities with a dynamic orientation toward the future. Hence, architectural efforts on the part of many contemporary pluralists to discover the total concrete character of a project are designed not only to make new environments meaningful but to make those environments sources of both memories and hopes.[55]

One of the most distinguished contemporary architects who has achieved worldwide praise is the Japanese architect Tadao Ando. His buildings tend to be pure geometric compositions of concrete, glass, steel, stone, and wood, most often described as deeply "spiritual." He has a powerful inner vision that ignores current movements, schools, or styles as he creates buildings with form and composition carefully related to nature, to the local environment, and to the life that will be lived within the buildings. He has linked international modernism with a profound concern for aesthetics. His buildings achieve unity between structure and nature. Influenced above all by Louis Kahn and Le Corbusier, between 1985 and 1988 he realized four buildings that firmly established his reputation, three of which are religious: the so-called Rokko Chapel and the churches of Light and Water. In the United States he has designed the Pulitzer Museum in St. Louis and the Modern Art Museum in Fort Worth, Texas. Down the road are plans for a Calder museum in Philadelphia; he has also designed a monastic guest house and prayer chapel for Saint John's Abbey in Collegeville, Minnesota.[56]

9

Developments in Liturgy and Sacred Architecture and Art Following World War II

IN GERMANY THE RESULTS OF LITURGICAL STUDIES COMBINED with pastoral efforts were evident in the remarkable document published in 1946 by the German Liturgical Commission entitled "Guiding Principles for the Design of Churches according to the Spirit of the Roman Liturgy."[1] In Rome the introduction of modern art into the liturgy was met with apprehension and misunderstanding. In 1924 a Pontifical Commission for Sacred Art in Italy had been established, followed the next year by the foundation of the Pontifical Institute for Christian Archeology. Beginning in 1933, the Commission for Sacred Art held study weeks on sacred art for the clergy; the concern of those meetings, however, was primarily to preserve the Christian artistic heritage rather than encourage the development of new styles of liturgical art and architecture.

Controversial art was placed in some of the French and German churches after World War II, which prompted the Congregation of the Holy Office to issue an instruction on sacred art on June 20, 1952.[2] The instruction gave general directives on the building of churches, their interior arrangement, and their appointment with pictures, statues, and liturgical objects. The document affirmed that new churches may be built in new architectural styles provided they do not look like profane buildings. The church buildings were to be houses of God and places for prayer, simply and practically constructed, without false ornamentation. Individual works of art in churches were to be designed so as to assist the liturgy and the worship of the congregation. They were not to be offensive to religious feeling or unworthy of the churches they adorned. The instruction reminded local ordinaries of their responsibility to oversee the images placed in worship spaces and to maintain standards of excellence in matters of sacred art and architecture.

After publication of the instruction, the Holy See was accused of being opposed to modern art, but that judgment was perhaps too harsh. In his commentary on the instruction, Cardinal Celso Costantini, an authority on sacred art and one of the principal organizers of the great exhibition of church art and artifacts during the Holy Year of 1950, emphasized that the masters of religious art were regularly representatives of their own times. In speaking of unusual images that should find no place in churches, the instruction was referring not to works executed in a modern style but to innovations in iconography representing false dogmas and endangering the faith and morals of the people. In 1953 Archbishop Giovanni Costantini, the president of the Pontifical Commission for Sacred Art in Italy, established the journal *Fede e Arte* in order to promote liturgical art, but the review was generally not sympathetic toward many of the new developments, especially those in France.

It was Cardinal Giacomo Lercaro (1891–1976), the archbishop of Bologna and a strong supporter of the liturgical movement in Italy, who promoted a more enlightened attitude toward the new developments in both church architecture and sacred art. He presided over the Bologna National Church Architecture Congress, which was held in 1955 in conjunction with a liturgical conference. The following year the Centro Studi e Informazioni per l'Architettura Sacra was founded and the journal *Chiesa e Quartiere* was begun. Unfortunately it ceased publication in 1978, shortly after Cardinal Lercaro died. A study center was established in Milan, where Cardinal Giovanni Montini (later Pope Paul VI) fostered the development of excellent church architecture. As a result, new churches designed by competent architects were built in the northern industrial centers around Milan and Bologna. The southern part of the country remained more traditional, although in recent years distinguished architects have been active in the promotion of quality church structures throughout Italy.

Religious communities in Spain commissioned well-known architects to design new churches that are impressive from a liturgical point of view. Although many new parish churches have been built in Spain since the Second Vatican Council, most of them are mediocre both liturgically and architecturally. In Belgium the Benedictines from the Abbey of St. André began in 1932 the publication of a superb journal, *L'Art d'Église*. It influenced church art and architecture not only in Belgium but in other parts of the world as well, especially in the years when the very talented Dom Frédéric Debuyst was the editor.

Pius XII's encyclical *Musicae Sacrae Disciplina,* issued on December 25, 1955,[3] and the instruction on sacred music and the sacred liturgy issued by the Sacred Congregation of Rites on September 3, 1958,[4] both raised questions about the placement of the organ and the choir in new churches. Only minor changes were made in the liturgy until the announcement of the Second Vatican Council by Pope John XXIII in January 1959. On June 5, 1960, however, John XXIII appointed a new Pontifical Liturgical Commission to prepare for the Second Vatican Council. Nevertheless, it was felt that a preliminary correction of the liturgical rubrics should be undertaken even before the council discussed the more general problems of the liturgy. Consequently, John XXIII published a new code of rubrics on July 26, 1960; it served an immediate need for sounder and clearer rubrics and it also was an important step in preparation for the liturgical renewal of the council itself.

Shortly after he announced the forthcoming ecumenical council, John XXIII established three secretariats and eleven commissions to prepare the council agenda. The pope invited the national hierarchies to send the Holy See proposals about the matters that should be dealt with at the council. Twenty percent of the suggestions dealt with the liturgy. Thirteen commissions were established to study the liturgical matters, the last of which was to deal with the question of sacred art, vestments, and church furnishings.

On December 4, 1963, Pope Paul VI promulgated the Constitution on the Sacred Liturgy (*Sacrosanctum Concilium*), chapter 7 of which deals with sacred art and furnishings but with church architecture only in a general way.[5] The chapter is not bolstered with strong theological reasons for its positions and in fact refrains from taking theological positions on artistic questions that are still open to discussion.

Paul VI had a keen interest in sacred art and addressed the topic on several occasions.[6] Shortly after the promulgation of the Constitution on the Sacred Liturgy, he met with a group of Italian artists in the Sistine Chapel, celebrated the eucharist with them, and then gave an address on the relationship between artists and the Catholic Church. In his discourse he pointed out that many of his predecessors had had close relationships with artists and architects, but none of them had invited artists as a group to a meeting to discuss their inspirations.[7] The most tangible reminder of that meeting is the gallery of contemporary religious art created by Paul VI in the Vatican Museum. He opened the gallery with an impressive allocution on June 23, 1973. Two hundred and fifty artists volunteered to send works that were intended to answer the question: Is there a valid modern religious art as distinct from sacred art which belongs to the liturgy? In his discourse Paul acknowledged that much of modern art is not immediately comprehensible but then went on to say that the church has in modern times visited incomprehension upon modern artists. Inviting artists to once again work for the church, Paul said "[W]e have not had the means to understand great things, beautiful things. . . . We have walked along crooked paths where art and beauty and the worship of God have been badly served. . . . Shall we make peace again? Here today? It must be left to you to sing the free and powerful song of which you are capable."[8]

Detailed norms on the construction of churches were set out in the instruction *Inter Oecumenici,* issued jointly by the Congregation of Rites and the Consilium on September 26, 1964.[9] Chapter 5 is entitled "Designing Churches and Altars to Facilitate Active Participation of the Faithful." It is one of the most important chapters in the instruction, but it should be interpreted in light of the earlier chapters, especially those on the eucharist and other sacraments. The text enunciates certain principles that, if taken seriously, would result in a renewed spirit according to which practical solutions to problems could be found. It promotes that cooperation between liturgists, architects, and artists which is always necessary if renovated and new churches are to have appropriate expressive and formative power.

On May 25, 1967, the Congregation of Rites issued an instruction *Eucharisticum mysterium* on worship and the eucharist. A lengthy document, the text deals primarily with the catechesis of the people concerning the eucharist, but there is also a concluding section on the cult of the eucharist as a permanent sacrament; it contains directives for reservation, devotion, processions, exposition, and congresses. Many of these and other norms were included in the General Instruction of the Roman Missal (nos. 253–80) issued by the Congregation for Divine Worship on April 3, 1969, and revised a number of times since that date, including the most recent revision.[10] In the 1983 edition of the Code of Canon Law, which went into effect on the First Sunday of Advent 1983, the norms on sacred places are contained in book 4, canons 1205–43; the norms on the veneration of the saints, images, and relics are contained in canons 1186–90. Other liturgical documents have been modified to conform to the new code.

In the conciliar and postconciliar norms, as well as the books, articles, and directives on liturgical theology and practice that have been issued by the mainline Protestant churches, there has been a rapid development in the understanding of the necessary rapport between artists, architects, and liturgists and those who exercise authority and ministry in the church. The implementation of ecclesial norms and directives by both Catholic and Protestant churches has of course been very uneven. Some remarkable developments have taken place in the last forty years, but in general the new and renovated churches and their appointments have been mediocre in quality. The official documents from the Holy See have usually set out broad principles that can be flexibly implemented and that enable patrons to take into account significant differences in situations. As the history of church architecture since the Second World War shows, competence is the key to the achievement of successful projects—competence in the architects, artists, liturgical consultants, and the clients for whom the churches are built.

CHURCH BUILDING SINCE WORLD WAR II

Following the Second World War, it became increasingly clear to liturgists and enlightened architects that churches destined to be the setting for the newly discovered concepts of the liturgy could not be built according to Gothic or baroque patterns, which were based on very different concepts of the liturgy and a totally different kind of social order. Protestant churches that recovered a regular practice of celebrating the eucharist each Sunday also realized that traditional "auditorium" churches had to be abandoned in favor of churches that focused not only on the pulpit but also on the altar and that attention had to be given to the assembly as the primary celebrant of the Sunday liturgy.

Theological developments, especially in the areas of theological anthropology, christology, ecclesiology, and sacramental theology, helped to restore to ordinary Christians a sense of personal worth, dignity, and mission in the church. Among Roman Catholics, the various forms of Catholic Action as well as movements such as the Young Christian Workers, Young Christian Students, and the Christian Family Movement, helped to ground the spirituality of ordinary Christians in the liturgy rather than in popular devotions. As a result, the church building more and more was looked upon as the house of God's people and as the assembly room for liturgical celebration by the whole community rather than simply by the ordained members of the community.

The application of the new theological and liturgical developments to church art and architecture was made only gradually but initially in France and Germany, especially by those associated with the Centre de Pastorale Liturgie in Paris and the Liturgical Institute in Trier. The latter promoted sound theological and pastoral education through the competent guidance of its faculty, including Johannes Wagner and Balthasar Fischer. Wagner was one of the consultors to the subcommission on sacred art established by Pope John XXIII to prepare for the Second Vatican Council.

In France the Dominican Fathers Marie-Alain Couturier (1897–1954) and Pie-Raymond Régamey played a very important role in promoting the work of competent artists through their publications. Régamey's thought was summarized and made available in the English translation of his book *Religious Art in the Twentieth Century* (1963). Some of Couturier's work has been collected and made available at Yale University through the generosity of the Menil Foundation. In 1938 the two friars had undertaken the direction of the journal *L'Art Sacré*, which had been founded two years earlier by Joseph Pichard. In a book called *L'Art Sacré Moderne*, Pichard had chronicled the new atmosphere that emerged between 1890 and 1914 and was resumed after World War I, a climate in which first attempts were made to develop a modern church architecture in Europe and in which modern sacred art was at least somewhat understood and appreciated.

Couturier was confined to the United States during World War II but returned to France in August 1945. His lectures and contacts with artists in the United States and Canada inspired him to develop new ideas about how the church and its environment should relate to modern architecture, sculpture, and painting. He set about attracting important artists for the appointment of a new church at Assy in the south of France. It was consecrated in June 1950. By that time Couturier had already corresponded with Henri Matisse about the design and appointment of a chapel for the Dominican nuns at Vence in southern France.[11]

The church at Assy, Notre-Dame de Toute Grâce, is a parish church in the French Alps near Mont Blanc. Designed by Maurice Novarina, it is not particularly distinguished from an architectural point of view, but the commissioning of outstanding artists from the secular art world to appoint the church aroused intense controversy surrounding the Dominican *l'art sacré* in postwar France. The artists were chosen not on the basis of their personal faith but rather on the quality of their work; most were non-Catholics. Fernand Léger, Marc Chagall, Jean Lurçat, Henri Matisse, Pierre Bonnard, Georges Braque, Georges Rouault, and Germaine Richier all designed works for the church at Assy. It was Richier's bronze crucifix that provoked the harshest antagonism, so much in fact that the local bishop felt obliged to ask for its removal. Many critics felt that the work captured in an extraordinarily stark, almost decadent way, the tragedy of the crucifixion but failed to express any sense of Christ's victory over death. Couturier answered his critics: For Christian art to exist at all, "each generation must appeal to the masters of living art, and today those masters come first from secular art; . . . there are no dead masters in art." The debate resulted in an official directive on sacred art issued by the French hierarchy in 1952, which managed to pacify the various parties. The controversy over the church at Assy, however, sharpened questions about contemporary liturgical art and provided a context for further responsible reflection.

The dispute over the church at Assy was only one facet of a much larger crisis in the French church caused by an ensemble of new directions taken in French Catholicism since 1946 that included the liturgical movement, modern art in churches, historical and biblical theologies, and approaches to pastoral theology. A particular problem in the eyes of the Holy See was the priest-worker movement, an experiment aimed at bringing the church more effectively into contact with the daily lives of ordinary people. In 1953 the worker priests were ordered not to accept any more recruits; the so-called new theology that had developed among the French theologians was summarily dismissed by Pius XII's encyclical *Humani Generis* in 1950; and the master general of the Dominicans, Emmanuel Suárez, removed the three French provincials from office and banished from their teaching posts some of the most distinguished theologians of the modern period, including Yves Congar, M. D. Chenu, H.-M. Feret, and Thomas Camelot. Pierre Boisselot, the director of Cerf, the large, innovative publishing house, was also sent into exile. Those active in art, including Régamey and Couturier, were to be closely supervised. Certainly under their editorship the pages of *L'Art Sacré* were beautiful, profound, and inspiring.[12] Looking back on Couturier's project at Assy, one senses that although the individual pieces in the church are often brilliant, as a whole the ensemble reflects such a disparity of styles that it is more like a museum than an integrated place for Christian worship.

The Chapel of the Rosary at the Dominican convent at Vence in the southern part of France was more successful as a worship space. Henri Matisse lived in Vence. The Dominican sisters there wanted to build a new chapel. Sister Jacques, who had nursed Matisse through an illness, asked him if he would consider decorating their chapel. Matisse agreed and Couturier was soon brought in on the project, working closely with Matisse, who conceived the entire design for the structure as well as its decoration. It was consecrated in June 1951. Matisse considered the project his masterpiece. His aim was to balance a surface of light and color against a solid wall printed discreetly with black line drawings. The decoration is concentrated in the stained glass of a group of full-length windows in the sanctuary and white glazed tile pictures on the walls opposite the windows. The latter are drawn with the greatest economy of line. There is a huge drawing of St. Dominic, one of the Virgin and Child in the midst of flowing clouds, and line drawings of the stations of the cross. Matisse also designed an elongated simple crucifix, several brilliant colored chasubles, and altar linen embroidered with fish. The outside of the chapel is white with blue roof tiles and a thin spirelike cross with a bell tower above it. In its simplicity, light, and color, the chapel is certainly one of the great works of liturgical art in the twentieth century.

Couturier was also asked to recommend some artists to appoint the Sacré Coeur church at Audincourt. There Novarina, the architect who had designed the church at Assy, gave the simple church interior at Audincourt a strip of window running completely around the interior immediately under the roof. Fernand Léger provided seventy meters of continuing glass to fill the space. The theme is the passion of Christ, but it is not shown in direct portrayal but rather is symbolized in emblems of the various stations and the instruments of the passion. It is recognized as a great work in which solid lumps of glass have been cemented together to form part of the wall. Jean Bazaine provided a large mosaic for the facade, which is not quite so successful. The work at Audincourt was an important step forward in liturgical art because of the unity and discipline with which the whole project was completed; it involved the support of the parishioners and provided a depth of experience for those who worshiped there.

In Germany it was the journal *Das Münster*, edited since 1947, which publicized excellent liturgical art and architecture. After World War II, numerous churches were built to replace those destroyed by bombing and to provide worship spaces for the growing German population. The gifted architects who designed the projects included Reinhard Hofbauer, Hans Schädel, Paul Schneider-Eisleben, Richard Jorg, Emil Steffan, Dominikus Böhm, and Rudolf Schwarz. Many of their new churches represented an intensely rational vision of space brought down to human scale and designed with good proportions. Their plans were generally based on a square or a rectangle, so that the assembly could gather close to the altar and feel integrated with what went on in the sanctuary.

Dominikus Böhm resumed his architectural career after the Second World War. In his new churches he strove for great simplicity of structure, but he achieved a profoundly spiritual atmosphere through decorative enrichment. One of the best examples of his work is the Maria Königen church in Cologne-Marienburg, built in 1954. The whole south wall of the church is a great curtain of superb stained glass with an intricate pattern of a stylized leaf design in a limited series of semitransparent silver-grey and grey-green tones that harmonize well with the leaves of the trees in the park outside. Fragments of antique glass in brilliant colors are used to accent points. The marvelous wall of shifting light stands in marked contrast to the severity of the rest of the church. Böhm is still acknowledged to have been one of the most original German church architects; his tradition was carried on effectively by his son Gottfried.

Rudolf Schwarz also resumed his commitment to church building after World War II. He felt that a religious building should be a mighty refuge; hence many of his postwar churches give the impression of being spiritual fortresses of enduring strength standing up against the outside secular world. For example, the solid towering walls of St. Michael's Church in Frankfurt, built in 1954, rise unbroken by windows. The church is illuminated only by a continuous band of windows just beneath the roof. The plan is an ellipse with trefoil chapels, so that the main body of the church is a great room surrounded by gently curving walls, producing a feeling of strength but also great calm. Schwarz felt that most human experience takes place in a menacing world where people have only a brief glimpse of light from above. He symbolized that experience in the church but tried to give the gathered community an assurance that God's light is always with those who assemble in the name of Jesus. This sense of tranquil harmony and simplicity is especially reflected in the small, unassuming church of St. Christophorus at Cologne-Niehl (1962). The building certainly points toward the future and the dominant role that the liturgy would play in the design of church buildings.

It was perhaps Emil Steffan's churches above all that emphasized the role of the assembly as closely involved with the presider in the celebration of the liturgy. He designed a remarkable series of churches, including St. Laurentius in Munich (1955), St. Elizabeth in Opladen (1957), and St. Maria-in-den-Benden in Dusseldorf-Wersten (1958). Their architecture is not markedly modern, but they have a human quality about them and certainly place their emphasis on the participation of the assembly in the liturgy.

In Switzerland there was a tradition of excellence in modern church architecture dating from the late 1920s. It was fostered by the Society of St. Luke, which began the publication of a yearbook on Christian art and architecture in 1927, first under the title *Ars Sacra* and after 1954 under the title *Sakrale Kunst*. The distinguished architects who designed Swiss churches after World War II included Fritz Metzger, Karl Higi, and August Boyer. Among the Swiss there was a conscious effort to develop a more organic approach to church building so that all the architectural elements— walls, ceiling, and floors—become parts of a whole and parts of each other. This continuity in structural materials and furnishings reflected the organic character of the assembly, which is hierarchical in nature but which is in fact the body of Christ. The term "hierarchical," however, did not imply elevation above or superiority to the laity but rather an ordered arrangement so that ordained clergy and laity might fulfill their proper roles in the assembly. One of the finest Swiss projects to embody this concern was Fritz Metzger's church of St. Franziskus at Basel-Riehen (1950). Its sanctuary and nave (an ellipse and trapezoid) blend into one symbolic form, though everything is organically directed toward the sanctuary and particularly is focused on the altar rather than on the assembly as a whole. In Switzerland a number of very competent artists were commissioned to produce works for new churches.

Following the construction of Le Corbusier's chapel at Ronchamp there was a major shift in the style of many church designs, especially in Germany and Switzerland. In general, there was a complete break with the axial symmetry that had governed church architecture since the peace of Constantine; unfortunately, many amateur architects tried to imitate the poetic style of Ronchamp but ended up creating pretentious monuments in which the liturgy was swallowed up in the decor and ambiance of the building. They failed to realize that Ronchamp was designed to fulfill a very special program—it was a pilgrimage chapel perched on top of a hill, unrelated to normal daily worship in a parish. Furthermore, Ronchamp was untouched by the vibrant liturgical movement in France at the time of its construction.

Even though the liturgical movement had been promoted in Austria since 1922 through the efforts of Pius Parsch, church architecture remained quite traditional until the mid-1990s. Several architects known as Group 4 designed successful churches in both Salzburg and Vienna. Other reputable churches were built at Innsbruck, Klagenfurt, Donawitz, and Graz. Italy was even more bound by tradition than Austria. Although many new parish churches were built in Spain after the Second Vatican Council, most of them are not distinguished.

In England, apart from new cathedrals at Coventry, Guildford, and Liverpool, new church buildings are relatively unknown to nonspecialists. They include some of the best and some of the worst examples attempting to challenge the utilitarianism of the modern movement. In Britain the shift from traditional planning and architecture to a modern interpretation of architecture was slow and fraught with turmoil. The dominant impression left by the new Anglican cathedral at Liverpool (1904–1961) and the Roman Catholic cathedral at Westminster (1895–1903) is one of traditionalism.

In England the most significant church building erected since World War II has been the new Anglican cathedral at Coventry, replacing the medieval cathedral bombed in 1940. At the instigation of the bishop of Coventry, it was decided to construct a new edifice among the ashes of the old. An architectural competition was held in 1951 with the original stipulation that the design should be in the Gothic style; fortunately that requirement was eventually withdrawn. After much discussion, a modern design by Sir Basil Spence was chosen. He sought to construct a building that would speak to both contemporary and future generations of worshipers, would witness to the central truths of the Christian faith, and would enshrine an altar for celebration in which the people could actively participate. He wanted to erect a building marked by continuity, unity, permanence, and vitality. To appoint the building he turned to some of the foremost artists living in Britain, including Graham Sutherland for the design of the great east-end tapestry, Jacob Epstein and Elizabeth Frink for sculpture, and John Piper and Lawrence Lee for the design of the windows. The sculpture in the building is very reflective of a Britain that had suffered intensely during the Second World War; much emphasis has been placed on the suffering of Christ with little hint of resurrection. In the midst of much controversy and opposition, the cathedral was completed in 1962. In general, the professional architectural journals and critics acclaimed the building a success, especially in the way it was related to the ruins of the old cathedral. The former had a superb tower and spire still standing, a gutted nave, and a charred cross.[13]

Spence turned the ruins of the old cathedral into an imposing forecourt to the new structure, which is joined to the old by a colossal arch. In the new cathedral there is a vast nave prefaced by a great western window-wall on which John Hutton has engraved thirty-five angels and thirty-one saints. The high altar is enormous. Behind and above it is Sutherland's green and gold tapestry, representing Jesus Christ the redeemer in the Glory of the Father; it dominates the whole cathedral. Other centers of focus are the Chapel of Christian Unity, the splendid baptistery window designed by John Piper, and the Chapel of Christ in Gethsemane.

Coventry is a truly modern cathedral, but there are serious weaknesses in the building, the most serious of which is its liturgical conservatism. The client's brief should have been crucial in the design of the building, but as often happens with competition-based designs such as the one that produced Coventry, requirements other than liturgical tend to dominate. The elongated nave and the massive, elevated altar clearly give the impression that the church is a spectator church, where the congregation looks at the altar rather than shares in the eucharistic celebration. The altar dwarfs the entire sanctuary. There is also the question whether the individualism of the artists was sufficiently subordinated to the unity of the church. For example, the brilliance of Piper's window certainly tends to outshine the baptismal font itself; likewise Sutherland's tapestry dominates the building and draws attention away from the altar. In spite of these serious reservations, the building did make English people and other visitors recognize that modern art and contemporary architectural styles are here to stay. The church not only stands as a symbol of a reconstructed Britain that was devastated by World War II but also as a symbol of the growth and change that are an inherent part of Christian life. Church buildings erected after Coventry were to some extent able to profit from its experience.

Two Roman Catholic cathedrals in Britain have been completed since the Second Vatican Council, and a third has undergone such major renovation as to be a new building. In Liverpool the church authorities wanted a cathedral that would give expression to the human belief in God and serve as an effective place for worship, but they also wanted a structure with a sufficiently broad architectural framework to accommodate other arts. Sir Edwin Luytens had designed a structure in 1934 but only the crypt was completed. In 1959 a competition for a new design was held. The program stipulated no particular style but insisted that Luytens's crypt be incorporated in the new design. Sir Frederic Gibbard won the competition with a circular plan and a central altar. The building was begun that same year and completed in 1967. From the start, the building posed the serious liturgical problems that are regularly caused by circular plans and central altars. The works of distinguished British artists have been included in the building, but unfortunately the cathedral has been plagued by engineering and construction problems. Gibbard confessed publicly that he did not really understand the principles of Roman Catholic liturgy set out in the Constitution on the Sacred Liturgy. The modern character of the cathedral is reflected in its polygonal shape with a circular sanctuary and in its tent-like exterior, surmounted by a crown over the sanctuary area. The congregation, gathered on three sides of the sanctuary, has been quite carefully associated with the action in the sanctuary area.[14]

In many ways a simpler but perhaps much more satisfying project was the building of the Roman Catholic Cathedral of Sts. Peter and Paul at Clifton/Bristol. Consecrated in 1973 and standing on an awkwardly shaped site, the building was designed as a diamond by Percy Thomas Partnership. It seats a thousand people in such a way that no worshiper is more than forty-five feet away from the presider in the sanctuary. Although it is not a very elegant building, it is pleasing to the eye and is a very effective shell for the celebration of the liturgy. In fact, the cathedral has been recognized for the excellent quality of its liturgy, especially its musical program. The artwork included in the building is both functional and impressive.

Much less satisfactory is the new cathedral structure at Brentwood. Many unkind remarks have been made about the postmodern project both before and after its construction, attacking both the idea in general and the design in particular. Brentwood's early Catholics had worshiped at a church built in 1861. That building was incorporated into successive structures. The first extension was added in 1972; it utilized the 1861 church as one segment of a much larger building. By the mid-1980s it was in need of repairs that would have cost a considerable sum of money; hence, the decision was made to demolish the 1972 addition and rebuild. The bishop commissioned Quinlan Terry, a well-known proponent of the neoclassical style of architecture, to design the building.

The main facade of the cathedral with its Doric columns and entablature and semicircular portico clearly proclaims the classical style. The walls of rough-surfaced Kentish rogastone contrast with the smooth stucco columns with their capitals and entablature of Portland stone. Surmounting the whole building is a small cupola after Bernini's style. The spire of the old cathedral is visible from the front of the building but is not conspicuous.

The interior contains a large open space with aisles on four sides divided off from the rest of the building by arches—three on the east and west sides, and five on the north and south sides. In the central area stand the altar, ambo, and bishop's cathedra, and there is seating for three hundred people. The areas beyond the arches accommodate five to six hundred more people, all seated on simple chairs. The south section of the church beyond the arches is the nave of the former cathedral, which serves as the Blessed Sacrament chapel. At one end of the chapel is an antique tabernacle of Italian design. In a niche in one of the walls is a statue of Our Lady and Child.

The altar is a thin marble table supported by eight stone Tuscan columns. It is a spindly structure lacking in strength of design. It is placed in the center of an open space under the lantern on a hexagonal platform raised two steps. The cathedra is of the same material and is placed in the central arch on the south side facing the altar. Opposite the throne on the same axis is an octagonally shaped ambo, much stronger in design than the altar.

In the northern section of the building near the main entrance is the baptismal font, which is octagonal in shape. Inside the structure there are three steps leading down to the water, which is about a foot deep. Adults to be baptized descend the steps into the water and then come up three steps on the other side. The font gives the impression of being cramped into an area that is much too small. The altar, ambo, cathedra, and font were all designed by Quinlan Terry and Raymond Erith.

The organ, originally built in 1881, is a three-manual instrument. It is located at the west end of the old Gothic nave in a new case designed by Terry to match the style of the rest of the church. The choir is placed behind the cathedra in formal choir stalls. The cathedral has had a distinguished musical program for many years.

Clearly the layout of the interior does not conform to the style of neoclassical churches. Christopher Wren would have a conventual east–west sanctuary. The Brentwood cathedral is laid out to encourage participation of the whole assembly gathered around the altar. That objective is admirable, but somehow the interior reminds one more of a ballroom than a place of worship. Classical architecture regularly drew attention to itself because of its beauty and form; it deliberately refrained from having a strong transcendent thrust. That seems to be the problem with the Brentwood cathedral—it lacks a sense of mystery and transcendence.[15]

MODERN CHURCH ARCHITECTURE IN IRELAND

The first modern church built in Ireland in the twentieth century was that of Christ the King at Turners Cross, Cork, designed in 1927 by the American architect Barry Byrne.[16] In Ireland, however, the design of churches in imitation of earlier styles of architecture continued well into the 1960s; most of these buildings were adorned with artificial veneers that simply presented earlier architectural styles but used new engineering and structural techniques.[17] In 1965 the Irish hierarchy established an Advisory Committee on Sacred Art and Architecture, whose members were either distinguished architects or specialists in theology.[18] Hence, the years after the Second Vatican Council witnessed a dramatic development of church building in Ireland.

Much of the inspiration for these remarkable buildings was provided by the Irish Episcopal Commission for Liturgy. The Irish Roman Catholic bishops were among the first members of the hierarchy to issue a directory on the environment and art of Christian worship.[19]

Since the council, various plans for church building and reform have emerged in Ireland as well as in other parts of the world. They can be broadly divided into four general categories: (1) longitudinal shape based on the traditional division of sanctuary and nave; (2) transverse emphasis, in which there is a careful planning of a close relationship between assembly and altar; (3) centralized plan, giving rise to more or less circular buildings; and (4) antiphonal plan, in which the assembly gathers on two opposite sides of an axial space containing the altar at one end, the ambo at another, and the presider's chair placed in close relation to both altar and ambo. These plans reflect an understanding of liturgical celebration ranging from that of spectator worship (longitudinal plan) to full, active, and conscious participation by the whole assembly (antiphonal plan).[20]

With the development of new technology and materials, including reinforced concrete, steel, factory-laminated wood, and new forms of colored glass, along with important advances in engineering, church architects were able to move away from the concept of a long, narrow space, dictated by the use of stone, brick, and wood, and respond more effectively to fresh concepts of space and light, more in keeping with the modern liturgical movement.[21] In Ireland, as in other parts of the world, modern church architecture stirred up lively public debate, with many people expressing a vociferous dislike for what was happening in the church. Despite the challenge, traditional sanctuaries were often hastily changed, sometimes with disastrous results, simply so that Mass could be celebrated facing the people.

Michael Scott was the leading architect of his generation following the Second World War; he was responsible for introducing the international style into Ireland. It was not until 1964, however, that he had a commission to build a church in Ireland.[22] Between 1967 and 1977, Liam McCormick established a reputation for being the most important church architect in Ireland. His buildings show great respect for the landscape, particularly the wilds of Kerry and Donegal. He was neither philosopher nor theologian but possessed a profound sense of what was right in solving particular architectural problems. At times he achieved an expression of sheer poetry, but at other times his sanctuaries are not sufficiently generous in scale to allow for proper ritual movements.[23] Likewise, the relationship between his sanctuaries and naves tend to reduce the laity to mere spectators. As is generally recognized, longitudinal plans tend to separate the altar from the people, thereby setting up a stage for the enactment of the liturgy. Effective use of new materials that allowed for flexibility is reflected in many of the churches built in the 1970s.

From 1975 onward there was a general effort to incorporate the demands of the liturgical movement and the directives of the Second Vatican Council and postconciliar norms into the design of church buildings in Ireland. There was an effort to break out of the mold of what a church should look like and to take account of the social and cultural context in which a church building would function. The emphasis was increasingly paced on the interiority of the church and its domestic character. In this regard, new churches reflected the liturgical theology of Frédéric Debuyst set out in his *Modern Architecture and Christian Celebration*.[24] Emphasis was placed on community and the close relationships experienced in the modern house.

A competition was held for the Chapel of Reconciliation at Knock in County Mayo (1989–1990). The commission was awarded to de Blacam and Meagher. The building constituted a modern presence in an otherwise rather dreary architectural landscape, dotted with various crosses, statues, and buildings of indifferent quality. Surrounded and covered with grass, the building appears to be an extension of the landscape. The inner space moves from a dimly lit periphery to bright light over the sanctuary area, which is rather an anticlimax because the furnishings lack a strong sense of presence.[25]

Circular buildings have a very long history in Ireland. That basic plan can easily be accommodated to the desire for a church in which the assembly encircles the altar on three sides with the church walls encircling the community. It was this background that inspired Liam McCormick to design the church of St. Aengus in Burt, County Donegal, in 1967. This building is considered to be McCormick's most important contribution in the development of Irish church buildings.

In the years since the Second Vatican Council, Richard Hurley has emerged not only as an exceptionally competent architect of church buildings but also as the author of articles and books in which he has set out a profound and clear liturgical theology and its implications for the design and appointment of sacred spaces. Among his exceptionally beautiful accomplishments was the design of the National Institute for Pastoral Liturgy in Carlow (1980). The institute was the brainchild of Msgr. Seán Swayne, a very gifted and tireless worker for liturgical reform and renewal in Ireland, also distinguished by his genuine spirit of Christian hospitality. The center was designed to train priests and laity in all matters of liturgical reform and renewal, including sacred art and architecture.[26] In fact, for many years an annual seminar was held at the center for practicing architects and artists who came from all over Ireland to share ideas and gain inspiration.

The brief for the project included gutting a whole wing of an extant building at St. Patrick's College and the creation of a gathering space, a room for eucharist, a Blessed Sacrament chapel, and a sacristy as well as space for a dining room, library, and parlors. The whole building was beautifully appointed. The gathering area was of special importance, since it would provide a place of welcome and for assembly before and after the liturgy; the area would flow over into the dining room. The room for the eucharist is right off the gathering area, which is partially two-storeys high and contains an open staircase. Hurley planned the space so that the room is oriented toward an informal antiphonal gathering surrounding a central area focused on the altar. The presider's chair was placed at one end of the axis, with the altar and ambo placed on the other side on an axis facing up the room. Everything in the room—walls, ceiling, light fixtures, and carpet—was off-white. The only color was added by the sap green of the large fig tree behind the presider's chair and a terra-cotta Madonna and Child sculpted by Benedict Tutty, O.S.B. Carefully crafted vestments and altar vessels also added to the vitality of the room. In some ways the ambiance was reminiscent of Cistercian churches, which traditionally have placed emphasis on interiority and simplicity; at Carlow the emphasis was not only on awe and mystery but also on the whole assembly as the celebrant of the liturgy. A totally different environment was created in the Blessed Sacrament chapel, an intimate area off the space for the eucharist, conveying a sense of peace and withdrawal, a place for personal prayer and quiet reflection. The exquisite tabernacle was designed and executed in silver by Peter Donovan.[27] The National Institute for Pastoral Liturgy has been moved to Maynooth, and the space at Carlow has reverted to St. Patrick's College.

Richard Hurley was also commissioned by the Cistercian nuns at Glencairn to renovate their church in keeping with the demands of the reformed liturgy. The altar was moved from the apse to the west end of the building, and the nuns' choir was placed between the ambo and the tabernacle now standing in the former apse. Benedict Tutty, O.S.B., designed and executed the tabernacle and processional cross; Phyllis Burke, the stained glass in the apse.[28]

In 1999 Richard Hurley was commissioned to renovate St. Mary's Oratory at St. Patrick's College in Maynooth, County Kildare. There are two chapels in the college, a major chapel built in 1879 and St. Mary's Chapel, originally a study hall designed by Augustus Welby Pugin but refurbished as a chapel in 1878. In 1967 the chapel was reordered when the sanctuary was moved from the west wall to the lengthy north wall, with the students surrounding the altar on three sides. That arrangement proved to be unsatisfactory. The latest renovation includes new woodblock flooring and oak paneling and a new pipe organ, with the addition of major artwork commissioned especially for the space as well as movable furniture. The main thrust of the plan is the restoration of the east–west axis of the chapel and the development of an antiphonal plan with the alignment of the major liturgical furnishings along the spine of the east–west axis. The pipe organ and the ambo are at one end of the chapel, the altar stands in the midst of the assembly, and the presider's chair is located in front of a devotional space where the tabernacle is located on the west wall. Standing between two stained glass windows is a large tapestry designed by Patrick Pye. Below it is an abstract painting by Kim En Joong, which surrounds the tabernacle designed by Benedict Tutty. The latter ensemble, designed by the architect, creates a vivid splash of color and presents a strong focus for personal prayer apart from the time for liturgical prayer.[29] Unfortunately, the colors in the painting are so bright that they contrast markedly with the muted colors in the stained glass windows and the Pye tapestry. As a result the painting draws undue attention to itself, even during the celebration of the liturgy. Nevertheless the space is indeed formative of the seminarians who worship there.

Several of the Irish cathedrals have also been reordered quite successfully. St. Macartan's Cathedral in Monaghan is a neo-Gothic building in the Ulster borderland diocese of Clogher in Northern Ireland. Originally dedicated in 1892, the cathedral was renovated under the wise direction of the current bishop, Joseph Duffy. In 1982 he called on the distinguished Dublin sculptor, the late Michael Biggs, to adapt the interior of the church to postconciliar liturgical needs. Originally the intention was to limit any changes to the sanctuary area and to retain existing furnishings, but that plan was fortunately rejected.[30]

The basic cruciform shape of the church and the concentration of natural light at the intersection of the nave and the transepts determined the place for the altar, which should be the focal point in any church. Four side areas of the church were given over to separate sacramental functions, relating them to the assembly, to one another, and to the eucharistic altar. The Blessed Mother's shrine and the stations of the cross were given their own special but secondary places and not simply treated as decor. A large crucifix, designed by the late Richard Enda King, rests with simple dignity against a pillar at the left of the altar and behind the ambo. Michael Biggs himself designed the altar, bishop's chair, and ambo, as well as lettering throughout the building. The strong, sturdy, and pleasing form of the altar dominates the cathedral from every angle and proclaims clearly, "I am what this building is about."[31]

Frances Biggs, Michael's wife, designed five extraordinary tapestries for the church, three to hang behind the bishop's chair, one to hang behind the baptismal font, and one to hang behind the tabernacle. The hanging behind the tabernacle is especially powerful, containing the image of a large broken Host symbolic of the body of Christ broken for all of us so that our bodies might be broken for one another. She also designed the stations of the cross, which have been executed in strong colors and very simple lines, more like cartoons for stained glass windows.[32]

In 1995 Richard Hurley was commissioned to carry out a major renovation of the cathedral of St. Mary and St. Anne in Cork. The sunken baptistery located immediately inside the great west door sets up a strong axis with the altar and bishop's chair located behind it. Unfortunately it does not allow baptism by complete immersion. The new sanctuary is thrust out into the nave of the church and accommodates the altar with the assembly arranged on three sides. The bishop's chair, the stalls for the presbytery, the pulpit, the baptismal font, and several other pieces were retained from the old cathedral, but they were moved to new positions in order to accommodate the new liturgical design. The work of distinguished artists has been wonderfully incorporated into the space, including paintings by Patrick Pye in the Lady Chapel at the back of the cathedral; stained glass by James Scanlon in the Blessed Sacrament chapel, located in a quiet area off the sanctuary; sculptures and shrines by Ken Thompson; a silver tabernacle by Peter Donovan; and the altar, ambo, and tabernacle pillar by Hurley himself.[33]

Roman Catholics constitute by far the largest majority of churchgoing Christians in Ireland. It is not surprising therefore that most of the

churches built in Ireland in the last forty years have been built for the celebration of Roman Catholic worship. The major Reformed churches in the
island were largely completed by the end of the nineteenth century. In the
last century the building of new Reformed churches was mainly confined
to Methodist and Presbyterian congregations.[34]

Irish architects and artists are certainly entitled to a sense of pride and
satisfaction when they reflect on what they have achieved in the last century in the field of church architecture and the environment for worship.
The best work in Ireland surely compares very favorably with what was
achieved in Europe and the United States. Developments in the liturgy and
in a renewed understanding of ecclesiology have given architects and artists
a rich opportunity to exercise their creativity. In reflecting on successful
Irish architectural projects, we are able to draw several conclusions that
have ongoing value in communal efforts to construct and appoint sacred
spaces in which the whole assembly of the faithful might worship God and
be transformed into vital communities of faith who are in turn transforming agents in establishing the reign of God in the world.

First of all, church leadership, especially on the part of bishops and pastors, is essential in encouraging and commissioning competent architects
and artists for church projects. That leadership was exercised by the Irish
Episcopal Commission for Liturgy in the development of the various editions of *The Place of Worship: Pastoral Directory on the Building and Reordering of Churches*. Such guidance has not been provided by most leaders in the
our churches.

Second, the most competent architects are most likely to design the
most effective buildings. They must, however, be capable of dialoguing
with their clients and be open to the development of a deep understanding
of the church's theology of worship.

Third, the best artists available should be commissioned to appoint liturgical spaces. They should be involved in the design and construction of the
building early in the development of the project rather than being commissioned to create art after the design of the building has been completed.
Like the architects, they must be willing to dialogue with their clients and
should see their role as one of ministry in the community.

Fourth, budgetary limitations should not necessarily determine what is
to be built and appointed. A master plan should be created so that long-
range projects can be envisioned. The great Romanesque and Gothic cathedrals were not built in a day; likewise, parish plans should be developed
always with the future of the community in mind.

CHURCHES IN THE UNITED STATES

Numerous churches were built or renovated in the United States since the Second Vatican Council. The majority of them have been nondescript, the work of second-rate architects; they have been appointed with items selected from traditional church goods catalogues. However, there are several that deserve comment because they have been designed by distinguished architects and appointed effectively with works of distinction.

Pietro Belluschi was for over fifty years one of the major modern architects in the United States. He first gained national attention for the simple religious buildings he designed in the Portland area in Oregon. In 1936 he designed a new chapel for the Finley Mortuary in Portland, a commission that brought him acclaim as a designer. His modernist principles were clear: he sought straightforward solutions to problems that were in sympathy with local materials, the existing landscape, and the people destined to inhabit the buildings.[35]

Shortly before World War II, Belluschi designed a small low-cost church of St. Thomas in a Portland suburb. The building bore the influence of Frank Lloyd Wright and also the American Arts and Crafts movement as it developed in the Pacific Northwest. It was this project above all that established Belluschi's reputation as a competent designer of modern buildings with spiritual dimensions. The eleven churches dating from this early period in Belluschi's career are characterized by a reverence for scientific values; rather severe, unornamented, rectilinear forms; warm interiors; textured materials; soft colored lighting; careful attention to the interior fixtures and the landscaping; and stylized art. Included are buildings for Methodists, Presbyterians, Lutherans, Catholics, and nondenominational religious communities.

In 1951 Belluschi became dean of architecture at Massachusetts Institute of Technology, a post he held until he retired in 1973. During that period he was influenced by the process philosophy of Alfred North Whitehead, the aesthetics of Paul Tillich, the architectural style of the Finnish architect Alvar Aalto, and the more philosophical aspects of Eastern mysticism, particularly Zen Buddhism; hence, his buildings sought to communicate an experience of transcendence and a strong appeal to emotions.

Belluschi did not seem to grasp the significant architectural implications of the liturgical developments set in motion by the Second Vatican Council, nor understand that primary emphasis must be placed on the whole assembly as the major celebrants of the liturgy. The church edifice is primarily a house for the assembly of God's people before it becomes a symbol of the faith of the community. His churches designed after the council continued to place very strong emphasis on the sanctuary area and to convey a sense of monumentality, as though a church must somehow look like a church and be distinctive from other buildings in the area. These flaws are reflected above all in his design for the Roman Catholic Cathedral of St. Mary in San Francisco. Collaborating with Pier Luigi Nervi, he designed a monumental building to be placed on a limited space in the midst of the city's late-nineteenth-century Victorian environment. He was successful in communicating a sense of mystery, but the assembly is dwarfed in the midst of a soaring concrete shell. The raised sanctuary area is defined by a rosewood screen, which forms the backdrop for the large white marble altar. The impression is given that the liturgy is a clerical celebration enacted before a passive assembly. The interior is illuminated by large expanses of glass designed by Gyorgy Kepes. Richard Lippold created a shimmering baldachino of thin aluminum rods forming the centerpiece of the church and focusing on the altar below. The building was completed in 1970. One cannot help wondering about the content of the liturgical brief that the diocesan authorities presented to Belluschi before he undertook the project.

Following his retirement from M.I.T., Belluschi continued to design religious buildings, especially in the Portland area. His projects include a chapel for the University of Portland. It is a multipurpose building of brick and cedar. Apart from the sunken sculptural baptismal font in the center of the narthex, the altar, dais, and chairs are removable so that the space can be used for other than religious purposes. The architect considered this the most successful of his later churches.

Saint James Cathedral in Seattle, Washington

The major renovation and restoration of St. James Cathedral, completed in 1994, was begun by Archbishop Raymond G. Hunthausen and carried out by his successor, Archbishop Thomas J. Murphy, under the direction of the cathedral rector, Rev. Michael G. Ryan. Father Richard Vosko of Albany, New York, served as the liturgical design consultant for the project. The building was originally designed by the prestigious New York architects Heins and La Farge, who submitted the original design for St. John the Divine Cathedral in New York and also the plans for St. Matthew's Cathedral in Washington, D.C.[36]

In the newly renovated church, the baptistery is carefully placed in the cathedral's main entrance so as to present the sacrament of baptism as the entrance or gateway to the church. It is meant to remind each person entering the church of that first sacramental encounter brought about by the saving waters of rebirth. Made of marble and slate and in the form of the classical quatrefoil, it resembles the cathedral's architectural shape with its rounded apses on the north, east, and south sides of the building. The holy water font at the west end of the baptistery is the cathedral's original baptismal font. The patterned terrazzo that surrounds the baptistery replicates the cathedral's original sanctuary floor. Surrounding the baptistery is an inscription from the very early Christian baptismal instruction in the First Letter of Peter: "But you are a chosen race, a royal priesthood, a holy nation, God's own people, that you may declare the wonderful deeds of God who called you out of darkness into marvelous light" (1 Pet. 2:9).

The altar, after the gathered assembly, is the primary symbol of Christ in the cathedral. It is placed in the center of the cathedral and so speaks of the abiding presence of Christ, who is in the midst of the community of believers as the head of his body, the church. It is at the altar that he nourishes his people in the celebration of the eucharist. The altar stands directly above the relics of Saints Adeodatus, Boniface, Fortunata, and Frances Xavier Cabrini, who worshiped in the cathedral when she was in Seattle in the early years of the twentieth century. The altar rests on a slate and granite platform in the center of the cathedral, immediately beneath where the cathedral's great dome once stood until it was destroyed during a heavy snowfall in 1916. In place of the dome a central skylight or *oculus Dei* has been constructed.

The ambo, the place were God's Word is proclaimed, stands at the head of the nave off to the right of the altar. It rests on a stone platform flanked by steps on both sides and bears an inscription from Isaiah 55:10, 11. The bishop's chair is directly opposite the ambo. It is symbolic of the bishop's role as chief pastor and teacher in the local diocese. The carved wooden pediment and columns that frame the chair are historic pieces taken from two earlier cathedras in the cathedral.

In accord with a directive from the *Caeremoniale Episcoporum* (1984) concerning the placement of the reserved Sacrament in cathedral churches, the Blessed Sacrament is reserved in a chapel separate from the main body of the church. A special effort has been made to incorporate in this special place of prayer a number of handsome artworks from the cathedral's past. There is an excellent representation of the Last Supper taken from the cathedral's old high altar. Rich red onyx wainscoting around the chapel walls is from the 1950 reredos. The bronze gates at the west entrance are from the cathedral's original baptistery. An oculus in the ceiling of the chapel gives a luminous quality to the chapel.

The reconciliation chapel, located in the north tower of the cathedral, replaces the old confessional boxes. Directly opposite the Blessed Sacrament chapel is the shrine of the Blessed Virgin Mary. The statue in this newly rebuilt shrine is the one popularly known as Our Lady of Seattle. It was brought from Europe to Seattle's first Catholic church, Our Lady of Good Help, in 1870. The cathedral also holds a statue of St. James the Apostle, the cathedral's patron saint, as well as statues of the Sacred Heart, St. Joseph, St. Anthony, the Infant of Prague, and St. Francis Xavier Cabrini. There is also an impressive collection of icons, which are enthroned for prayer and veneration on the church's major solemnities and feasts, such as the Annunciation, Christmas, Epiphany, and Easter. The cathedral's fine stained glass windows, installed in the 1920s, are the work of the Connick Studios of Boston.

In order to improve the cathedral's acoustics for both music and the spoken word, numerous painted acoustical tiles covering the entire ceiling have been removed and replaced by detailed plaster coffers built into the ceiling. They give the cathedral a dramatic new appearance and considerably enrich its ambiance. The organ in the high gallery dates from the very beginning of the cathedral. The organ in the east apse, built by Casavant Frères, is a modest instrument that will eventually be rebuilt and expanded. The pipes will be rearranged so that the central stained glass window representing the sacrament of baptism will be fully exposed. The carved oak choir stalls, which ring the east apse of the cathedral, have become the primary area for the choir and for the performance of music.

The renovation and renewal of this cathedral are eminently satisfactory, putting a lie to the frequently heard objection that recently renovated churches are boring and devoid of excellent art that appeals to the creative imaginations of churchgoers. The Cathedral of St. James is rich in its artistic appointments, thoroughly in accord with conciliar and postconciliar directives concerning the celebration of the liturgy, and functional in terms of sacramental rites.

Cathedral of St. John the Evangelist, Milwaukee, Wisconsin

Theological and liturgical concerns were primary in the renovation of the Cathedral of St. John the Evangelist in Milwaukee, Wisconsin. This emphasis was surely due to the theological and liturgical competence of the archbishop, Rembert Weakland, O.S.B., and the project director, Father Carl Last. Father Richard Vosko served as the liturgical design consultant.

The cathedral is built of cream-colored brick. Since the laying of the cornerstone on December 9, 1847, the external appearance of the building has changed very little, except for the addition of a wonderful tower rebuilt above the clock in 1893. It is one of the admired pieces of architecture in the city. The cathedral has been designated a Milwaukee landmark and is listed in the National Register of Historic Places.

The cathedral was rededicated on February 9, 2002. The reordering was based on two understandings of what a Catholic cathedral is meant to be. It is, first of all, a house for God's people, the community that regularly gathers there to celebrate the liturgy, as well as the people of the archdiocese, for whom the cathedral is their mother church. The church is the people; hence the cathedral renovation was designed around the occupants. It was shaped so that the people could effectively celebrate the liturgy and so be transformed into dynamic, outgoing Christians as a result of those celebrations.

The cathedral also stands as a symbol of Christian faith for all the people of the archdiocese. The style, the design, and the appointments all say something important about those who worship within its walls. In a sense the fabric of the building is like the skin of the human body. It covers and protects the assembled community, but just as healthy skin on the human body promotes and reflects the health of the whole body, so the style and design of the church building both reflect and affect the faith-life of the worshipers. As a symbol of the community's faith, the cathedral building speaks not only to the faithful but also to the wider community and to the secular world, as well as to those who might visit the church. It is for that reason that the exterior of the church is well cared for and so invites people to enter and to pray.

In the Archdiocese of Milwaukee, the local cathedral assembly has for many years striven to be church in various ways: in outreach to the community, in its patronage of the arts, and in its excellent liturgical celebrations. Hence, the renovations that have been made to the cathedral reflect the sound Christian principle of social justice that the cathedral should always be at the service of God's people. The cathedral as a whole speaks of God, but of a God who loves and welcomes every person, especially the poor and marginalized. The cathedral project included not only changes in the fabric and appointment of the building itself but also revitalization of the whole cathedral city block. Unused buildings were removed to make room for an atrium, a new ministry center, and a prayer garden. The convent has been converted into an assessment center for women and children run by the government with private and religious partners.

The interior of the cathedral has been completely repainted, restoring the original vibrant color palette of terra-cotta, gold, ivory, and taupe, thus creating a beautiful warm space. Since the sacrament of baptism is the means whereby we enter the church, the location of the baptistery near the main entrance of the cathedral speaks well of the experience of baptism as the womb from which new Christians are born. From the life-giving waters of the font, Christian pilgrims respond to God's invitation and process to the altar and beyond, ready to serve not only God but also God's people and the world beyond the walls of the cathedral. The tomb-shaped baptismal pool signifies the Christian's passage from death to new life in Christ. It is two feet deep and is made from granite and marble. With three steps down at the east end, the font is suitable for the immersion of both adults and children. The upper font is from the 1943 cathedral renovation; its basin is carved from pink marble and supported by three pillars. It has been refashioned to be the source of water flowing into the larger pool. It serves as a holy water font and may also be used for the baptism of infants. Balusters, originally in the cathedral sanctuary, surround the lower pool. The baptistery is on an axis with the altar; it directs Christians to the place where they gather for the nourishment needed to live out their baptismal commitment.

Because of its significance, size, and location, the baptismal font also becomes the center of other sacramental rituals that are rooted in and recall the sacrament of baptism. As the cathedral's central holy water font, it serves as a regular reminder of baptism for all who enter and leave the cathedral. It is the place where the body is received at a funeral, for it is a symbol of the origin of the Christian life of the one who has died. Wedding couples are welcomed at the font; confirmands renew their baptismal promises around the font before they are anointed in the sacrament of confirmation. When baptismal promises are renewed at the beginning of the eucharist, especially during the Easter season, the font is a visible symbol of the sacrament that is at the root of each Sunday renewal. Directly south of the baptistery is the ambry, the place where the holy oils that are blessed and consecrated by the bishop during Holy Week are stored and displayed. There is the oil of catechumens used at baptism, the oil of chrism used at baptism, confirmation, and holy orders, and oil for the anointing of the sick. All the parishes of the archdiocese come to the cathedral for the holy oils needed for their sacramental celebrations.

The altar is the table for the celebration of the paschal sacrifice of the

Lord Jesus as well as the table for the eucharistic banquet. It is an important symbol of Christ himself. Because of its identity, the altar calls for a prominent and central place in the church. Situated in the midst of the assembly, the cathedral altar is the focus of the action of the gathered church. It signifies the presence of Christ in the midst of the people who come to be nourished at the eucharistic table. The altar stands on a predella, or platform, of Tennessee marble three steps high on the central axis of the building, providing access from all sides. The mensa, or tabletop, is a square of Italian marble that establishes a strong but dignified presence in the midst of the great pillars of the cathedral. The Doric columns that form its base as well as the dentil decoration have been fashioned from the cathedral's former devotional altars. In keeping with an old tradition, relics of martyrs and other saints have been honored by placing them beneath the altar as a reminder that the sacrificial life of the saints is always rooted in the sacrifice of Christ.

Suspended twenty-eight feet above the altar are a crown and crucifix, which serve to emphasize the altar as the symbolic center of the cathedral and the place where the sacrifice of Christ is regularly celebrated in the eucharist. The crown symbolizes the crown of thorns transformed into a crown of glory as Christ raised up on the cross draws all humanity with him into the kingdom of heaven. The overall symbolism is based on the Gospel of John, which presents Jesus as thoroughly incarnate yet the divine Lord whose inner glory shines forth, especially at the hour when he is lifted up on the cross and gives his life for the salvation of the world. Hence, the cross is inserted into the crown to show that Jesus was transformed and glorified by his love and fidelity to his Father's will. The crown and cross were designed by the distinguished Italian sculptor Arnaldo Pomodoro in collaboration with Giuseppe Maraniello, who created the figure of Christ, which is made of burnished bronze, revealing the strength of his humanity. Critics have asserted that the crown and cross are really overpowering and that they tend to draw too much attention to themselves and away from the altar, which is the central symbol in the cathedral, apart from the gathered assembly.

The ambo is the place where God's Word in the sacred scriptures is proclaimed to the assembly. Its prominence in the church serves as an appropriate reminder to the assembly that they are nourished at one celebration but at two tables, the table of God's Word and the table of the Lord's body. The ambo is built on a platform extending forward from the apse. The ambo is high enough to be visible throughout the cathedral and yet can serve effectively for smaller gatherings as well as for celebrations of the

Word and morning and evening prayer. It is constructed of marble to harmonize with the altar.

The cathedra is the bishop's chair. The word "cathedral" comes from the Greek word *kathedra,* meaning "chair" or "throne." The cathedra is a symbol of the bishop's role as chief teacher, liturgist, and pastor of the local church. Thus, the cathedral building derives its name from the fact that the bishop is the symbol of unity in the diocese. The cathedra is placed on the axis extending south from the altar, with two of the cathedral's strong pillars as a backdrop. Resting on a platform three steps high and constructed from Collemandina rosso marble from the former Communion rail, the cathedra is the place from which the archbishop presides over cathedral celebrations; it is also the place from which he may choose to preach.

Directly across from the cathedra is the chair from which priests preside in the archbishop's name. The cathedra is reserved for the archbishop or other bishops to whom he may grant its use. The presider's chair is made of the same marble as the cathedra.

Like the cathedra and the priest-presider's chair, the seating for the rest of the assembly, who are in chairs, faces the altar; at the same time it allows people to see one another, thus reinforcing the unity of the body of Christ. The flexible seating allows people to gather round the altar and at the same time provides for processions and other movements called for by the liturgical rites. The flexible seating can be expanded for large gatherings or it may be arranged for more intimate celebrations. It also can accommodate nonliturgical events, such as concerts, which are in keeping with the role of the cathedral as a center for the arts in the Milwaukee area.

The former baptistery of the cathedral now serves as a dignified and beautiful chapel for the reservation of the Blessed Sacrament. Marking the entrance to this chapel is the newly restored cathedral sanctuary lamp, which hangs from the archway overhead. The polished and brushed bronze tabernacle, decorated with eucharistic symbols, is from the 1943 church and is enthroned on a plinth fashioned from parts of the sanctuary baldachino. The stained glass windows in the chapel depict events in the life of Christ. Visible and in close proximity to the main altar, this chapel provides a fitting place for personal prayer and adoration.

The former vesting sacristy has been converted into a day chapel that can accommodate small groups for daily Mass; it is accessible from the outside through the east entrance of the cathedral and from the parking lot. The altar and ambo have been fashioned from the white oak of the former confessionals. The crucifix and devotional art, including statues of St. Joseph and the Little Flower, were part of the 1943 rebuilding of the cathedral. The entrance to the main reconciliation chapel is through the day chapel; it houses a carved statue of the Sacred Heart as well as a crucifix of bronze and rosewood. A secondary reconciliation chapel is in the northwest corner of the cathedral, located in relation to the baptistery. This location serves as a reminder that reconciliation, like baptism, leads to the altar.

The area where the choir, cantors, organists, and other musicians minister is in the apse at the east end of the cathedral. From this flexible area they are able to lead the sung prayer of the assembly. A new chancel organ by Nichols & Simpson will join the organ in the choir loft, a splendid instrument built by Robert Noehren and installed in 1966. Both organs will be able to be controlled by the console located in the apse.

There are several devotional shrines in the cathedral. A major shrine is dedicated to the Blessed Mother under the title Mother of the Church. It contains a newly commissioned bronze and gilt statue resting on a pedestal whose bas relief features people from a number of the ethnic and cultural communities that comprise the Archdiocese of Milwaukee.

A second shrine dedicated to Blessed John XXIII stands near the entrance to the Blessed Sacrament chapel. The life-size bronze statue honors the saintly pope who inaugurated the reforms of the Second Vatican Council. Along the sides and rear walls of the cathedral are the fourteen stations of the cross depicting the passion and death of Jesus. Also along the walls are the twelve dedication crosses, which were anointed with sacred chrism during the rededication celebration.

The large, fine stained glass windows in the cathedral portray the twelve apostles and St. Paul. They were designed and crafted by T. C. Esser Company of Milwaukee and constructed of Norman slab glass and German and English antique glass, hand-cut and then leaded together. Below each central figure is a symbol with a medallion expressing in pictorial form the text of the Apostles' Creed. Above these windows are the portraits of the archbishops of Milwaukee. In the alcoves at the west entrances to the cathedral, there is a Venetian mosaic inlay of Our Lady of Perpetual Help on the south side and a white oak statue of Moses on the north side. These popular devotional pieces were first installed in 1943.

Perhaps one of the most admirable aspects of the cathedral renovation project is its relationship to the wider world and its concern for social justice through its commitment to the poor, the homeless, the sick, and the other marginalized people in the world. Certainly any description of the cathedral itself would be incomplete without reflecting on the revitalization of the rest of the cathedral block, which is an inseparable and crucial part of the overall cathedral project. A new atrium connects the cathedral and the Archbishop Weakland Center. What was originally the school has been completely renovated, so that it effectively houses various pastoral and outreach ministries. These ministries implement the vision that Archbishop Weakland and his auxiliary bishop, Richard J. Sklba, set out in their 1997 pastoral letter, "Eucharist without Walls: A Vision of the Church for the Year 2002." The "Beyond the Door" ministry provides a place where the area homeless and urban poor are fed on a daily basis. The St. Vincent de Paul Society has expanded its clothing center, while Catholic Charities has set up a mental health and drug abuse counseling clinic. St. Ben's Clinic provides medical health screening and services. The building also houses the archdiocesan AIDS ministry and Alcoholics Anonymous and AL-ANON counseling and support groups for the downtown community. The old convent on the northeast corner of the block serves as an annex to the ministry center and has been converted to serve as a community assessment and service center for homeless women and children. It not only provides a safe environment for women and their children but serves as a coordination place to help people access permanent housing, counseling, job training, and other services available through area agencies.

The atrium also serves as a gathering place where the blessing of candles, palms, and the Easter fire occurs. It is the building that links the cathedral itself with the other buildings housing the pastoral and outreach ministries. The west wall of the atrium allows people to walk through the new prayer garden and courtyard and into the cathedral itself. When they leave the cathedral and pass by the various ministries in the center, they are invited to participate in the many outreach ministries that take place on the entire cathedral block.

The Cathedral of St. John the Evangelist is indeed the "mother church" of the archdiocese, because it nourishes not only the spiritual life of God's people in the area but also responds effectively to their many physical needs. The cathedral is an image of that holiness and catholicity to which all God's people are called.

Cathedral of Our Lady of the Angels, Los Angeles, California

In the midst of the enormous sprawling city of Los Angeles and on the edge of the busy Hollywood Freeway stands a new cathedral constructed from powerful blocks of architectural concrete. The cathedral was consecrated on September 2, 2002. The soft tones of the structure evoke the spirit of early California's adobe mission churches. A rather dramatic angu-

lar structure, the Cathedral of Our Lady of the Angels catches the sunlight
and casts shadows along the building's surface in moving patterns.[37] As a
matter of fact, the use of light to structure planes and inner spaces is characteristic of the cathedral's distinguished architect, José Rafael Moneo,
Pritzker Prize winner and former chair of the department of architecture
at Harvard University. His work is both contemporary and rooted in the
sunlit antiquity of the Mediterranean rim. The cathedral has been built in
part to replace the previous cathedral, which was badly damaged in the
1994 earthquake. Certainly the cathedral's asymmetrical and angular silhouette departs quite sharply from conventional notions of church design,
especially in Roman Catholic churches.

The design of the cathedral developed as a result of a carefully constructed dialogue between the architect and Cardinal Roger Mahony, the
archbishop of Los Angeles. The cardinal wanted the building to evoke California's rich Spanish history and to adhere closely to the requirements for
liturgical celebration set out by the Roman Catholic Church since the Second Vatican Council. He wanted the church to speak to contemporary
worshipers in their own idiom, a complex requirement because of the
multicultural character of the worshipers in the Archdiocese of Los Angeles. Moneo wanted a structure where people could withdraw from the fre-
netic pace of daily life.

A large plaza outside the main doors of the cathedral contains the Gateway Pool, a fountain inscribed with the words, "I shall give you living
water," in the thirty-seven languages in which the eucharist is celebrated in
churches of the archdiocese. The plaza also has a water wall and a circular
marble fountain, a bronze memorial to Native Americans, and a shrine to
our Lady of Guadalupe. There is also a fountain constructed of stone from
Jerusalem, given by the Skirball Foundation and meant to celebrate the historic bonds between Judaism and Catholicism, as well as a children's garden and a grove of olive trees, linking southern California to the
Mediterranean origin of the Christian church.

The mostly windowless exterior and the Spanish mission-style walls that
surround the entire complex facilitate an experience of transcendence,
peace, and quiet in the midst of an often troubling and complicated world.
There is no imposing central portal such as one regularly finds in the great
Romanesque and Gothic cathedrals. Instead, the main entrance is posi-
tioned off to one side, marked by thirty-foot-high bronze doors designed
by sculptor Robert Graham. Doors have traditionally been important
thresholds in religious places, gateways into sacred spaces that are holy
because of the community that gathers within and the cultic actions that

are carried out in the space. Doors open up to what often seems impossible in daily life. Hence, the great bronze doors of the Los Angeles cathedral signal a procession from ordinary life to a new world where transformation is meant to take place.[38]

The inner doors of the cathedral depict on the lower register forty mythological symbols of spirituality from around the world interwoven among grape vines. On the upper level there are Old World images of Mary that were transported to the New World, including the Virgin of Loreto, the Black Madonna of Montserrat, the Virgin of the Cave, the Apocalyptic Virgin Immaculately Conceived, Mater Dolorosa, and the Virgin of the Rosary. Of course, there is also the Virgin of Guadalupe. Above the entryway is an eight-foot statue of Mary, Our Lady of the Angels, a modern Madonna with bare outstretched arms and a dark braid down her back. The passing sun forms a halo over her unveiled head through an opening in the gold wall behind her. As a naturalistic sculptor, Robert Graham deliberately bared Mary's arms, making her at home in Los Angeles, where both climate and culture approve of women appearing in public with bare arms. Clothed in a long gown, Mary is a strong woman whose outstretched hands are capable of hard work. She is indeed a *mulier fortis,* but also a lowly woman raised up to the heights of heaven; she is majestic but without throne or crown.[39]

The great bronze doors do not lead directly into the nave of the church but rather to an ambulatory bathed in light from splendid alabaster windows. During services the building is illuminated and sound is carried on mountings shaped like forty-foot trumpets with their narrow ends rooted in the ceiling. Designed by Moneo himself, they are generally disliked, even by the architect himself. Along the right side of the walkway are small chapels, including the chapel of the Blessed Sacrament, where the eucharist is reserved. Another chapel dedicated to Mary contains a statue of Our Lady of the Angels. Other chapels will be dedicated and furnished at a later time when funds become available. The ambulatory carries worshipers up a slight incline to the back of the nave and a full-immersion baptismal font designed by Father Richard Vosko, who also served as liturgical art consultant for the entire project. Behind the pool are five cotton-and-viscose tapestries designed by John Nava, an esteemed California artist known for his still life and portrait work. They contain a naturalistic image of the baptism of Jesus in the River Jordan. A nearby ambry contains the sacred oils for sacramental anointings.

The nave itself is over 300 feet long and over 130 feet high. No pillars block worshipers' views because the chapel structures on each side support the roof of the cathedral. The sanctuary area opens out to narrow transepts that allow worshipers unhindered views of the altar from the seats, which can accommodate three thousand worshipers. The crimson altar table, designed by Cardinal Mahony, is enormous. Four bronze angels are affixed around the base. The ambo stands to the right of the altar. To the left of the altar stands the cathedra, the bishop's chair; it incorporates a variety of woods from different countries. With an open design in the back and a wooden frame, it comes across as fussy rather than strong. The cardinal's coat of arms is above the chair. Soft light from alabaster windows filters through the interior of the church.

On either side of the nave are twenty-five tapestries also designed by John Nava. They depict 135 holy men and women selected by the arch-diocese's multicultural commission. The average height is about ten feet. Included are a variety of people of different nationalities, ages, occupations, and vocations from both past and present. The tapestries were designed to relate effectively to the interior architectural plan of the building with regard to color, texture, light, and scale.[40] The figures are intensely realis-tic; worshipers who recognize the figures will see them as saints; others are apt to find little sense of transcendence in the images.

A Dobson pipe organ rises five stories in the right transept; it contains over six thousand metal and wooden pipes and over a hundred stops. Space behind the altar provides seating for clergy and other liturgical ministers. The organ console and choir, placed in full view behind the ambo and altar, create a kind of stage, not unlike what one finds in seeker-service churches, such as Philip Johnson's Crystal Cathedral near Anaheim, California. A larger-than-life bronze figure of Christ hangs on a movable cross in the sanctuary area. On the wall behind the altar there are seven Nava tapestries based on images from the Book of Revelation; they relate the local church of Los Angeles to the New Jerusalem. The north ambulatory provides for additional chapels which will be dedicated in the future. The chapel for the sacrament of reconciliation is already open.

The crypt of the cathedral contains a chapel of St. Vibiana, an ancient Roman martyr who is the patron of the archdiocese. The chapel houses the original altar from the former St. Vibiana Cathedral. Along the hallways of the mausoleum are the back-lit stained glass windows from the former cathedral. There is also a campanile rising over 150 feet from the ground. It is designed to hold eighteen bells and is topped by a twenty-six-foot cross.

It is the actual experience of worshipers and ministers that determines the effectiveness of a church building. Certainly those who have designed and appointed the cathedral have striven for grace of line, play of light and shadow, discretion of adornment, and beauty in color and texture. It is their fondest hope that this house will indeed be a house of prayer.

Intense controversy has surrounded the design and construction of this 189-million-dollar building. Eloquent objections were raised by those who felt that the money should have been used to alleviate the conditions of poverty in the archdiocese. In fairness, however, it must be noted that the cathedral has already drawn very large numbers, both worshipers and tourists. It is one of the few places in downtown Los Angeles that is open on weekends, and it is located in an area of the city that for decades had no middle-class residential base but is beginning to acquire one through gradual gentrification of downtown Los Angeles. More important, the huge, poor Hispanic population of the area has already found a safe and stable public space that remains open for long hours without an admission fee. The poor people are there in large numbers leaving simple bouquets, notes, and *ex voto* objects at the small outdoor shrine dedicated to our Lady of Guadalupe. Actually the cathedral complex comprises three buildings: the cathedral itself, a center, and a residence for the cardinal and the priests who serve the cathedral. The center provides office space, outreach to the poor, and space for conferences and meetings of various kinds.

PROTESTANT AND ANGLICAN CHURCHES

Among Protestant churches, auditoriums continue to be built as churches, especially by Pentecostals and Evangelicals. Such a design is in fact always preferred by megachurches and churches committed to so-called seeker-services. These churches either emphasize the entertainment model or continue the frontier revival tradition of worship. Seeker-service churches would include the well-known Willow Creek Community Church in Barrington, Illinois; the Garden Grove Community Church (the Crystal Cathedral) near Anaheim, California; and the Community Church of Joy in Phoenix, Arizona. The megachurches have generally departed from strict adherence to the liturgical requirements of any of the mainline Protestant denominations.[41]

Among Protestants, Edward A. Søvik has often been commissioned to build churches in the United States since the Second Vatican Council. He has articulated his theories about church building effectively in a number of publications.[42] His primary concern has been to provide worship spaces in which the community and its various functions are primary. His churches have often been described as multipurpose in design and use; they provide a room of generous proportions called a "centrum" for the community's liturgical celebrations. This room is not a traditional sanctuary or nave but a meeting place for people in which they can accomplish a variety of tasks, including worship, but also other activities that are appropriate to the life of the community. Because the furniture arrangement is flexible, the room can accommodate worship services, concerts, dramas, meetings, and sometimes even meals. Søvik regularly used portable altars and lecterns, and chairs rather than pews. The only permanent fixtures in his churches are usually the organ and a large baptismal pool with flowing water. Among his best church buildings are Our Savior's Lutheran Church in Jackson, Minnesota; Trinity Lutheran Church in Princeton, Minnesota; and Trinity Methodist Church in Charles City, Iowa.[43] He has also been responsible for the reordering of the Roman Catholic Cathedral in Indianapolis, and the Roman Catholic Church of the Good Shepherd in State College, Pennsylvania.

Liturgical scholars and consultants are in general agreement that most Episcopal congregations in the United States have not taken seriously the demands that a reformed and renewed liturgy places on the space for gathering and celebrating the paschal mystery. As John Runkle has noted,

> The general state of architecture and liturgical design in the Episcopal Church is in decline. Once known for its architectural leadership, our tradition now has many existing church buildings growing ever more dysfunctional to the needs of the people and its liturgy. Most new designs are superficial, either mimicking styles of days gone by or serving as self-absorbed, personal statements of a designer's ego. The Episcopal Church appears content to wander in an architectural wilderness. The desire to move beyond this apathetic state and create church buildings relevant to our time is rarely seen.[44]

It is quite impractical to argue for a definitive form of Episcopal church architecture, since "the liturgical beliefs and practices of local Episcopal congregations exist on a spectrum from conservative, low church, and evangelical to liberal, high church, and Anglo-Catholic."[45]

There is one new church in the Episcopal tradition that has received considerable comment—St. Gregory's Episcopal Church in San Francisco, designed by John Goldman. The church is based on an early Roman adaptation of the basilica as illustrated in Louis Bouyer's *Liturgy and Architecture*.[46] The presider and assistant leaders take their places at the head of the congregation, which is arranged antiphonally on both sides of raised platforms, at the head of which stands the lectern, opposite from the presider. For the liturgy of the eucharist the community moves into an adjacent space and surrounds the altar. The baptismal font stands outside the building proper. Apart from the placement of the font, most liturgists would agree with the excellent arrangement of the community, the presider, the ambo, and the altar. It is with good reason that in 1996 the building won an award from the American Institute of Architects as Best Religious Building of the Year.

Many Episcopalians, however, would be quite disconcerted by the liturgy that actually takes place in the building, for it seems to be an eclectic collage of rites and appointments taken from diverse liturgical traditions, far removed from anything that appears in the Book of Common Prayer and vastly different from what one would find at Grace Cathedral in the same city. The majority of Episcopalians in this country would probably be shocked by the multipurpose use of the eucharistic space, where parish suppers, coffee hours, workshops, dances, talent shows, and concerts all take place where the altar normally stands. A sense of mystery is undoubtedly lost when a coffee urn and donuts are placed on the altar immediately after the eucharist has been celebrated. Though the sense of transcendence is present at least in some of the artwork in the church, at St. Gregory's the sense of transcendence seems generally to be lost in the actual celebration of the liturgy, which often appears to be gimmicky. The community's outreach to the poor and marginal in the area is admirable, but the primary horizontal dimension of the community's concerns runs the risk of obliterating the centrality of the emphasis on God and God's transcendence in Christian worship in general and in the Book of Common Prayer in particular. A number of Christian denominations experimented with multipurpose spaces during the 1960s and 1970s, but most of them moved to more permanent spaces, which are generally reserved for celebrations of the liturgy.

A much more satisfactory project has been the renovation of the Episcopal Cathedral in Philadelphia. In December 1998 the Episcopal bishop of Pennsylvania invited Richard Giles to become the dean of the Philadelphia cathedral. He had served for years as vicar in Huddersfield in England and authored a successful book on church renovation, *Pitching the Tent*.[47] The bishop's motive was undoubtedly to put in place a dean who would successfully renovate the local cathedral. Giles met many challenges with amazing success as he transformed a conservative community into an assembly at home in an imaginatively renewed space. He has described the

essential package Episcopalians expect to find when they enter a church building: a rusty St. George's shield, red doors and red carpets, gloomy interiors in which you can barely see a hand in front of you, pews and more pews, choir stalls filling the chancel, a pipe organ, fenced altars, pointed windows, and as large an acreage as possible of wood paneling, stained dark brown—all combined in a liturgical space of bowling alley proportions, utterly inappropriate for expressing the theology of participation and inclusion.[48]

What the cathedral community now finds as a result of working with Giles and architect George Yu is a bishop's chair set in a semicircular stone presbyterium that continues all around the perimeter of the worship space where the people, initiated through baptism into the priestly community, sit on chairs arranged antiphonally. The baptistery, an actual pool into which water from the old font cascades, is placed in the south aisle, a somewhat awkward place at present, but eventually there will be a new gatehouse building on the south side from which all areas and activities of the cathedral site can be accessed. Within the liturgical area of the nave, there is an ambo similar in design to the *bema* of a synagogue; it is a long lectern with a bench behind it. A dignified altar table has replaced the original stone high altar.

Giles has noted that in his native England many of the cathedrals in the Anglican Communion have undergone some renovation, but only one

> has been renovated radically in accordance with a theological and liturgical rationale. That is Portsmouth, where David Stancliff's inspired work has provided us with a model of how a cathedral can become a space in which the Easter experience comes alive as we move through the space in worship.[49]

In the United States, the renovated cathedral in Philadelphia might well be for North American Episcopalians what Portsmouth cathedral is for the English Anglicans. The renovation, however, is but the first step in renewing the community itself made of living stones built into the temple of God. Episcopalians need to ask very serious questions about their liturgical spaces but also about their ecclesial identity. Only when the latter questions concerning doctrinal, liturgical, and moral issues are confidently answered can they come up with honest and creative answers to their architectural questions.

10

Twentieth-Century
Monastic Architecture

JUST AS BENEDICTINES WERE LEADING FIGURES IN THE MODERN
liturgical movement, so they were leaders in commissioning major architects to build monastic churches and renovate old ones in the twentieth
century. Their decisions, however, were not driven by a primary concern
for architectural style but rather by sound theological and liturgical programs. Commissioning competent architects, they trusted the architects'
ability to translate theological and liturgical programs into forms that, over
the years, would shape both the theological and liturgical life of their communities. The structures illustrate the rich diversity in approach to traditional monastic living that is possible in the modern and even the
postmodern world. The communities were especially sensitive to the environments in which their buildings were erected, to the honest use of materials, and to the economic issues that the communities would face in the
upkeep of their buildings.

Monastic communities following the Rule of Benedict stand in the biblical tradition; but, as Christians, their members are called to bring that tradition into dialogue with contemporary cultures as they seek to be
responsible for the place, the environment which is their gift, their
promise, and their challenge. In their more faithful periods, Benedictine
communities have tried to respond to the biblical teaching on landedness
through their vow of stability, their commitment to simplicity and sharing
of goods, and their policy of hospitality.[1] They have tried to realize that the
world is not simply something given to people for utilitarian purposes; it
is home at the present time, even for pilgrim people on their way into the
kingdom of God.[2]

Writing for cenobites, Benedict stressed the community's responsibility to share its goods with the poor and the stranger.[3] His concern was for reverence, proper care, and appropriate use of material things.[4] He seemed to grasp the importance of a certain rootedness, a grafting on the particular locality in which the community finds itself.[5] The attitude toward the world that he tried to instill was one of stewardship, inspired by the second chapter of Genesis, in which humans are placed in the garden not as masters but rather as stewards.[6] As a result, Benedictine communities throughout history have sought to establish creative, harmonious relationships with their environments. While affirming the primacy of the human person over the rest of creation, they have enhanced their surroundings. But in the same way that they have regularly humanized their environments, so also has the environment humanized them.[7]

The Benedictine tradition has something important to say about human life in the contemporary world, plagued as it is with problems of pollution, energy, and consumption. In seeking to establish a balanced order of relationships between humanity and the rest of creation, among human beings themselves, and between humans and God, Benedict stressed the importance of reverence for the physical world and the role of a humane environment in helping monastic men and women develop as people whose lives are committed to the search for God. Throughout history, of course, the implementation of Benedict's teaching has been conditioned by both cultural and ecclesial factors.

With the end of the Second World War, many monastic communities in the Western world launched extensive building programs. The end of the war brought pressures for expansion as the number of candidates for monastic life dramatically increased, along with the number of students enrolled in monastic schools. In general, the buildings put up soon after the war were erected in the same style as their predecessors, the traditional Gothic or Romanesque style. As a result of greater reflection on the various roles played in liturgical celebrations, however, and increasing awareness of theological, liturgical, and architectural developments in Europe, monastic communities encouraged their church architects to depart from the longitudinal plan, according to which the pews in the nave, the choir stalls for the monks, and the altar ran along a single axis. Efforts were made to accommodate large congregations, especially in those monasteries committed to school work. Likewise, special attention was given to the placement of the monastic choir, which generally distinguishes monastic from parochial churches. Efforts were made to locate the choir so that it could relate to the rest of the worshiping community without standing as a barrier between the congregation and the altar.[8]

MOUNT SAVIOUR MONASTERY

The first monastic church in the United States to depart from the longitudinal form was that erected at Mount Saviour Monastery in Pine City, New York. The monastery was founded in 1951 by Damasus Winzen, a monk of Maria Laach in Germany. In laying plans for his new community, he proposed a monastery without a school or parish commitments. He stressed simplicity of life and hospitality for guests, whom he wanted drawn into the community's worship and work.[9]

To design a temporary, low-cost chapel that would be useful after the completion of a permanent monastery, Winzen turned to Joseph Sanford Shanley of New York.[10] It was Winzen's own theological, monastic, and liturgical background, however, that determined the design of the new chapel. To avoid stratification of clerical and lay areas so prominent in longitudinally planned churches, Winzen proposed an octagon, permitting the altar to be central. All could gather around it, the monks forming an inner circle with the guests close behind.[11] In Shanley's original plan the chapel occupied the southern corner of a square, with the other monastic buildings jutting out at the northwest and northeast. No attempt was made to adopt a consciously modern style; a simple building was designed to rest on top of rolling hills.

Mount Saviour experienced a steady growth throughout the 1950s, so in 1959 the monks set about developing a total monastic plan, lest the buildings develop in chaotic fashion. The central area of the property was divided into nine squares, with the chapel occupying the central square; the four corner squares were assigned to other buildings. In Winzen's mind the altar was the center of monastic life; it was appropriate, then, that all other buildings and activities be built around the altar. The chapel as a whole combined the octagon, a Christian symbol of resurrection, with the form of a cross. The southeast square of the plan contained an existing guest house. A house for oblates and novices was projected for the square at the southeast. The most secluded square to the northwest was set aside for an inward-looking building housing the monastic dormitory and library. A more open building was planned for the northeast corner, housing the busy activities associated with the kitchen, refectory, chapter room, and laundry.

The new buildings that were finally erected were designed by Ronald Cassetti. He respected Shanley's earlier work on the chapel but expanded its capacity. It was ready for use by Christmas 1963. The dormitory-library building is an enclosed square, but the lines are more active and outward-looking. The chapel is obviously central and dominant; its horizontal roof line, stretching outward from the central spire, ties the building to the ground. The interior has a sense of simplicity and clarity. A pair of stairways in the northern arm of the chapel descend to the crypt, which houses both the Blessed Sacrament and a fourteenth-century sculpture of the Madonna and Child. The overall monastic complex communicates tranquility and peace.

MONASTERY OF CHRIST IN THE DESERT, ABIQUIU, NEW MEXICO

Since the community had grown in numbers, the monastic chapter at Mount Saviour decided in 1964 to make a foundation in New Mexico.[12] Winzen sent Father Aelred Wall to explore possible sites. He chose a 115–acre ranch in the canyon of the Chama River, thirteen miles by dirt road from the nearest highway. Wall contacted George Nakashima, a long-time friend who had designed many of the church furnishings at Mount Saviour, and asked him to plan a series of simple, inexpensive buildings for the property in New Mexico, since the monks hoped to concentrate on primitive monastic ideals. The buildings were designed around an existing farmhouse on a parched slope rising from the flat bottomland along the river and extending to the foot of the steep, craggy, rust-colored canyon walls. The original farmhouse was converted into a kitchen, refectory, provisional chapel, and guest house. Five two-celled adobe units were built behind the farmhouse for the monks. All structures were built of adobe, since the community wanted to link itself with the culture and tradition of the southwest.

The monastic church, a towerlike structure, rests on somewhat higher ground above the cells. Stark and stately in its simplicity, the interior of the building is flooded with light. A square red sandstone altar table is set on a base of fieldstone cut from the monastery grounds. Two statues in the chapel, one of Our Lady and the other of John the Baptist, were executed by sculptor Ben Ortega of Tesuque, New Mexico. They preserve much of the natural contour of the gnarled juniper out of which they were carved. The well-known artist Ben Shawn, a personal friend of Nakashima, designed a wood processional cross with a relief figure of Christ that was executed by Shawn's son, Jonathan. An adobe guest house has been erected at some distance from the other buildings, and because of growth in the monastic community in Abiquiu, additional structures have been added to the complex in recent years.

PORTSMOUTH ABBEY,
PORTSMOUTH, RHODE ISLAND

Between 1958 and 1963 a number of other Benedictine monasteries engaged in extensive building programs, including St. Gregory's Abbey in Portsmouth, Rhode Island; St. John's Abbey in Collegeville, Minnesota; Annunciation Monastery in Bismarck, North Dakota; and St. Louis Abbey in St. Louis, Missouri.

Monks settled at Portsmouth in 1919 and opened a boys' school in 1926. Located near the shore of Narragansett Bay, the physical facilities of the monastery and school developed in the early years around an old manor house built in the 1860s.[13] When Aelred Graham became prior in 1951, the community began to discuss plans for a new church and monastery. After considering several architects, the community chose Pietro Belluschi. In 1957 he presented the monks at Portsmouth his plans for an octagonal church with a gallery for enlarged assemblies and retrochoir behind the altar.[14] In his design for the church, he moved away from his traditional longitudinal plan to develop a more centralized plan. Reflecting the octagonal plan of San Vitale in Ravenna, the church makes effective use of wood and local fieldstone. Focus is placed on the altar through a filigree sculpture of thin, taut wire designed by the New York abstractionist Richard Lippold. Unfortunately, the retrochoir behind the altar is not integrated with the major worship space but rather appears as an additional room behind the sanctuary. In the church, eight laminated wood bents mark the corners of the inner octagon and rise through the gallery to an octagonal clerestory that is surmounted by a needlelike spire. The choir and sacristies form a link with the three-storey monastery wing behind and to the north of the church. To the south the monastery connects with the students' dining room. The church, monastery, and dining hall are scaled in sympathy with the earlier buildings on the property. Color and texture are provided by the blue-gray local stonework of the lower walls, the dark brown stain on the vertical wood siding, and the copper roofing. The elements are modestly sized, avoiding a monumental appearance.

SAINT JOHN'S ABBEY, COLLEGEVILLE, MINNESOTA

There is no doubt that a major accomplishment in the history of monastic architecture is the church at Saint John's Abbey in Collegeville, Minnesota.[15] Both the monastery and the university expanded considerably after the Second World War. Consequently, before attention could be given to a new church, the community had to settle on a comprehensive plan for the whole campus so that the future of the abbey and the university could be somewhat projected and the placement and design of the buildings could respect both the mission of the abbey and the contours of the 2,400–acre property with its gentle, rolling hills, lakes, and woods. In 1953 twelve distinguished architects from various parts of the world were invited to prepare a comprehensive plan. The community decided to work with Marcel Breuer, the Hungarian Jew who had been associated with Walter Gropius and the Bauhaus. The monastic wing, the first unit constructed, was completed in 1955.

Although Abbot Baldwin Dworschak surely played a key role in securing the community's acceptance of Breuer's imaginative designs for the new church, the community's longtime involvement in liturgical and theological scholarship was a critical asset. The abbey church, contemporaneous with Coventry Cathedral in England, is one of the first, if not the first, cathedral-scale church buildings designed for active participation of the entire liturgical assembly. In light of the extraordinary developments in our understanding of liturgical space since the Second Vatican Council, it is easy to criticize certain aspects of the building; nevertheless, its profound respect for the importance and priority of the whole assembly as the principal celebrant of the liturgy is both pioneering and remarkable. As completed, the church is a trapezoid covered by a thin concrete shell that is pleated into deep folds on either side. The shell rises from the ground by means of narrow concrete piers; the intervening space is closed with plate glass windows looking into enclosed gardens, which in turn are closed off by parallel cloister corridors linking the church and the new monastery wing. A kite-shaped chapter house is attached to the east cloister.

In the church, the altar, located along the central axis, divides the plan into two similar trapezoids. The choir stalls are arranged around the altar, with the abbot's place facing across the altar toward the nave. The wider end of the main trapezoid is occupied by the congregation. At the rear of the nave is a balcony raised on concrete piers independent of the walls. The north wall is a textured screen resembling a honeycomb. It is filled with stained glass designed by a relatively unknown artist, probably the least impressive element in the ensemble. The window was a great disappointment to Breuer, who had hoped that his friend and Bauhaus collaborator Josef Albers would be commissioned to design the glass. A rather abstract figure of the triumphant Christ, to be designed by Ben Shawn, was planned for the large space behind the abbot's throne, but it was never actually commissioned, since some of the monks feared that the church would become a museum. A shrine at the rear of the church contains an elegant twelfth-century wooden figure of Our Lady of Wisdom and her Child, which originated in southern France.

Abutting the north wall is a low atrium housing a depressed square baptistery. Overlooking the baptistery is a remarkable sculpture of John the Baptist, patron of the abbey and university, designed by Doris Cesar. Before the atrium stands the bell banner, the most memorable feature of the church. It provides a striking entrance to the church under its sweeping parabolic arch and reflects the sunlight into the north stained glass wall of the church. Holding aloft both the bells and a cross, in a single gesture it proclaims faith and inspires hope.[16]

The church was consecrated in 1961. At the time no one suspected the complex developments in religious and liturgical life that would be set in motion by the Second Vatican Council. The same church building undoubtedly would not be built today because the celebration of the liturgy has been considerably simplified so that the whole community, including the nonordained monks and the laity, might fully participate as a unified assembly. Likewise, the monks no longer think of the abbey primarily in hierarchical terms but rather as a fraternity whose symbol of unity and direction is the abbot; hence, the abbot uses the throne only for the most solemn celebrations of the liturgy.

There are various accommodations that have already been made and others yet to be made so that the church might serve the changing needs of both the monastic community and the university. For example, the Blessed Sacrament is no longer reserved on the main altar but is housed in a small, temporary chapel at the rear of the church. A more permanent placement is yet to be arranged. At the weekday eucharist, the principal celebrant presides from a chair placed near the altar, facing the choir stalls rather than the nave; both monks and guests take their places in the stalls. The regular practice of concelebration has eliminated the need of the numerous small private Mass chapels in the crypt. In themselves, these chapels are truly gems, housing as they do beautifully designed altars, crucifixes, and pieces of sculpture executed by some of the most admired modern artists, including Meinrad Burch-Korrodi, Peter Watts, and Lambert Rücki.

ANNUNCIATION MONASTERY, BISMARCK, NORTH DAKOTA

Impressed by the new buildings at Collegeville, the Benedictine Sisters at Annunciation Monastery in Bismarck, North Dakota, asked Marcel

Breuer to help them plan a new monastic complex on a site five miles north of the city, overlooking a branch of the Missouri River.[17] The land still has an almost primitive beauty; the low hills are worn smooth by strong winds, with few trees on the exposed slopes. There is a sense of great space and distance. Initially Breuer designed a convent and a school for young girls. The elements of the complex are connected by covered but open walkways which serve to pull them into unity and also to define courtyard spaces and give the scheme an appropriate human scale. The bell tower rises above the rest of the construction; from afar it makes a distinctive silhouette in the otherwise empty landscape, and from nearby it marks the approach to the chapel. At the left there is what was designed as a monastic wing and community room; adjacent is the main chapel. Next to that is a smaller chapel for the students, flanked on either side by the sister's refectory and the students' dining room; to the left is the college wing. In recent years a new building has been constructed for the monastic community, and the original Breuer buildings have been occupied by the growing university.

The exteriors of the original Breuer buildings show an interesting juxtaposition of forms, patterns, materials, and textures. The basic pattern is rectilinear, made up of projecting slabs and columns of white-painted concrete, which casts sharp shadows into the in-filling panels. These are alternately of black shade-screening for windows and light buff-colored local brick, which blends well with the concrete.

The exterior buttresses of the main chapel are of rough concrete and take the lateral thrust of the chapel roof, which is painted white on the inside, along with the fieldstone walls. The reredos screen is gold-leafed; the baldachino is lacquered primary blue; the floor is polished black brick; and the pews and choir stalls are of dark-stained oak. There are glass-in-concrete windows, designed by the architect, on either side of the choir area. These replace the transept as a means of marking off the choir area from the nave. A plaster screen wall at the left permitted the sick and infirm sisters to join in the celebrations; the screen at the right encloses the sacristy.

The materials used had such quality that applied finishes were not necessary. The factor of availability in the sparsely settled region was important. It was also thought desirable to use materials that would have the character of permanence and would age gracefully. After finishing the main monastic complex, Breuer also designed a number of other buildings for the university nearby. He was convinced that contemporary architecture should show organic growth but not be a replica of the past. Each building should be young and living, expressing the culture of its own time. Surely this conviction shows through his work.

SAINT LOUIS ABBEY, SAINT LOUIS, MISSOURI

Unlike the buildings at Mount Saviour, Collegeville, and Bismarck, the monastery and school complex at St. Louis Abbey in St. Louis, Missouri, seems to have been designed primarily on the basis of aesthetic and functional principles rather than clearly delineated theological and liturgical grounds. Founded in 1955 by monks from Ampleforth Abbey in England, the new community engaged Gyo Obata, a Japanese American architect, to design buildings to serve the monastic community and an upper and lower school. A monastic wing, a church, and a number of school buildings were erected; however, it is the church, consecrated in 1962, that has attracted most attention.[18] Obata proposed a circular plan, which the monks decided to use in a congregation-altar-retro-choir sequence, with the altar in the center. The covering concrete shell is composed of two superimposed circles of twenty parabolic vaults each, supported by twenty parabolic ribs containing a skylight. The lower and larger of the circles of vaults shelters an ambulatory marked off from the seating area partially by a screen and also by the choir stalls and benches. Certainly one has an immediate feeling of closeness to the altar, but it is difficult to orient oneself to liturgical actions elsewhere in the building. The obvious problem in a geometrically centered sanctuary is that ministers, especially presiders and preachers, cannot avoid having members of the assembly behind them. Although the church space at St. Louis Abbey may be experienced as sacred in some sense, on the liturgical level the building raises serious problems which are not easily solved, in spite of the fact that modern architecture is generally adaptable. Some modifications were made to the building in 1995, and a new monastery residence was completed in 2001.

SAINT MARY'S ABBEY, MORRISTOWN, NEW JERSEY

The Second Vatican Council raised complex questions for monasteries, not only in the area of liturgy but also in the broader area of monastic life and its relationship with the church and the world. For example, the council stressed the value of monastic enclosure, the contemplative dimension of monastic life, and the primacy of liturgy and personal prayer over ministry outside the monastery. It also called for the integration of what were formerly called lay brothers and sisters into the unity of the community so they might be more closely united with the life and work of the monastery.

Some of these issues were already being discussed when Victor Christ-Chaner of New Canaan, Connecticut, was commissioned in 1961 to draw up a master plan for Saint Mary's Abbey in Morristown, New Jersey. A new abbey and church were built there between 1964 and 1966. Christ-Chaner thought of monastic life as basically inward-looking; hence, the wings of the monastery are turned in on one another around small courts with narrow windows recessed into broken wall surfaces.[19]

The church is square, surrounded by protrusions serving as ventilation and stairwells. The building serves as a circulation center for monks and students descending to the lower level, which houses the monastic common room, refectory, kitchen, and students' dining room. The architect carved out a church area within the church building by means of a curved, six-foot-high wall surrounding the actual space for liturgical celebrations. One enters the church by way of a small cube containing a large holy water font. In the church itself, a congregation-altar-choir sequence has been followed, with semicircular tiers of choir benches behind the altar. A Blessed Sacrament Chapel and a Lady Chapel stand as white prismatic enclosures on either side of the sanctuary. The jutting in and out of the walls within the interior and the marked contrast between the white walls within and the dark mahogany furniture and the red-brick primary walls of the building do make for a rather busy space, but the monks have tried to use it intelligently.

WESTON PRIORY, WESTON, VERMONT

In contrast to the rather monumental buildings just described stand the much simpler buildings at Weston Priory in Weston, Vermont. Founded in 1953 by Abbot Leo Rudloff, the community has sought to discard the nonessentials that tend to clutter human life.[20] The original building at Weston was an old farmhouse and attached barn. During early renovations, the small barn was converted into an unpretentious, rustic chapel. In 1960 a dormitory wing was added to the side of the chapel opposite the original house. Four years later, a Burlington architect, Julian Goodrich, was asked to add a nave to the original chapel, which in turn became the choir. Using native fieldstones from the property and old barn timbers, he fashioned a worship space that is both hospitable and modest. The monks line the walls of the choir with the altar in their midst, while the rest of the assembly occupies a narrow nave flanked on the right by an aisle and on the left by a cloister corridor. The Blessed Sacrament Chapel is a small room, two steps down from the head of the right-hand aisle, with a pleasant chapter room beyond it. To accommodate the large number of guests who come to celebrate liturgy with the monks in pleasant weather, they have developed a barn chapel which opens up to welcome overflowing crowds. None of the buildings is architecturally sophisticated, but the beauty and honesty of natural materials generally used very well are in themselves inspiring, although there are those who find the complex at Weston somewhat affectedly simple.

SAINT VINCENT ARCHABBEY, LATROBE, PENNSYLVANIA

The Second Vatican Council encouraged a stronger emphasis on people, acknowledging their greater importance relative to the institutions of any authentic religion. This is clearly reflected in many of the buildings that have been erected by monastic communities in the last fifty years. The primacy of persons is surely evident in the new monastery at Saint Vincent Archabbey in Latrobe, Pennsylvania. Founded in 1846, the community is the oldest Benedictine foundation in the United States. Over the years the monks erected numerous buildings to accommodate a very large community, a seminary, and a college. In 1963, however, a serious fire destroyed a sizable section of the monastery. Under the leadership of Archabbot Rembert Weakland, the community commissioned Tasso Katselas to design a new monastery building. Finished in 1967, the edifice groups on seven floors an immense network of cells, common rooms, chapels, and accommodation for the aged and infirm. Conscious that the building would serve a busy community deeply involved in academic and pastoral work where the stress is apt to be on individual apostolates, the architect concentrated on the cenobitic dimensions of Benedictine life and sought to create an interior environment that would synthesize respect for persons and at the same time support and encourage communication among the brethren.[21]

Special attention was given to the design of the two hundred cells. Katselas realized that a monk spends much of his life in his cell; hence, he sought to create a space that functioned favorably for the individual. He felt that the cell of a monk engaged in work that necessitates much contact with the larger world and church should foster a contemplative spirit and focus attention inward. As one enters a cell in the monastery, an exterior view is denied; it is only suggested. One must make a special effort to walk to an elevated window niche which is V-shaped. Light floods the room, but it can be controlled by a drape, which may be drawn to cover the niche. The closet in each cell projects into the corridor, sculpting the corridor space so that a definition of the cell and the corridor is established from within as well as without. In the same way as the exterior surfaces of the building have been broken up by the projecting window niches, so have the corridors within the building been broken up by the projecting closets.

The recreation floor has rooms for personal enrichment as well as for community exchange. It is raised above the terrace level with a deep overhang and is oriented toward an adjacent lake. It captures a panoramic view as opposed to the controlled view from the cells. The terrace level itself opens out onto gardens and a private sitting area. There is also a roof terrace for walking. A keen sense of circulation both within and outside the building has been fostered. The new monastery is linked with the complex of older buildings on campus by means of a concrete bridge.[22]

Since the new monastery does in fact function well, many of the architect's goals have been achieved. However, from the exterior the edifice is rather overwhelming. If the design had been more discreet, the building would have been less monumental and probably would have been integrated more effectively with the other buildings on the campus. The highly sculptured surface communicates a sense of complexity and generates a busy atmosphere rather than a climate of simplicity and peace.[23]

SAINT PROCOPIUS ABBEY, LISLE, ILLINOIS

Among the most handsome buildings erected by monastic communities since the Second Vatican Council are those designed for the monks of Saint Procopius Abbey in Lisle, Illinois. Founded by Saint Vincent Archabbey in 1885, the community eventually opened a college (now called the Benedictine University of Illinois) on a large campus in the Chicago suburb of Lisle. By 1964 they had decided to build a new monastery and church on a wooded hill across from the college campus. Edward Dart was selected to design the buildings. His impressive structures present themselves as an ascending, well-integrated spiral that calmly leads its twelve construction units to the chapel; hence one has the impression of a small village rather than an institution. The whole is carefully related to the countryside. The residential blocks, each containing eight to twelve rooms, harmonize with one another so as to form dwellings that are expansive but not grandiose. One senses a profusion of air and space, rather than embellishments.

A visitor approaches the church through a sheltered court and enters a one-storey, glass-walled narthex beyond which rises an open belfry directly above the Lady Chapel. Walking through the main doors, one stands in a low-beamed space that functions as a foyer both to the monastery to the left and to the church. Straight ahead is a holy water font cut from a large block of red-gray granite. The church itself is designed as two distinct spaces, a room within a room. The highest portion extends over the altar and choir. This area is bathed in light from a large clerestory window. The monks occupy benches facing the altar, similar to those used by the lay community in the lower space. The monks wanted a flexible choir arrangement, and so they opted against traditional choir stalls. The present arrangement, however, is not without problems. It makes antiphonal singing difficult and tends to inhibit a sense of community among the monks when they gather for the liturgy of the hours, since they are strung out in a bank of benches where they see only the backs of the monks in front of them. Nor are they effectively related to the assembly of guests who gather in the other bank of benches.

The altar, ambo, and presider's chair, all simply and directly constructed of heavy oak, are movable within the asymmetric sanctuary. However, the space comes across as very austere, since there is little or no ornamentation. A similar concern for natural beauty and detail is manifested in the monastic refectory and chapter room. Dart's buildings are both strong and tranquil; they are intrinsically discreet but naturally elegant. It is with good reason that the project at Saint Procopius was awarded the highest architectural honor by the American Institute of Architects in 1973.

MOUNT ANGEL ABBEY, SAINT BENEDICT, OREGON

Because of the interest among architects and historians of architecture in the work of the Finnish architect Alvar Aalto, the monks of Mount Angel Abbey in Oregon commissioned him to design a library to serve both the monastic community and the seminary.[24] It was dedicated in 1970. Before the library was built, the beauty of Mount Angel rested in its setting, situated as it is on an isolated plateau rising in the center of the plane of Salem at the center of a ring of mountains. Great volcanic peaks stand in the distance. Aalto maintained that, if possible, libraries should be built facing

north; hence it is the northern end of the Mount Angel library that affords
the most spectacular view.[25]

Constructed primarily of buff brick and teakwood, the building itself is
rigorous and yet modest. Its fan-shaped plan is quite characteristic of
Aalto's style. Organic unity, another characteristic, is evident above all in
the interior. Standing at the library control area, one senses the volume of
the building with its rhythms and counter-rhythms, its overhead and lateral lighting, and the cascade of various floor levels. One gets the impression of standing on a ship and looking at the various decks below. Aalto
surely exploited the ground levels of the property effectively.[26]

The building and its function are unified. It is all library—a place for
people who want to explore the world of books and who want to be
enriched by that experience. Aalto sought to relate that new world of
knowledge to the old world of nature, which one can admire through the
numerous bay windows in the building. Likewise, he wanted to relate that
new world to the familiar world of other people, whom one can see at the
various reading desks and in the conference room, which opens onto the
main entrance.[27] His concern for people is manifested in the attention he
has given to details. The library is a superb example of a humanizing environment that promotes the best in the Benedictine tradition: a deep commitment to what is good, what is beautiful, and what is true.

SAINT BENEDICT'S MONASTERY, SAINT JOSEPH, MINNESOTA

In the 1980s Frank Kacmarcik and Theodore Butler, who had worked
together on a number of successful church building and renovation projects, linked their talents to work on a major project for Saint Benedict's
Monastery in Saint Joseph, Minnesota. A college had originally developed
out of a simple high school and college program for the Benedictine sisters
themselves, but the number of laywomen grew steadily until it was rather
difficult to distinguish between what was college and what was monastery.
So the sisters decided to build a significant entrance to the monastery that
would give them their own gathering space and would emphasize the
church as the dominant building on campus. The entrance to the old chapel
was reversed and a large gathering hall was erected. It is a handsome building and is used creatively by the sisters both for meeting guests and for community and college events.

Architecturally the renovation of the church has been described as impeccable. The dome was the determining factor in positioning the altar so that the community gathers on four sides of the altar. No matter how one stands or sits when presiding, there are always people behind—which makes communication difficult. Likewise, the placement of the lectern has not been thought out adequately; one reads and preaches across the altar with part of the community sitting behind. A beautifully designed large chest for relics has been placed beneath the altar. Unfortunately, with its striking structure and its gold inlaid cubes, it comes across as the central focus in the building and draws too much attention to the relics, which are of secondary importance in the Catholic liturgy.

The space has been considerably lightened by the use of Remy glass made in Germany, replacing the stained glass in all the windows. A separate chapel for reservation of the Blessed Sacrament has been handsomely designed. In many ways the renovation is remarkable; whenever possible, pillars, statues, and other parts of the original chapel have been retained in the new structures, so there is an effective sense of continuity much appreciated by the community. However, there are some inherent problems. One gets the impression that architectural concerns were primarily determinative of the arrangements and that more concern should have been given to the liturgical requirements.

WORTH ABBEY CHURCH, WEST SUSSEX, ENGLAND

One of the major church buildings of the English post–World War II period is the Worth Abbey Church under the patronage of Our Lady Help of Christians, in West Sussex, England. Designed by Francis Pollen (1926–1987), the building exhibits one architect's effective response to the Second Vatican Council. Pollen had entered the Liverpool cathedral competition in 1959 with a fan-shaped design, a plan he continued to favor for Catholic parish churches. As an architectural student he came under the influence of Edwin Luytens, but then about 1958 he suddenly launched into a version of the new brutalism. He became firmly committed to modernism but critical of the intellectual and physical shallowness of the word in England, a concern he shared with both the brutalists and exponents of liturgical reform.

Pollen originally designed a building at Worth containing four separate side chapels for the four school houses; he intended to place the chapels within a large square with a pyramidal roof supported by the walls of the four chapels. To expand the seating of the main worship space from five hundred to eight hundred, it was proposed that two of the chapels be placed in a crypt, thus invalidating the pyramid concept. The roof was changed to a cone rising from a ring beam, 110 feet in diameter, supported by eight irregularly spaced columns. Two remaining chapels, placed behind the central altar, were redesigned as snail-like walls of brick wrapped around two further columns, perhaps influenced by Niemeyer's chapel of the president's palace in Brasilia (1958). These borrow light from the main worship space over the walls which stop short of the ceiling. The altar is rather large and elongated with the mensa supported by four legs. A smaller but more substantial design would have given the altar a more powerful and symbolic presence in the church.

The plan of the church consists of a circle inscribed in a square, but it avoids some of the confusion inherent in Gibbard's Liverpool cathedral design by confining the assembly to three-fourths of the circle, with a stepped monastic choir occupying the space behind the altar and between the two chapels. The monks sit on simple chairs in the choir; the arrangement, however, calls for a more stable and permanent accommodation. The main floor of the church is dished toward the center.

The cone is supported by two ring-beams with a continuous narrow clerestory between them and bearing on the brick-clad concrete columns. The cone is open at the top, allowing a continuous clerestory in the form of a lantern. The descending central cylinder channels light down onto the altar and acts as a visual focus. The spatial effect of the cone, when seen in isolation from inside the church, is startling. There is a balcony at the rear of the church, so that the overall seating accommodates about a thousand people. Suspended over the altar is a large wooden cross with a bronze corpus designed by Arthur Pollen, the architect's father. He also designed a bronze sculpture of the Madonna and Child, which occupies a small niche facing outward in the wall of one of the small chapels. The internal space of the church can contract or expand depending on the lighting; hence it can easily be accommodated to both large and small groups, to the public celebration of the liturgy and to personal prayer. It is definitely a contemplative space. The church is regularly used for large diocesan celebrations, since it is in fact the largest church in the diocese of Arundel and Brighton. It was consecrated on July 13, 1975.

Referring to his work at Ronchamp, Le Corbusier said that "the requirements of religion have had little effect on the design; the form was an answer to a psycho-physiology of the feelings." Such a personal and emotional response to a church building would surely be alien to the doctrinal and liturgical demands of most Christian communities today; professionalism requires a proper understanding of the program for a church building. It is that carefully delineated program which the clients are often unable to produce. The church at Worth Abbey represents a healthy confrontation of tradition and modernity in both liturgy and architecture, resulting in the reconciliation of what often appears to be conflicting tendencies. It exemplifies architecture responding effectively to both artistic and liturgical needs. In 1993 a piazza outside the church, designed by the architect, was added, so that all structural work has been completed.

The church at Worth certainly fulfills Peter Hammond's hopes for responsible church building. As he remarked,

> It is only when church architecture is placed squarely within its social context, only when the design of the house of God is related both to modern architectural thinking and also to the work of the theologian, the liturgist, the pastor and the sociologist, that we shall begin to realize the potentialities that lie open to us. When that happens—and not until then—we may hope to discover the secret of an architecture that is at once traditional, in the true sense of that much abused word, and wholly of its time: an architecture that is capable of becoming a vital factor not merely in the reform of the liturgy but, through the renewal of the Church's common prayer, in the transformation of the whole life of the Christian community.[28]

Undoubtedly Pollen's knowledge of the practical and spiritual aspects of the eucharist and other tenets of the Roman Catholic liturgy gained from a lifetime's experience helped him to eliminate superfluous elements and to create an environment that promotes rather than hinders both personal and communal religious experience. The monastic community at Worth played a major role in providing the architect with a clearly articulated brief describing the nature of the community and its apostolates, its commitments to prayer and work, and its relationship with the larger diocese and church in Britain. The relationship underscores the importance of imaginative church building which facilitates the active participation of the entire assembly in the celebration of the liturgy.

SAINT MEINRAD ARCHABBEY, SAINT MEINRAD, INDIANA

The Archabbey Church of Our Lady of Einsiedeln at St. Meinrad, Indiana, was originally dedicated on March 21, 1907.[29] A Romanesque structure, it was originally designed by Br. Adrian Werwer, a Franciscan from St.

Louis. The building is made of hand-cut sandstone quarried in the early 1900s on St. Meinrad property. In 1968 the community began renovating the church to reflect the principles of the Second Vatican Council. The monastic choir was retained in the apse of the church, the galleries were removed, and the altar was placed in the center of the nave so that the whole community could gather around it during the celebration of the eucharist. In 1993 the archabbot appointed a committee of monks to oversee the planning and completion of an extensive renovation of the church. The completely renovated church was dedicated on September 30, 1997. The renovation was designed and guided by the architectural firm of Woolen, Molzan and Partners of Indianapolis, Indiana. The firm had previously designed new buildings for the monastery and library.

There are six vaults in the church. In keeping with the Romanesque style, the community explored medieval forms as inspiration for most of the new artifacts to be installed in the church. As a monastic church, the archabbey church is primarily meant to accommodate the monks and their guests for the celebration of the liturgy of the hours and the eucharist. Immediately inside the doors of the church and under the first vault stands a newly designed and executed font created from a mixture of limestone and epoxy. Under the second vault stands a newly designed altar measuring five feet square and forty inches in height. In the Middle Ages altar coverings were often made of precious thread and adorned with jewels. Later developments resulted in the attachment to the wooden or stone altar frames of precious metal plates engraved with rich symbols and biblical personages. This style of altar covering, called the *pala d'oro* (covering of gold), can still be found in Europe, for example, in the Romanesque churches of St. Mark in Venice and St. Ambrose in Milan. Among the most famous altars adorned in this manner is that in the cathedral of Charlemagne in Aachen, Germany, built in the ninth century. It was the *pala d'oro* form and specifically the Aachen altar that served as a model for the design of the altar in the archabbey church. There are seventeen gilded bronze panels on each of the four sides. Each of the four sides of the altar expresses a particular theme in the life of Christ. The craftsmanship is well executed, but unfortunately, being quite small and intricate, the panels do not read clearly from a distance. The placement of the altar, directly under the second bay as one enters the church and physically separated from the monastic choir area, allows both monks and guests to gather around the altar during the eucharist. Thus, the altar is the primary symbol of the body of Christ in the church.

The monastic choir and places for guests have been located in the third and fourth bays of the church. In the 1968 renovation, the choir stalls that had served the community since 1907 were removed and replaced by simple wooden chairs. In planning for the recent renovation, the monks chose to return to traditional choir stalls for their seating during the liturgy of the office and the liturgy of the word during the eucharist. The four rows on each side of the church are tiered so as to help the monks in their singing and to enhance the acoustics within the church. Guest seating has been provided in a bay next to the monastic choir stalls. Along the side walls of the church are benches that house the heating, ventilation, and air-conditioning units and serve as additional seating when a large number of guests is present.

The ambo, from which the scriptures and other spiritual writings are proclaimed during the eucharist and the liturgy of the hours, stands at the head of the bay containing the choir stalls. Each of the three sides of the ambo has three bronze panels containing representations of holy men and women whose writings are read during the divine office.

The presider's chair was originally executed about 1909 for use by the abbot. It is a rather elaborate, highly carved piece of furniture. It has been repaired and restored and is now used by both the archabbot and other priests who preside at the liturgy.

The Blessed Sacrament Chapel is located in the apse of the church. Set within the main body of the church and yet carefully placed so that it is not a distraction during the celebration of the liturgy, the chapel provides easy access from either side of the nave; the large organ facade spanning the apse provides a sense of privacy for personal prayer and adoration. The taber-nacle, created from elements of the original high altar in the church, rests beneath a tower also fashioned from the old high altar, which had been removed from the church in 1968. In addition to benches lining the wall of the chapel, there are chairs and kneelers in the area. Two sanctuary lamps, part of the original archabbey church, are hung just inside the two entrances to the chapel.

There are three shrines in the church. Immediately to the right as one enters the church from the main doors is the shrine of Our Lady of Ein-siedeln, the patron of the archabbey. The statue of the Black Madonna was given to Saint Meinrad for its centennial in 1954 by the founding abbey, the Swiss Abbey of Maria Einsiedeln.

A shrine honoring St. Meinrad, the patron of the archabbey, contains a seven-foot triptych constructed of oak, walnut, and purpleheart woods. It also contains a relic of the martyr. Hand-painted scenes depict various episodes in the life of the ninth-century Benedictine monk as well as representations of the early settlers of the monastery, the abbots who played significant roles in the history of the community, and the abbots involved in the renovation of the church. The central panel contains a scene of the holy woman offering support to Meinrad so he could serve God as a hermit.

The third shrine contains the archabbey's collection of relics. It is in this shrine that the monastic community wakes the dead members. Enclosed within the shrine is the necrology, the listing of all the deceased monks of the archabbey. The three shrines are meant to inspire remembrance of the rich history of the community and to honor all those who have built the abbey by their faithful service and dedication.

One of the most attractive aspects of the renovation is the new marble floor. An impressive figure of the risen Christ looms high upon the wall of the apse. It was designed and executed by Dom Gregory de Wit, a Benedictine of the Abbey of Mont César in Louvain. In one hand Christ holds the book of life; in the other a laurel wreath as a crown of victory. The striking image has greeted visitors to the church for over a half century. The stained glass windows in the church, depicting the various ways in which holy men and women have lived out the Christian faith, were installed in 1908.

The monastic community is rightly proud of the renovated church. Some visitors might find the diversity of artistic styles in the building rather disconcerting, but the monks themselves see the renovation not so much as a tribute to the artisans who have contributed to the project as an expression of gratitude to God, who has nurtured the life of the community for over a hundred and fifty years.

GETHSEMANI ABBEY, TRAPPIST, KENTUCKY

Cistercian monks and nuns also follow the Rule of Benedict and so stand in the Benedictine tradition. Since the Second Vatican Council most of their communities have engaged in building or renovations projects. Gethsemani, the home of Thomas Merton, is probably the best known Cistercian monastery in the United States. The size of the community increased considerably after the Second World War; consequently, extensive architectural renovation was necessary throughout the abbey. In 1962 two of the lay brothers went to consult William Schickel, a designer and architectural consultant, at Loveland, Ohio. They acknowledged that there was much going on in the world of design and planning about which they knew little or nothing, and so they wanted to work out a relationship with Schickel that would bring fresh influence to bear on the developments in the monastery. At first, Schickel simply designed furniture that could be made by the monks in their shops. Out of this association grew some general design consultation about interior planning on projects already in progress. The relationship between Schickel and the monks gradually enlarged, so that he eventually became involved in the renovation of the monastery church, cloister, and courtyard.

As Schickel has written, three main concerns influenced the accommodation of the traditional, one-hundred-year-old, pseudo-Gothic church and its adjoining cloister and courtyard: monastic and liturgical usefulness, excellent aesthetic quality, and economic feasibility.[30] In executing the program, all concerned tried to realize that honest renewal always involves a certain collaboration with one's ancestors. They also acknowledged that all human works should contribute positively to human evolution; hence they must be related to the best in contemporary culture. A basic principle underlying the work was expressed in Alfred North Whitehead's statement that the art of progress is the ability to maintain order amidst change and change amidst order.

A number of polarities, then, had to be fused into a unified whole. There was, on the one hand, an existing one-hundred-year-old structure, molded by various historical assumptions and psychological factors. On the other hand, there was a large community searching for God amidst the complex culture of the 1960s. The old abbey buildings had come into being in an American wilderness; their design was without question influenced by the neighboring Shaker community of the nineteenth century in the area of Bardstown, Kentucky. The founding monks had built in a very sensible fashion; but when it came to the church, they attempted within a basic rectangular building, constructed on the practical premises of brick walls and hand-hewn timber, to build by means of lath and plaster the interior shell of a neo-Gothic church. It was probably for the monks of that time something awesome and deeply religious because if its pseudo-elegance, but it was a building that was culturally nostalgic and regressive. It was clearly a case of style without a sound theological or liturgical program. As such it burdened the monastery for a hundred years.

What seemed most desirable in the 1960s was a light and airy space, a building standing without sham and looking forward toward the future. Accordingly, the plaster replicas of a Gothic interior were torn down, which immediately brought the shape and form of the interior into a close, honest relationship with the rest of the monastery buildings. The same basic approach was taken in the renewal of the cloister and the courtyard. It was no small achievement that a large community of varied backgrounds and ages could arrive at a consensus to take the drastic actions that were necessary to revolutionize their surroundings. That is in itself a tribute to the adaptability and resilience of the Benedictine spirit.[31]

ABBEY OF OUR LADY OF NEW MELLERAY, PEOSTA, IOWA

In 1973, the Cistercians at the Abbey of Our Lady of New Melleray near Dubuque, Iowa, voted to remodel the north wing of their monastery for the permanent location of their church.[32] The monastery was founded in 1849 by monks from Mount Melleray in Ireland. Following the Civil War, the community engaged a local architect, John Mullany, to design a complex of permanent buildings. Mullany had been associated for a time with Augustus Welby Pugin, the distinguished English architect. Mullany's designs reflect Pugin's influence in his preference for pitched roofs and arched windows, and his use of asymmetry and vertical forms. By 1875 the north and east wings were occupied by the monks. Their church was temporarily located on the second floor of the east wing, until it was moved in the 1920s to the second floor of the north wing. Mullany's plans called for a permanent church to be constructed as the south building running parallel to the north wing; however, when construction was resumed on the south wing in the 1950s, the original plans for the church were set aside. When the monks turned their attention to a permanent church in the 1960s, it was suggested that the north wing be razed and a circular church built in its place, but those plans were not accepted by the community. By 1973 they decided instead to remodel the north wing to house a permanent church and hired Willoughby Marshall, Inc., to draw up the original architectural plans.

A second floor was removed from the north and old kitchen wings so as to allow the use of the full height of the north wing for the church and of the old kitchen wing for a chapter house. As a result, an open space of great simplicity was created. Under the direction of Frank Kacmarcik and Theodore Butler, the project was carried through to completion. With the unnecessary partitions and ornamentations stripped away, a space of exceptional beauty emerged as a marvelous shelter capable of revealing God as mysteriously transcendent but also warmly immanent in wood and stone, and above all in the community of monks and their guests gathered for worship. The beams and purloins were sandblasted so as to appear in natural finish. Douglas fir was used for decking in the roof, which arches forty-nine feet above the red-gray tile used as paving throughout the project. The native, light honey-colored sandstone walls have been left bare; they are pierced by arched windows running along both sides of the building and filled with clear glass so that sunlight plays on the walls and furnishings, thus changing the mood of the church throughout the day. In a sense the space is grand, but it does not dwarf those who gather for worship; it rather generates an atmosphere that is unified, mysterious, and inspiring.

In order to offset the length of the church, the sanctuary at the east end and the guest area at the west end have both been elevated somewhat, thus facilitating visibility and pulling the two ends of the building toward one another. As a monastic church the building is used primarily for the celebration of the liturgy of the hours seven times a day and also for the daily celebration of the eucharist. The latter has rightly placed the strongest claims in determining the furnishings of the space, but through effective lighting the sanctuary area recedes in prominence during the liturgy of the hours. A gray-black opalescent granite altar centers the space in the sanctuary. The rest of the furniture is made from solid butcher-block red oak with oiled finish. On each side of the church is a single row of choir stalls; a tracker-action organ stands at the foot of the choir stalls on the right. Pews at the rear of the church rest on slightly raised tiers, accommodating about eighty guests. The community at the time of renovation insisted on a single wrought iron grate separating the monks from the guests, which is problematic during the eucharist, above all during the Communion rite.

Of special interest is the successful handling of the place for the reserved eucharist. The monks wanted to emphasize the primacy of the eucharistic celebration, but they also wanted the reserved sacrament related to the larger eucharistic space. Hence, the reserved sacrament stands in a large tabernacle house of red oak directly behind the presider's chair in the sanctuary. The edifice provides an effective backdrop for the sanctuary area and can accommodate several monks for eucharistic devotion and personal prayer. Apart from the processional cross, the only image in the church is an icon of Our Lady of Vladimir mounted on a wrought iron stand. This is in keeping with the Cistercian tradition, which on the one hand has maintained a strong devotion to the Mother of God but on the other hand has been reserved in its attitude toward paintings and sculptures in monastic buildings. The overall effect of the renovation project is powerful; it has been and will continue to be formative of both the monastic community and their guests. It rightly received an honor award from the American Institute of Architects.

MEPKIN ABBEY, MONCKS CORNER, SOUTH CAROLINA

The new church and other monastic buildings at Mepkin Abbey in South Carolina are eminently successful from both architectural and liturgical points of view. In 1949 a group of Trappist monks came from the Abbey of Gethsemani in Kentucky to bring the monastic life to Mepkin. The property, a splendid old plantation, belonged to Henry and Clare Booth Luce, who donated it for the foundation of a new monastery. The monks built a provisional church in 1950 and worshiped there for about forty years. In 1989, before the arrival of hurricane Hugo, the community began discussions concerning a renovation of that temporary edifice. The arrival of the hurricane and the destruction it left in its path, however, delayed the project until 1991, when the community, now under the direction of a vibrant young abbot, Francis Kline, took up the process once again.

After interviews with several liturgical consultants, the community chose Frank Kacmarcik with Theodore Butler as architect. They discussed at length their identity as a community—how they worshiped together, how they prayed as individual monks, how they celebrated the liturgy with retreatants and guests, and how the eucharist and the liturgy of the hours related to each other in their daily life. During their deliberations they found they were examining the whole of their monastic life: what it had been, how it was currently expressed, and what they hoped for in the future. It was clear that a monastic, theological, and liturgical program was uppermost in their minds, rather than a particular style of building. It was also clear that the emerging floor plan of an entirely new church and the relationship of proposed spaces in the church were, in fact, expressing their identity as a monastic community and their vision for the future. The centrality of the altar to the entire space; the relation of the choir to the altar; the relation of retreatants to the monastic community; the placement of casual visitors; the creation of a smaller, more intimate space for personal prayer and eucharistic devotion; the very location of the building itself in the monastic complex—all these factors they discovered spoke of a theology of monastic life, their vision of church, and their faith in the risen Lord.

The new church provides both monks and guests with a wonderful experience of God's transcendence and immanence in the community. One is aware of others, but not too aware. There is a profound sense of beauty in all that is there—in the altar, in the lighting, in the organ, in the woodwork, especially the ceiling, in the holy water font, and above all in the people. The church was dedicated in November 1993. Since then an impressive bronze statue of Mary and the young Christ child has been placed at the head of the choir, near the presider's chair. Since 1993, a new monastic wing for the elderly and infirm monks, a new refectory for the monks and their guests, and a spacious library and conference center have been built.

This chronicle has shown that since the Second World War various monastic communities have struggled to understand what it means to be grafted onto a locality, what it means to be heir to a living Benedictine tradition, and what it means to be part of a contemporary church and world. They have struggled to be responsible for their landedness as gift, promise, and challenge, and have tried to come to grips with the temptation to greed, presumption, and complacency. Historically, Benedictines have had a strong tradition of creative architecture. At one time William of Volpiano, Lanfranc, and Suger of St. Denis were the European leaders in architectural developments. They were outstanding leaders precisely because they looked to the future and refused to be limited by the accomplishments of the past. In our own era, monastic communities have made a positive contribution to that living tradition. But in times of great cultural uncertainty and insecurity like our own, there is a strong temptation to indulge in romanticism and nostalgia, to settle for forms that are known and familiar, and to abdicate one's responsibility to share in the creation of a new future. Speaking in Milwaukee in June 1979 at a symposium on environment and art in Catholic worship, Archbishop Rembert Weakland seemed to be well aware of the temptation when he warned that "the further Church art, architecture, and music are removed from the contemporary idioms and styles of our time, the more likely it is that they will be sterile and artificial."[33]

The challenge that confronts us was put in even a more provocative way by Armand Veilleux, a Canadian Cistercian and an expert on primitive monasticism:

The only way to belong to a community, a church, a civilization is to help build it. Are we going to be part of a new humanity, or shall we be found cultural runaways once more one revolution behind? In world evolution one assists in every epoch of in-depth change at the emergence of new species but at the same time at the forming of vast fields of fossils. The question facing every community, every monastic order, at this turning-point in human and ecclesial history is as follows: Shall we choose to be members of the new species or shall we rather go to enrich the collection of fossils? The latter alternative is not wanting in attractiveness, for fossils are sought after and marveled at. May we at least have the courage to make our choice in full cognizance rather than let ourselves be passively pigeon-holed by history.[34]

11

Sacred Art from 1900 to the Present

MUCH OF THE ART PRODUCED IN THE LAST CENTURY WAS pessimistic, turned in on itself, reflecting cultures that were often deeply disturbed and disturbing. Much of it was abstract and involved complicated installations in galleries. Several examples will clarify the point. Between 1976 and 1982, Magdalena Abakanowicz, a Polish artist, produced a series of body works called *Alternations*. Included are eighty *Backs,* all different, though alike, eighty human backs without heads, without legs to their thighs, without hands to their arms. They have no centers or fronts; they are hollow, each hiding his own emptiness by crouching submissively. Although they have no sexual distinguishing marks, the artist formed them from burlap and glue on the plaster cast of a muscular male. Their isolation yet their potential for life, so sadly negated by their condition, comes through with a massive pathos.[1] They are reminiscent of T. S. Eliot's "hollow men . . . headpiece filled with straw."[2] They are powerful expressions of the human need for transcendence and immanence to overcome humankind's isolation, introversion, and loneliness.

In 1981, Maggi Hambling was artist in residence at the National Gallery in London. While there she saw a one-man show by the great actor-clown Max Wall, who went on to play Vladimir in Samuel Beckett's *Waiting for Godot.* Hambling developed a friendship with Wall and created a number of powerful portraits, including *The Search Is Always Alone,* where we see the clown scuffling forward, seemingly unaware or, perhaps more exactly, refusing to be daunted by an awareness of how cold and isolated his world really is. It is not by accident that he strides across an egg-shaped stage, symbolic of new life and creativity.[3]

Roderick Barrett painted *Players* in 1989. There are five players, two of whom are clearly playing. The man on the far right raises his arms to beat his drum, yet he seems to lift them with a convulsive fury as though in terrible protest or pain. The boy on the far left plays with a child's hoop. Closer inspection reveals that he is tangled up in the hoop and seems to be entrapped in an emptiness. The clown wearing a funny hat and a striped suit holds an umbrella as if to say that life is really a wet and miserable business. The two other players are enigmatic, perhaps figures of Adam and Eve. The woman stares out blankly at us. She is lonely, as the rigid man beside her is lonely. In fact every player is alone; they stand together yet are isolated from one another—images of the loneliness that longs for self-transcendence and communion.[4]

Francis Bacon has been called one of the most important artists of the second half of the twentieth century. Even those who dislike his work are forced to admit that it is memorable and horribly expressive. He was obsessed with the wretchedness of existence and the terrible vulnerability of being human. He professed to see no hope for humanity. Certain images recur again and again in Bacon's paintings, the best known of which is the screaming pope, after Diego Velázquez's famous portrait of Pope Innocent X. In one of his portraits Bacon depicts the tortured expression of a blood-spattered pope, imprisoned in a tubular construction resembling an unpadded throne. The background, painted in dramatic, vertical strokes, cruelly blurs out the screaming figure as he sits helplessly with clenched fists.[5] In another portrait, *Head Surrounded by Sides of Beef,* the pope is pushed down to the bottom half of the canvas. Bacon has built the suggestion of a cage or cell and has marked the pope with an arrow, as if this tense and tortured image were an exhibit in the artist's chamber of horrors. Bacon himself relied on a famous image, Rembrandt's painted *Carcass of Beef,* and has hung the animal's flesh on either side of this human animal. Rembrandt painted his carcass with reverence, but Bacon simply sees raw meat, dangling behind the papal chair.[6]

There is no doubt that we live in a world in which there is much loneliness and much suffering—some of it is physical suffering that comes from illness, from abuse, from old age; much of it comes from depression and anxiety about life. Unfortunately, traditional institutionalized religious bodies in many ways seem unequipped to respond to this crisis of meaning. In fact, contemporary art forms often simply image back to people the isolation and loneliness they already know in their own lives.

Two distinguished American artists in the last century did in fact seek to relate both themselves and their viewers to the more ultimate realities in human life. Barnett Newman (1905–1970) was well known for the creation of what he called his "zips," which resulted from placing a strip of masking tape down the center of a canvas. For example, in painting *Covenant* in 1949, he placed the tape down the center of a small canvas, painted a deep reddish brown, and then applied a warm orange pigment down its length. Newman came from a Jewish tradition which affirms that God, who cannot be named, entered human history and made a covenant with his people, an act of gracious love. In his painting, Newman expressed this by two zips. The one on the right, a bright orange, symbolized the rich gift of God; the one on the left, a black zip, expressed human mortality, which recedes when related to the presence of God. The deep red behind the zips was carefully chosen as a symbol of our earthen existence. The painting expresses the human being rejoicing because of a relationship with God that gives meaning to existence.[7]

Barnett Newman and Mark Rothko (1903–1970) were friends and colleagues. In a sense their paintings are somewhat similar, for both used rich background colors and then applied lines of other colors to the canvas. For example, Rothko's *Black, Brown, and Maroon* is a richly contemplative painting seeking to draw the viewer beyond the present moment. The soft maroon background mesmerizes the viewers, calling them into a consideration of the deeper aspects of life. Concentrated attention on the rich colors produces a sense of awe and quiet.[8] Both Newman and Rothko produced what might be called imageless paintings; their work is religious but certainly not specifically Christian.

On a walking tour with some friends, the German artist Harald Duwe, who died in 1984, asked whether the painting of Christian subjects was still a possibility. Eventually he answered his own question with a painting, *Abendmahlsbild* (Last Supper). It shows a group of men, actually Duwe's friends from the walking tour, surrounding a dinner table on which, besides bread and wine, we see the head, the heart, the hands, and the feet of Christ being served. The realism is deeply disturbing. Viewers are not excluded from the scene, because the width of the laden table is spread before their very eyes. Thus, all viewers are involved in the scene. A single Judas is not specifically exposed. In discussing his painting, Duwe explained that all of us are potentially like Judas, for the Christian West has continually cut Christ's body through betrayal.[9] He reminds us that the eucharist we celebrate so regularly is always bittersweet, for over it hangs the question, "Is it I, Lord?"

In the introduction to his *Images du Christ*, published in 1980, Frederik van der Meer complained that there was hardly any room left for Christ in art from the modern period.[10] Certainly images of Christ, his mother, and the saints have not been so prominent as they were in Romanesque, Gothic, Renaissance, and baroque periods, but in the modern period, and especially in the last century, there were in fact various portrayals of Jesus, his mother, and the saints produced in modern cultures, especially non-European cultures. Some of those images have been powerful; others have been challenging; and some have been blasphemous. In the latter category one thinks of Andres Serrano's photograph of a crucifix in a container of urine, or Art Spiegelman's cover on *The New Yorker* during Holy Week in 1995. As the Easter Bunny was hung on a cross that was superimposed on an American tax form, the caption read: "Theology of the Tax Cut." Other controversial images, offensive to many Christians, would be found in Terrence McNally's play *Corpus Christ,* and in the book *INRI,* published in Paris, which attempted to reinterpret Christianity by depicting on the cover a nude woman in the role of the crucified Christ.

Distinguished modern theologians and art historians, including Hans Urs von Balthasar, Paul Tillich, John Dillenberger, Horton Davies, Margaret Miles, H. R. Rookmaaker, Jeremy Begbie, George Pattison, and Jane Dillenberger, have all analyzed the interface of religion and culture; some have surveyed the history of Christian imagery since the expansions of Christianity into Africa, the Americas, and Asia.[11] They observe that the Christian colonizers frequently went forth not to serve but to rule. The link between mission and imperialism was clearly shown in a painting by Vicente Manansala, in which a priest is depicted blessing the first large cross planted on Philippine soil. Indigenous laborers do the work while Spanish soldiers carrying spears bark orders at them.[12] There is little doubt that the cross, a Christian symbol of the execution of an innocent victim, has at times been turned into a sword against Muslims in the Crusades, against Native Americans in the Indian wars, against blacks in the slave trade and slavery, and against Jews in the long association of Christianity with anti-Semitism.[13] The contemporary Taiwan theologian Choan-Seng Song has pointed out how historically the *pax Romana* was replaced by the *pax Christiana* and how Jesus, rather than being pictured as the humble friend of the poor and marginalized in the world, was increasingly portrayed as the lawgiver, judge, and cosmic lord. In Renaissance art the humble stable where he was born became a royal palace and his Blessed Mother and St. Joseph were transformed into personages of the royal court.[14]

There have been, however, a number of very distinguished artists who have worked with traditional Christian themes, and their works are deeply religious and sacred. Others have taken traditional Christian themes but have interpreted them in nontraditional ways that are purely secular. Examples should clarify these observations.

The French Catholic painter Georges Rouault (1871–1958) was surely one of the most powerful religious artists of modern times. Although he belonged to no particular group of painters, he is usually classified as an expressionist, since his works project strong emotion by means of vivid color and distorted form. At the age of fourteen, he was apprenticed to a maker of stained glass, a craft that certainly left a mark on his style. Subject matter was immensely important to Rouault. He was in fact a moralist who regarded the sins and foibles of humanity not with bitterness or amused tolerance but with a profound pity and regret. He held deep religious beliefs, which usually set his work apart from that of his contemporaries. He linked his own faith in Jesus Christ to the victims of poverty, injustice, and war. The Christian character of his painting is manifested both in his choice of subject and in his general attitude toward life. He was a man of great integrity. In the early years of his career, religious works were conspicuously absent, but from 1914 on the characters of the Christian story regularly replaced the secular characters who had formerly filled his canvases. Hence, the sorrows of the mocked Christ echo those of the clown so frequently portrayed in his early work. "My only ambition," Rouault once remarked, "is to be able one day to paint Christ so movingly that those who see him will be converted."[15] He never shows Christ in majesty or in judgment, but always Christ as a victim, Christ being mocked, Christ weighed down by the sins of the world. His depictions of Jesus are variations of the Suffering Servant, as we see him rebuked by brutish soldiers. His well-known *Miserere* series parallels Christ's passion with the experience of the poor and the victims of war.[16] One of the etchings from the series bears the caption "Don't we all wear makeup?" It speaks clearly of the artist's rejection of hypocrisy and insincerity.[17] He achieved a high degree of spirituality and left an impressive collection of transcendent images that may rightly take their place with some of the finest Byzantine mosaics, Romanesque frescoes, and Russian icons.[18] His works have rightly found a place in Christian churches.

Recent years have witnessed much discussion of Christianity's role in the persecution of the Jews. There is no doubt that images of Jesus in medieval art influenced the Middle Ages in their attitude toward the Jews and that modern passion plays have often been prejudiced in their presentation of the Jewish people. Some of the most powerful correctives of that unfortunate tradition, however, have been rendered by Jewish artists who see the passion of Jesus not as an expression of anti-Semitism but rather as one of the most effective ways to combat anti- Semitism.[19]

Among the most notable of those representations are those by the Jewish artist Marc Chagall (1887–1985), who was haunted by the crucified Jesus throughout his life.[20] A Russian-born Jew, he settled for a time in Vitebsk, but the element of fantasy in his work disconcerted the authorities, who wanted art to be realistic and to communicate a social message. After some years in the United States, he made his home in France, near Nice. His fantasies are indeed strange but not sinister; they communicate a sense of lyrical innocence. His cows give the impression that they can in fact jump over the moon, images probably rooted in the Jewish dreamworld of his childhood. Certainly his background was deeply religious. Much of his work was inspired by his Jewish spirituality and was explicitly illustrative of biblical themes. In Chagall's work there is often a glimpse of a world that is alive; there is a sense of the fundamental unity of the universe, all moved by divine energy. His cocks crow, his moons rise, David plays his harp, the whole world is in color. There is a sense of the timeless and the miraculous pervading his work.[21] His colors are often stunning, but in spite of their beauty, which can certainly be spiritually uplifting, some critics claim his religious works do not often transcend the level of folklore and fairy tales.[22]

Chagall's delight in dreamworlds does not mean that he is indifferent to events in the contemporary world. He was convinced that each day Christ is recrucified, villages are burned, refugees are forced to flee into the night. Chagall's *White Crucifixion*, painted in 1938, clearly links the suffering of Jesus with the suffering of the Jews at the hands of the Nazis. In the painting, Jesus is at the center of a score of atrocities committed against the Jews—murders, pogroms, exile, and the destruction of synagogues. Jesus' clear identification with the Jewish people and their suffering is shown by the fact that his head is covered by the traditional ceremonial headcloth, a prayer shawl serves as his loin cloth, and a menorah stands at the foot of the cross. Chagall's *Yellow Crucifix*, painted in 1943 when the world was learning of the horrors of the Nazi concentration camps, also emphasizes the Jewishness of Jesus in life and death, for he wears the phylacteries of a devout Jew on his head; he has prayer straps on his arms; and at his right hand is the scroll of the Torah.[23]

Reflecting on Jesus as rabbi in his *Illustrated Jesus through the Centuries*, Jaroslav Pelikan asked:

Would there have been such anti-Semitism, would there have been so many pogroms, would there have been an Auschwitz, if every Christian church and every Christian home had focused its devotion on images of Mary not only as Mother of God and Queen of Heaven but also as the Jewish maiden and the New Miriam, and on icons of Christ not only as the Cosmic Christ but as Rabbi of Nazareth, the Son of David, come to ransom a captive Israel and a captive humanity?[24]

Another Jewish artist who created impressive works based on Christian themes was Jacob Epstein (1880–1959). He was American-born but spent most of his mature life in England. His sculptures regularly caused outcries and often scandal because of the nude figures, which were thought to be either obscene or blasphemous. Nonetheless, Epstein was entrusted with several important church commissions which show his ability to interpret Christian themes with conviction and sympathy. They include an early work from 1926, *The Visitation*, which shows a young woman obviously perplexed by the angel's appearance but open to the unexpected. Then there is the quite powerful *Lazarus*, still wrapped in his winding cloths, which is housed in the chapel of New College in Oxford. Among his better known works is the *Madonna and Child* commissioned for the Holy Child Convent in Cavendish Square, London; it truly vibrates with feeling but somehow seems to dangle on the facade of the building. For the Llandaff Cathedral he sculpted *Christ in Majesty* in 1955. Much better known is his large sculpture *St. Michael and the Devil* on the front of Coventry Cathedral, which was completed shortly before Epstein's death. The devil is a nasty creature, no match for the overpowering archangel.[25]

In the last century, England was home to a significant number of distinguished artists who created impressive works with a religious theme. Among some of the best known are those who settled in Ditchling Common along with Eric Gill and the other members of the Guild of St. Joseph and St. Dominic. The story of the guild exercised a dominant influence over Catholic art in Britain for about seventy years, beginning in the early years of the twentieth century. It was in London that three of the key figures met at the Arts and Crafts Centre by the Thames at Hammersmith: the stone carver Eric Gill, calligrapher Edward Johnston, and Hilary Pepler. In 1907, Gill left Pepler and Johnston and moved to Ditchling High Street in rural Sussex and was joined by Pepler in 1915. Gill moved from High Street in 1913 and bought a house, Hopkins Crank, and two acres of land at the Common's south end. In 1917, Father Vincent McNabb, the prior of the Dominicans at Hawkesyard in Staffordshire, arrived in Ditchling and brought with him an ardent Catholicism that inspired Gill and Pepler with hope for transforming society's ills.[26]

Eric Gill was born in Brighton on February 22, 1882, the son of a Nonconformist parson. Together with his wife and children, Eric became a Catholic in 1913. He began his career as a cutter of inscriptions. From Johnston he learned the visual alphabet, which he used in various memorials and later in his distinguished printing types: Gill Sans, Perpetua, and Joanna. Work on inscriptions led him to direct stone carving, but he was probably best known for his work in relief.

Shortly after becoming a Catholic, Gill was invited to submit designs for a set of stations of the cross for Westminster Cathedral. Completed in 1918, they are still admired as a masterful achievement. In 1918, Gill, his wife, Mary, Hilary Pepler, and Desmond Chute all became novices of the Third Order of St. Dominic. The three men founded the Guild of St. Joseph and St. Dominic in 1920, but in 1924 Gill left Ditchling for the remote Welsh village of Chapel-y-ffin. He worked there for four years and then in 1928 moved back closer to London, to a large house near High Wycombe, Pigotts, which became his home and that of his extended family until he died on December 17, 1940. In addition to being a distinguished carver in stone and wood, Gill was also a prolific graphic artist, his masterpiece being a series of wood engravings made to illustrate the Four Gospels and published by the Golden Cockerel Press. He is also well known for his writings on art and life in a secular society: *Art—Nonsense* (1929), *Necessity of Belief* (1936), and *Sacred and Secular* (1940). His work was inspired by papal teachings on social justice and the economy, the tenets of distributism, and the theories of Ananda Coomaraswamy, Jacques Maritain, and W. R. Lethaby.[27] His Christian social views were strongly reflected in his relief entitled *Christ Driving the Money Changers from the Temple* at Leeds University. There the money changers are his contemporary British businessmen and businesswomen.

Even after Gill's departure from Ditchling, the Guild continued to attract competent, imaginative artists until it was finally disbanded in 1989. Among the better known members of the Guild were Dunstan Pruden (1907–1974) and John Valentine KilBride (1897–1982). Pruden, a distinguished silversmith, moved to Ditchling in 1932 and became a member of the Guild in 1934. He fulfilled hundreds of commissions for ecclesiastical metalwork, including chalices, ciboria, candlesticks, and croziers. He was deeply committed to the faithful use of materials and strove always to maintain the highest quality of finish. The high point of his career was the creation of a gold chalice for the Metropolitan Cathedral in Liverpool in 1959.[28]

John Valentine KilBride set up shop as a weaver at Ditchling in March 1925, joined the Guild a year later, and remained a faithful member until his retirement in 1981. Along with his partner, Bernard Brocklehurst, he revived the fashion for Gothic, plain silk woven vestments cut in a conical shape for the Roman Catholic Church. From the sixteenth century, priests had worn Roman-style vestments, stiff, ornamental, brocade garments, heavy, often embellished with elaborate braid. During the Second World War, KilBride and his family moved to Scotland, but in 1946 they returned to Ditchling, where five of his children were employed in their father's workshop. Following her father's retirement for health reasons in 1981, Jenny KilBride took over the management of the workshop. She and her brother Thomas and their cousin Ewan Clayton were among the six remaining members of the Guild when it disbanded in 1989.[29]

Henry Moore (1898–1986) has rightly occupied a position of international eminence. Although his religious works are rare, he showed himself capable of adapting to the needs of a client without losing any sense of his own integrity as an artist. By the 1930s he was recognized as the leading avant-garde sculptor in England. Moore's most important religious work was unveiled in 1944. As the vicar of St. Matthew's Church in Northampton, Walter Hussey had shown a passion for contemporary religious art. He persuaded Moore to carve a Madonna and Child for the church. Hussey was encouraged by Kenneth Clark, who wrote of Moore:

> I consider him the greatest living sculptor and it is of the utmost importance that the Church should employ artists of first-rate talent instead of the mediocrities usually employed. . . . His sketches promise that this will be one of his finest works. I am sure it will shed luster on your church.[30]

In the correspondence between Hussey and Moore, Moore reflected on the significant difference between secular and religious art: "It's not easy to describe in words what this difference is, except by saying in general terms that the 'Madonna and Child' should have an austerity and nobility and some touch of grandeur (even hieratic aloofness) which is missing in the everyday 'Mother and Child' idea." [31] The Northampton sculpture, rather more than life-size, is placed in the north nave aisle. Mary looks down the aisle and greets the visitor. The child is human yet hieratic. The figures have an intense dignity and beauty that are captivating.

Moore's religious works, and especially his Northampton sculpture, are excellent examples of the humble way in which a creative artist is able to adapt himself to the requirements of a client without losing any sense of integrity. He approached the commission with the right spirit, recognizing that the Christ child and his mother are not merely ordinary people. The result is simple, deeply moving, and, like all Moore's work, truly monumental.[32]

Certainly one of the most distinguished and prolific sculptors specializing in religious subjects during the last century was Ivan Meštrović (1893–1962).[33] He was born in Yugoslavia but became an American citizen in 1954. From 1917 to the outbreak of World War II he carved numerous religious sculptures, including a series of walnut reliefs depicting the *Life of Christ* and a series of *Virgin and Child* images in wood and bronze, a subject that Meštrović would return to regularly. They manifest delicate curvilinear and lyrical qualities and exhibit attenuated limbs, sinuous lines, and graceful elegance. Outstanding among the latter groups is the *Ashbaugh Madonna,* dating from 1917. It was carved from French walnut and now is housed in the Snite Museum on the campus of the University of Notre Dame.

At the outbreak of World War II, Meštrović was torn by political strife and war in his homeland. In Zagreb he was arrested and put in prison and under house arrest for four and a half months. Eventually he made his way to Venice and finally to Rome. In 1946, he began work on a seven-ton block of Carrara marble, which within a year he transformed into a sorrowful and inspiring scene of the dead Christ and his three comforters. From 1947 to 1955, he was a professor of sculpture at Syracuse University in New York. While there he devoted himself almost exclusively to religious subjects and portraits. In 1955 he joined the faculty at the University of Notre Dame, where the campus provided a congenial setting for his work. Plaster sketches done while at Syracuse were cast in bronze, including his *Moses* and *The Return of the Prodigal Son.* The former stands in the Notre Dame Memorial Library; the latter in the Basilica of the Sacred Heart on campus. One of Meštrović's great desires was to see his Rome *Pietà* installed in a religious setting. In 1956 it was brought from the Metropolitan Museum of Art in New York to Notre Dame and placed in one of the apsidal chapels in the Basilica of the Sacred Heart.

During his years at Notre Dame, Meštrović completed several important sculptures for various buildings on campus, including a large *Last Supper* and a bronze *Madonna and Child.* A large *Last Supper* was completed in 1957 for the North Dining Hall. Perhaps his finest work at Notre Dame was the *Christ and Samaritan Woman at Jacob's Well*, completed in 1957.[34] Some critics see his work as mainly derivative, but others appreciate it as an artful expression of communication.

Some of the most interesting modern religious paintings have been done by Stanley Spencer (1891–1959), the British artist who spent most of his life in his native village of Cookham-on-Thames.[35] Much of his work was a celebration of the life of that village. Early in life his faith seems to have been one of a simple Nonconformist kind, but his service in World War I and complications in his marriage changed him so that his ideas became increasingly unorthodox. Without abandoning Christianity, he came to regard sexual experience as a kind of religion and a manifestation of the divine. He had a rather fantastic imagination. Two paintings in which his visionary character is apparent are *The Nativity*, painted in 1912, and *Elizabeth and Zachary*, painted in 1912–1913. Both communicate a deeply religious sense of unearthly stillness and expectancy. He painted huge canvases of the resurrection of the dead and of Christ preaching, all localized in his Berkshire village, which he seems to have regarded as an earthly paradise. His resurrections, however, are simply scenes of resuscitation rather than spiritual transformation through the Spirit of Christ. His major work was the mural in the Sandham Memorial Chapel at Burghclere in Hampshire, with its altar-piece of *The Resurrection of the Soldiers*.

The clumsy figures with which he peopled his canvases are usually dressed in bizarre clothes. For example, in his *Saint Francis with the Birds*, the saint, a very corpulent figure, is shown with one of his hands back to front and is wearing a shabby dressing gown that belonged to Spencer's father.[36] As would be expected, Spencer's *Baptism of Christ* is set in a bathing pool on the Thames. Christ is surrounded by the Cookham villagers in their bathing suits. *Christ Carries His Cross* is set in front of the artist's home in Cookham. *The Crucifixion* was commissioned for the chapel of Aldenham School in a northwest suburb of London. Traditionally, representations of the crucifixion in art have portrayed the scene in such a way as to induce quiet meditation. Christ is almost always shown from the front either alone or flanked by two thieves and his Mother and St. John. In Spencer's unconventional painting, the figure of Christ, with head in profile and gazing upward, is seen from the back. It is not Christ who dominates the painting but rather his tormentors. Sadistically, even gleefully, they pound their black nails into the flesh of Jesus while one of the crucified thieves, his face contorted with hatred, shrieks at Christ, whose suffering as a man is emphasized rather than his divinity. Characteristically, Spencer situated this horrendous event in his native village. By placing the crucifixion in a contemporary setting, Spencer emphasized his conviction that the meaning of the events in the life of Christ transcends time and space and is just as significant in our lives today as when they occurred many years ago. When Spencer lectured about his painting of the crucifixion to the students of the Aldenham School, he explained that he painted the crucifiers in contemporary garb because, he said, "It is your governors and you who are still nailing Christ to the Cross."[37] Spencer had hoped that his deeply felt series of paintings entitled *Christ in the Wilderness* would find a place in a church, but they languished in Britain until they were sold to an Australian art museum.[38]

An effort to emphasize the contemporary character of biblical events was laid out by the Canadian artist William Kuralek in a series of nativity scenes for a children's book in which the Christ child is situated in the most ordinary places. There is the child as a little Innuit boy, cuddling a husky in the shelter of an igloo. There is the child in a Rocky Mountain cattle shed. There is the child as a black baby in the arms of his black mother eating Christmas dinner with the Salvation Army. There is the child as a Native American seeking shelter for the night at a country mission.[39] Kuralek's point is that the Christ who is not inculturated in modern society through the power of the Spirit is not really the Christ of Christianity, for Christ in a real sense continues to be incarnated among his people through the gift of the Holy Spirit.

Inculturation is also the concern of a Native American artist from Canada. Stanley Peters has sculpted a provocative picture of the crucifixion called *Totem Cross*. Instead of Christ on the cross he has placed a thunderbird. Eyes in each wing and on the cross represent the eyes of the whole world focused on the cross. A circle below the bird's feet contains four colors—red, yellow, black, and white—symbolizing all the races of the earth. The cross challenges viewers to consider how much they can absorb Christ into their own culture without losing his distinctiveness. Certainly Christians traditionally have spoken of Christ as an animal, as the Lamb of God who is led to sacrifice. Native Americans would assert, however, that the lamb has little meaning for them, for they do not have lambs in their tradition, in their literature, in their memory. In their tradition the thunderbird is a messenger from God to the people. In a limited sense the bird fulfills the same role in their stories as Christ does in the gospel. Hence, the thunderbird on the cross has the same kind of impact for Native Americans in Canada as the sacrificial lamb has for Europeans and many other Christians.[40]

In a similar vein, artists from India have painted the birth of Jesus as occurring within their own tradition. For example, Angela Trinidade has painted Mary and Joseph in typical Indian clothing. Mary wears the wide skirt and *chaddar*, or shawl, of village women. The pillars in the background are old and worn, covered with Hindu or Buddhist carving. The cattle are the typical hump-backed cattle of India. The family might be any family in rural India, except for the striking beam of light coming from the star. Like Angela Trinidade, Frank Wesley has painted the nativity in a very humble setting. The mother wears a simple undecorated sari. She sits beside a *charpoy*, a bed made of interwoven ropes. The light, however, comes not from the star but from the infant. Wesley has sought to make visible the quality that John's Gospel calls "the light of the world."[41] He has also painted a striking picture entitled *Christ with the Rich Young Man*. Both figures in the painting wear circlets in their ears. The shape of their eyebrows and the slant of their eyes and their mouths are all modeled on classical Hindu art. Jesus has a *tip*, a circle painted in the middle of his forehead, as a symbol of purity. These paintings say that Jesus has entered into the lives of Indians in order to share their lives as one of them.[42]

Although Australia has been represented as one of the most secular countries in the modern world, the country has produced distinguished artists whose works are deeply religious.[43] Brett Whiteley is a well-known Australian artist, born in 1939. He is mainly self-taught. In 1979–1980 he painted powerful images of the crucifixion, including *My God, My God . . . Why . . .* and *The Giving Up*. In 1980 the young Australian sculptor Joel Elenberg died of cancer. During his terminal illness he lived in the Whiteley home. The paintings of the crucifixion are Whiteley's memorial and reflection as well as his anger over the death of his friend. In a sense it is Elenberg who is hanging on the cross. The paintings represent different moments in the act of dying. Whiteley was obviously inspired by the great images of Christ's cruel death on the cross in the history of art, especially those by Grünewald, Cimabue, Duccio, and Sassetta. But he did not simply copy the work of other masters. The hands in his paintings are reminiscent of those in Grünewald's painting for the Isenheim altarpiece, but Whiteley has considerably enlarged and distorted them even further until they seem to extend beyond the canvas. The gold leaf in the background is similar to that used by early Sienese artists, but in Whiteley's work it has become like a mirror in which the viewer is almost enabled to see who it is that is looking at the crucifixion. In fact, the viewer is called into the painting as one who shares in the suffering of the victim.

Certainly the crucifixion has traditionally been one of the most power-ful images in the history of Western art. It seems each period has found a distinctive way in which to represent this profound mystery of the death of Jesus Christ, the God-man who endured death so that others might live. The crucifixion has always been a sign of contradiction and radical chal-lenge. Brett Whiteley's crucifixions were wrung from the depths of his soul at a time of deep sorrow and crisis. Until Elenberg's death, Whiteley had never been able to paint a crucifixion. With the loss of a dear friend, he was inspired and responded with works of profound sorrow and power.[44]

Alan Oldfield's work is much more serene. Born in 1943, he painted a series of nine major works based on the *Revelations of Divine Love* of Julian of Norwich. The paintings build into a series with repetitive themes; they are genuinely narrative in that they seek to encapsulate the truth of the mystical experiences of Julian, the fourteenth-century anchorite from Nor-wich. Oldfield is a Christian believer; he studied carefully the account of Julian's visions and found their theology of compassion and optimism very convincing. The paintings are superbly crafted and manifest in an amazing way the transcendence of the divine. For example, in *The Theophany,* Old-field has painted the vision as it was described by Julian.[45]

In the painting, Julian stands to the right, clothed in a dark blue tunic and a brown cloak; she holds a small sphere in her hand. Behind her is a dark blue drape; in front of her are a wall, a curtain, and a cross—all fifteenth-century devices to indicate the distinction between this world and heaven. Christ stands outside the wall, bathed in bright gold light. He wears a pale blue garment that contrasts with the earth-color of Julian's cloak. In the painting everything is clear and well ordered, symbolizing Julian's famous words, "All shall be well, all manner of things shall be well."[46]

Many of the works of these artists are set out against a typical Australian background. For example, John Perceval has painted *Christ Dining in Young and Jackson's.* The scene takes place in a famous Melbourne hotel on Flinders Street. At first Christ is indistinguishable from the other guests. He is clearly in the midst of a celebration. Under his table is a greyhound; a woman swings across the room bearing a typical Australian dinner of baked chicken and potatoes. There is a bustle of activity and noise. When painted in 1947, the painting offended viewers who forgot that Brüghel and various Renaissance painters pictured Christ in a similar situation.[47] Perce-val painted other pictures that are typically Australian and deeply religious. In the late 1940s he was living with the Merric Boyd family, where religion was simply an essential part of life. Prayer was a regular part of the daily routine. Perceval's *Christmas Eve*, which dates from this period, is a bucolic celebration of life in suburban Melbourne. The stable is a partly constructed house near a bay that is recognized as Port Phillip. Gum trees straggle in the forefront; a fowl is being plucked for Christmas dinner.[48] *Crossing the Red Sea* was painted in 1947–1948. In the foreground is a Christ-like figure with a halo. He is Perceval's Moses, a gentle fatherlike figure, not the Old Testament patriarch. The child he holds is the artist's own son. One hand blesses the friendly lions, a goat, and some fish, while the other reaches out to a woman who sits at his feet. From the raging waters, a stream of people, some with crutches, come to him as they are watched over by an angel. Perceval has taken a great biblical narrative and domesticated it by setting it along Port Phillip Bay shoreline. He simply recreates the mood and complexity of the biblical account. Hence, with him the crossing of the Red See is both history and myth.[49]

Margaret Preston is another distinguished Australian artist whose themes were often religious. *Adam and Eve in the Garden of Eden, The Expulsion,* and *Christ Turning Water into Wine* were all completed in 1953. The overriding mood is a mild protest. She wanted her paintings to have real Australian incident and feeling. Consequently, Adam and Eve are black Aborigines surrounded by flannel flowers, gum trees, kangaroos, emus, echidna, and koalas. Preston's painting of Christ is charming in an unsophisticated way. She has situated the miracle at Cana in an Australian landscape. Wedding guests are crowded on the veranda under a corrugated iron roof, a pair of kangaroos play near a gum tree, Christ lifts his hands in blessing over giant water jugs while Mary watches from the door of the house. Preston lived to be eighty-eight; her religious prints were the most innovative of her creative output, especially in the last years of her life.[50]

Arthur Boyd is undoubtedly the best known, most prolific, and most distinguished painter in Australian history. In 1920 he was born into a deeply religious family, a number of whom were well-known artists. After the Second World War, Boyd turned to the Bible for inspiration, subject matter, and a means to express his horror at the tragedies of war in contrast to the tranquility he knew at home. In 1946–1947 he painted *The Mining Town,* actually a rather amusing portrayal of Christ driving the money changers out of the temple. It stands in marked contrast to El Greco's paintings of the same scene. The print is situated in suburban Melbourne. At the left a miniature Christ drives out the money changers, who tumble down the steps of the church, setting up a chain reaction. The foreground teems with activity with more than seventy-two people, thirteen pigs, and many birds and dogs. A cripple runs out of the way, a kite-flyer snatches a pig escaped from a turned-over cart. Only two lovers in an enclosed garden are oblivious of what has happened.[51]

Two paintings from 1947–1948, *Angel Spying on Adam and Eve* and *The Expulsion*, are intriguing. The first invites the viewer to look in on a very intimate scene, as Adam and Eve embrace in a moment of privacy. An angel spies on the scene, gazing greedily on the pair. The innocent couple are naked, whereas the angel is fully clothed in red. At the feet of Adam and Eve is a ram, often in Boyd's paintings a symbol of sexual desire. But in this painting the ram is white; it may well evoke the Christian symbol of the Lamb of God or Christ. Adam and Eve, as well as the angel, are credible as they engage in fundamental human actions of love and envy. The light in the painting is soft. Everything in the print speaks of sensuality yet deep reverence for all that is most human. This painting contrasts with *The Expulsion*, in which Adam and Eve are driven out of paradise by a screaming, avenging angel. Their nakedness is no longer innocent, and the greenery is no longer idyllic but rocky and threatening. Pain has replaced tranquility, as exile becomes a reality.[52]

In 1947 Boyd also painted *Moses Leading the People*. Moses is a great, grim-faced patriarch who leads his people out of Egypt. He wears a bright red tunic, but his passion is for freedom. Behind him the chosen people struggle to follow. A man grabs at a tree for support, another struggles up a slope while a woman clutches her little child. There are no specifically religious symbols in the painting; the focus is simply on Moses, the savior of his people, who are heedless of the dangers of the Australian bush. In 1946 Boyd painted two other canvases of the Moses epic: *The Golden Calf* and *Moses Throwing Down the Tablets of the Law*. Both contain explicitly religious symbols.[53]

There are two paintings from 1979–1980 that are more controversial: *Crucifixion, Shoalhaven* and *Crucifixion and the Rose*. In 1959 Boyd and his wife moved to England, but during the 1970s they frequently returned to Australia, where Boyd bought property along the Shoalhaven River. By that time his interests had shifted to what might be interpreted as contemporary cultural and political issues, and his hope was to make a contribution to social progress and enlightenment. His *Crucifixion, Shoalhaven* and *Crucifixion and Rose* startle because of the juxtaposition of the cross, Christianity's most powerful symbol, and the Australian landscape.[54] The cross stands not on Golgotha but in the waters of the Schoalhaven River. In the first painting Boyd has broken with a two-thousand-year tradition by placing a woman on the cross. The image is frontal, nude, and uncompromising. In 1987 Boyd said in an interview with Rosemary Crumlin, "I do not wish to separate the idea of suffering by allowing just the male to be seen. There has been an awakening consciousness of the potential and force of women in our time."[55]

In the second picture, the Christ-figure is male. Again, the image is frontal and nude. A single rose, a traditional symbol of the Virgin Mary, in Christian iconography, the *Rosa Mystica*, floats by the cross. Boyd, however, has given the rose a new meaning. It is the English rose, a symbol of English culture that cannot take root in the rugged Australian landscape and culture. As Boyd said in 1982, "The rose represents the desperate attempts of the Europeans to impose their culture on an essentially primitive landscape. It floats because it cannot take root. If it does, it destroys...."[56]

Boyd's paintings, however, raise the complex question: Is the crucifixion of Jesus simply about suffering in the world, or is it not above all about the death and resurrection of the Word made flesh in Jesus Christ, the one who triumphed over sin, suffering, and death through God's own intervention in the world through the power of the Holy Spirit. As a matter of fact, neither the female nor the male bodies on Boyd's crosses are really images of the incarnate Word of God. They are rather images of Australia suffering at the hands of European colonizers.

A similar radical change in the symbolism of the crucifix occurred during Holy Week in 1984 in New York City. Both the Episcopal Cathedral of St. John the Divine and Union Theological Seminary used crucifixes with female figures as central symbols. Edwina Sandys created a sculpture called *Christa*, which was exhibited at the Episcopal Cathedral. The corpus was hung in the traditional posture; hence, there was no doubt that the figure was female. At Union Theological Seminary James M. Murphy's *Christine on the Cross* was quite different. A woman stood with both her arms nailed to the vertical beam of the cross and with her legs splayed on the lower cross beam. The sculpture clearly expressed the violence and hostility of both physical and emotional rape committed against women.[57]

Both crucifixes subverted the traditional interpretation of the Christian cross. Both elicited strong emotional, at times even religious responses; both elicited outrage. But they helped at least some viewers to realize more fully how all humanity has participated in the pain of crucifixion.[58] An important question, however, needs to be asked: Were the crucifixes properly employed as part of the Christian celebration of Holy Week? I do not think so, for the essential focus during that great week is not simply on the evil that we humans perpetrate against one another but on the triumph over that evil made possible by the death and resurrection of the God-man, Jesus Christ, the Son of God.

Contemporary Aboriginal artists have created numerous works that are deeply religious but also highly symbolic. Their works express the actual rules and rites by which the Australian Aborigines live. For thousands of years they have painted their beliefs, but in the last forty years or so, there has been a surge of extraordinary images coming from the many groups of Aborigines living in Australia. Painting has become for many of these people like a new face, a way to transmit their identity to the outside world. It is a powerful way to transmit their culture, their myths, their stories, and their practices.[59] For example, the Aboriginal people of Turkey Creek in Western Australia are predominantly Catholic, but they sustain not only their Catholic faith with its beliefs and rituals but also their traditional rituals and customs; apparently they experience little tension in combining their two belief systems.

Until he died in 1991, George Mung Mung was an artist, teacher, and leader among his people in Turkey Creek. He painted in ochres the landscapes and life of his people. But he was also a skilled wood carver. His *Mary of Warmun* (The Pregnant Mary) was created about 1983. The wood was cut from a tree deep in the remote Bungle Bungle Range of Western Australia. He wanted to make an image that would never break. The result is a sculpture that is immensely powerful and deeply religious. To create the image, Mung Mung went deep into his Aboriginal roots, into his belief in his ancestral spirits, and into his responsibility to maintain a proper relationship with the land and his community, where he served as an elder. But he also reflected deeply on his Catholic faith in Mary as the mother of Jesus, the Son of God. The figure is that of a young, unmarried Warmun woman. Her body is painted with the traditional designs. She is pregnant and carries her child in her womb-shield beneath her heart. The unborn child is already a little man, who literally dances within her. Mung Mung's image is undoubtedly one of the greatest images of Mary and her child produced in the last century.[60]

The paintings of the Warmun community at Turkey Creek reflect a landscape that is brown and hard, with huge rocks in the midst of desertlike country, and the myths are often concerned with long journeys in search of food and water. In contrast, the Nauiyu Nambiyu community lives in the lush tropical land along the deep-flowing Daly River. This is a land of plenty to be enjoyed by the hundred and fifty members of the community and is the setting for the myths, stories, and symbols of the people.

The art produced in Daly River rejoices in the abundance of food, water, and luscious scenery. Most of the artists at Daly River are women; they sit together to reminisce and tell stories about the coming of the Catholic mission in 1956 but also stories about the pre-Christian days and the Aboriginal heritage, which has some elements in common with Christian spirituality as well as a belief in the unity of body, land, and spirit.[61]

Miriam-Rose Ungunmerr-Baumann, who was born in 1950, is an artist, a school principal, and a leader of the Nauiyu Nambiyu people of Daly River. She is an acknowledged leader among Aboriginal communities in the Northern Territory of Australia and is deeply respected in both civic and church circles. The fourteen stations of the cross, commissioned in 1974 for the rebuilding of the white church, which is the physical and sometimes spiritual center of the community, were designed and executed by Ungunmerr-Baumann. They have become well known and important even among non-Aboriginal people. Her fourteenth station shows men carrying the body of Jesus to the tomb. Their faces and bodies are ceremonially painted. Along the central figure of Jesus is a huge snake, a frightening yet mysterious figure in both Aboriginal and Christian iconography.[62] In her painting, it symbolizes the powers of evil overcome by the death of Jesus. Ungunmerr-Baumann herself considers the stations a work of her youth. She now is quite reflective and discerning about the complexity of including Aboriginal elements into non-Aboriginal traditions in this way.[63]

There are two contemporary British artists whose work is profoundly religious: Peter Eugene Ball and Albert Herbert. Ball was born into a simple family in Coventry in 1943. He took classes at the Coventry College of Art from 1957 to 1962, then joined a local historian in surveying Anglo-Saxon, Norman, and Gothic architecture. It was then that he found Romanesque and Celtic art forms especially inspiring. He has always been proud of his roots and has been very suspicious of the bureaucracy, politics, and elitism surrounding the arts. His first church commission came in 1975 for a crucifix for Westminster Cathedral. Since then church commissions have played a very important part in Ball's artistic creations. Some of the more important works include a memorial at Preston-on-Stour Church (1981), a crucifix and figurative candleholders for Birmingham Cathedral (1983), a small crucifix for Portsmouth Cathedral, a large *Christus Rex* for Southwell Minster (1987), *Christus* and *Pietà* for Winchester Cathedral (1990), *Madonna and Child* for Southwark Cathedral (1990), *Light of the World*, a *Saint*, and *Christ Condemned* for Southwark Cathedral in recent years; as well as a nativity scene, *Holy Family*, and shepherds and kings for Winchester Cathedral (1991).

Ball does not wear his religious sentiments publicly; in fact, he has denied that he is a Christian. Dogma, the church as an institution, and the ordained clergy in his mind all imply constriction, convention, and conformity. Above all he wants to preserve his creative freedom and to maintain the spark of sacred fire that burns in his life. Ball often uses wood or metal that has already been used for other things—taken from a building, a junk shop, or from the sea. All his work is figurative, reduced to essentials. One of his most impressive crucifixes began with a battered piece of beech branch. Ball saw how the forked piece of wood could be the trunk and arms of Christ, how the defects in the wood could suggest the dereliction of Christ's condition, and how the arms could suggest his exaltation. The end result was a profound theological statement about Christ's death and resurrection.[64]

Ball uses very ordinary things to communicate a sense of the extraordinary and to achieve a profound sense of transcendence. His works tend to be very quiet and contemplative. As he himself said of his work,

> They don't shout at you. It's as though they were mute. This silence, I think it's something very important, more important than any statement. They may not speak, but you're aware of something coming from them all the same. Jesus was like that, presumably. Without his even speaking there was that presence. People were awed by it.[65]

Two of Ball's most impressive religious works are in Winchester Cathedral—his *Christus* and *Pietà*. The *Christus*, about five feet high, is made of oak extracted from a house in the process of demolition, a cross-beam that suggested to Ball the trunk and outstretched arms of a man. The long, slender, robed trunk is reminiscent of ancient Syrian representations, whereas the dislocated foot and elongated arms are Ball's own creations. The pierced hands and feet are traditional. Ball has added gold, green, and brown coloring by carefully applying brass, copper, gold leaf, and paint. There are circular whirls on the robe, so that Christ is conceived not simply as a sacred figure but as a cosmic figure as well. The sculpture hangs from the north central wall of the north transept about twenty feet from the floor. The robed figure does not hang on a cross, since the significance of the cross is included in the form of Christ's body. Ball comments about the crucifixion, "I've always been interested in a Christ that's compassionate yet aloof, like the Romanesque Christ, almost hieratic; not quite involved with humanity yet representing them. To me this is not an agonized Christ but very calm, compassionate but almost resigned."[66]

The *Pietà* was acquired by Winchester Cathedral in 1990. The Roman Catholic community, who occasionally worship in the cathedral, wanted to make a contribution to the Anglican Cathedral and suggested a sculpture for the Lady Chapel. Peter Ball was selected to produce a number of maquettes of the Blessed Virgin Mary as she related to Christ. The *Pietà* was finally chosen as the subject. The resulting sculpture reveals Ball's indebtedness to medieval form and substance, especially in the shape of Mary. Her face, hands, and body carry the strong emotional characteristics of German expressionism, especially the work of the distinguished sculptor Ernst Barlach (1870–1938), whose art exemplified the deep sense of alienation experienced by many in the Western world in the years before his death. Unlike Michelangelo's *Pietà*, in which the anatomically correct large body of Christ falls artistically across the lap of Mary by the introduction of her flowing robes and spread knees, Ball's figures are taut and unrelated. The sculpture has a vertical direction that harmonizes with the architectural style of the chapel. Mary's face is the face of a mature grieving woman whose heart must have been broken by the torture and death of her beloved Son. Mary is faithful and persevering in her loyalty. The dead body of Christ limply stretches backwards and is painted gold: his face is regal and noble, the face of one who died for our sins but has been raised from the dead.[67]

Albert Herbert has been described as one of "the most significant religious painters to emerge in England during the 1980s."[68] Sister Wendy Becket claimed that "no one who sees his work can doubt that we have here that rarest of phenomenon, the great religious artist."[69] After World War II he was given a grant to study at the Wimbledon School of Art; from there he received a scholarship to the Royal College of Art. While studying in Italy, he was charmed by Italian Catholicism, and in 1958 he became a Roman Catholic. He was attracted by Catholicism as the way to truth rather than as an institution with traditions and rituals.

In the 1970s he turned his attention to biblical subjects. He claimed that he had no interest in the historical factuality of the stories and had read many theological interpretations; he looked at the stories as symbols and as metaphors revealing something of the divine. In 1987 he was approached by an enterprising Anglican priest to produce the fourteen stations of the cross. Herbert was delighted that some of his work might find a place in a church. He produced detailed sketches and then painted the stations in oil on board; they were certainly original—challenging, devout, and expressionistic. One shows Jesus being stripped of his garments; clutching hands grab at him while leering faces peer out of the darkness. An especially ugly face gawks out at the viewer in order to draw the viewer into the act. In another painting showing Jesus being taken down from the cross, he is lovingly embraced by a man in contemporary dress; a modern house is pictured at the right of the painting. The Christ events are set out as really happening in the lives of people today. Unfortunately, the parish council rejected Herbert's work as too disturbing.[70] Patrick Reyntiens observed shrewdly:

> They are beautiful and moving and one wonders if there was not too much experience and truth in them to be other than disturbing to the congregation using them for devotion. This unhappy example of incomprehension and alienation on the part of perspective clients shows up all too clearly the hazards and the near-impossibility of effecting commissions of true quality within the consciousness of the Church, however much good will towards such activities is claimed to exist.[71]

Both the content and the placement of a sculpture were questioned in England when Mark Wallinger's *Ecce Homo* was installed in July 1999 on a plinth in the northwest corner of Trafalgar Square in London. The plinth, which rises about twenty-five feet from the sunken square, was originally intended for a statue of William IV but has been empty since the square was opened in 1843.[72]

Wallinger's sculpture was the first of three new works to be displayed on the plinth for a brief period. It was selected to be shown during the turn of the twentieth century to mark the two thousandth anniversary of the birth of Jesus Christ. The title of the sculpture, *Ecce Homo*, is applied to Christ as he was shown to the people by Pontius Pilate and implies that the viewer is one of those who behold Christ and condemn him. The statue is not a conventional sculpture; it is a cast, in synthetic resin and white marble dust, of the whole body of a young man; the figure is life-size. The model wore a rubber cap during the casting; hence Christ appears to be both bald and clean shaven. The model had to keep his eyes shut during the casting; consequently Christ bears an enigmatic expression almost of passivity, if not simple endurance. He does not wear a royal robe, but only a loincloth cast from a towel around the young man's naked body. A crown of gold-plated wire encircles his head. Standing on the edge of the plinth, the figure is dwarfed by the other sculptures in the square.

The figure is meant to represent the historic Christ, not Christ as a victim of some contemporary catastrophe. But he is simply an ordinary young man; he looks like a young man about to dive into a pool for a swim.

Wallinger had hoped that his sculpture would remind people of the sad record of religious and racial intolerance and that they are in so many ways forced to make a choice between Barabbas and Christ. One thing is quite certain: there is no sense of transcendence communicated in the sculpture. It is hard to imagine anyone standing in front of the statue and exclaiming, "My Lord and my God!" It is not surprising, then, that the reactions to the sculpture have been very mixed.

Not all contemporary realistic art, however, is lacking a sense of the transcendent. Leonard McComb's golden sculpture *Portrait of a Young Man Standing* was shown as part of an exhibit centering on "The Journey" at the Lincoln Cathedral in England. The naked figure upset the dean and some of the cathedral patrons because it was too real. The young man, a modern Adam waiting to be called, is slender and muscular; one hand is clenched in tension, the other hangs free in quiet repose. He looks strongly and with profound reverence toward God and gleams from head to foot, a creation of burnished bronze and gold leaf. The sculpture proclaims the wonders of God as the Creator of this beautiful human body. Like all of us before God, the young man is unashamed and open to be seen in all his defenselessness.[73]

A similar sense of mystery and transcendence is communicated in Winchester Cathedral by Antony Gormley's statue *Sound II*. The figure is a naked young man standing in the waters of the flooded crypt. This setting evokes the image of Christian baptism as the man opens his hands to receive the Spirit of new life.[74]

A sense of urgency and missionary zeal has been created by Elizabeth Frink in her somewhat realistic *Walking Madonna* standing outside Salisbury Cathedral. Mary, walking with purpose and compassion as a member of the community of the risen Christ, proceeds to bring the love of the Lord where love is absent. She strides through the cathedral close, as if she has just left the cathedral and is about to go into the city.[75]

An artist who has won wide respect for his Christian art, especially outside his native Japan, is Sadao Watanabe (1913–1996). He died on January 8, 1996, but he left the world a rich legacy of both Old and New Testament prints rendered in the folk idiom of Japan, a country that has traditionally been quite resistant to Christianity.[76] His prints are marked by their warm earthen colors, their simple lines, their powerful expressiveness, and the unique way in which he conveyed the message of the Bible. The human figures are flat or two dimensional with masklike faces. The hands are often elongated and the eyes are extremely large. The decorative patterns often remind one of the whimsical paper cutouts of Henri Matisse. The clear outlines and bold colors are reminiscent of stained glass and Georges Rouault's expressionism. The prints are at one and the same time very simple, almost naive or primitive, yet profound and sophisticated.[77]

Watanabe had an innate appreciation for God's creation and a deep love of flowers, plants, animals, and birds, motifs that appear again and again in his prints. As a youngster he came under the influence of a primary-school teacher who was a Christian; she invited him to attend church with her. That was the beginning of his journey into Christianity. He was baptized when he was seventeen. His conversion was not dramatic; it was simply a response to the words of Jesus, "Come to me, all you who labor and are burdened, and I will refresh you." He was deeply inspired by God's love manifested concretely by Jesus' death on the cross.[78]

As a young man struggling to support himself by designing and dying patterns for kimonos, Watanabe became a member of a prominent group of craftsmen trained in the traditional art of textile dyeing and printing.[79] It was in that context that he met his teacher, Serizawa, who had rediscovered the art of *katazome*, a craft using stencils for printing patterns on cloth. Watanabe took the process and transferred it to the creation of prints on paper. Other Japanese artists have used the method very successfully, but most have chosen subjects closely associated with the Japanese folk tradition—actors, theatrical scenes, Japanese architecture, and Buddhist and Shinto figures. Only Watanabe turned to the Christian religion as his sole source of inspiration. In that regard he dared to be different in a country that has traditionally prized homogeneity, where fitting in is a whole way of life and where Christianity is looked upon as a Western import.[80]

Watanabe's characters and settings were most often supplied by a biblical text, but the inner meaning, the heart of what he sought to communicate, he found at the deeper level of personal prayer and contemplation. In his larger prints, the flow of lines in the backgrounds and in the attired figures set a dynamic mood for the scene, but it is above all in the eyes and hands that the biblical story is told. For example, in his *Flight into Egypt*, the elongated hand of Mary literally caresses and encompasses the Christ child. The eyes of both Mary and Joseph indicate their deep but anxious concern for the safety of the child. The vast space in the distance isolates them in the midst of their worry. Likewise, in *Veronica's Handkerchief*, a theme not based on the Bible but rather rooted in tradition, the eyes of Jesus and Veronica communicate a sense of mutual love given and received. In *The Walking on the Water*, the agitated waves indicate Peter's panic as he sinks into the water. In the tradition of folk art, the message and the meaning are communicated quite directly, not subtly. The title or the biblical text are usually enough to invite the viewer to enter into Watanabe's inner vision.

Watanabe was a prodigious artist. He made almost five hundred large prints and hundreds of smaller ones, but very few departed from biblical or other Christian themes. The latter include *Saint Francis of Assisi Preaching to the Birds, Saint Francis Xavier and the Padres Arriving in Japan,* as well as prints of St. Benedict, St. Scholastica, and John Calvin.[81]

The acceptance or rejection of Christian art by clients and other viewers raises a number of questions about the placement of art in churches or liturgical settings, especially when the art is being commissioned. First of all, there is an intellectual question about the reason for commissioning a piece of art; then there are the liturgical questions, and finally there are aesthetic questions about form, space, color, and light.

Rationale. When a piece of art is commissioned for a church, both the commissioner and the artist need to know why the work is being commissioned. Is it because the pastor and the community want to enhance the liturgy and the setting for worship or because they want to inspire the devotion of the faithful by enriching the church environment? Or is the work being commissioned because a benefactor or a group wants to give money to the church for a particular project? Those who commission a work should ask themselves whether they believe that the primary purpose of the donor or group is to enrich the church setting for liturgical worship or for devotional purposes or whether it is to enhance the social status of the donor. It is important that pastors and parish communities are aware of the various motives in the minds of potential donors. It is to be expected that donors will take an interest in the proposal and the progress of an artistic creation, but it is not at all acceptable for the donor to attempt to dictate terms either to the artist or to the pastor or the parishioners. If the donor insists that funds will be forthcoming only if all his or her desires are met, the project is off to a very bad start and unfortunate compromises are apt to be made along the line, much to the frustration of the artist and also of the pastor and the parish members.[82]

Form and space. The question of form is very important because it is apt to determine how the work will be viewed. Certainly form is an elusive term that can include shape, light, and context.[83] How will each and every aspect of the work fit into the whole liturgical or devotional context, and how will it fit into the setting in which it will be placed? Form, then, involves space. For example, John Piper's brilliant tapestry is most appropriate in Chichester Cathedral, in the south of England, a building distinguished by the excellent quality of artistic pieces throughout the interior. It is almost shockingly bright but relieves the dull interior of the cathedral's sandstone. It hangs behind the high altar and is liturgically appropriate because of its trinitarian theme. It consists of a semi-abstract representation of the Trinity in the form of an equilateral triangle with the Father symbolized by a white light, the Son by a *tau* cross, and the Holy Spirit by a flamelike wing or tongue of fire. The other panels of the tapestry are filled with symbols of earth, fire, air, and water in the upper part and of the four evangelists in the lower part. The symbols speak for themselves; no explanation is necessary.[84] If one has any reservations, it might well be that the tapestry is so brilliant and complex that it draws attention to itself and away from the altar during the celebration of the liturgy.

Much less successful is the tapestry by Ursula Benker-Schirmer for the shrine of St. Richard of Chichester, which backs up to the tapestry by Piper. There are numerous symbols, including a chalice, a candle, a fig tree, and a fish, but the symbols are not at all easily recognized, nor are they integrated into a whole; consequently, the tapestry comes across as a fragmented collage.[85]

The form of an artistic piece will also determine whether the piece fits in with what is already present in the building. The architectural style plays an important role in this regard. For example, how does a contemporary piece fit into a Romanesque or Gothic structure? It is generally felt that Peter Ball's work, though very contemporary, fits in well with both Romanesque and Gothic structures because it conveys a sense of being well-worn and old. It would probably find a less suitable place in a Renaissance or baroque church.

Germain Richier's crucifix at Assy caused enormous emotional and liturgical concern when it was placed in the church, because it was felt that it simply conveyed the horror of Christ's death on the cross without any sense of victory over sin and death. The celebration of the eucharistic liturgy, which places primary demands on a Roman Catholic church, is always a celebration not simply of the death of Jesus but also of his triumph over death through his resurrection. In this case the liturgy places special demands on artworks that play an essential role in the celebration. Richier's crucifix would probably be more appropriately placed in a devotional space within the church rather than in the sanctuary area where the eucharist is celebrated regularly.

Color and light. Form is also related to color and light. Light is a very important element in any iconography pertaining to God within the Christian tradition. In the New Testament, Christ proclaims clearly, "I am the light of the world"; the opposite of light, of course, is darkness, which also plays an important role in the Christian tradition, referring to sin and death. In the Gothic period, churches were filled with stained glass windows, because patrons felt that the glass reflected all that was good and beautiful. The light was soft and diffused because of the colors used in the windows, especially blues and reds. The light conveyed the mystery of God and the saints. The Protestant Reformers, however, reacted to this sense of mystery; for them the appropriate light was daylight flooding into the church. Hence, the Protestant church builders of the seventeenth and eighteenth centuries tended to place plain glass in their church windows.

There should also be space for darkness in churches, places where people are able to find their own sinfulness and come to terms with it, especially in spaces that are given over to the sacramental celebration of reconciliation. When one enters a Gothic church, it is darkness that one first of all encounters, for the architects wanted to communicate that we are a people who walk in darkness. Christianity is a salvation religion for pilgrim people who gradually make their way to the light of Christ. This pilgrim path should condition the placement of art in churches and should play an important role in how they are illuminated. In the new Cathedral of Los Angeles, the pilgrims do not enter the church immediately but gradually make their way down a long passageway before coming face to face with the baptistery and the altar. The whole church is permeated with soft light coming from alabaster windows; the light is gentle and quiet, in keeping with the sand-colored walls and the muted colors of the environment in southern California.

Questions of lighting, both natural and enhanced, are important when considering the appropriateness of a particular painting, sculpture, or tapestry. So too are questions of color. Bright colors carelessly placed can distract a worshiper's attention from what is in fact of primary importance in a liturgical celebration. When a tabernacle is placed in close proximity to the eucharistic altar and is highlighted by a colorful hanging as a backdrop, the focus of attention even during the liturgy can easily be drawn to the tabernacle rather than to the action at the altar.[86] If for architectural reasons the tabernacle must be placed in the sanctuary or apse of the church, the lighting on the tabernacle should be reduced or eliminated during the eucharistic celebration. At other times, the lighting on the tabernacle may be enhanced so as to promote eucharistic devotion.

Purpose and function. Probably the most important questions concerning the design and placement of art in a church relate to the purpose and function it will serve. A church building is meant to enhance a community's experience of mystery; it is meant to facilitate an experience of God so that people might center their lives on God. A simple and attractive beauty in everything that is placed in the church will invite people to experience the mystery of God. An invitation and access to the transcendence of God should be provided by expressions of God's immanence in all that is placed in the church and all that is done there. Every object and every appointment must be authentic, not pretentious or counterfeit. Different cultural groups in our contemporary world are apt to have different styles of celebration and quite different forms of artistic expression. How will the work enhance the liturgical worship of the community and promote the life and goals of the church? How will it encourage the community to be a eucharistic community? How will it facilitate the preaching of the word and the celebration of the sacraments? How will it promote the devotional life of the community in such a way that their devotional life will be consonant with their liturgical life? How will the work challenge and rightly confront the community, which might often be indifferent, lethargic, and blind to the injustice, the prejudice, and the poverty in their world? Unlike much of modern art, which often communicates a political message and functions as propaganda, art placed in our churches should be in keeping with the gospel. Images are truly Christian when they are in tune with the paschal mystery of Jesus Christ.[87]

Conclusion

THE EXPRESSION OF CHRISTIAN FAITH ALWAYS INVOLVES A TENSION between the human modes of communication and the transcendent God who is mystery, the God who cannot be confined by any human images or categories. Nevertheless, though our symbols cannot contain or restrict God, they can be avenues through which God approaches us and through which we respond to God's approach. The Old Testament assures us that God made a covenant with us through human events and history and called us as a covenanted people to respond to the divine initiative in an effort to shape those human events and history. That covenant was renewed and enriched by Jesus Christ himself, who became flesh so that we could share in God's own divine life. As we have seen, Christians have never hesitated to employ a great variety of art and architectural forms in their celebration of the paschal mystery of Jesus Christ. Certainly God does not need our celebrations, but we do need them, and we are only able to celebrate with human forms that give rise to our own cultural identity. Those celebrations of our Christian faith of necessity involve the whole person, since we are not only rational, intellectual beings; we are beings with bodies, senses, imaginations, emotions, and memories. If we acknowledge that no human words or architectural or artistic forms can exhaust the infinite mystery of God, but that countless forms can become channels through which God comes to us and we go to God, then we need concrete criteria to judge those forms that are especially useful in our celebrations of the Christian mystery.[1]

The experience of God's mystery is discovered above all when we are conscious of God's presence and have centered our lives in God. That experience flourishes in a climate of hospitality, of welcome, in which people are present to one another as the body-persons they are, as members of the body of Christ, comfortable with one another, gathered together with one another, capable of seeing and hearing all that is enacted within the worshiping assembly. An attractive beauty in all that is said and done, used or observed is the best way to facilitate the experience of mystery, for God is not only goodness and truth; God is also beauty. We should be able to sense a transcendent reality in everything that is seen, heard, touched, and smelled in the celebration of the Christian mysteries. It is above all God's Spirit in our hearts and communities that gives us access to the otherness, the transcendence, and the holiness of God. However, the symbols that express God's presence in our midst must be authentic; they must never be pretentious, counterfeit, or tawdry.

Our contemporary challenge is to open up the symbols, especially the basic ones of people, bread, wine, water, oil, and the imposition of hands, so that we may experience them as truly authentic and consequently may appreciate their symbolic meaning and value. Our Western culture, with its emphasis on individualism and competitiveness, which has tended toward efficiency, functionalism, and productivity, has made us insensitive to the symbolic nature of persons and things. We need to depose the false god called "ego" and replace it with the true and living God. Above all, in keeping with the medieval axiom *Sacramenta sunt propter homines,* "Sacraments are for people," we need to affirm the primacy of persons over things and to have faith in the fact that we are members of the body of Christ and temples of God's own Holy Spirit.[2]

Certainly no architectural or artistic forms have a legitimate place in our liturgical celebrations if they are not honest and appropriate in form.[3] Good quality is perceived and appreciated only by those who are able and willing to assume a contemplative distance from experience and to see, hear, touch, and taste symbols for what they truly are. We tend to experience things and events in pragmatic terms, whereas contemplative experience implies that we see beyond the facade of what takes place and discern the honesty and genuineness that have gone into the making of events and their diverse components. This applies to architecture, music, sculpture, painting, silver and gold smithing, stained glass, pottery, and the crafting of furniture as well as to any other art forms that might make up a worship experience. The composition of our worship experience must be capable of bearing the weight of mystery, reverence, and awe that are essential characteristics of sound liturgical experience. The various components must also serve a ministerial role in the celebration; they are not ends in themselves and certainly should never interrupt the flow of celebrations, which have their own distinctive rhythms and structures.[4]

There are important elements in the liturgical environment that contribute significantly to the overall experience of mystery, especially the seating of the assembly and the placement of the major liturgical actions, as well as light, acoustics, color, texture, spaciousness, silence, stillness, and even temporary decorations. The architectural and artistic environment is appropriate when it is beautiful, hospitable, and inviting—when it creates a certain sense of emptiness and appears to be incomplete when the celebrating assembly is absent. It is appropriate when it brings the members of the body of Christ closely together so that they are able to see and hear one another as well as everything that is part of the liturgical rites.[5]

Both sacred architecture and art should function as *loci theologici*, for it is often in these forms, as well as in scripture and tradition, that the presence and power of God operating through the Spirit are revealed and mediated into the lives of Christian persons and communities. There is neither one source nor one method of coming to an experience of the divine. Sacred architecture and art invite us to see with our eyes as well as with our intellects. Verbal symbols of the divine must be complemented by a variety of nonverbal symbols. As has often been asserted, religion and religious experience are communicated, shared, and sustained not primarily through creeds and theological statements but through symbols, myths, metaphors, and rituals. Sacred buildings and sacred art are above all symbolic; they can be important sources through which God comes to us in a great diversity of cultural forms.[6]

The meaning of the cultural forms that architecture and art assume is not immediately clear because, like all symbols, the forms must be interpreted. The interpretation we give will be conditioned by the worldviews we bring to the task of interpretation. People coming out of a primal culture will interpret their world and their experience in vastly different ways from those coming from a classical or modern culture. Great sensitivity is then required by architects and artists as well as pastoral ministers as they seek to create or renovate spaces in which the Christian assembly celebrates and encounters the paschal mystery of Jesus Christ through the power of the Holy Spirit.

Certainly the New Testament, which is normative for Christians, asserts the primacy of persons and communities over things. It is the paschal mystery of Jesus Christ celebrated by the Christian assembly that provides the foundational meaning for all places of worship. Their meaning is always derivative; apart from the centrality of the paschal mystery and the assembly which is the body of Christ, they easily degenerate into mere monuments, often very impressive monuments, but monuments nonetheless. Over the centuries, the architectural forms of Christian

churches and their artistic appointments have taken diverse forms reflective of the structure of the liturgical rites and the theological underpinnings
of such rites. However, the church buildings themselves and their appointments have also conditioned both positively and negatively the ways in
which the liturgy has been celebrated and the theological understanding of
the liturgy. Architectural and artistic styles have reflected both the phenomenon of inculturation and that of tradition. In fact architectural and
artistic traditions are simply records of inculturation from the past; as such
they provide us with a storehouse of models and resources for proper inculturation today.[7]

Throughout history, the church has not adopted any particular style of
sacred architecture or art as its own; rather the church has admitted styles
from every period in keeping with the cultures and conditions of various
peoples and the requirements of the liturgical rites as understood and practiced at a particular time. History in this regard can be instructive, but it is
not necessarily determinative or normative, since each generation of Christians has manifested its own shifts in ecclesial and liturgical consciousness,
with corresponding shifts in the architectural and artistic forms by which
that consciousness has been expressed. As the history of architecture and
art clearly shows, the church has been responsible for the birth and development of a great architectural and artistic treasury. In our own time and
place, architects and artist should be given relatively free scope in the
church, but they must have both a clear understanding of the requirements
of the sacred liturgy and a profound understanding of the paschal mystery
of Jesus Christ and the dignity and role of the community of the faithful
who celebrate that sacred mystery. It is the responsibility of patrons who
commission architects and artists to provide such a sound liturgical and theological brief to both architects and artists. The architectural and artistic
models that are proposed by architects and artists should be carefully eval-
uated in light of sound liturgy and theology.

The basic architecture of the church building as well as the altar, the baptistery, the ambo, the place for the faithful, including the various ministers,
the place for the reservation of the Blessed Sacrament, and all objects used
in the liturgical celebrations should be carefully designed and selected in
consultation with experts in liturgy, theology, architecture, and art so that
everything is capable of making a visual or other sensory contribution to
the beauty of the celebration and the transformation of the Christian community of persons. This basic requirement was admirably expressed in the
concluding statement on *Environment and Art in Catholic Worship* by the
American Bishops' Committee on the Liturgy:

When the Christian community gathers to celebrate its faith and vision, it gathers to celebrate what is most personally theirs and most nobly and truly Church. The actions of the assembly witness the great deeds God has done; they confirm an age-old covenant.

With such vision and depth of the assembly can the environment be anything less than a vehicle to meet the Lord and to encounter one another? The challenge of our environment is the final challenge of Christ: We must be ready until he returns in glory.[8]

Notes

1. Culture: The Context for Theology, Liturgy, and Sacred Architecture and Art

1. Bishops' Committee on the Liturgy, *Environment and Art in Catholic Worship* (Washington, D.C.: National Conference of Catholic Bishops, 1978); United States Conference of Catholic Bishops, *Built of Living Stones: Art, Architecture and Worship* (Washington, D.C.: United States Catholic Conference, 2000); Walter C. Huffman and S. Anita Stauffer, *Where We Worship* (Minneapolis: Augsburg Publishing House, 1987); Canadian Conference of Catholic Bishops, *Our Place of Worship* (Ottawa: Canadian Conference of Catholic Bishops, 1999); Irish Episcopal Commission for Liturgy, *The Place of Worship: Pastoral Directory on the Building and Reordering of Churches* (Dublin and Carlow: Veritas and Irish Institute of Pastoral Liturgy, 1994); Evangelical Lutheran Church in America, *Principles for Worship* (Minneapolis: Augsburg Fortress, 2002), 67–96.

2. See Christopher Irvine and Anne Dawtry, *Art and Worship* (Collegeville, Minn.: Liturgical Press, 2002), 1–15; Keith Walker, *Images or Idols? The Place of Sacred Art in Churches Today* (Norwich: Canterbury Press, 1996), 64–105.

3. See *Icons of American Protestantism: The Art of Warner Sallman*, ed. David Morgan (New Haven: Yale University Press, 1996).

4. See Samuel Laeuchli, *Religion and Art in Conflict* (Philadelphia: Fortress Press, 1980).

5. William A. Dryness, *Visual Faith: Art, Theology, and Worship in Dialogue* (Grand Rapids: Baker Academic, 2001), 11–23.

6. Bernard Lonergan, *Method in Theology* (New York: Herder & Herder, 1972), xi. Since the 1970s new directions have developed in the study of culture; they have critiqued and displaced earlier static notions and stress the importance of cultural processes as dynamic, often fragmented, and at times conflictual. See Kathryn Tanner, *Theories of Culture: A New Agenda for Theology* (Minneapolis: Fortress Press, 1997). In the following discussion of cultures the author wishes to acknowledge his dependence on the work of Thomas Berry, available from the Riverside Center for Religious Research, Riverdale, New York, and also the work of Joe Holland, espe-

cially *Varieties of Postmodern Theology,* which he co-edited with David Ray Griffin and William Beardslee (Albany, N.Y.: State University of New York Press, 1989).

7. Michael Paul Gallagher, *Clashing Symbols: An Introduction to Faith and Culture* (London: Darton, Longman & Todd, 1997), 11–12; Aylward Shorter, *Towards a Theology of Inculturation* (London: Geoffrey Chapman, 1988), 4; Lonergan, *Method in Theology,* xi; D. Amalorpavadass, "Réflexions théologique sur l'inculturation," *La Maison-Dieu* 179 (1989): 58–66.

8. For a historical account of the role of images in American religions, see David Morgan, *Visual Piety: A History and Theory of Popular Religious Images* (Berkeley: University of California Press, 1998); *The Visual Culture of American Religions,* ed. David Morgan and Sally M. Promey (Berkeley: University of California Press, 2001); Colleen McDannell, *Material Christianity: Religion and Popular Culture in America* (Bloomington: Indiana University Press, 1995).

9. Philip Bock, *Modern Cultural Anthropology* (New York: Knopf, 1969), 319. See Christopher Dawson, *Religion and Culture* (London: Sheed & Ward, 1948); idem, *Religion and the Rise of Western Culture* (New York: Sheed & Ward, 1950).

10. R. Kevin Seasoltz, "Anthropology and Liturgical Theology: Searching for a Compatible Methodology," in *Liturgy and Human Passage,* Concilium 112, ed. David Power and Luis Maldonado (New York: Seabury Press/A Crossroad Book, 1979), 3–13.

11. Christopher Dawson, *Progress and Religion: An Historical Enquiry* (New York: Sheed & Ward, 1938); idem, *Enquiries into Religion and Culture* (New York: Sheed & Ward, 1933); idem, *The Making of Europe: An Introduction to the History of European Unity* (New York: Sheed & Ward, 1937); idem, *The Historic Reality of Christian Culture* (New York: Harper, 1960).

12. See Peter C. Phan, "Contemporary Theology and Inculturation in the United States," in *The Multicultural Church: A New Landscape in U.S. Theologies,* ed. William Cenkner (New York: Paulist Press, 1996), 109–30.

13. Monica Sjoo and Barbara Mor, *The Great Cosmic Mother: Rediscovering the Religion of the Earth* (San Francisco: Harper & Row, 1987).

14. See Thomas Kane, *The Dancing Church: Video Impressions of the Church in Africa* (New York: Paulist Press, 1992).

15. See John A. Saliba, *Understanding New Religious Movements* (Grand Rapids: Wm. B. Eerdmans, 1996); also The Irish Theological Commission, *A New Age of the Spirit? A Catholic Response to the New Age Phenomenon* (Dublin: Veritas, 1994); Richard Woods, "What Is New Age Spirituality?" *The Way* 33 (July 1993): 175–88.

16. For an account of Pope Gregory the Great and his relations with the English, especially through Augustine of Canterbury, see Bede, *A History of the English Church and People,* trans. Leo Sherley-Price (Baltimore: Penguin, 1955); also Jeffrey Richards, *Consul of God: The Life and Times of Gregory the Great* (London: Routledge & Kegan Paul, 1980).

17. Ian Bradley, *Celtic Christianity: Making Myths and Chasing Dreams* (New York: St. Martin's Press, 1999), 9; also Mary Condren, *The Serpent and the Goddess:*

Women, Religion, and Power in Celtic Ireland (San Francisco: Harper & Row, 1989).

18. Virgil Elizondo, *Guadalupe: Mother of the New Creation* (Maryknoll, N.Y.: Orbis Books, 1997).

19. See Rosemary Crumlin, ed., *Aboriginal Art and Spirituality* (North Blackburn: Collins Dove, 1991).

20. Geraldine Brooks, "The Painted Desert," *The New Yorker*, July 28, 2003, 60–67.

21. See Joseph E. Brown, *The Spiritual Legacy of the American Indian* (New York: Crossroad, 1982); Åke Hultkrantz, *The Religions of the American Indians* (Berkeley: University of California Press, 1979).

22. Arthur Versluis, *Native American Traditions* (Shaftsbury, Dorcet: Element, 1994), 33–37.

23. See Paulette Molin and Arlene B. Hirschfelder, *Encyclopedia of Native American Religions: An Introduction* (New York: Facts on File, 2000).

24. Ibid., 44.

25. Clara Sue Kidwell, Homer Noley, George E. "Tink" Tinker, *A Native American Theology* (Maryknoll, N.Y.: Orbis Books, 2001), 13–15.

26. Versluis, *Native American Traditions*, 18. See also Robert A. Murray, *Pipes on the Plains* (Washington, D.C.: National Park Service, U.S. Department of the Interior/ Pipestone Indian Shrine Association, 1975).

27. Ibid., 38–42.

28. Ibid., 29, 52.

29. Ibid., 43–44.

30. Ibid., 73–85. See also Frederick J. Dockstader, "North American Indian and Inuit Art," in *A History of Art* (Ann Arbor: Borders Press, 1995), 488–502; Peter Nabokov, *Native American Architecture* (New York: Oxford University Press, 1989).

31. Ibid., 87–89.

32. See Shawn Copeland, "African American Catholics and Black Theology: Interpretation," in *African-American Catholics and Black Theology: An Interpretation*, ed. Gayraud Wilmore (Durham, N.C.: Duke University Press, 1989), 228–48.

33. See J. Mbiti, *African Religions and Philosophy* (New York: Praeger, 1969); A. Shorter, *African Christian Spirituality* (Maryknoll, N.Y.: Orbis Books, 1980); Cyprian Davis, "Black Spirituality," *U.S. Catholic Historian* 8 (1989): 39–46.

34. See Andrew Wilson-Dickson, *The Story of Christian Music from Gregorian Chant to Black Gospel* (Minneapolis: Fortress Press, 1992), 191–206.

35. See Vincent L. Wimbush, "Reading Texts through Worlds, Worlds through Texts," in *Black and Catholic: The Challenge and Gift of Black Folk: Contributions of African American Experience and Thought to Catholic Theology*, ed. Jamie T. Phelps, 2nd ed. (Milwaukee: Marquette University Press, 2002), 59–73.

36. Marcus Roser, "Church Architecture in Africa," *Worship Net*, no. 8 (October 1996): 3–4.

37. Anton Wessels, *Images of Jesus: How Jesus Is Perceived and Portrayed in Non-European Cultures* (Grand Rapids: Wm. B. Eerdmans, 1990), 110–11. See also Robert Brain, "African Art," in *A History of Art*, ed. Lawrence Gowing (Ann Arbor: Borders Press, 2002), 504–20.

38. Patrick Jones, "Sweet, Sweet Spirit in This Place," *New Liturgy*, nos. 118–19 (Summer–Autumn 2003): 23–25.

39. See Robert Brancatelli, "*Religiosidad Popular* as a Form of Liturgical Catechesis," *Worship* 77 (May 2003): 210–24.

40. See Timothy Matovina, "Liturgy, Popular Rites, and Popular Spirituality," in Virgil Elizondo and Timothy Matovina, *Mestizo Worship: A Pastoral Approach to Liturgical Ministry* (Collegeville, Minn.: Liturgical Press, 1998), 81–91.

41. See Timothy Matovina, "San Fernando Cathedral and the Alamo: Sacred Place, Public Ritual, and Construction of Meaning," *Journal of Ritual Studies* 12 (Winter 1998): 1–13.

42. Donna Pierce, "Portraits of Faith," in Eliot Porter and Ellen Auerbach, *Mexican Churches* (Albuquerque: University of New Mexico Press, 1987), 13–20. See also Jonathan Yorba, *Arte Latino: Treasures from the Smithsonian American Art Museum* (New York: Watson-Guptill Publications, 2001).

43. Richard E. Nisbett, *The Geography of Thought: How Asians and Westerners Think Differently . . . and Why* (New York: Free Press, 2003), xiii.

44. See Ronald Takaki, *Strangers from a Different Shore: A History of Asian Americans* (New York: Penguin Books, 1989); David Palumbo-Liu, *Asian/American: Historical Crossings of a Racial Frontier* (Stanford: Stanford University Press, 1999).

45. See *Images of Asia*, special issue, *The Way* 39 (April 1999).

46. See *Frontiers in Asian Christian Theology: Emerging Trends*, ed. R. S. Sugirtharajah (Maryknoll, N.Y.: Orbis Books, 1994); and idem, *Asian Faces of Jesus* (Maryknoll, N.Y.: Orbis Books, 1993); Peter C. Phan, *In Our Tongues* (Maryknoll, N.Y.: Orbis Books, 2003).

47. *Journeys at the Margin: Toward an Autobiographical Theology in American-Asian Perspective*, ed. Peter C. Phan and Jung Young Lee (Collegeville, Minn.: Liturgical Press, 1999), xvi–xvii.

48. See Chung Hyun Kyung, *Struggle to Be the Sun Again: Introducing Asian Women's Theology* (Maryknoll, N.Y.: Orbis Books, 1990), 104.

49. Phan, *Journeys at the Margin*, xvii.

50. See, e.g., Jung Young Lee, *A Theology of Change: A Christian Concept of God in Eastern Perspective* (Maryknoll, N.Y.: Orbis Books, 1979).

51. See Aloysius Pieris, *An Asian Theology of Liberation* (Maryknoll, N.Y.: Orbis Books, 1988), 51–58.

52. Phan, *Journeys at the Margin*, xvii.

53. Caroline Humphrey and Piers Vitebsky, *Sacred Architecture: Explore and Understand Sacred Spaces* (London: Thorsons, 2003), 92–93.

54. Ibid., 104–5.

55. *Christ for All People: Celebrating a World of Art,* ed. Ron O'Grady (Maryknoll, N.Y.: Orbis Books, 2001), 74–75.

56. Ibid., 32–33.

57. See Masao Takenaka, *The Place Where God Dwells: An Introduction to Church Architecture in Asia* (Hong Kong: Christian Conference of Asia, 1995).

58. See Stephen Happel, "Classicist Culture and the Nature of Worship," *Heythrop Journal* 21 (July 1980): 294. Happel's treatment of classical versus empirical culture is derived from Bernard Lonergan's works, especially *Method in Theology,* xi–xii, 301–2, 305–19, and *Doctrinal Pluralism* (Milwaukee: Marquette University Press, 1971), 1–91.

59. See Robert Marks, *The Origin of the Modern World* (Lanham, Md.: Rowman & Littlefield, 2002).

60. See Arthur Mirgeler, *Mutations of Western Christianity* (Notre Dame: University of Notre Dame Press, 1968), 103–20.

61. See A. J. N. W. Prag, "Archaic Greek Art," in *History of Art,* ed. Gowing, 114–30; idem, "Classical Greek Art," in ibid., 132–48; K. B. Tompkins, "Hellenistic Art," in ibid., 150–64.

62. See Martin Henig, "Roman Art," in *History of Art,* ed. Gowing, 178–210.

63. See Nathan D. Mitchell, "The Amen Corner: 'Liturgical Language: Building a Better Mousetrap,'" *Worship* 77 (May 2003): 250–63; Keith Pecklers, *Dynamic Equivalence* (Collegeville, Minn.: Liturgical Press, 2003).

64. Walter J. Ong has explored at length the complex question of orality and literacy. See, e.g., *Interface of the Word: Studies on the Evolution of Consciousness and Culture* (Ithaca, N.Y.: Cornell University Press, 1977); idem, *Orality and Literacy* (New York: Methuen, 1982); idem, *The Presence of the Word: Some Prolegomena for Cultural and Religious History* (New Haven: Yale University Press, 1967); *Time, Memory, and the Verbal Arts: Essays on the Thought of Walter Ong,* ed. Dennis L. Weeks and Jane Hoogestraat (Selinsgrove, Pa.: Susquehanna University Press, 1989).

65. See *Romanesque: Architecture, Sculpture, Painting,* ed. Rolf Toman, photographs by Achim Bednorz (Cologne: Könemann, 1997); George Zarnecki, *Romanesque* (New York: Universe Books, 1971); Bernhard Schütz, *Great Cathedrals* (New York: Harry N. Abrams, 2002); Michael Camille, *Gothic Art: Glorious Visions* (New York: Harry N. Abrams, 1996).

66. See Louis Dupré, *Passage to Modernity: An Essay in the Hermeneutics of Nature and Culture* (New Haven: Yale University Press, 1993).

67. Paul Vignaux, *Nominalisme au XIVe Siècle* (Montreal: Inst. d'études médiévales, 1948); Marilyn McCord Adams, *William Ockham,* Publications in Medieval Studies 26, 2 vols. (Notre Dame: University of Notre Dame Press, 1987).

68. See Donald K. McKim, *The Cambridge Companion to Martin Luther* (New York: Cambridge University Press, 2003).

69. Galileo Galilei, *The Achievement of Galileo,* ed. with notes by James Brophy

and Henry Paolucci (Smyrna, Del.: Bagehot Council, 2003); *The Cambridge Companion to Galileo,* ed. Peter Machamer (New York: Cambridge University Press, 1998).

70. See Diogenes Allen, *Christian Belief in a Postmodern World: The Full Wealth of Conviction* (Louisville: Westminster John Knox Press, 1989); David Ray Griffin, William A. Beardslee, and Joe Holland, *Varieties of Postmodern Theology* (Albany, N.Y.: State University of New York Press, 1989); David Tracy, *Plurality and Ambiguity: Hermeneutics, Religion, and Hope* (San Francisco: Harper & Row, 1987).

71. Peter Matheson, *The Imaginative World of the Reformation* (Edinburgh: T. & T. Clark, 2000), 26–27.

72. See Alister McGrath, *In the Beginning: The Story of the King James Bible and How It Changed a Nation, a Language, and a Culture* (New York: Doubleday, 2001), 5–23.

73. See Richard Viladesau, *Theological Aesthetics: God in Imagination, Beauty, and Art* (New York: Oxford University Press, 1999), 6.

74. Frank Burch Brown, *Religious Aesthetics* (Princeton, N.J.: Princeton University Press, 1989), 77–111.

75. Herbert Marcuse, *One-dimensional Man* (Boston: Beacon Press, 1966).

76. H. R. Rookmaaker, *Modern Art and the Death of Culture* (Leicester: Inter-Varsity Press, 1970), 160–90.

77. Suzi Gablik, *Has Modernism Failed?* (New York: Thames & Hudson, 1984); Samuel Laeuchli, *Religion and Art in Conflict* (Philadelphia: Fortress Press, 1980).

78. See Frank C. Senn, "'Worship Alive': An Analysis and Critique of 'Alternative Worship Services,'" *Worship* 69 (1995): 194–224.

79. See S. Grenz, *A Primer on Postmodernism* (Grand Rapids: Eerdmans, 1996); Michael Warren, *Seeing through the Media* (Harrisburg, Pa.: Trinity Press International, 1997); David Lyon, *Jesus in Disneyland: Religion in Postmodern Times* (Cambridge: Polity, Blackwell, 2000); *The Postmodern God: A Theological Reader,* ed. Graham Ward (Malden, Mass.: Blackwell, 1997).

80. See Paul Lakeland, *Postmodernity: Christian Identity in a Fragmented Age* (Minneapolis: Fortress Press, 1997).

81. Philippa Berry and Andrew Wernick, *Shadow of Spirit: Postmodernism and Religion* (London: Routledge, 1992); *Postmodern God,* ed. Ward.

82. Jean-Luc Marion, *Being Given: Toward a Phenomenology of Givenness* (Stanford, Calif.: Stanford University Press, 2002).

83. Robert Venturi, *Complexity and Contradiction in Architecture* (New York: Museum of Modern Art, 1977).

84. Graham Ward, "Postmodernism," in *The Oxford Companion to Christian Thought,* ed. Adrian Hastings, Alistair Mason, and Hugh Pyper (New York: Oxford University Press, 2000), 551–52.

85. Eleanor Heartney, *Postmodernism* (London: Tate, 2001).

86. See George Pattison, *Art, Modernity, and Faith* (London: SCM Press, 1998).

87. See R. Kevin Seasoltz, "Another Look at Sacrifice," *Worship* 74 (2000): 402–6; idem, "Human Victimization and Christ as Victim in the Eucharist," *Worship* 76 (2002): 110–19.

88. See the excellent sociological analysis of the contemporary American scene in the works of Robert Wuthnow: *The Crisis in the Churches: Spiritual Malaise, Fiscal Woe* (New York: Oxford University Press, 1997); *After Heaven: Spirituality in America since the 1950s* (Berkeley: University of California Press, 1998); *Creative Spirituality: The Way of the Artist* (Berkeley: University of California Press, 2001); *All in Sync: How Music and Art Are Revitalizing American Religion* (Berkeley: University of California Press, 2003).

2. The Response of the Churches to Cultural Shifts

1. See Eamon Duffy, *Saints and Sinners: A History of the Popes* (New Haven: Yale University Press, 1997), 133–94; John Hale, *The Civilization of Europe and the Renaissance* (New York: Simon & Schuster, 1995); Frank C. Senn, *Christian Liturgy: Catholic and Evangelical* (Minneapolis: Fortress Press, 1997), 267–392.

2. *Luther's Works*, ed. Jaroslav Pelikan and Helmut T. Lehmann (St. Louis: Concordia; Philadelphia: Fortress Press, 1955–1986), XXXVI, 11–126.

3. Paul V. Marshall, "Liturgy," in *The Encyclopedia of Christianity* (Grand Rapids: Eerdmans, 2003), 3:325; James F. White, *Protestant Worship: Traditions in Transition* (Louisville: Westminster John Knox Press, 1989), 36–49.

4. Marshall, "Liturgy," 325; White, *Protestant Worship*, 58–69.

5. Marshall, "Liturgy," 325; White, *Protestant Worship*, 94–105.

6. Marshall, "Liturgy," 326; White, *Protestant Worship*, 79–91.

7. See Theodor Klauser, *A Short History of the Western Liturgy: An Account and Some Reflections* (New York: Oxford University Press, 1979).

8. James F. White, *Roman Catholic Worship: Trent to Today* (Collegeville, Minn.: Liturgical Press, 2003), 1–23.

9. J. A. Jungmann, *Pastoral Liturgy* (New York: Herder & Herder, 1962), 80–89.

10. Ibid., 25–46. See also Louis Bouyer, *Liturgical Piety* (Notre Dame: University of Notre Dame Press, 1955), 1–9; Keith F. Pecklers, "History of the Roman Liturgy from the Sixteenth until the Twentieth Centuries," in *Handbook for Liturgical Studies: Introduction to the Liturgy*, ed. Ansgar J. Chupungco (Collegeville, Minn.: Liturgical Press, 1997), 153–64.

11. R. Kevin Seasoltz, *The New Liturgy: A Documentation* (New York: Herder & Herder, 1966), xviii–xxi.

12. Ibid., xvii–xxi.

13. See Rudolf Wittkower, *Art and Architecture in Italy, 1600–1750* (New Haven: Yale University Press, 1999).

14. Bouyer, *Liturgical Piety*, 10–22.

15. J. D. Crichton, *Lights in the Darkness: Forerunners of the Liturgical Movement* (Collegeville, Minn.: Liturgical Press, 1996), 77–81.

16. James F. White, *The Cambridge Movement: The Ecclesiologists and the Gothic Revival* (New York: Cambridge University Press, 1962).

17. R. W. Franklin, "Guéranger: A View on the Centenary of his Death," *Worship* 49 (1975): 318–28; idem, "Guéranger and Pastoral Liturgy: A Nineteenth Century Context," *Worship* 50 (1976): 146–62.

18. Olivier Rousseau, "German Ecclesiology in the Nineteenth Century," in *The Progress of the Liturgy* (Westminster, Md.: Newman Press, 1951), 51–68.

19. Michael Himes, *Ongoing Incarnation: Johann Möhler and the Beginnings of Modern Ecclesiology* (New York: Crossroad, 1997); Avery Dulles, "A Half Century of Ecclesiology," *Theological Studies* 50 (1989): 419–42.

20. See Avery Dulles, *Models of the Church* (Garden City, N.Y.: Doubleday, Image Books, 1991).

21. Richard N. Berube, "Christological Models and Their Sacramental Implications," *The Living Light* 15 (1975): 180–83.

22. Karl Rahner, "Ende oder Anfang?" in *Das Konzil von Chalkedon: Geschichte und Gegenwart,* ed. Aloys Grillmeier and Heinrich Bacht (Würzburg: Echter-Verlag, 1954), 3:3–49.

23. Berube, "Christological Models and Their Sacramental Implications," 185.

24. Ibid., 183–84. See also Hans Urs von Balthasar, *The God Question and Modern Man* (New York: Seabury, 1967), 150.

25. Ibid., 184–86, 190–91.

26. Ibid.

27. Roger Haight, *The Experience and Language of Grace* (New York: Paulist Press, 1979); Wolfhart Pannenberg, *Anthropology in Theological Perspective* (Philadelphia: Westminster Press, 1975).

28. See Karl Rahner, *Foundations of Christian Faith: An Introduction to the Idea of Christianity* (New York: Seabury Press, 1978); Edward Schillebeeckx, *Christ, the Experience of Jesus as Lord* (New York: Seabury Press, 1980).

29. Michael Kunzler, *The Church's Liturgy* (New York: Continuum, 2001), 75–165.

30. See Alexander Schmemann, *For the Life of the World* (Crestwood, N.Y.: St. Vladimir's Seminary Press, 1989).

31. Edward Robinson, *The Language of Mystery* (London: SCM Press, 1987), 5–28.

32. Quoted by Edward Robinson, *The Image of Life* (Exeter: Religious and Moral Education Press, 1980), 4.

33. Naum Gabo, letter to Herbert Read (1942), *Horizon* 10 (July 1944); quoted by Robinson, *Image of Life,* 4.

34. Robinson, *Language of Mystery,* 29–41.

35. Rembert Weakland, "Aesthetic and Religious Experience in Evangelization," *Theology Digest* 44 (Winter 1997): 319.

36. Ibid., 319–20.

37. Ibid., 320.

38. Charles R. Morris, *American Catholics: The Saints and Sinners Who Built America's Most Powerful Church* (New York: Random House, 1997), 158–64.

39. See Gordon Lathrop, "New Pentecost or Joseph's Britches? Reflections on the History and Meaning of the Worship Ordo in the Megachurches," *Worship* 71 (November 1998): 521–38.

40. Weakland, "Aesthetic and Religious Experience in Evangelization," 322.

41. Thomas F. O'Meara, *Seeing Theological Forms*, Monograph No. 6 (Belmont, Calif.: Archives of Modern Christian Art, 1997), 4.

42. Margaret R. Miles, *Image as Insight: Visual Understanding in Western Christianity and Secular Culture* (Boston: Beacon Press, 1985), xi–xii; Caroline Walker Bynum, *Jesus as Mother: Studies in the Spirituality of the High Middle Ages* (Berkeley: University of California Press, 1982); eadem, *Holy Feast: The Religious Significance of Food to Medieval Women* (Berkeley: University of California Press, 1987).

43. The work of a number of modern scholars serves as both a complement to and corrective of that literary history of Christianity. See, e.g., Graydon F. Snyder, *Ante Pacem: Archaeological Evidence of Church Life before Constantine* (Macon, Ga.: Mercer University Press, 1985); Paul Corby Finney, *The Invisible God: The Earliest Christians on Art* (New York: Oxford University Press, 1994). Paul Bradshaw has recently shown how much interpretation of early church documents must be corrected in light of scholarly investigations in the past twenty years. See *The Search for the Origins of Christian Worship: Sources and Methods for the Study of Early Liturgy*, 2nd ed. (New York: Oxford University Press, 2002).

44. R. Kevin Seasoltz, "Artistic Images of Jesus," *Worship* 73 (1999): 15–16; see also William S. Taylor, *Seeing the Mystery: Exploring Christian Faith through the Eyes of Artists* (Ottawa: Novalis, 1989), 7–8.

45. Robinson, *Language of Mystery*, 62.

46. See David N. Power, "Worship in a New World: Some Theological Considerations," *The Changing Face of Jewish and Christian Worship in North America*, ed. Paul F. Bradshaw and Lawrence A. Hoffman (Notre Dame: University of Notre Dame Press, 1991), 166; also *The Presence of Transcendence*, ed. Lieven Boeve and John C. Ries (Leuven: Peeters, 2001).

47. Richard R. Gaillardetz, "North American Culture and the Liturgical Life of the Church: The Separation of the Quests for Transcendence and Community," *Worship* 68 (1994): 403–16.

48. See R. Kevin Seasoltz, "Symbolizing Immanence and Transcendence," *Worship* 50 (1976): 398; also *Sacramental Presence in a Postmodern Context*, ed. L. Boeve and L. Leijssen (Leuven: University Press, 2001).

49. See Stephen Happel, "Symbol," in *The New Dictionary of Sacramental Worship*, ed. Peter Fink (Collegeville, Minn.: Liturgical Press, 1990), 1237–45; Nathan Mitchell, "Sign, Symbol," in *The New Westminster Dictionary of Liturgy and Worship* (Louisville: Westminster John Knox Press, 2002), 438–40.

50. See Paul Tillich, *Dynamics of Faith* (New York: Harper, 1957), 41–43.

51. Philip Wheelwright, *The Burning Fountain: A Study in the Language of Symbolism* (Bloomington: Indiana University Press, 1968). See also Avery Dulles, *Models of Revelation* (Garden City, N.Y.: Doubleday, 1983), 131–34; idem, *The Craft of Theology: From Symbol to System* (New York: Crossroad, 1995). Mary Collins has explored many of these issues in depth in her various works. See, e.g., her *Contemplative Participation: Sacrosanctum Concilium Twenty-five Years Later* (Collegeville, Minn.: Liturgical Press, 1990); eadem, *Worship: Renewal to Practice* (Portland, Ore.: Pastoral Press, 2003).

52. See R. Kevin Seasoltz, "The Language of Liturgical Celebrations: A Matter of Form," *Liturgy* 4 (Spring 1985): 27–33.

53. Salvatore Marsili, *Anamnesis* (Turin: Marietti, 1974), 1:94.

54. Hans Urs von Balthasar, *The Glory of the Lord: A Theological Aesthetics*, 7 vols. (San Francisco: Ignatius Press, 1982–). Other works include Frank Burch Brown, *Religious Aesthetics: A Theological Study of Making and Meaning* (Princeton, N.J.: Princeton University Press, 1989); Jeremy S. Begbie, *Voicing Creation's Praise: Towards a Theology of the Arts* (Edinburgh: T & T Clark, 1991); *Theologie und Ästhetik*, ed. Günter Pöltner and Helmuth Vetter (Vienna: Herder, 1985); Patrick Sherry, *Spirit and Beauty: An Introduction to Theological Aesthetics* (Oxford: Clarendon Press, 1992); Richard Viladesau, *Theological Aesthetics: God in Imagination, Beauty, and Art* (New York: Oxford University Press, 1999).

55. Richard Viladesau, *Theology and the Arts: Encountering God through Music, Art and Rhetoric* (New York: Paulist Press, 2000), 11–58.

56. Ibid., 123–24.

57. Margaret Miles, *Image as Insight: Visual Understanding in Western Christianity and Secular Culture* (Boston: Beacon Press, 1985), 9.

58. Viladesau, *Theology and the Arts*, 134.

59. Leonid Ouspensky, *Theology of the Icon*, vol. 1, trans. Anthony Gythiel (Crestwood, N.Y.: St. Vladimir's Seminary Press, 1992), 138–39.

60. Viladesau, *Theology and the Arts*, 144–51.

61. David Tracy, *The Analogical Imagination: Christian Theology and the Culture of Pluralism* (New York: Crossroad, 1982). See also Andrew Greeley, *The Catholic Imagination* (Berkeley: University of California Press, 2000), 5–9.

3. Sacred Architecture and Art
in the Bible and the Early Church

1. Susan White, "The Theology of Sacred Space," in *The Sense of the Sacramental: Movement and Measure in Art and Music, Place and Time*, ed. David Brown and Ann Loades (London: SPCK, 1995), 31.

2. Ibid., 32–33.

3. Ibid., 34–35.

4. See F. J. Foakes Jackson, "Stephen's Speech in Acts," *Journal of Biblical Literature* 49 (1930): 283–86; M. Simon, "St. Stephen and the Jewish Temple," *Journal of Ecclesiastical History* 2 (1951): 127–42.

5. François Louvel, "Le mystère de nos églises," *La Maison-Dieu* 63 (1960): 5–6. See also Johannes Quasten, "The Conflict of Early Christianity with the Jewish Temple Worship," *Theological Studies* 2 (1941): 481–87.

6. Mircea Eliade, *Images and Symbols: Studies in Religious Symbolism* (Princeton, N.J.: Princeton University Press, 1991).

7. Alexander Schmemann, *The World as Sacrament* (London: Longman, Darton & Todd, 1965), 16.

8. Ibid., 140–41.

9. John Habgood, "The Sacramentality of the Natural World," in *The Sense of the Sacramental: Movement and Measure in Art and Music, Place and Time*, ed. David Brown and Ann Loades (London: SPCK, 1995), 27–28.

10. Joel P. Brereton, "Sacred Space," in *The Encyclopedia of Religion*, ed. Mircea Eliade (New York: Macmillan, 1995), 9:526–35. See also Mircea Eliade, *The Sacred and the Profane: The Nature of Religion* (New York: Harper & Row, 1959), 20–67; idem, *Patterns in Comparative Religion* (New York: Sheed & Ward, 1958), 367–87.

11. Demetrius Dumm, *Flowers in the Desert: A Spirituality of the Bible* (New York: Paulist Press, 1987), 62. See also Robert L. Cohn, "Liminality in the Wilderness," in *The Shape of Sacred Space: Four Biblical Studies*, AAR Studies in Religion 23 (Chico, Calif.: Scholars Press, 1981), 7–23.

12. S. White, "Theology of Sacred Space," 37.

13. Ibid., 38–39. See also Walter Brueggemann, *The Land: Place as Gift, Promise, and Challenge in Biblical Faith* (Minneapolis: Fortress Press, 2002).

14. See Ignazio M. Calabuig, *The Dedication of a Church and an Altar: A Theological Commentary* (Washington, D.C.: United States Catholic Conference, 1980).

15. Arnold van Gennep, *The Rites of Passage* (Chicago: University of Chicago Press, 1960); Victor Turner, *The Ritual Process: Structure and Anti-structure* (Chicago: Aldine, 1969); idem, *Drama, Fields, and Metaphors: Symbolic Actions in Human Society* (Ithaca, N.Y.: Cornell University Press, 1974); Victor Turner and Edith Turner, *Images and Pilgrimage in Christian Culture: An Anthropological Perspective* (New York: Columbia University Press, 1978).

16. Turner and Turner, *Images and Pilgrimage*, 111–12.

17. See Eliade, *Images and Symbols: Studies in Religious Symbolism*.

18. Diana Eck, "Mountains," in *Encyclopedia of Religion*, ed. Eliade, 9:130–34; see also Cohn, "Mountains in the Biblical Cosmos," in *Shape of Sacred Space*, 25–41.

19. Yves Congar, *The Mystery of the Temple* (London: Burns & Oates, 1962), 3–6.

20. Ibid., 7–19.

21. Ibid., 20–49.

22. Ibid., 49–53. See also Jean Daniélou, *Le Signe du temple ou de la présence de Dieu* (Paris: Gallimard, 1942); H.-M. Féret, "Le temple du Dieu vivant," in *Prêtre et Apôtre* (Paris: Bonne Presse, 1947), 103–5, 135–37, 166–69, 181–84.

23. Congar, *Mystery of the Temple,* 54–79.

24. Leslie J. Hoppe, *The Synagogues and Churches of Ancient Palestine* (Collegeville, Minn.: Liturgical Press, 1994); Robert Wilken, *The Land Called Holy: Palestine in Church History and Thought* (New Haven: Yale University Press, 1992); L. Michael White, *Building God's House in the Roman World: Architectural Adaptations among Pagans, Jews, and Christians* (Baltimore: Johns Hopkins University Press, 1990); Steven Fine, *This Holy Place: On the Sanctity of the Synagogue during the Greco-Roman Period* (Notre Dame: University of Notre Dame Press, 1997).

25. Paul F. Bradshaw, *The Search for the Origins of Christian Worship: Sources and Methods for the Study of Early Liturgy* (New York: Oxford University Press, 2002), 36.

26. Congar, *Mystery of the Temple,* 112–50.

27. François Louvel, "Le mystère de nos églises," *La Maison-Dieu* 63 (1960): 16; Lucien Cerfaux, *The Church in the Theology of St. Paul* (New York: Herder & Herder, 1959), 145–55.

28. R. Kevin Seasoltz, *The House of God* (New York: Herder & Herder, 1963), 76–77.

29. Ibid., 83–84.

30. See Rafael Aguirre, "Early Christian House Churches," *Theology Digest* 12 (Summer 1985): 151–55.

31. Noële-Maurice Denis-Boulet, "La leçon des églises de l'antiquité," *La Maison-Dieu* 63 (1960): 24.

32. *Passio Sancti Justini et Socii* 3, in L. Michael White, *The Social Origins of Christian Architecture,* vol. 2, *Texts and Monuments for the Christian Domus Ecclesiae in Its Environment* (Valley Forge, Pa.: Trinity Press International, 1997), 42–43.

33. L. M. White, *Social Origins of Christian Architecture,* vol. 1, *Building God's House in the Roman World: Architectural Adaptation among Pagans, Jews, and Christians* (Valley Forge, Pa.: Trinity Press International, 1990), 110.

34. *First Apology* 67.3.8. English trans. by Thomas B. Falls, *Writings of St. Justin Martyr* (New York: Christian Heritage, 1948), 106.

35. L. M. White, *Social Origins of Christian Architecture,* 2:19.

36. *Vita Alexandri Severi* 49.6, cited in C. Kirsch, *Enchiridion fontium historiae Ecclesiae et Antiquiae* (Freiburg: Herder, 1914), 284.

37. *Epistula* 39.4. English trans. by Sister Rose Bernard Donna, *St. Cyprian's Letters* (Washington, D.C.: Catholic University of America Press, 1964), 101.

38. Bradshaw, *Search for the Origins of Christian Worship,* 79.

39. Arthur Vööbus, ed. and trans., *The Didascalia Apostolorum in Syriac* (Louvain: Corpus SCO, 1979), 12, 130–31. English extracts in Sebastian Brock and Michael Vasey, *The Liturgical Portions of the Didascalia,* Grove Liturgical Studies 29 (Bramcote: Grove Books, 1982).

40. L. M. White, *Social Origins of Christian Architecture,* 1:7–8.

41. Robin Margaret Jensen, *Understanding Early Christian Art* (New York: Routledge, 2000), 61.

42. Ibid., 21.

43. L. M. White, *Social Origins of Christian Architecture*, 1:8.

44. Ibid., 62, 74–78, 83, 93–97.

45. Ibid., 44, 50, 54–55.

46. Eusebius, *The History of the Church from Christ to Constantine*, trans. G. A. Williamson (Minneapolis: Augsburg, 1965), 328.

47. Jean Lassus, "Origine de la basilique chrétienne," *Bible et Terre Sainte* no. 181 (1976): 8; Enrico Cattaneo, *Arte e liturgia dalle origini al Vaticano II* (Milan: Vita e Pensiero, 1982), 26–42.

48. See Matilda Webb, *The Churches and Catacombs of Early Christian Rome: A Comprehensive Guide* (Portland, Ore.: Sussex Academic Press, 2001).

49. See Marcel Metzger, *History of the Liturgy: The Major Stages* (Collegeville, Minn.: Liturgical Press, 1997), 37–39.

50. Hervé-Marie Legrand, "The Presidency of the Eucharist according to the Ancient Tradition," *Living Bread Saving Cup*, ed. R. Kevin Seasoltz (Collegeville, Minn.: Liturgical Press, 1987), 196–221.

51. Paul Corby Finney has addressed this complex question in what is considered a ground-breaking study of "normative" Christian attitudes toward visual art, inquiring whether Christians, either because of the Jewish roots or because of their belief in an invisible God were originally opposed to the creation and veneration of sacred images. See *The Invisible God: The Earliest Christians on Art* (New York: Oxford University Press, 1994).

52. Jensen, *Understanding Early Christian Art*, 15.

53. Ibid., 9–10.

54. Margaret Miles, *Image as Insight* (Boston: Beacon Press, 1985), 47.

55. Emile Mâle, *Early Churches of Rome* (London: Ernest Benn, 1960), 24.

56. Miles, *Image as Insight*, 48.

57. Jensen, *Understanding Early Christian Art*, 11. See also Sister Mary Charles Murray, "Art and the Early Church," *Journal of Theological Studies* 28 (October 1977): 303–45; Aidan Nichols, *The Art of God Incarnate: Theology and Image in Christian Tradition* (London: Darton, Longman & Todd, 1981).

58. Jensen, *Understanding Early Christian Art*, 26–30.

59. Ibid., 30–31.

60. Ibid., 62–63.

61. Ibid., 68–69.

62. Ibid., 68–93.

63. Ibid., 84–85.

64. Ibid., 77–84.

65. Ibid., 87.

66. Ibid., 181–82.

67. Ibid., 182.

4. Post-Constantinian Period

1. Anscar J. Chupungco, "History of the Roman Liturgy until the Fifteenth Century," in *Handbook for Liturgical Studies,* ed. Anscar Chupungco, vol. 1 (Collegeville, Minn.: Liturgical Press, 1997), 131–41.

2. Roger Stalley, *Early Medieval Architecture* (New York: Oxford University Press, 1999), 17–22. See also Marcel Metzger, *History of the Liturgy: The Major Stages* (Collegeville, Minn.: Liturgical Press, 1997), 64–112.

3. Ibid.,17–35.

4. François Louvel, "Le mystère de nos églises," *La Maison-Dieu* 63 (1960): 5–23.

5. Metzger, *History of the Liturgy,* 76–77.

6. R. Kevin Seasoltz, *The House of God* (New York: Herder & Herder, 1963), 90–100.

7. Patrick Nuttgens, *The Story of Architecture* (London: Phaidon Press, 1997), 9–120.

8. Hervé-Marie Legrand, "The Presidency of the Eucharist according to the Ancient Tradition," in R. Kevin Seasoltz, *Living Bread, Saving Cup* (Collegeville, Minn.: Liturgical Press, 1987), 196–221.

9. Richard Krautheimer, *Early Christian and Byzantine Architecture* (Baltimore: Penguin Books, 1965), 25–26.

10. L. Michael White, *The Social Origins of Christian Architecture,* vol. 1, *Building God's House in the Roman World: Architectural Adaptation among Pagans, Jews, and Christians* (Valley Forge, Pa.: Trinity Press International, 1990), 23.

11. Ibid., 2:136–39.

12. Robin Margaret Jensen, *Understanding Early Christian Art* (New York: Routledge, 2000), 88–91.

13. Margaret R. Miles, *Image as Insight: Visual Understanding in Western Christianity and Secular Culture* (Boston: Beacon Press, 1985), 48–55.

14. Eusebius, *The History of the Church from Christ to Constantine,* trans. G. A. Williamson (Minneapolis: Augsburg, 1965), book 10, 383–84.

15. Enrico Cattaneo, *Arte e liturgia: Dalle origini al Vaticano II* (Milan: Università Cattolica del Sacro Cuore, 1982), 29–31.

16. Matilda Webb, *The Churches and Catacombs of Early Christian Rome: A Comprehensive Guide* (Portland, Ore.: Sussex Academic Press, 2001), 41–44.

17. Seasoltz, *House of God,* 218–20.

18. See A. Grabar, *Martyrium: Recherches sur le culte des reliques et l'art chrétien antique,* Collège de France, Fondation Schlumberger pour les Études byzantines (1946; London: Variorum Reprints, 1972).

19. John Lowden, *Early Christian and Byzantine Art* (New York: Phaidon, n.d.), 34–38.

20. See the various articles on the symbolism of the cross in *Bibel und Liturgie* 76, no. 3 (2003): 162–99.

21. Gabriele Finaldi et al., *The Image of Christ* (London: National Gallery Company, 2000), 108–11.

22. Paulinus, *Poem* 27.522–83, trans. P. G. Walsh, *The Poems of St. Paulinus of Nola,* Ancient Christian Writers Series (New York: Newman Press, 1975), 289–92.

23. Jensen, *Understanding Early Christian Art,* 94. See also Jean-Michel Spieser, "De l'anonymat à la gloire des images de Rome à Byzance du IIIe siècle," *Le Monde de la Bible: Le Christ dans l'art des origines au XVe siècle,* no. 114 (October 1998): esp. 9–24.

24. Jensen, *Understanding Early Christian Art,* 95.

25. Ibid., 97.

26. Ibid., 98.

27. Finaldi, *Image of Christ,* 108–11.

28. Ibid., 110.

29. Ibid., 110–11.

30. Thomas F. Mathews, *The Clash of the Gods: A Reinterpretation of Early Christian Art* (Princeton, N.J.: Princeton University Press, 1993).

31. Ibid., 10.

32. Ibid., 3–22.

33. Ibid., 12.

34. Ernst Kantorowicz, "The 'King's Advent' and Enigmatic Panels in the Doors of Santa Sabina," *The Art Bulletin* 26 (1944): 206–31. For a brief account of the life and work of Andreas Alföldi, see *Andrew Alföldi 1895–1981,* ed. Harry Woolf (Princeton, N.J.: Princeton University Press, 1982); see also Andreas Alföldi, "Die Ausgestaltung des monarchischen Zeremoniells am Römischen Kaiserhofe," *Mitteilungen des deutschen archäolgischen Instituts, Römische Abteilung* 49 (1934): 1–118. For a brief biography of André Grabar, see Richard Krautheimer, Ihor Sevcenko, and Ernst Kitzinger, *Speculum* 66 (1991): 723–25.

35. André Grabar, *Christian Iconography: A Study of Its Origins,* The A. W. Mellon Lectures in the Fine Arts, 1961, The National Gallery of Art, Washington, D.C. (Princeton, N.J.: Princeton University Press, 1968), esp. 13–14.

36. See Sister Mary Charles Murray, "Art and the Early Church," *Journal of Theological Studies,* n.s., 28 (1977): 304–45; eadem, *Rebirth and Afterlife: A Study of the Transmutation of Some Pagan Imagery in Early Christian Funerary Art* (Oxford: BAR International Series, 1981), 55–60.

37. Mathews, *Clash of the Gods,* 23; see also Eamon Duffy, *Saints and Sinners: A History of the Popes* (New Haven: Yale University Press, 1997), 16–27.

38. Mathews, *Clash of the Gods,* 177–79.

39. Ibid., 180.

40. Jensen, *Understanding Early Christian Art,* 94.

41. Ibid., 94–95.

42. Ibid., 97.

43. Ibid., 97–98.

44. Ibid., 98. See also Spieser, "De l'anonymat à la gloire des images de Rome à Byzance du IIIe siècle," 18–21.

45. Jensen, *Understanding Early Christian Art*, 106; see also Spieser, "De l'anonymat à la gloire des images de Rome à Byzance du IIIe siècle," 18.

46. Jensen, *Understanding Early Christian Art*, 107.

47. See M. Collinet-Guerin, *Histoire du nimbe des origines aux temps modernes* (Paris: Nouvelles Éditions Latines, 1961).

48. Jensen, *Understanding Early Christian Art*, 112.

49. Ibid., 119–20.

50. See Robin Jensen, "Moses Imagery in Jewish and Christian Art: Problems of Continuity and Particularity," in *Society of Biblical Literature 1992 Seminar Papers* (Atlanta: Scholars Press, 1992), 389–418.

51. Jensen, *Understanding Early Christian Art*, 122.

52. Ibid., 124–26. It is interesting that apart from John DeRosen's apsidal mosaic of the triumphant Christ in the National Shrine of the Immaculate Conception in Washington, D.C., where he is portrayed as a severe judge, and Graham Sutherland's apsidal tapestry in Coventry Cathedral, where Christ is also a stern figure, modern representations of Christ usually portray him as gentle, with long hair and a mild expression.

53. Ibid.

54. See Henri Leclercq, "Croix et crucifix," in *Dictionnaire d'archéologie chrétienne de liturgie*, ed. Fernand Cabrol (Paris, 1914), 3:3045–144; Julien Ries, "Cross," trans. Kristen Anderson, in *The Encyclopedia of Religion*, ed. Mircea Eliade (New York: Macmillan, 1987), 2:155–66; Spieser, "De l'anonymat à la gloire des images de Rome à Byzance du IIIe siècle," 22–23.

55. Spieser, "De l'anonymat à la gloire des images de Rome à Byzance du IIIe siècle," 22.

56. This substitutionary view of sacrifice has more recently been qualified by emphasis on God as the self-sacrificing one whose whole life has been characterized by self-giving, expressed above all by the gift of Jesus' own life on the cross and in the eucharist.

57. Jensen, *Understanding Early Christian Art*, 133–34.

58. Massey Shepherd, "Christology: A Central Problem of Early Christian Theology and Art," in *The Age of Spirituality*, ed. K. Weitzmann (New York: Metropolitan Museum of Art, 1979), 110.

59. Ibid., 137.

60. Jensen, *Understanding Early Christian Art*, 118.

61. Ibid., 150.

62. Ibid., 142. See John 1:29; 1 Cor. 5:7; Rev. 5:6–14.

63. Jensen, *Understanding Early Christian Art*, 143.

64. Ibid., 143.

65. Ibid., 145–46.

66. Ibid., 147.

67. Ibid., 150. See also Louis Tongeren, *Exaltation of the Cross: Toward the Origins of the Feast of the Cross and the Meaning of the Cross in Early Medieval Liturgy* (Paris/Leuven: Peeters, 2000).

68. Jensen, *Understanding Early Christian Art*.

69. Ibid., 152–54. See Jürgen Moltmann, *The Crucified God: The Cross of Christ as the Foundation and Criticism of Christian Theology* (New York: Harper & Row, 1974); Edward Schillebeeckx, *Jesus: An Experiment in Christology* (New York: Seabury, 1979); idem, *The Experience of Jesus as Lord* (New York: Seabury, 1980); Thomas Weinandy, *Does God Suffer?* (Edinburgh: T & T Clark, 2000).

70. See Dermot Lane, *Keeping Hope Alive* (New York: Paulist Press, 1996), 112–31; Luke Timothy Johnson, *The Creed* (New York: Doubleday, 2003), 285–95; Hans Schwarz, *Eschatology* (Grand Rapids: Eerdmans, 2000), 280–301.

71. Jensen, *Understanding Early Christian Art*, 156–59; see also J. G. Davies, "Factors Leading to the Emergence of Belief in the Resurrection of the Flesh," *Journal of Theological Studies*, n.s., 23 (1972): 448–55; A. H. C. Van Eijk, "Resurrection Language: Its Various Meanings in Early Christian Literature," *Studia Patristica* 12 (1975): 271–76; J. E. McWilliam Dewart, *The Shape of Death and Resurrection* (Collegeville, Minn.: Liturgical Press, 1986); Pheme Perkins, *Resurrection* (New York: Doubleday, 1984); Jaroslav Pelikan, *The Shape of Death: Life, Death, and Immortality in the Early Fathers* (New York: Abingdon, 1961); and Caroline Walker Bynum, *The Resurrection of the Body in Western Christianity, 200–1336* (New York: Columbia University Press, 1995) 43–51.

72. Jensen, *Understanding Early Christian Art*, 159.

73. Ibid., 160.

74. Ibid., 162–63.

75. Ibid., 164.

76. Ibid., 166.

77. Ibid., 167.

78. Ibid., 169–71.

79. On the complex subject of nudity, see J. Z. Smith, "The Garments of Shame," *History of Religion* 6 (1966): 217–38.

80. Jensen, *Understanding Early Christian Art*, 173.

81. Ibid., 175.

82. For an interpretation of nudity in baptism, see Henri Leclercq, "Nudité baptismale," in *Dictionnaire d'archéologie chrétienne de liturgie*, ed. Fernand Cabrol (Paris, 1914–), vol. 12.2 (1936), 1801–5. The *Apostolic Tradition* also described the initiates stripping off their clothes and entering the water naked: 21.3, 5, and 11.

83. Jensen, *Understanding Early Christian Art*, 178.

84. Ibid., 180–82.

85. Cyril of Jerusalem, *Catechetical Lec.*, 10.5, trans. A. Stephenson, *The Works of Saint Cyril of Jerusalem*, vol. 1, Fathers of the Church Series (Washington, D.C.: Catholic University of America Press, 1969), 198.

5. Romanesque and Gothic Architecture and Art

1. See *The Rule of St. Benedict in Latin and English with Notes*, ed. Timothy Fry, O.S.B. (Collegeville, Minn.: Liturgical Press, 1981), 3–151; P. Schmitz, *Histoire de l'Ordre de Saint-Benoît*, 7 vols. (Maredsous: Éditions de l'Abbaye, 1942–1956); L. Daly, *Benedictine Monasticism: Its Formation and Development through the 12th Century* (New York: Sheed & Ward, 1965); R. Southern, *Western Society and the Church in the Middle Ages* (Harmondsworth: Penguin Books, 1970), 214–99; C. Butler, *Benedictine Monachism: Studies in Benedictine Life and Rule* (reprint, London: Longmans, Green, 1961); S. Hilpisch, *Benedictinism through Changing Centuries*, trans. L. J. Doyle (Collegeville, Minn.: Liturgical Press, 1958).

2. Timothy Gregory Verdon, "Monasticism and Christian Culture," in *Monasticism and the Arts*, ed. Timothy Gregory Verdon (Syracuse: Syracuse University Press, 1984), 1.

3. Ibid., 2.

4. See George Zarnecki, *Romanesque* (New York: Universe Books, 1971), 14–54; Roger Stalley, *Early Medieval Architecture* (New York: Oxford University Press, 1999), 37–57; Rolf Toman, ed., *Romanesque Architecture, Sculpture, Painting* (Cologne: Könemann, 1997), 32–255.

5. Stalley, *Early Medieval Architecture*, 37–51.

6. Ibid., 121–27.

7. C. H. Lawrence, *Medieval Monasticism: Forms of Religious Life in Western Europe in the Middle Ages* (New York: Longman, 1984), 76–96; see also J. Hourlier, "Le monastère Saint Odilon," *Studia Anselmiana* 50 (1962): 5–21.

8. Lawrence, *Medieval Monasticism*, 146–52.

9. See Terryl N. Kinder, *Cistercian Europe: Architecture of Contemplation* (Grand Rapids: Eerdmans, 2002); idem, *Architecture of Silence: Cistercian Abbeys of France*, photography by David Heald (New York: Harry N. Abrams, 2000); *Studies in Cistercian Art and Architecture*, 4 vols., ed. Meredith Parsons Lillich. (Kalamazoo, Mich.: Cistercian Publications, 1980, 1984, 1987, 1993).

10. Conrad Rudolph, *The "Things of Greater Importance": Bernard of Clairvaux's Apologia and the Medieval Attitude toward Art* (Philadelphia: University of Pennsylvania Press, 1990), 287–93.

11. Kinder, *Cistercian Europe*, 374–88.

12. See Janet Backhouse, *The Illuminated Manuscript* (Oxford: Phaidon, 1997).

13. Michael Curran, "Early Irish Monasticism," in *Irish Spirituality*, ed. Michael Maher (Dublin: Veritas, 1981), 10–21.

14. See Kathleen Hughes, *Early Christian Ireland: Introduction to the Sources* (Ithaca: Cornell University Press, 1972); eadem, *Church and Society in Ireland, A.D. 400–1200* (London: Variorum, 1987); Kathleen Hughes and Ann Hamlin, *Celtic Monasticism: The Modern Traveler to the Early Irish Church* (New York: Seabury,

1981); *Ireland in Early Medieval Europe: Studies in Memory of Kathleen Hughes*, ed. Dorothy Whitelock (New York: Cambridge University Press, 1982).

15. See Brian de Breffny and George Mott, *The Churches and Abbeys of Ireland* (London: Thames and Hudson, 1976), 7–104; Roger Stalley, "Middle Ages," in *Sacred Places: The Story of Christian Architecture in Ireland* (Dublin/Belfast: Royal Institute of the Architects of Ireland and Royal Society of Ulster Architects, 2000), 6.

16. Peter Harbison, *Irish High Crosses* (Drogheda: Boyne Valley Honey Company, 1994).

17. For an anthology of texts, see D. Bevington, *Medieval Drama* (Boston: Houghton Mifflin, 1975), 225–788; also *The Staging of Religious Drama in Europe in the Later Middle Ages: Texts and Documents in England*, ed. P. Meredith and J. E. Tailby (Kalamazoo: Medieval Institute Publications, 1983).

18. See Salvatore Paterno, *The Liturgical Context of Early European Drama* (Potomac, Md.: Scripta Humanistica, 1989), 25–40; Johannes Quasten, *Music and Worship in Pagan and Christian Antiquity*, trans. Boniface Ramsey (Washington, D.C.: National Association of Pastoral Musicians, 1983), 121–28.

19. See Richard B. Donovan, *The Liturgical Drama in Medieval Spain* (Toronto: Pontifical Institute of Mediaeval Studies, 1958), 13–14.

20. See Johan Huizinga, *The Waning of the Middle Ages: A Study of the Forms of Life, Thought, and Art in France and the Netherlands in the XIVth and XVth Centuries* (New York: St. Martin's Press, 1967).

21. See, e.g., *The Art of Gothic: Architecture, Sculpture, Painting*, ed. Rolf Toman (Cologne: Könemann, 1999); David Macauley, *Cathedral: The Story of Construction* (Boston: Houghton Mifflin, 1973); Ian Dunlap, *The Cathedrals' Crusade: The Rise of the Gothic Style in France* (New York: Taplinger Publishing Company, 1982); Titus Burckhardt, *Chartres and the Birth of the Cathedral* (Bloomington, Ind.: World Wisdom Books, 1996); Jean Body, *French Gothic Architecture of the Twelfth and Thirteenth Centuries* (Berkeley: University of California Press, 1983); John Harvey, *The Gothic World, 1100–1600: A Survey of Architecture and Art* (New York: Batsford, 1950); Otto von Simson, *The Gothic Cathedral: Origins of Gothic Architecture and the Medieval Concept of Order*, 3rd ed. (Princeton, N.J.: Princeton University Press, 1988); Wim Swaan, *The Late Middle Ages: Art and Architecture from 1350 to the Advent of the Renaissance* (Ithaca: Cornell University Press, 1977).

22. Robert Barron, *Heaven in Stone and Glass: Experiencing the Spirituality of the Great Cathedrals* (New York: Crossroad, 2000), 11–12.

23. Ibid., 16.

24. Ibid., 19.

25. Ibid., 21–27.

26. Ibid., 79–85.

27. Nathan Mitchell, *Cult and Controversy* (Collegeville, Minn.: Liturgical Press, 1982), 375–89.

28. Miri Rubin, *Corpus Christi: The Eucharist in the Late Medieval Culture* (New York: Cambridge University Press, 1991), 164–287.

29. Ibid., 271–87.

30. Gabriele Finaldi et al., *The Image of Christ* (London: National Gallery Co., 2002), 104–57.

31. Ibid., 29–37.

32. Jeffrey F. Hamburger, *Nuns as Artists: The Visual Culture of a Medieval Convent* (Berkeley: University of California Press, 1997).

33. Ibid., xix.

34. Ibid., 10–20.

35. Ibid., 63.

36. Ibid., 66–80

37. Ibid., 80.

38. Ibid., 82.

39. Ibid., 84–96.

40. Ibid., 96.

41. Ibid., 222.

6. Renaissance, Baroque, and Reformation Periods

1. Lawrence Gowing, *A History of Art* (Ann Arbor: Borders Press, 2002), 641–58.

2. See *The Renaissance: Basic Interpretations,* ed. Karl H. Dannenfeldt (Lexington: Heath, 1974); *Humanity and Divinity in Renaissance and Reformation,* ed. John W. O'Malley et al. (New York: Brill, 1993); *Science, Culture and Popular Belief in Renaissance Europe,* ed. Stephen Pumfrey et al. (Manchester: Manchester University Press, 1991); *Renaissance Society and Culture,* ed. John Monfasani and Ronald G. Musto (New York: Italica Press, 1991); Peter Burke, *The Italian Renaissance: Culture and Society in Italy* (Princeton, N.J.: Princeton University Press, 1986); John Dillenberger, *Images and Relics: Theological Perceptions and Visual Images in Sixteenth-century Europe* (New York: Oxford University Press, 1999); Anthony Levi, *Renaissance and Reformation* (New Haven: Yale University Press, 2002).

3. Ross King, *Brunelleschi's Dome: How a Renaissance Genius Reinvented Architecture* (New York: Walker & Co., 2000).

4. See Laurie Schneider Adams, *Key Monuments of the Italian Renaissance* (Oxford: Westview, 2000).

5. Louis Bouyer, *Liturgical Piety* (Notre Dame: University of Notre Dame Press, 1954), 5–6.

6. See Anne Mueller von der Haegen, *Giotto di Bondone, about 1267–1337* (Cologne: Könemann, 1998); Bruce Cole, *Giotto and Florentine Painting, 1280–1375,* (New York: Harper & Row, 1976).

7. See Bruce Cole, *Masaccio and the Art of Early Renaissance Florence* (Bloomington: Indiana University Press, 1980).

8. See Georges Didi-Huberman, *Fra Angelico: Dissemblance and Figuration*, trans. Jane M. Todd (Chicago: University of Chicago Press, 1995); Christopher Lloyd, *Fra Angelico* (London: Phaidon, 1992).

9. See Ludwig Goldscheider, *Donatello* (New York: Oxford University Press, 1941).

10. See Ronald Lightbown, *Sandro Botticelli* (Berkeley: University of California Press, 1978).

11. See *Leonardo da Vinci: Master Draftsman*, ed. Carmen C. Bambach (New Haven: Yale University Press, 2003); Clayton Martin, *Leonardo da Vinci: The Divine and the Grotesque* (London: Royal Collection Enterprises, 2002); Pietro C. Marani, *Leonardo da Vinci: The Complete Paintings* (New York: H. N. Abrams, 2002).

12. Peter Murray and Linda Murray, *The Oxford Companion to Christian Art and Architecture* (Oxford: Oxford University Press, 1996), 274–75.

13. See Alexander Nagel, *Michelangelo and the Reform of Art* (New York: Cambridge University Press, 2000); Diana Stanley, *Michelangelo* (New York: HarperCollins, 2000); James H. Beck, *Three Worlds of Michelangelo* (New York: W. W. Norton, 1999).

14. See Roger James and Nicholas Penny, *Raphael* (New Haven: Yale University Press, 1983); James H. Beck, *Raphael* (New Haven: H. N. Abrams, 1976).

15. Robert Coughlan, *The World of Michelangelo 1475–1564* (New York: Time Incorporated, 1966).

16. See Donna Spivey Ellington, *From Sacred Body to Angelic Soul: Understanding Mary in Late Medieval and Early Modern Europe* (Washington, D.C.: Catholic University of America Press, 2001).

17. Ibid.

18. Gowing, *History of Art*, 660–74.

19. Stephen Kemperdick, *Rogier van der Weyden* (Cologne: Könemann, 1999), 12–16.

20. Ibid.

21. Ibid., 46–49.

22. The following paragraphs about Gossaert's work are dependent on the exhibition entitled "Seeing Salvation," held at the National Gallery in London, February 26–May 7, 2002. See Gabriele Finaldi et al., *The Image of Christ* (London: National Gallery Company, 2002), 44–47; Neil MacGregor, *Seeing Salvation: Images of Christ in Art* (London: BBC, 2000), 11–15.

23. MacGregor, *Seeing Salvation*, 60–63.

24. Ibid.; Finaldi, *Image of Christ*, 72–73.

25. See Brian Tierney, *Foundations of the Conciliar Theory* (Cambridge: Cambridge University Press, 1955).

26. See M. H. Carré, *Realists and Nominalists* (Oxford: Oxford University Press, 1946).

27. See Bernard McGinn, *The Mystical Thought of Meister Eckhart* (New York: Crossroad, 2001); Oliver Davies, *Meister Eckhart* (London: SPCK, 1991).

28. Karl Suso, *With Greater Liberty*, trans. Joseph T. Lienhard (Kalamazoo: Cistercian Publications, 1993), 137.

29. Bruce Mansfield, *Erasmus in the Twentieth Century: c. 1920-2000* (Toronto: University of Toronto Press, 2003); István Pieter Bejczy, *Erasmus and the Middle Ages* (Boston: Brill, 2001).

30. *The Cambridge Companion to Martin Luther* (New York: Cambridge University Press, 2003).

31. Bruce Gordon, *The Swiss Reformation* (New York: Manchester University Press, 2002).

32. T. H. L. Parker, *Calvin: An Introduction to His Thought* (New York: Continuum, 2002).

33. Eamon Duffy, *The Stripping of the Altars: Traditional Religion in England c. 1400—c. 1580* (New Haven: Yale University Press, 1992).

34. R. William Franklin and Joseph M. Shaw, *The Case for Christian Humanism* (Grand Rapids: Eerdmans, 1991), 131.

35. See P. N. Brooks, *Cranmer in Context* (Minneapolis: Fortress Press, 1989); and E. G. Rupp, *Studies in the Making of English Protestant Tradition* (Cambridge: Cambridge University Press, 1947).

36. Franklin and Shaw, *Case for Christian Humanism*, 131-32.

37. See Geoffrey Cuming, *A History of Anglican Liturgy* (London: Macmillan, 1982); and P. N. Brooks, *Thomas Cranmer's Doctrine of the Eucharist* (London: Macmillan, 1965).

38. Franklin and Shaw, *Case for Christian Humanism*, 134-35.

39. James F. White, *Protestant Worship: Traditions in Transition* (Louisville: Westminster John Knox, 1989), 122-29.

40. Ibid., 129-31.

41. James F. White, *Roman Catholic Worship: Trent to Today* (Collegeville, Minn.: Liturgical Press, 2003), 1-23.

42. *Summa Th.* III, q. XXV, a. 3.

43. *Enchiridion symbolorum, definitionum et declarationum de rebus fidei et novum*, ed. H. Denzinger, rev. A. Schönmetzer, 36th ed. (Freiburg: Herder, 1976) (abbreviated DS), 1867.

44. See DS 2532.

45. Meister Eckhart, "This Is Another Sermon," in *Meister Eckhart*, trans. Raymond Blakeney (New York: Harper & Row, 1941), 108.

46. Margaret R. Miles, *Images as Insight: Visual Understanding in Western Christianity and Secular Culture* (Boston: Beacon Press, 1985), 101.

47. Frank Senn, *Christian Liturgy: Catholic and Evangelical* (Minneapolis: Fortress Press, 1997), 529-30.

48. See Daniel W. Hardy, "Calvinism and the Visual Arts: A Theological Introduction," in *Seeing Beyond the Word: Visual Arts and the Calvinist Tradition*, ed. Paul Corby Finney (Grand Rapids: Eerdmans, 1999), 1–16.

49. Carl C. Christensen, *Art and the Reformation in Germany* (Athens, Ohio: Ohio University Press, 1979), 81.

50. For example, Westminster Abbey, as well as the cathedrals at Peterborough, Oxford, Gloucester, Bristol, and Chester. See Tim Tatton-Brown, *The English Cathedrals* (London: New Holland, 2002), 82–95.

51. Horton Davies, *Worship and Theology in England: From Cranmer to Baxter and Fox, 1534–1690* (Grand Rapids: Eerdmans, 1996), 351.

52. John Calvin, *Institutes of the Christian Religion* (Chicago: Encyclopaedia Britannica, 1990), 1:11.12.

53. Ibid., 1:11.7.

54. J. P. Ramseyer, "Liturgical Art," *New Catholic Encyclopedia* (New York: McGraw-Hill, 1967), 8:887–89.

55. See George Hay, *The Architecture of Scottish Post-Reformation Churches, 1560–1848* (Oxford: Clarendon Press, 1957).

56. See A. L. Mayer, "Renaissance, Humanism und Liturgie," *Jahrbuch für Liturgiewissenschaft* 14 (1934): 123–70.

57. Louis Bouyer, *Liturgical Piety* (Notre Dame: University of Notre Dame Press, 1954), 6.

58. See Niels Rasmussen, "Liturgy and Liturgical Arts," in *Catholicism in Early Modern History: A Guide to Research*, ed. John O'Malley (St. Louis: Center for Reformation Research, 1988), 273–98.

59. See M. L. Lewine, "The Roman Church Interior, 1527–1580" (Ph.D. diss., Columbia University, 1960); *Baroque Art: The Jesuit Contribution*, ed. R. Wittkower and I. Jaffe (New York: Oxford University Press, 1972); *Diccionario Histórico de la Compañía de Jesús*, 4 vols., ed. Charles E. O'Neill and Joaquin Domínguez (Rome: Institutum Historicum S.I., 1999), 1:246–52.

60. *Luther's Works*, ed. Jaroslav Pelikan and Helmut T. Lehmann (St. Louis: Concordia Publishing House; Philadelphia: Fortress Press, 1955–1986), 53:69.

61. Miles, *Image as Insight*, 113–17.

62. Ibid., 119–20.

63. See Helen Digby, *Rembrandt* (New York: Barnes & Noble, 1995); Ernst Van de Wetering, *Rembrandt: The Painter at Work* (Berkeley: University of California Press, 2000); Claudio Pescio, *Rembrandt and Seventeenth-century Holland* (New York: Bedrick Books, 1995).

64. See Peter Robb, *The Man Who Became Caravaggio* (New York: Henry Holt, 2000); Helen Langdon, *Caravaggio: A Life* (New York: Farrer, Straus & Giroux, 1999); Leo Bersani and Ulysses Dutoit, *Caravaggio's Secrets* (Cambridge, Mass.: M.I.T. Press, 1998).

65. See Jonathan Brown, "El Greco: Between the Renaissance and the Counter Reformation," in *Art and Religion: Faith, Form and Reform*, ed. Osmund Overly

(Columbia: University of Missouri-Columbia, 1986), 40–66. See also Brown's "El Greco, the Man and the Myths," in *El Greco of Toledo* (Boston: Little, Brown, 1982), 15–33; idem, "The Redemption of El Greco in the Twentieth Century," in *El Greco: Italy and Spain* (Washington, D.C.: National Gallery of Art, 1984), 29–32; and *El Greco: Essays by David Dance and John Elliott* (London: National Gallery Co., 2003).

66. See David Summers, *Michelangelo and the Language of Art* (Princeton, N.J.: Princeton University Press, 1981).

67. See Richard L. Kagan, "El Greco and the Law," in *Figures of Thought: El Greco as Interpreter of History, Tradition, and Ideas,* ed. Jonathan Brown (Washington, D.C.: National Gallery of Art, 1986), 84–86.

68. Miles, *Image as Insight,* 122–23.

69. Ibid., 124.

70. Ibid.

71. Ibid., 124–25.

7. Seventeenth, Eighteenth, and Nineteenth Centuries

1. Frank C. Senn, *Christian Liturgy: Catholic and Evangelical* (Minneapolis: Fortress Press, 1997), 538–39.

2. R. William Franklin and Joseph M. Shaw, *The Case for Christian Humanism* (Grand Rapids: Eerdmans, 1991), 140.

3. Ibid., 140–41.

4. Ibid., 141.

5. Senn, *Christian Liturgy,* 531. See also Friedrich Kalb, *Theology of Worship in Seventeenth-century Lutheranism* (St. Louis: Concordia, 1965); and Guenther Stiller, *Johann Sebastian Bach and Liturgical Life in Leipzig* (St. Louis: Concordia, 1984).

6. See Ronald S. Wallace, *Calvin's Doctrine of the Word and Sacrament* (Edinburgh: Oliver & Boyd, 1953); and Duncan Forrester and Douglas Murray, *Studies in the History of Worship in Scotland* (Edinburgh: T. & T. Clark, 1924).

7. G. W. O. Addleshaw and Frederick Etchells, *The Architectural Setting of Anglican Worship* (London: Faber & Faber, 1948), 45.

8. Horton Davies, *Worship and Theology in England: From Watts and Wesley to Martineau, 1690–1900* (Grand Rapids: Eerdmans, 1996), 38.

9. For the historical background of the introduction of the vernacular into England and Anglican worship, see Alister McGrath, *In the Beginning* (New York: Doubleday, 2001), 24–36.

10. Ibid., 40.

11. *Parentalia: Or Memoirs of the Family of the Wrens, but Chiefly of Sir Christopher Wren, Compiled by his Son Christopher* (London, 1750; reprint, Farnborough,

1965), 320. See also Christopher Hibbert, *London's Churches* (London: Macdonald, 1988); Lisa Gardner, *The Outlandish Life of Sir Christopher Wren* (New York: HarperCollins, 2003).

12. Franklin and Shaw, *Case for Christian Humanism,* 141.

13. Senn, *Christian Liturgy,* 533.

14. See W. Jardine Grisbrooke, *Anglican Liturgies of the Seventeenth and Eighteenth Centuries* (London: SPCK, 1958); and Addleshaw and Etchells, *Architectural Setting of Anglican Worship.*

15. Senn, *Christian Liturgy,* 531–32; Franklin and Shaw, *Case for Christian Humanism,* 141.

16. See Frank Swinnerton, *The Georgian Scene: A Literary Panorama* (New York: Farrar & Rinehart, 1934).

17. See David Lowes Watson, "Methodist Spirituality," in *Protestant Spiritual Traditions,* ed. Frank Senn (Mahwah, N.J.: Paulist Press, 1986), 217–73.

18. See J. Ernest Rattenbury, *The Eucharistic Hymns of John and Charles Wesley* (London: Epworth Press, 1948).

19. James White, *Protestant Worship: Traditions in Transition* (Louisville: Westminster John Knox Press, 1989), 152.

20. Senn, *Christian Liturgy,* 548–50.

21. Davies, *Worship and Theology in England,* 44.

22. Ibid., 46.

23. Ibid., 51.

24. Hans Sedlmayr and Hermann Bauer, "Rococo," *Encyclopedia of World Art* (New York: McGraw-Hill, 1966), 12:267–68.

25. Enrico Cattaneo, *Il Culto Cristiano in Occidente: Note storiche* (Rome: C.L.V. Edizioni Liturgiche, 1978), 539–80.

26. See H. A. Ladd, *The Victorian Morality of Art: An Analysis of Ruskin's Esthetic* (New York: Long, 1932).

27. Senn, *Christian Liturgy,* 569.

28. Ibid., 570.

29. Guilio Romano Ansaldi, "Neoclassic Style," *Encyclopedia of World Art,* 10:518, 523, 530, 538–41.

30. Pugin's most effective propaganda was contained in his 1836 illustrated volume *Contrasts: Or A Parallel between the Noble Edifices of the Middle Ages and the Corresponding Buildings of the Present Day: Showing the Present Decay of Taste.*

31. Augustus Welby Pugin, *The True Principles of Pointed and Christian Architecture* (Edinburgh: J. Grant, 1895).

32. *A. W. N. Pugin: Master of Gothic Revival,* ed. Paul Atterbury (New Haven: Yale University Press, 1995).

33. Henry-Russell Hitchcock, *Architecture: Nineteenth and Twentieth Centuries* (Baltimore: Penguin Books, 1958), 97–101.

34. See David Wathen, *Morality and Architecture: The Development of a Theme in Architectural History and Theory from the Gothic Revival to the Modern Movement* (Oxford: Clarendon, 1977).

35. Michael Day, *Modern Art in English Churches* (London: Mowbray, 1984), 5.

36. Ibid., 8, 11. See also E. P. Thompson, *William Morris: Romantic to Revolutionary* (New York: Pantheon Books, 1976).

37. See Peter J. Davey, *Architecture of the Arts and Crafts Movement* (London: Phaidon, 1995).

38. See Ralph Adams Cram, *My Life in Architecture* (Boston: Little, Brown, 1936).

39. See M. Schuyler, "Works of Cram, Goodhue and Ferguson," *Architectural Record* 29 (1911): 1–44.

40. Ibid., 8, 11.

41. Franklin and Shaw, *Case for Christian Humanism,* 142.

42. See Hugh McLeod, *Religion and the People of Western Europe 1789–1970* (Oxford: Oxford University Press, 1981); and E. P. Thompson, *The Making of the English Working Class* (New York: Vintage Books, 1963).

43. See James F. White, *The Cambridge Movement* (Cambridge: Cambridge University Press, 1979).

44. Senn, *Christian Liturgy,* 567–77.

45. Franklin and Shaw, *Case for Christian Humanism,* 145–46.

46. R. William Franklin, "Pusey and Worship in Industrial Society," *Worship* 75 (1983): 386–411.

47. See *Pusey Rediscovered,* ed. Perry Butler (London: SPCK, 1983); *Essays Catholic and Radical,* ed. Kenneth Leech and Rowan Williams (Milton Keynes: Bowerdean Press, 1983); Geoffrey Rowell, *The Vision Glorious* (Oxford: Oxford University Press, 1983); and Louis Weil, *Sacraments and Liturgy* (Oxford: Basil Blackwell, 1983).

48. See Johann Augustus Neander, *History of the Planting and Training of the Christian Church* (Edinburgh: T. & T. Clark, 1842).

49. Franklin and Shaw, *Case for Christian Humanism,* 148–50.

50. See E. B. Pusey, *A Course of Sermons on Solemn Subjects, Preached in St. Saviour's Church, Leeds* (Oxford: J. H. Parker, 1845, 1847); idem, *Sermons During the Season from Advent to Whitsuntide* (Oxford: J. H. Parker, 1848).

51. Franklin and Shaw, *Case for Christian Humanism,* 150–54.

52. See C. Hartley Graatan, "The Meaning of Grundtvig: Skill plus Culture," *Antioch Review* 18 (1958): 76–86; Holger Begtrup, *The Folk High Schools of Denmark* (London: Oxford University Press, 1936).

53. Henning Høirup, "Grundtvig and Kierkegaard: Their Views of the Church," *Theology Today* 12 (1955): 330.

54. Franklin and Shaw, *Case for Christian Humanism,* 159–60.

55. See Manfred Probst, *Gottesdienst in Geist und Wahrheit: Die liturgischen Ansichten und Bestrebungen Johann Michael Sailers* (Regensburg: Friedrich Pustet, 1976); Olivier Rousseau, *The Progress of the Liturgy: An Historical Sketch from the Beginning of the Nineteenth Century to the Pontificate of Pius X* (Westminster, Md.: Newman Press, 1951), 51–68.

56. See Mario Rosa, "Italian Jansenism and the Synod of Pistoia," *Historical Investigation, Concilium* 17 (New York: Paulist Press, 1966), 34–49; Cattaneo, *Il Culto Cristiano in Occidente*, 516–38.

57. Louis Bouyer, *Liturgical Piety* (Notre Dame: University of Notre Dame Press, 1955), 10–22.

58. See Cuthbert Johnson, *Prosper Guéranger (1805–1875): A Liturgical Theologian*, Studia Anselmiana 89, Analecta Liturgica 9 (Rome: Pontificio Ateneo Anselmo, 1984).

59. See R. Kevin Seasoltz, *The New Liturgy: A Documentation, 1903–1965* (New York: Herder & Herder, 1966), iv.

60. Rousseau, *Progress of the Liturgy*, 69–80.

61. Ansgar Dreher, "Zur Beuroner Kunst," in *Beuron 1863–1963: Festschrift zum hundertjährigen Bestehen der Erzabtei St. Martin*, ed. Virgil Fialo (Beuron: Beuroner Kunstverlag, 1963), 358–94.

62. Jeanne Halgren Kilde, *When Church Became Theatre: The Transformation of Evangelical Architecture and Worship in Nineteenth-century America* (Oxford: Oxford University Press, 2002), 3–21.

63. Ibid., 4–6.

64. Ibid., 9.

65. Ibid., 198.

66. Ibid.

67. Lewis Mumford, *The City in History: Its Origins, Its Transformations and Its Prospects* (New York: Harcourt Brace, 1961), 458.

68. Christian Norberg-Schulz, *Meaning in Western Architecture* (New York: Rizzoli, 1974), 170.

69. Ibid., 173–74.

70. Ibid., 175. See Frank Lloyd Wright, *The Natural House* (New York: New American Library, 1954).

71. Ibid.

72. Ibid., 185.

73. Ibid.

8. Architectural and Liturgical Reforms
in the Twentieth Century

1. Frank C. Senn, *Christian Liturgy: Catholic and Evangelical* (Minneapolis: Fortress Press, 1997), 609. See also Michael Kammen, *Mystic Chords of Memory: The Transformation of Tradition in American Culture* (New York: Alfred A. Knopf, 1991), 299–305.

2. Senn, *Christian Liturgy*, 610.

3. Louis Bouyer, *Liturgical Piety* (Notre Dame: University of Notre Dame Press, 1955), 1–22.

4. See Ernest B. Koenker, *The Liturgical Renaissance in the Roman Catholic Church* (Chicago: University of Chicago Press, 1954), 80–93.

5. See Paul Bradshaw, *The Search for the Origins of Christian Worship*, rev. ed. (New York: Oxford University Press, 2002).

6. Senn, *Christian Liturgy*, 610–11.

7. Henry-Russell Hitchcock and Philip Johnson, *The International Style: Architecture since 1922* (New York: W. W. Norton, 1932), 17–18.

8. Walter Gropius, *The New Architecture and the Bauhaus* (Cambridge, Mass.: M.I.T. Press, 1965), 21, 32.

9. Christian Norberg-Schulz, *Meaning in Western Architecture* (New York: Rizzoli, 1974), 186.

10. Le Corbusier, *Towards a New Architecture* (1927; reprint, New York: Dover, 1986), 141; see also Le Corbusier, *My World* (New York: Galerie Denise René, 1971).

11. Hitchcock and Johnson, *International Style*, 33–34.

12. Ibid., 44–50.

13. Ibid., 50–68.

14. Ibid., 76–77.

15. Norberg-Schulz, *Meaning in Western Architecture*, 193–94.

16. *Acta Sanctae Sedis* 36 (1903): 329–39.

17. Ibid., 330.

18. Decree of the Sacred Congregation of the Council, December 22, 1905, *Acta Sanctae Sedis* 38 (1905): 400–406.

19. See Sonya A. Quitslund, *Beauduin: Prophet Vindicated* (New York: Newman Press, 1973).

20. R. Kevin Seasoltz, *The New Liturgy: A Documentation, 1903–1965* (New York: Herder & Herder, 1966).

21. Romano Guardini, *The Spirit of the Liturgy*, trans. Ada Lane, intro. Joanne M. Pierce (New York: Crossroad, 1930, 1998).

22. The *Jahrbuch* ceased publication in 1941 but was resumed in 1950 under the title *Archiv für Liturgiewissenschaft*.

23. Ildefons Herwegen, *Kirche und Seele: Die Seelenhaltung des Mysterienkultes und ihr Wandel in Mittelalter* (Münster: Aschendorff, 1928).

24. See Jerome M. Hall, *We Have the Mind of Christ: The Holy Spirit and Liturgical Memory in the Thought of Edward J. Kilmartin* (Collegeville, Minn.: Liturgical Press, 2001), 16–31.

25. Seasoltz, *New Liturgy*, xxx.

26. Koenker, *Liturgical Renaissance in the Roman Catholic Church*, 19–20.

27. See Msgr. Goellner, "Monitum de vitandis exaggerationibus in re liturgica," *Periodica de re morali, canonica, liturgica* 27 (1937): 164.

28. Pius Parsch, *The Church's Year of Grace*, trans. William G. Heidt, 5 vols. (Collegeville, Minn.: Liturgical Press, 1957).

29. Josef A. Jungmann, *Die Frohbotschaft und unsere Glaubensverkündigung*

(Regensburg: Friedrich Pustet, 1936). The book was translated and abridged by William A. Huesmann, ed. Johannes Hofinger, *The Good News Yesterday and Today* (New York: W. H. Sadlier, 1962).

30. See John Allyn Melloh, "A Prophet Vindicated: Proclaiming the Good News," in *Source and Summit: Commemorating Josef A. Jungmann, S.J.*, ed. Joanne M. Pierce and Michael Downey (Collegeville, Minn.: Liturgical Press, 1999), 63–77.

31. Koenker, *Liturgical Renaissance in the Roman Catholic Church*, 16.

32. Senn, *Christian Liturgy*, 620–21.

33. Hugo Schnell, *Twentieth Century Church Architecture in Germany* (Munich: Schnell & Steiner, 1974), 33.

34. Susan White, *Art, Architecture and Liturgical Reform: The Liturgical Arts Society (1928–1972)* (New York: Pueblo, 1990).

35. The original German edition was published in 1949, an English translation in 1951/1955: Josef A. Jungmann, *Missarum Sollemnia: The Mass of the Roman Rite*, trans. F. A. Brunner, 2 vols. (New York: Benziger Bros., 1951, 1955). See John F. Baldovin, "The Body of Christ in Celebration: On Eucharistic Liturgy, Theology, and Pastoral Practice," in *Source and Summit*, ed. Pierce and Downey, 49–61.

36. Hitchcock and Johnson, *International Style*, 422.

37. Peter Collins, "Auguste Perret," in *Contemporary Architects*, ed. Muriel Emanuel (New York: St. Martin's Press, 1980), 624; Hitchcock and Johnson, *International Style*, 313–14.

38. See Robert A. Krieg, *Romano Guardini: A Precursor of Vatican II* (Notre Dame, Ind.: University of Notre Dame Press, 1997).

39. Schnell, *Twentieth Century Church Architecture in Germany*, 35.

40. Hitchcock and Johnson, *International Style*, 314.

41. Konstantin Bagarov, "Dominikus Böhm," in *Contemporary Architects*, ed. Emanuel, 108.

42. See G. E. Kidder Smith, *The New Churches of Europe* (New York: Holt, Rinehart & Winston, 1964).

43. Gontran Goulden, "Otto Bartning," *Contemporary Architects*, ed. Emanuel, 74.

44. See Kidder Smith, *New Churches of Europe*.

45. Rudolf Schwarz, *Vom Bau der Kirche* (Heidelberg: L. Schneider, 1947); Eng. trans. *The Church Incarnate*, trans C. Harris (Chicago: J. Regnery, 1958).

46. Konstantin Bagarov, "Rudolph Schwarz," in *Contemporary Architects*, ed. Emanuel, 726.

47. Philippe Potié, *Le Corbusier: Monastery of Sainte-Marie de la Tourette* (Paris: Foundation Le Corbusier/Birkhauser, 2001). See also Thomas O'Meara, *A Theologian's Journey* (New York: Paulist Press, 2002), 154–55.

48. Norberg-Schulz, *Meaning in Western Architecture*, 213.

49. Ibid., 213–16.

50. Robert Venturi, *Complexity and Contradiction in Architecture* (New York: Museum of Modern Art, 1977); idem, *Learning from Las Vegas* (Cambridge: M.I.T. Press, 1972).

51. Charles Moore, *Body, Memory and Architecture* (New Haven: Yale University Press, 1977).

52. See Kenneth Frampton, *Modern Architecture: A Critical History* (London: Thames & Hudson, 1992).

53. Norberg-Schulz, *Meaning in Western Architecture*, 218.

54. Ibid., 213.

55. Ibid., 220.

56. Masao Takenaka, *The Place Where God Dwells: An Introduction to Church Architecture in Asia* (Hong Kong: Christian Conference of Asia, 1995), 70–73. Unfortunately, for economic reasons the guest house designed by Ando will not be built.

9. Developments in Liturgy and Sacred Architecture and Art Following World War II

1. R. Kevin Seasoltz, *The New Liturgy: A Documentation, 1903–1965* (New York: Herder & Herder, 1966), 617–23.

2. Instruction of the Holy Office (June 30, 1952), *Acta Apostolicae Sedis* 44 (1952): 542–46.

3. Encyclical Letter of Pius XII (December 25, 1955), *Acta Apostolicae Sedis* 48 (1955): 5–25.

4. Instruction of the Sacred Congregation of Rites (September 3, 1958), *Acta Apostolicae Sedis* 50 (1958): 630–63.

5. Constitution on the Sacred Liturgy (December 4, 1963), *Acta Apostolicae Sedis* (1964): 97–138.

6. See his address to participants in a national congress of diocesan liturgical commissions of Italy on liturgy and sacred art in *Notitiae* 3 (1967): 33–36; and his address to the Pontifical Commission for Sacred Art in Italy in *Notitiae* 6 (1970): 3–6.

7. *Le nobili espressioni, L'Osservatore Romano,* May 8–9, 1964.

8. Quoted in Peter Hebblethwaite, *Paul VI* (New York: Paulist Press, 1993), 613–14.

9. *Acta Apostolicae Sedis* 56 (1964): 877–900.

10. See *General Instruction of the Roman Missal* (Washington, D.C.: United States Conference of Catholic Bishops, 2003).

11. Marie-Alain Couturier, *Sacred Art* (Austin: University of Texas Press, 1989). See also Joanna Weber, *Couturier's Vision* (privately printed, 1989).

12. See Thomas O'Meara, "'Raid on the Dominicans': The Repression of 1954," *America* 170 (February 5, 1994): 8–16.

13. See Louise Campbell, *Coventry Cathedral: Art and Architecture in Post-war Britain* (New York: Oxford University Press, 1996).

14. *The Metropolitan Cathedral of Christ the King Liverpool: The History of Liv-*

erpool's Catholic Cathedral (Liverpool: Trustees of the Roman Catholic Archdiocese of Liverpool, n.d.).

15. See Paul Walker, "Brentwood Cathedral: The Appearance of Tradition," *Church Building* (Autumn 1992): 31–33; idem, "Brentwood Cathedral: Putting on the Style," *Church Building* (Winter/Spring 1993): 27–31.

16. For more on church architecture in Ireland, see R. Kevin Seasoltz, "In the Celtic Tradition: Irish Church Architecture," in *Ars Liturgiae: Worship, Aesthetics and Praxis: Essays in Honor of Nathan D. Mitchell*, ed. Clare V. Johnson (Chicago: Liturgy Training Publications, 2003), 231–52.

17. Richard Hurley, *Irish Church Architecture in the Era of Vatican II* (Dublin: Dominican Publications, 2001), 21–25.

18. Ibid. The committee included J. G. McGarry (chairman), Wilfrid Cantwell, Ray Carroll, A. D. Devane, Austin Flannery, Richard Hurley, Cahal McCarthy, W. H. H. McCormick, Gerard Montague, James White, and Brendan Devil (secretary).

19. Irish Episcopal Commission for Liturgy, *The Place of Worship* (Dublin: Veritas; Carlow: Irish Institute of Pastoral Liturgy, 1994). For a detailed commentary, see R. Kevin Seasoltz, "The Place of Worship," *Worship* 69 (1995): 175–78.

20. Richard Hurley, "20th Century," in *Sacred Places—The Story of Christian Architecture in Ireland* (Dublin: Royal Institute of the Architects of Ireland; Belfast: Royal Society of Ulster Architects, 2000), 14.

21. See Michael J. Crosbie, *Architecture for the Gods* (Mulgrave, Australia: Image Publishing Group, 1999).

22. Hurley, "20th Century," 15; see also his *Irish Church Architecture in the Era of Vatican II*, 45–46.

23. Hurley, *Irish Church Architecture*, 48–49.

24. Frédéric Debuyst, *Modern Architecture and Christian Celebration* (Richmond, Va.: John Knox Press, 1968).

25. Hurley, *Irish Church Architecture*, 78–79.

26. Richard Hurley, "The Eucharist Room at Carlow Liturgy Center: The Search for Meaning," *Worship* 70 (1976): 238–50.

27. Hurley, *Irish Church Architecture*, 95.

28. Ibid., 95–96.

29. Richard Hurley, "St Mary's Oratory, St. Patrick's College, Maynooth, Co. Kildare," *Irish Architect* (October 1999): 18–20.

30. *A Cathedral Renewed: St. Macartan's Monaghan*, ed. Eltin Griffin (Blackrock: Columba Press, 1998); see also R. Kevin Seasoltz, "A Cathedral Renewed: St. Macartan's, Monaghan," *Worship* 74 (2000): 268–70.

31. See Joseph Duffy, "Michael Biggs: Liturgical Artist," *Doctrine and Life* 44 (February 1994): 110–15.

32. *A Cathedral Renewed*, ed. Griffin, 50–55. See also Frances Biggs and Donal Neary, *The Way of the Cross* (Dublin: Veritas, 2002).

33. Richard Hurley, "Cathedral of St Mary and St Anne, Cork," *Irish Architect* (March 1997): 29–34.

34. Hurley, "20th Century," 17–18.

35. See Meredith L. Clausen, *Spiritual Space: The Religious Architecture of Pietro Belluschi* (Seattle/London: University of Washington Press, 1992).

36. The information concerning the Cathedral of St. James has been derived from the booklet compiled by Michael G. Ryan, *Saint James Cathedral: Guide to the Restoration* (Seattle: Corporation of the Catholic Archbishop of Seattle, 1994).

37. The information concerning the cathedral has been drawn mainly from the following sources: Michael Downey, *The Cathedral at the Heart of Los Angeles* (Collegeville, Minn.: Liturgical Press, 2002); Jack Miles, "Our Lady of the Freeways: Is Los Angeles' New Cathedral Worth the Price?" *Commonweal* (February 28, 2003), 13–17; John Broder, "New Los Angeles Cathedral Evokes Survival in Adversity," *The New York Times*, August 30, 2002, A1, A14; Richard Lacayo, "To the Light House," *Time*, September 2, 2002, 64–66; Mary-Cabrini Durkin, *Short Tour of Our Lady of the Angels* (Strasbourg: Éditions du Signe, 2002).

38. Richard S. Vosko, "The Threshold of Transformation," in Jack Miles, Peggy Fogelman, and Noriko Jujinami, *Robert Graham: The Great Bronze Doors for the Cathedral of Our Lady of the Angels* (Venice, Calif.: Wave Publishing, 2002), 7–8.

39. Jack Miles, "Our Lady of Los Angeles," in Miles et al., *Robert Graham: The Great Bronze Doors*, 13–46.

40. *Art for the Cathedral of Our Lady of the Angels, John Nava: The Cathedral Tapestries from Proposal to Installation*, Catalogue for an Exhibition at the Judson Gallery of Contemporary and Traditional Art, Los Angeles, California, October 13, 2002–January 25, 2003.

41. See Frank C. Senn, "'Worship Live': An Analysis and Critique of 'Alternative Worship Services,'" *Worship* 69 (1995): 194–224.

42. See, e.g., Edward A. Søvik, *Architecture for Worship* (Minneapolis: Augsburg Publishing House, 1973).

43. Frank C. Senn, *Christian Liturgy: Catholic and Evangelical* (Minneapolis: Fortress Press, 1997), 673–74.

44. John Runkle, ed., *Searching for Sacred Space: Essays on Architecture and Liturgical Design in the Episcopal Church* (New York: Church Publishing, 2002), 1.

45. Brantley Gasaway, "Highly Effective Episcopal Architecture: Integrating Architecture and Worship to Reflect a Church's Identity," in *Searching for Sacred Space*, ed. Runkle, 63.

46. Louis Bouyer, *Liturgy and Architecture* (Notre Dame: University of Notre Dame Press, 1967).

47. Richard Giles, *Pitching the Tent* (Collegeville, Minn.: Liturgical Press, 1999).

48. Richard Giles, "The Making of a Cathedral," in *Searching for Sacred Space*, ed. Runkle, 186–87.

49. Ibid., 204.

10. Twentieth-Century Monastic Architecture

1. References are to *RB: The Rule of Benedict in Latin and English with Notes,* ed. Timothy Fry (Collegeville, Minn.: Liturgical Press, 1981), 58:60, 61 (stability), 53:56 (simplicity and sharing of goods), 53 (hospitality).

2. See Johannes Baptist Metz, *Theology of the World,* trans. William Glen-Doepel (New York: Herder & Herder, 1969).

3. *RB* 53:36.

4. *RB* 32.

5. See *Consider Your Call,* ed. Daniel Rees (London: S.P.C.K., 1978), 141. The importance of "being grafted onto the local community" is developed by Gabriel Marcel, *Mass Society,* trans. G. S. Fraser (Chicago: Regnery, 1969), 93.

6. René Dubos, "Franciscan Conservation versus Benedictine Stewardship," in *A God Within* (New York: Scribner, 1972), 153–74.

7. See David Steindl-Rast, "The Environment as Guru," *Cross Currents* 24 (Summer-Fall, 1974): 148–53.

8. Howard Niebling, "Modern Benedictine Churches: Monastic Churches Erected by American Benedictines since World War II" (Ph.D. diss., Columbia University, 1973), 147–49. The dissertation was summarized in two articles published in *American Benedictine Review* 26 (June 1975): 180–226; (September 1975): 298–340.

9. Damasus Winzen, "Of Persons and Places," *American Benedictine Review* 1 (Winter 1950): 554–55.

10. Niebling, "Modern Benedictine Churches," 172. Shanley's work was reviewed by Maurice Lavanoux in *Liturgical Arts* 38 (February 1970): 62–63.

11. Winzen described his approach to the chapel in a letter published in the *Mount Saviour Chronicle,* no. 2 (October 1953).

12. See Edward Rice, "Return to St. Benedict," *Jubilee* 13 (September 1965): 33–39. The monastery is described in an early booklet issued by the community entitled "Monastery of Christ in the Desert." For a more recent assessment of the monastery, see Charles A. Fracchia, *Living Together Alone: The New American Monasticism* (New York: Harper & Row, 1979), 155–67.

13. William Wilfrid Bayne, O.S.B., "Thirty-three Years of Portsmouth History," *American Benedictine Review* 3 (Winter 1952): 315–39.

14. The project was described in the Fall 1957 issue of *Portsmouth Bulletin.*

15. The genesis and design for the monastery and church, with emphasis on the relationship between the architect and the community, are discussed in Whitney Stoddard, *Adventure in Architecture: Building the New Saint John's* (New York: Longmans Green, 1958). The development of the monastery from its inception in 1856 until 1956 has been recounted by Colman Barry, *Worship and Work* (Collegeville, Minn.: Saint John's Abbey, 1956).

16. The church is described in a booklet published by the Abbey: "Abbey and University Church of Saint John the Baptist." It was also critiqued in various architectural journals: *L'Art d'Église* 27 (1959): 145–54; 29 (1961): 97–107; *Architectural Record* 80 (November 1961): 132–42; *L'Architecture d'Aujourd'hui* 33 (March 1962): 40–47; *Architect and Building News* (June 13, 1962): 686–87.

17. See "North Dakota Community for the Benedictine Sisters," *Architectural Record* 82 (December 1963): 95–102; "Annunciation Priory–Bismarck, North Dakota," *Liturgical Arts* 32 (February 1964): 50–59; Frédéric Debuyst, "La Prieuré de l'Annonciation à Bismarck," *L'Art d'Église* 29 (1961): 108–11.

18. Columba Cary-Elwes, "La prieuré Saint-Louis," *L'Art d'Église* 29 (1961): 116–17; see also "A School in Praise of God," *Architectural Forum* 57 (November 1957): 122–27.

19. Niebling, "Modern Benedictine Churches," 267–79.

20. For an account of the origins of the monastery, see Leo Rudloff and John Hammond, "The Weston Story," *American Benedictine Review* 13 (1962): 390–400; Rudloff, "Weston Priory," *American Benedictine Review* 5 (1954): 168–90; and Peter M. Miller, "The Monks at Weston," *Jubilee* 3 (March 1956): 40–47; Fracchia, *Living Together Alone*, 86–103.

21. Tasso Katselas, "L'abbaye Saint-Vincent à Latrobe," *L'Art d'Église* 142 (1968): 132–38.

22. "St. Vincent Monastery," in *Religious Buildings*, ed. Jeremy Robinson and Patricia Markert (New York: McGraw-Hill, 1979), 38–42.

23. Ibid., 68–69.

24. Stanley Abercrombie, "Aalto's Second Coming," *Portfolio* 1 (December-January 1979–1980): 56–61.

25. Frédéric Debuyst, "La bibliothèque d'Alvar Aalto à Mount Angel," *L'Art d'Église* 155 (1971): 146.

26. Ibid., 146–53.

27. Ibid.

28. Peter Hammond, *Liturgy and Architecture* (London: Barrie & Rockliff, 1960), 173.

29. The information about the church at St. Meinrad is derived from the archabbey publication *The Renewed Heart of Saint Meinrad: The Art and Architecture of the Archabbey Church of Our Lady of Einsiedeln* (St. Meinrad, Ind.: Saint Meinrad Archabbey Press, 1998).

30. William Schickel, "Unifying the Old and the New," *Liturgical Arts* 36 (August 1968): 146–53.

31. For further reflections on the project, see Thomas Merton, "Note on the New Church at Gethsemani," *Liturgical Arts* 36 (August 1968): 100–101; Matthew Kelty, "Gethsemani: Impressions on a Renovation," *Liturgical Arts* 36 (1968): 101–7.

32. The history of the monastery and church is set out in a booklet entitled *An Historical Sketch of the Abbey Church* (Dubuque, Ia.: New Melleray Abbey, n.d.);

the spirit of the community is described in another booklet: *New Melleray Abbey: Cistercians of the Strict Observance* (Dubuque, Ia.: New Melleray Abbey, n.d.).

33. Quoted in "U.S.A.: National Symposium on Environment and Art," *Notitiae* 160 (November 1979): 659.

34. Armand Veilleux, "Monasticism and Culture-Encounter," *Tjuringa* (May 1975): 48.

11. Sacred Art from 1900 to the Present

1. See Wendy Becket, *Contemporary Women Artists* (New York: Universe, 1988), 16–17; also P. Jacob and M. Abakanowicz, *Magdalena Abakanowicz* (Richmond, Va.: Virginia Museum of Fine Arts, n.d.).

2. T. S. Eliot, "The Hollow Men," in *Collected Poems 1909–1935* (New York: Harcourt, Brace & Company, 1936), 101.

3. Becket, 46–47. See also *Max Wall, Pictures by Maggi Hambling* (London: Catholic Portrait Gallery Catalogue, 1983).

4. Wendy Becket, *Art and the Sacred* (London: Rider, 1992), 32–34.

5. *The Art Book* (London: Phaidon, 1994), 23.

6. *Sister Wendy's 1000 Masterpieces* (New York: DK Publishing, 1999), 17.

7. Patrick Negri, "Barnett Newman," in Rosemary Crumlin, *Beyond Belief: Modern Art and the Religious Imagination* (Melbourne: National Gallery of Victoria, 1998), 106–7. See also Harold Rosenberg, *Barnett Newman* (New York: Harry N. Abrams, 1978); Barnett Newman, *Northwest Coast Indian Painting* (New York: Betty Parsons Gallery, 1946).

8. Negri, "Mark Rothko," in Crumlin, *Beyond Belief,* 108–9.

9. Horst Schwebel, "Harald Duwe," in Crumlin, *Beyond Belief,* 132–33.

10. F. van der Meer, *Images du Christ dans la sculpture des Alpes et des Pyrenees* (Antwerp: Fonds Mercator, 1980), 79.

11. Anton Wessels, *Images of Jesus* (Grand Rapids: Eerdmans, 1990).

12. Amarao Takenaka, *Christian Art in Asia* (Tokyo: Kyo Bun Kwan, 1975), 18, fig. 97.

13. See Heinz Schreckenberg's encyclopedic collection of more than a thousand pictures in *The Jews in Christian Art and Spirituality* (New York: Continuum, 1996).

14. *Third Eye Theology: Theology in Formation in Asian Settings,* ed. Choan-Seng Song (Maryknoll, N.Y.: Orbis Books, 1979), 12.

15. Quoted by Winefride Wilson, *Christian Art since the Romantic Movement* (London: Burns & Oates, 1965), 55.

16. Georges Rouault, *Miserere* (Boston: Boston Book and Art Shop, 1963). See also G. De San Lazzaro, *Homage to Georges Rouault* (New York: Tudor, 1971).

17. José María Faerna, ed., *Rouault* (New York: Harry N. Abrams, n.d.), 5.

18. Wilson, *Christian Art since the Romantic Movement,* 55.

19. See Michael J. Cook and Terrence E. Dempsey, "Images of Jesus in the Arts: Stumbling Blocks or Stepping-stones?" *Proceedings of the Center for Jewish Christian Learning* [University of St. Thomas, St. Paul, Minnesota] 10 (Fall 1995): 57.

20. Jane Dillenberger, *Secular Art and Sacred Themes* (Nashville: Abingdon Press, 1969), 35; Horton Davies and Hugh Davies, *Sacred Art in a Secular Century* (Collegeville, Minn.: Liturgical Press, 1978), 44–47.

21. John Lane, *The Living Tree: Art and the Sacred* (Hartland, U.K.: Green Books, 1988), 106–8.

22. Wilson, *Christian Art since the Romantic Movement*, 68–69. See also *Chagall*, text by Marcel Brion (New York: Harry N. Abrams, 1961), 46.

23. Cook and Dempsey, "Images of Jesus in the Arts," 57.

24. Jaroslav Pelikan, *The Illustrated Jesus through the Centuries* (New Haven: Yale University Press, 1997), 21.

25. See Richard Buckle, *Jacob Epstein, Sculptor* (Cleveland: World, 1963).

26. *Eric Gill and the Guild of St. Joseph and St. Dominic*, ed. Timothy Wilcox (Hove: Hove Museum and Art Gallery, 1990), 7–13.

27. Ibid., 15–21, 37–41; Wilson, *Christian Art since the Romantic Movement*. See also Judith Collins, *Eric Gill—Sculpture* (London: Lund Humphries, 1992).

28. *Eric Gill and the Guild of St. Joseph and St. Dominic*, ed. Wilcox, 70–73.

29. Ibid., 61–69.

30. Walter Hussey, *Patron of Art* (London: Weidenfeld & Nicholson, 1985), 30.

31. Ibid., 33.

32. Wilson, *Christian Art since the Romantic Movement*, 85.

33. See Laurence Schmeckebier, (ed.), *Ivan Meštrović: Sculptor and Patriot* (Syracuse: Syracuse University Press, 1959).

34. Anthony J. Lauck, Dean A. Porter, Steven A. Bennett, and Don Vogl, *Ivan Meštrović: The Notre Dame Years* (Notre Dame, Ind.: Art Gallery, University of Notre Dame, 1974), 5–19.

35. See Fiona MacCarthy, "Stanley Spencer, English Visionary," in *Stanley Spencer: An English Vision* (New Haven: Yale University Press, 1997), 1–60; Nicholas Wolterstorff, "Painting God in Our Village: The Religious Dimension of Stanley Spencer's Painting," *Image* (Winter 1997–1998): 27–38.

36. Wilson, *Christian Art since the Romantic Movement*, 69–70.

37. *Stanley Spencer: An English Vision*, 62–63.

38. Keith Walker, *Images or Idols? The Place of Sacred Art in Churches Today* (Norwich: Canterbury Press, 1996), 45.

39. William Kuralek, *A Northern Nativity* (Plattsburgh, N.Y.: Tundra Books, 1976), 1, 2, 15, 19.

40. William S.Taylor, *Seeing the Mystery: Exploring Christian Faith through the Eyes of Artists* (Ottawa: Novalis, n.d.), 59–60.

41. Ibid., 36–38.

42. Ibid., 44–45.

43. See Rosemary Crumlin, *Images of Religion in Australian Art* (Kensington: Bay Books, n.d.).

44. Crumlin, *Images of Religion in Australian Art*, 118–21.

45. *Revelations of the Divine Love of Julian of Norwich*, ed. H. Backhouse and R. Pipe (London: Hodder & Stoughton, 1987), 68.

46. Crumlin, *Images of Religion in Australian Art*, 140–41.

47. Ibid., 32–33.

48. Ibid., 34–35.

49. Ibid., 36–37.

50. Ibid., 40–45.

51. Ibid., 144–45.

52. Ibid., 146–47.

53. Ibid., 148–49.

54. Ibid., 158–61.

55. Ibid., 158.

56. Quoted in Sandra McGrath, *The Artist and the River* (Sydney: Bay Books, 1982), 61.

57. Janet Walton, *Art and Worship: A Vital Connection* (Collegeville, Minn.: Liturgical Press, 1988), 105–7.

58. Ibid., 106.

59. Geraldine Brooks, "The Painted Desert," *The New Yorker* (July 28, 2003): 61–67.

60. *Aboriginal Art and Spirituality*, ed. Rosemary Crumlin (North Blackburn: Collins Dove, 1991), 34, 38.

61. Eileen Farrelly, "Dark River," in *Aboriginal Art and Spirituality*, ed. Crumlin, 42.

62. See Oodgeroo Noonuccal and Kabul Oodgeroo Noonuccal. *The Rainbow Serpent* (Canberra: Australian Government Publishing Service, 1988).

63. *Aboriginal Art and Spirituality*, ed. Crumlin, 44–45, 135.

64. See *Icons of the Invisible God: Selected Sculpture of Peter Eugene Ball*, ed. Elaine Kazimierczuk (Newark: Chevron Books, 1999).

65. Quoted by Walker, *Images or Idols?* 161.

66. Ibid., 162.

67. Ibid., 163–65.

68. Patrick Reyntiens, "Gallery," *The Tablet*, November 11, 1989.

69. Sister Wendy Becket, "Albert Herbert," *Arts Review* 7 (November 1989): 772.

70. Walker, *Images or Idols?* 172–78.

71. Reyntiens, *The Tablet*, November 11, 1989.

72. See Neil MacGregor with Erika Langmuir, *Seeing Salvation: Images of Christ in Art* (London: BBC, 2000), 112–15.

73. Sister Wendy Becket, *Art and the Sacred* (London: Rider, 1992), 5.

74. *Westminster Cathedral* (Andover: Pitkin Guides, 1998), 5; Walker, *Images or Idols?* 93–95.

75. *Salisbury Cathedral* (Andover: Pitkin Guides, 1999), 11.

76. Anne H. Pyle, "A Personal Remembrance of Sadao Watanabe (1913–1996)," *Lutheran Quarterly* 11 (Summer 1997): 151–54.

77. Ibid.

78. Masao Takenaka, *Biblical Prints by Sadao Watanabe* (Tokyo: Shinkyo Shuppansha, 1986), 25; see also *Printing the Word: The Art of Watanabe Sadao* (New York: American Bible Society, 2000).

79. Ibid.

80. Pyle, "Personal Remembrance of Sadao Watanabe (1913–1996)," 66.

81. Ibid.

82. Christopher Irvine and Anne Dawtry, *Art and Worship* (Collegeville, Minn.: Liturgical Press, 2002), 52–53.

83. Ibid. 53. See also Karen Stone, *Image and Spirit: Finding Meaning in Visual Art* (Minneapolis: Augsburg, 2003).

84. Ibid., 62.

85. Ibid.

86. Ibid., 60–61.

87. See Bishops' Committee on the Liturgy, *Environment and Art in Catholic Worship* (Washington, D.C.: National Conference of Catholic Bishops, 1978), 35, 48–50; National Conference of Catholic Bishops, *Built of Living Stones: Art, Architecture and Worship* (Washington, D.C.: United States Catholic Conference, 2000), 49–56.

Conclusion

1. Bishops' Committee on the Liturgy, *Environment and Art in Catholic Worship* (Washington, D.C.: National Conference of Catholic Bishops, 1978), 7–9.

2. Ibid., 11–12.

3. *General Instruction of the Roman Missal* (Washington, D.C.: United States Conference of Catholic Bishops, 2002), nos. 288–318, pp. 97–108.

4. Bishops' Committee on the Liturgy, *Environment and Art,* 14–15.

5. Ibid., 16.

6. Gesa Elsbeth Thiessen, "Exploring a *Locus Theologicus*: Sacramental Presence in Modern Art and Its Hermeneutical Implications for Theology," in *The Presence of Transcendence,* ed. Lieven Boeve and John C. Ries (Leuven: Peeters, 2001), 213–22.

7. Peter Jeffery, "A Chant Historian Reads *Liturgiam Authenticam* 3: Language and Culture," *Worship* 78 (May 2002): 236.

8. Bishops' Committee on the Liturgy, *Environment and Life,* no. 107, p. 52.

Index